THE OXFORD ANTHOLOGY OF
Writings from North-East India

THE OXFORD ANTHOLOGY OF
Writings from North-East India

POETRY AND ESSAYS

edited by
Tilottoma Misra

UNIVERSITY PRESS

OXFORD
UNIVERSITY PRESS

YMCA Library Building, Jai Singh Road, New Delhi 110 001

Oxford University Press is a department of the University of Oxford. It furthers the University's objective of excellence in research, scholarship, and education by publishing worldwide in

Oxford   New York

Auckland   Cape Town   Dar es Salaam   Hong Kong   Karachi   Kuala Lumpur
Madrid   Melbourne   Mexico City   Nairobi   New Delhi   Shanghai   Taipei   Toronto

With offices in

Argentina   Austria   Brazil   Chile   Czech Republic   France   Greece   Guatemala
Hungary   Italy   Japan   Poland   Portugal   Singapore   South Korea   Switzerland
Thailand   Turkey   Ukraine   Vietnam

Oxford is a registered trademark of Oxford University Press
in the UK and in certain other countries

Published in India
by Oxford University Press, New Delhi

© Oxford University Press 2011

The moral rights of the author have been asserted
Database right Oxford University Press (maker)

First published 2011

All rights reserved. No part of this publication may be reproduced,
or transmitted in any form or by any means, electronic or mechanical,
including photocopying, recording or by any information storage and
retrieval system, without permission in writing from Oxford University Press.
Enquiries concerning reproduction outside the scope of the above should be
sent to the Rights Department, Oxford University Press, at the address above

You must not circulate this book in any other binding or cover
and you must impose this same condition on any acquirer

Every effort has been made to trace the copyright holder of some of the pieces
included in this volume. The publisher would be pleased to hear from the owner
of copyright so that proper acknowledgement can be made in future editions.

ISBN-13: 978-0-19-806749-8
ISBN-10: 0-19-806749-6

Typeset in 10.5/12.5 Adobe Garamond Pro
by Excellent Laser Typesetters, Pitampura, Delhi 110 034
Printed in India by Rakmo Press Pvt. Ltd., New Delhi 110 020
Published by Oxford University Press
YMCA Library Building, Jai Singh Road, New Delhi 110 001

Contents

Acknowledgements ix
Introduction xi

POETRY

ARUNACHAL PRADESH
Mamang Dai
   The Voice of the Mountain 3
   The Sorrow of Women 5
   An Obscure Place 5

ASSAM
Navakanta Barua
   Judas 7
   Bats 8
   Silt 9

Nilmani Phookan
- Poem — 10
- After a Couple of Days — 11
- Mating Music — 12

Hiren Bhattacharya
- The Lone Prayer for Poetry — 12
- The Earth my Poem — 13
- Sylvan Song — 13
- Let There be Crop — 14

Harekrishna Deka
- Another One — 15
- A Word for Love — 15
- Towards Freedom — 16

Nilim Kumar — 17
- I had Nothing to Offer — 17
- To my Son — 17

Sameer Tanti
- The Night of Kadams in Bloom — 20
- As the Night Thickens the Stars Nod Off — 20

Anubhav Tulasi
- Prodigal — 21
- The Infernal Playground — 24

Jiban Narah
- Rhythm — 25
- Colours — 26
- Mother — 26
- The Subaltern — 27

Shaktipada Brahmachari
- One Birth of Love, Another of Household Duties — 28
- Assassin, Turn Horse — 28

Anupama Basumatary
- Seasons — 29
- Earthy — 29

Aruni Kashyap
- Journeys — 30
- Me — 32

MANIPUR

Rajkumar Bhubonsana
   Should Light be Put Out or Mind Kept in Dark   35
   The Smell of Pomegranate   40
   E-nga   40

Robin S. Ngangom
   Poetry   41
   Gangtok, February 1998   42
   The First Rain   44
   Everywhere I Go   46

Yumlembam Ibomcha
   For the Next Birth   47

Saratchand Thiyam
   Shillong   48
   Hillworld   50
   Hill   51
   Pokhran, Kargil, Gaisal   52

Gambhini Devi
   Hansapadika   53
   A Village Girl   53

Memchoubi
   Red Chingthrao   54
   The Goddess of Lightning   55

Thangjam Ibopishak
   I Want to be Killed by an Indian Bullet   56
   Gandhi and Robot   57

MEGHALAYA

Desmond Kharmawphlang
   Letter from Pahambir   59
   Poems during November   60
   The Conquest   61

Esther Syiem
   Retelling Nam's Tale   62

Kynpham Sing Nongkynrih
   The Colours of Truth   66

The Ancient Rocks of Cherra	66
A Day in Sohra	67
A Farewell Letter of Cherries	68

MIZORAM

Mona Zote
What Poetry Means to Ernestina in Peril	71
Girl with Black Guitar and Blue Hibiscus	72

Cherrie L. Chhangte
Rain	73
Night	74
Plea	75
What does an Indian Look Like	76

Lalrinmawii Khiangte
Betrayal	76
For a Better Tomorrow	77

L. Biakliana
Cry of Mizo Women	78
True Love	79

NAGALAND

Temsula Ao
Blood of Others	81
The Old Story Teller	83
The Spear	85

Easterine Iralu
Genesis	87

Monalisa Changkija
Mist over Brahmaputra	88
One of these Decades	89
Shoot	90

Nini Lungalang
Mirror	91
I Will Be	92
Rock	93

TRIPURA

Chandrakanta Murasingh
O Poor Hachukrai	95

Of a Minister	96
The Python's Call from the Deserted Tong	96
Your Dreams	97

Pijush Raut
Feelings	98
Picnic	98

Bijoy Kumar Debbarma
Eklavya of the Longtarai	99

Jogmaya Chakma
The Martyr's Altar	100

Narendra Debbarma
The Border	101

ESSAYS

Mrinal Miri
The Spiritual and the Moral	105

Birendranath Datta
North-East India and its Socio-Cultural Milieu	118

Esther Syiem
Social Identity and the Liminal Character of the Folk: A Study in the Khasi Context	128

Thingnam Kishan Singh
Encounters and Literary Engagements: A Critique of History and Literature in Manipur	142

Sanjoy Hazarika
There Are No Shangri-Las Left	157

Udayon Misra
Peasant Consciousness as Reflected in the Oral Literature of Assam: A Study of Two Assamese Ballads	164

Moushumi Kandali
The Colonial Impression on Vaishnavite Art Form of Assam: A Study of the Sculptural Reliefs of the Srihati Satra	186

Tayenjam Bijoykumar Singh
'Kurukshetragi Peeraang'—Ratan Thiyam's Gift to Mothers	200

Margaret Ch. Zama
Mizo Literature: An Overview — 205

Tilottoma Misra
Crossing Linguistic Boundaries: Two Arunachali Writers in Search of Readers — 214

Cherrie L. Chhangte
'Loneliness in the Midst of Curfews': The Mizo Insurgency Movement and Terror Lore — 237

Sukalpa Bhattacharjee
Narrative Constructions of Identity and the Sylheti Experience — 245

Charles Chasie
A Naga View of the World — 259

Easterine Iralu
Should Writers Stay in Prison? — 272

Chandrakanta Murasingh
Kokborok: Her People and Her Past — 276

Patricia Mukhim
Land Ownership Among the Khasis of Meghalaya: A Gender Perspective — 285

Robin S. Ngangom
Contemporary Manipuri Poetry: An Overview — 297

Anungla Aier
Folklore, Folk Ideas and Gender among the Nagas — 301

Notes on Contributors — 309
Copyright Statement — 325

Acknowledgements

It goes without saying that an anthology of this kind cannot be put together without the advice and support of people who have experience and knowledge in different areas. I am thankful to all the friends from the seven states of north-east India who have been so generous with their suggestions and help throughout the rather long period of gestation that this anthology has had to go through. Although it is not possible for me to thank each one individually, yet I would like to express my gratitude especially to Margaret Zama of Aizawl, Sukalpa Bhattacharjee and Kynpham Sing Nongkynrih of Shillong, Tayenjam Bijoykumar Singh of Imphal, Saroj Chaudhuri of Agartala, Rupanjali Barua of Guwahati, and Kallol Choudhuri of Hailakandi for helping me in every possible way with the collection and translation of the works and in contacting the authors for their permission. Without their constant help and cooperation, this anthology would not have been possible.

I wish to thank all those authors who have helped me in the selection and translation of their own works and the translators who have not only allowed me to include their translations in this collection but have also offered their generous help and suggestions for improvement of some of the translations.

I am also thankful to my daughter Sanghamitra and son Arindam for their help in preparing the manuscript. To the editorial team at Oxford University Press I owe a special word of thanks for bearing with me through difficult times and supporting me in various stages of the work.

Introduction

An intense sense of awareness of the cultural loss and recovery that came with the negotiation with 'other' cultures is a recurrent feature of the literatures of the seven north-eastern states. Each small community or linguistic group has responded through its oral or written communication to the encounters with the majoritarian cultures from either mainland India or from outside the borders of the country, in its own distinctive manner. The main waves of cultural invasion that have wrought significant changes in the literary world of the region originated in the Bhakti movement, followed by the various reformist dispensations of the nineteenth century, colonialism and the Christian missionary activities that accompanied it, and the new culture of development that has become a part of global culture. Each of these encounters resulted in different forms of resistance as well as appropriations. The clash of cultures has often led to the loss of traditional forms and the adoption of new cultural icons that threatened the existing ones. While there have been attempts at reviewing and critiquing one's own society and culture in the light of the new ideas that have invaded the region from time to time, yet whenever the xenophobic fear of the 'outsider' has seized a community, a tendency to retreat into the cocoon of cultural isolation has been quite evident. In Assam, Manipur, and Tripura, this process of cultural intermixing began long before the advent of colonialism. Shaiva, Shakta, and Vaishnava forms of Hinduism together with Buddhism and Islam spread their distinctive influences in the region, while the Tai-Ahoms who entered Assam from the east and ruled the country for almost 600 years till the advent of the British in 1826, made immense contribution towards the creation of a syncretic culture in the region. It is significant that the literature of the pre-colonial period in all these three kingdoms was deeply rooted in the wonderfully mixed cultural life of their respective societies. Colonialism, however, superimposed a Eurocentric concept of modernity derived from the Enlightenment on the literatures of the region, thereby creating a rupture between the past and the present. The Christian missionaries took the lead in ushering in a print culture by establishing printing presses and bringing out textbooks, books on grammar, and Christian literature and journals in the local languages. The standardization of the Assamese language that took place as a result of this encounter, however, led to the marginalization of the other spoken dialects of the language, thus creating a distance between the oral and the written. This interference with what a recent historian has termed the 'robustly polyglot character'[1] of the pre-colonial administration of Assam, helped the colonial administrators to cope with the problem of managing the bewildering and mindboggling heterogeneity of speech which they encountered in the colonial province of Assam which constitutes much of what is called the 'North-East' today. The initial attempt of the British to impose a standardized form of Bengali to serve as the vernacular of Assam, met with stiff resistance from the Assamese literati of the time who received unexpected support from the American Baptist missionaries. The creation of a standardized print language in Assam was, therefore, the result of a joint effort by the missionaries and the Assamese intellectuals schooled in the metropolitan culture of Calcutta in the nineteenth century. This language, which emerged as the medium for the new literary creations of the nineteenth century, contained elements from many existing speech practices of the various indigenous communities of the region as well as from Persian, Hindi, Bengali, and other languages of the neighbouring communities

---

[1] Bodhisattva Kar, 2008, 'The Tongue has No Bones; Fixing the Assamese Language *c.* 1800–*c.* 1930', *Studies in History*, Vol. 24, No.1, February.

with which the pre-colonial rulers of Assam used to carry on political and commercial intercourse. The modern Assamese language has, therefore, been termed as a 'philologist's paradise'[2] because of the heterogeneous elements mobilized within its structure.

The Assamese language in its various oral forms has also served as the lingua franca amongst many of the hill people in the neighbouring states of Arunachal Pradesh and Nagaland. But these oral forms of the language have remained as pidgin languages and are, therefore, termed as 'non-language' even by the speakers who use these forms of the language for communicating with people from the neighbouring tribes.[3] It may be noted that before the advent of identity politics amongst the various ethnic communities in the region whose mother tongue is not Assamese, the writers from the different communities used the Assamese language as the medium for creative writing. This resulted in the language acquiring distinctive characteristics because of the infusion of elements peculiar to the culture of the different indigenous communities. In this collection, the translations from the Assamese writings of Lummer Dai and Yeshe Dorjee Thongchi belonging to the Adi and the Sherdukpan communities respectively, an excerpt from an Assamese novel of the Karbi writer Rong Bong Terang, poems of the Mishing poet Jiban Narah, and those of the Bodo poet Anupama Basumatari, would show how a language acquires new dimensions and vibrancy when handled by writers from other cultures.

While setting out to compile this anthology, the most daunting task has been to make the best possible selection from the available works in English and in translation. Of the three generations of writers of the post-Independence period included here, a significantly large number of the younger writers are writing in English. A variety of reasons may be cited for this phenomenon. Many of them have had the privilege of being educated in English-medium schools and they are more capable of handling that language rather than their mother tongues. This new band of writers writing in English is bound to grow in number because most of the hill-states of the region have adopted English as the official language, thus ensuring that it would be the first language of the new generation of literates and it would be used to the best advantage both in the professional as well as in the academic arena. While whether the English language would be able to replace the regional languages

---

[2] Maheswar Neog, 2004, *Essays in Assamese Literature*, Delhi: Omsons, p. 1.

[3] See my essay, 'Crossing Linguistic Boundaries: Two Arunachali Writers in Search of Readers' in this volume.

in creative writing may be a contested question, it is a fact that some of the best writings from the North-East have been produced in acquired languages, including English. Moreover, given the small sizes of the linguistic groups to which many of the writers belong, it is understandable that the aspiring writers should choose to write in a language through which they can reach out to a wider reader base. Indeed, many of the writers writing in English have reaped the benefits of acquiring a worldwide audience through national and international forums. Reflecting on this phenomenon, Nigel Jenkins, a Welsh scholar who has edited a collection of Khasi poetry in English and Welsh, has expressed the hope that the Khasis would go back to their own language after the 'purging of the clutter' that is under way at present. He says: 'It is a painful fact of literary life for certain young writers that although Khasi is their everyday medium, they are not sufficiently confident in the language to make poems in it. This real or imagined incapacity is largely the fault of an education system which obliges secondary school pupils to abandon their native tongue and matriculate in English.'[4] In contrast, a completely different view has been expressed by Salman Rushdie who finds no reason to be apologetic about the choice of the English language by Indian and diasporic writers. Commenting on the status of the Indian writers 'working in English', he says: 'English is the most powerful medium of communication in the world; should we not then rejoice at these artists' mastery of it, and at their growing influence? To criticize writers for their success at "breaking out" is no more than parochialism (and parochialism is perhaps the main vice of the vernacular literatures).'[5]

In the present anthology, the English poetry of Temsula Ao, Mamang Dai, Robin S. Ngangom, Desmond Kharmawphlang, Esther Syiem, Kynpham Sing Nongkynrih, Thanesia, Cherrie L. Chhangte, Lalrinmawii Khiangte, Easterine Iralu, Monalisa Changkija, Nini Lungalang, and Aruni Kashyap represent the new voices in the literature of the North-East. These poets have effectively combined the music, rhythm, and patterns of their own languages and cultures with the forceful communicative power of the English language.

---

[4] Nigel Jenkins, 1995, 'Introduction', *Khasi in Gwalia: An Anthology of Poetry and Prose from the Khasi Hills in North-east India,* West Glamorgan: Alun Books, p. 18.

[5] Salman Rushdie, 'Introduction', in Salman Rushdie and Elizabeth West (eds), 1997, *The Vintage Book of Indian Writing (1947–1997)*, Vintage.

The lack of first-rate translations of Indian literature in vernacular languages has been mentioned by most editors who have compiled anthologies of Indian writings. Though the effort of Sahitya Akademi and some other institutions in collecting and publishing Indian writings in translation is laudable, yet many areas have still remained untouched. Despite the claims of some scholars that 'in India we keep translating every moment of our active life' and that much of the pre-colonial literature in India was founded on translations of the epics and the puranas,[5] it is sad that some of the best writings in the Indian languages can be read only by the readers who belong to the same linguistic community as that of the author.

Most of the communities from north-east India can pride themselves for possessing a vibrant storytelling tradition. The culture of the 'face-to-face communities'[6] which is distinguishable from the abstract nature of social relationships in the 'modern' world, is a distinguishing feature of the oral and it has continued as the dominant influence on the literary creations from the region. After the introduction of print culture into the region during the colonial times, collecting, re-telling, and printing the folklore of the different communities became an important part of the colonial ethnographic agenda of mapping the region for more effective administrative control over the bewildering variety of races that the British encountered here. P.R.T Gordon, J. Shakespeare, T.C. Hodson, Major A. Playfair, J.P. Mill, Sidney Endle, and many other colonial ethnographers had collected, translated, and printed a rich body of folklore material, the latest in the line being the valuable additions made by Verrier Elwin in the post-Independence period. Collecting and printing the oral and written literature of one's own community also became a part of the nationalist agenda of identity-assertion. People whose history and civilization had been pushed to the margins as not conforming to the norms of the Eurocentric concept of modernity, took up the task of re-creating their past and re-inventing tradition so as to represent the present as a stage in the continuous process of marching from the past to the future. Amongst many indigenous communities of Africa and America too there has been a resurgence of a conscious attempt to adopt elements from their own oral tradition in order to create a modern literature of their own which would resist the colonial project of a denial of history or literature to

---

[6] This phrase has been used by Madhu Dubey in 'Postmodern Geographies of the U.S. South', in Saurabh and Ishita Dubey (eds), 2006, *Unbecoming Modern: Colonialism, Modernity, Colonial Modernities*, p. 101.

the colonized. But Temsula Ao, whose own writings display a sensitive blending of the oral and the written, claims that the 'new literature, rich with indigenous flavour' that is being created by the modern storytellers and poets from the North-East, does not seem to have a political agenda like the postcolonial literature that is emerging in Africa and amongst the Native Americans in recent times. Drawing a dividing line between African and native American literatures and that of north-east India, she says:

> ... the people of North East India seem to have attained a new 'maturity' in their perceptions about themselves, that the 'other' of their position vis-à-vis mainland India was not 'them' elsewhere but very much within their own sense of isolation in an oral culture. Once articulated through the written text, similarities of worldviews with other cultures have helped forge new affinities, and at the same time enabled them to accept the differences as only uniqueness of any given culture rather than as denominators of any deficiency or inferiority.[7]

This new-found confidence that attempts to erase the boundaries between subaltern traditions and 'Great Traditions', however, in itself, is an assertion of a political awareness on the part of communities that have been seen as living in 'enchanted spaces'[8] bearing unpronounceable names. Significantly, for mainland India, the region known as the 'North-East' has never had the privilege of being at the centre of epistemic enunciation, except perhaps at some ancient time when Assam was recognized as the centre of occult knowledge associated with tantric worship, magic, and astrology, and, strangely enough, the imagination of the 'mainland' has even today not outgrown those constructs of the mysterious 'other'.

The sense of being denied fair representation in the great Indian civilizational discourse or even in the nationalist discourse, has deeply affected the emerging literati of many of the regions of north-east India in the post-Independence era. A recurrent note in the journalistic as well as academic writings of Assam from the colonial times till the present has been the resentment at the province being turned into a virtual colonial hinterland of Calcutta. Assamese creative literature of the post-Independence era, however, displays a more mature sensibility of focusing on the more complex issues facing the composite state of Assam in the years immediately following Independence. For instance,

---

[7] Temsula Ao, 'Writing Orality', in Soumen Sen and Desmond Kharmawphlang (eds), 2007, *Orality and Beyond*, New Delhi: Sahitya Akademi, p. 109.

[8] The term has been borrowed from Saurabh Dube, 'Mapping Oppositions: Enchanted Spaces and Modern Places', in *Unbecoming Modern*.

the problems of forging new cultural identities through interaction with different communities living within undivided Assam becomes the subject matter of much of Assamese fiction of this period. The crisis of identity brought about by the re-drawing of boundaries that began with the Partition of the Subcontinent affected the Assamese self-representation more than any of the other states in the region. This crisis has been best reflected by the writers from the state in their works of fiction.

Making a choice between the path of armed resistance and the road to peace through dialogue has long remained the unresolved issue before the post-Independence generation of the region, and this becomes the central theme of Birendra Kumar Bhattacharyya's novel *Mrityunjay* published in 1970. Birinchi Kumar Barua's *Xeuji Pator Kahini* (1954), which he wrote under the pseudonym 'Rasna Barua' and from which an excerpt has been included in this anthology, is a sensitive portrayal of the relationship between the indigenes and the immigrant tea-plantation labourers who constitute a sizeable proportion of the population of the state and whose status, vis-à-vis the locals, still remains uncertain. Rong Bong Terang writes about the transformation brought about by 'modernization' to a secluded Karbi village. His *Rongmilir Hanhi* (1981) traces the process of social mobilization amongst the new generation of the hill-people who learn to articulate their demands for the protection of their distinct identity on the eve of India's Independence. Moushumi Kandali takes up from where Terang left. In her story, *Lambada Machor Seshot* ('The Crossroads of Mukindon') written in a refreshingly original style, she holds up a disturbing portrait of the dilemma faced by the younger generation of the same Karbi community, poised at the crossroads between a traditional way of life and a metropolitan modernity with its alluring temptations that can sweep away the ground beneath their feet.

The invasion of an alien culture that lays exclusive claim to modernity and progressiveness and compels the indigenes to be apologetic about their own culture has been the subject matter of much of the satirical writings from the region. In Assamese literature, Anglophiles had been the target of ridicule in the works of many nineteenth-century satirists, including Lambodar Bora and Lakshminath Bezbaroa. Saurabh Kumar Chaliha's *Golam* (1974) is thematically in the same tradition, though structurally it represents the innovative style which was introduced into modern Assamese short-fiction by Chaliha. The stories by Wan Kharkrang, S.J. Duncan, and Kynpham Sing Nongkynrih of Meghalaya are also in the tradition of the comic satire, exposing the social and academic pretensions of a newly emerging urban middle class amongst the small ethnic communities. While S.J. Duncan gives a hilarious version of the old story of the women being smarter than men in business matters and Kharkrang tells a simple comic tale of the effect of sartorial changes on a would-be sahib, Nongkynrih's is a ruthless exposure of the intellectual emptiness of a new class of people with academic pretensions.

While the first generation of fiction writers from Arunachal Pradesh represented here by Lummer Dai and Yeshe Dorjee Thongchi wrote in Assamese because that was the language through which they received their school and college education in the early years after Independence, the situation has changed now after the shift in the language policy of the government. The new official policy is guided by the agenda of 'integration' of the tribes with the Indian 'mainstream' through the induction of Hindi as the medium of instruction in secondary schools. At present, however, the new generation has accepted the prime position of English in the intellectual sphere of the country and would rather write in that universally powerful language than in their mother tongue or any of the Indian languages. The change in the medium of expression has brought about some significant innovations in the choice of the subject matter as well, and this has happened within a short span of a decade or so. Lummer Dai and Thongchi have sought to depict the sensitive questioning of the values represented by the traditional institutions which give little space to the voices of the youth and the women. These two writers may be considered counterparts of the litterateurs of the Indian Renaissance of the nineteenth century who encountered the challenges posed by the ideals of 'modernity' and 'progress' aggressively pushed forward by the European Enlightenment. Mamang Dai's *The Legends of Pensam* (2006) is written in lyrical prose and evokes the memories of an entire community of people. It represents the predicaments of the sensitive young minds in contemporary Arunachal Pradesh, who too are at crossroads and find it difficult to come to terms with the inevitable break with the enchantment of the past and to re-model their lives according to the demands of the changing times. In her powerfully lyrical style, in verse as well as prose, Mamang Dai depicts the experiences of the new generation inhabiting what she calls the 'in-between' places of the mind.

A sizeable number of the selected stories is about the growing awareness of the effect of the wanton destruction of the forests and wildlife in the name of development. Yeshe Dorjee Thongchi's 'The

Forest Guard', Monalisa Changkija's 'The Hunter's Story', Vanneihtluanga's 'Innocence Wears Another Look', and Arupa Patangia Kalita's 'The Conflict' reveal this growing awareness about the problem of the ecological balance being disturbed in the states across the North-East.

It is surely not a coincidence that the dominant theme of the fiction writing included in this collection happens to be that of violence perpetrated by various militant outfits as well as by the armed forces in their counter-insurgency operations. Violence features as a recurrent theme because the story of violence seems to be a never-ending one in this region and yet people have not learnt 'to live with it', as they are expected to do by the distant centres of power. Writers across the states of Assam, Manipur, Nagaland, and Tripura are deeply concerned about the brutalization of their societies by the daily experience of human rights violation and the maiming of the psyche of a whole people by the trauma caused by violence. Manoj Goswami, Imran Hussain, Atulananda Goswami, Temsula Ao, Manorama Das Medhi, Yumlembam Ibomcha, Tayenjam Bijoykumar Singh, Shekhar Das, Kallol Choudhury, Haribhushan Pal, and Bimal Choudhury, all depict their perceptions of the traumatic experience of a people living in the midst of terror and fear and yet cherishing hopes that human values will triumph some day and a new dawn of peace would emerge out of this trial by fire. The feeble child born in the midst of every possible form of adversity in Manorama Das Medhi's 'A Time to Come' holds out some promise of a new life against all odds.

Not all the states of the 'North-East' have produced an equally large harvest of good poetry in the last 50 years and it is even more difficult to come across translations that are reasonably satisfying. Ultimately, therefore, a compromise had to be made between established names and quality translations so that at least some of the representative names from each region could be included in this anthology. The selection has not been totally fair in the case of the states that have a richer production of poetry. An honest attempt has, however, been made to include at least some of the significant poets who have initiated new trends in the modern poetry of the region. Another problem faced has been the need to maintain a judicious balance so that the amount of space allocated to the states with a richer corpus of literary works is not disproportionately large. This has, however, not always been possible and the only way to justify the selections is to assert discreetly that for the purpose of this anthology at least the whole of the 'North-East' should be viewed as one unit.

Three Assamese poets, Nilmani Phookan, Navakanta Barua, and Hiren Bhattacharya have dominated the post-Independence poetic scene of Assam with their distinctive styles that bear the marks of a variety of influences from Anglo-American and European modernist poetry, combining these with elements from the classical Indian tradition. Phookan and Barua delve deep into the world of a modern man, trying to discover logical connections between the shattered images of a modern post-war situation and the inner world of a poet which strives to establish some logical connections between the inner and the outer world. Navakanta's language has great evocative power and his poems as well as novels reflect a deep sense of history. Some of the most memorable images in his poetry spring from this historical sense. Nilmani Phookan has been considered as a gifted poet whose poems are 'concentrated as well as chiseled'.[9] Though his craft has received much attention from critics, his treatment of a variety of themes that signify the tragic dilemma of the modern man deserve equal attention. Hiren Bhattacharya's poems are unique in their capacity to bind together a deep commitment to a socialist cause, especially in his early poetry, with his brilliant handling of words which gives his language a life of its own. According to Harekrishna Deka, it is difficult to capture in translation 'the hypnotic magic of the sounds' in the poetry of Hiren Bhattacharya.[10] Harekrishna Deka's early poetry seeks to explore the human unconscious, but his mature poetry concentrates on 'the facets of hideous violence confronting man' and the complex relationships of urban life.[11] All these poets have assimilated a variety of trends from the modernist poetry of England, America, and Europe with the tradition which they have inherited from Indian literature of the past. Their innovative handling of language, form, and imagery has left its mark on the new generation of Assamese poets. The younger group, represented here by Nilim Kumar, Anubhav Tulasi, Sameer Tanti, Jiban Narah, Anupama Basumatari, and Aruni Kashyap, reflect the heterogeneous sensibilities of a truly polyglot culture. Images, metaphors, myths, and folklore drawn from the different linguistic communities of the region have enriched their poetic language and given it a life of its own. Similarly, the poets from the Barak valley of Assam, like their counterparts in Tripura, have given a new dimension to

---

[9] Hirendra Nath Dutta, 2005, 'Introduction', *One Hundred Years of Assamese Poetry*, Guwahati: Publication Board Assam, p. 16.

[10] Harekrishna Deka, 'The Modern Era in Assamese Poetry: From Romanticism to Modernism' (unpublished essay).

[11] Hirendranath Dutta, p. 17.

the Bengali language by bringing in the unique experiences of a diasporic community. Some of the Bengali poems of Shaktipada Brahmachari and Pijush Raut have been included here.

The rich and powerful poetic voices from Manipur have been represented here by the selections from the poetry of Yumlembam Ibomcha, Saratchand Thiyam, R.K. Bhubonsana, Robin S. Ngangom, Gambhini Devi, Memchoubi, and Thangjam Ibopishak. The history of modern Manipuri literature, as has been discussed in the article by Thingnam Kishan Singh in this collection, marks a significant departure from the general pattern that is visible in the emergence of a new literature during the colonial period in the other states of the region. The Christian missionaries could not make much of an inroad into the Manipur valley where a vibrant Vaishnava culture patronized by the ruling dynasty of the kingdom was strongly entrenched. This Vaishnava tradition continued to exercise its hegemonic power over the cultural arena throughout the colonial period and it almost seemed as if the Manipuri writers had not taken any notice of the entry of the British into the region after the Anglo-Manipuri war of 1891. It is significant, therefore, that the birth of modernism in Manipuri literature in the early years of the twentieth century was not marked by the missionary enterprise of translating Christian texts and Bunyan's *Pilgrim's Progress*, but by the growing awareness of the indigenous Meitei identity which had been suppressed during the rule of the Manipuri kings who had offered active patronage to the alien Vaishnava culture. The roots of the present-day militant identity movement in Manipur, therefore, can be traced back to the early part of the twentieth century which was marked by the efforts of the writers to re-invent a glorious Meitei past for Manipur. The poems in this collection, even in their translated form, display a maturity and vigour of expression that come from a sensitive tapping of the rich resources of the Meitei language. Modern Manipuri poetry, according to Ngangom, was born amidst the ravages of the Second World War, of which Manipur remains a forgotten theatre.[12] The political events that followed soon after the War—the departure of the British, the questionable accession of the kingdom of Manipur to the Indian Union, the disillusionment with the new political arrangement, and the subsequent militant resistance movement were all reflected in the literature of the post-War period. The

---

[12] Robin S. Ngangom, 2007, 'Contemporary Manipuri Poetry: An Overview', *Muse India*, Issue 16, November–December.

anti-romantic trend that characterizes much of the modernist literature of post-War Manipur is reflected in the work of all the poets included in this selection. The poetry that has been published in the 1980s and 1990s, unlike the writings of the 'angry young poets' of the 1970s, is marked by a deeper probe into the social reality and the journey inwards into the tortured soul of the poet.

The history of modern Manipuri fiction is in many respects similar to that of poetry. Though the tradition of the prose narrative can be traced back to an ancient text *Numit Kappa* written probably in the tenth century AD, modern fiction in Manipur emerged in the first half of the twentieth century.[13] After the events of the Second World War which left their indelible marks on the popular psyche of this eastern state, fiction writers abandoned the romantic tradition of the Bengali novel which had inspired a few earlier writers, and wrote boldly about the new social realities and the changing patterns of human relationship. The short stories included in this volume are picked from the writings of the post-1970s when fiction writers began to display a deep concern about the destruction of the traditional way of life and the wanton violation of human rights by the different militant organizations and the security forces involved in counter-insurgency operations.

The scribal tradition is a recent one amongst the Nagas and before the development of a script for the Naga languages through the efforts of the American Baptist missionaries, literature was confined only to the oral form. Amongst the 14 major Naga tribes, speaking about 30 different languages, there is a rich tradition of the oral. So adaptations and transcreations of oral literature constitute a significant part of print literature in modern times. Since, under the initiative of the missionaries most of the Naga writers from the first group of literates honed their literary skills on translations of the Gospels, written literature of the early phase took on a moralistic note. Amongst the Ao Nagas, who were the first to come into contact with the Christian missionaries stationed at the adjacent district of Sibsagar in Assam, the first printed book was one of alphabets in the Roman script published in 1880 by Rev. Edward Clark who came to work among the Ao Nagas in 1876. The story of Ao literature was later repeated in other areas of the Naga Hills where Christianity gradually spread in the twentieth century. For example, the Tenyidin (Angami) language was given a written form

---

[13] For details, see Tayenjam Bijoykumar Singh, 2002, 'Fiction in Manipur', *New Frontiers*, Vol. V.

by the missionaries in the third decade of the twentieth century, but secular literature in its written form began to take shape only under the initiative of the Angami Literature Committee in the 1970s.[14] The literature that developed in the different Naga languages during the early years of their acquiring written forms, bore the recognizable stamp of the style, imagery, and diction of the Bible.

The change came after the outbreak of the war between the Naga underground army and the Indian government forces which completely transformed the cultural ethos of the people, bringing in significant changes in what was considered the 'Naga way of life'. The possibility of making quick money by providing supplies to the military contractors or amassing wealth through corruption in government service, raised great expectations about 'progress' and 'development' which are inimical to the notions of a distinctive old-world tradition. Commenting on this change, Temsula Ao says, 'The sudden displacement of the young from a placid existence in rural habitats to a world of conflict and confusion in urban settlements is also a fallout of recent Naga history and one that has left them disabled in more ways than one.'[15] In the rural areas too, the regrouping of villages during the operations of the Indian army against the Naga underground resulted in displacements of another kind that also snapped traditional ties. The post-1950s generation of Naga writers have journeyed through territories of the mind which are distant from the world of simple Christian pieties upheld by the newly converted Christian writers of the earlier period. The new literature, most of which is in English, has sprung from the staccato cry of the machine guns and reflects the revolutionary ideals of the militants as well as the disillusionment with their ways that followed. The course of the struggle has also transformed the whole idiom of poetry as well as prose fiction and words with sinister connotations have crept into the vocabulary of common speech.[16] In a recent biographical note, Easterine Iralu writes about her experience of growing up in Nagaland: 'Curfews and continued periods of gun-fire were all a part of growing up in Nagaland.'[17] Yet, the new literature that is emerging from Nagaland is

---

[14] D. Koulie, 'Tenyimia Folklore and Verse: Quest for Beyond', in S. Sen and Desmond Kharmawphlang (eds), *Orality and Beyond*, p. 128.
[15] Temsula Ao, 2006, *These Hills Called Home: Stories from a War Zone*, New Delhi: Zubaan, p. x.
[16] Ibid., pp. 11–12.
[17] Easterine Iralu in *ICORN International Cities of Refuge Network*, Norway, Autumn 2006.

not all soaked in blood. The old storytelling tradition, which is common to all oral cultures of indigenous people, has been creatively integrated into modern literary genres to give a distinct identity to the literature of this region.

Modern Mizo literature too draws from a rich oral tradition. While much of the secular prose literature is derived from myths and folktales, the poetry draws inspiration from the rich corpus of folk songs that the various Mizo groups possess. As has been discussed in Margaret Zama's article 'Mizo Literature: An Overview', included in this anthology, the coming of Christianity to Mizoram infused a 'non-secular mindset' which determined the character of the songs and narratives written during the early phase of written literature in Mizoram. The Christian missionaries entered the Lushai Hills, then a district in the colonial province of Assam, in the last decade of the nineteenth century, accompanied by British colonization. As in Nagaland and Meghalaya, the Roman script was adopted for the Luesi dialect of the Duhlian language which became the standardized Lushai language, by the Christian missionaries. The first major literary task accomplished by them was the translation of the Bible into the Lushai language. The rich secular tradition of oral literature of the pre-colonial period was almost marginalized in order to underscore the success of the 'civilizing' mission of the British. But the natural genius of the people stood out even during the height of the religious phase, in the writings of Biakliana and others. During the period of insurgency when normal life was paralysed in the hills, a new trend developed in Mizo literature which was subversive in nature but reflected the anguish of the people traumatized by violence. The Mizo militant movement and the counter-insurgency programme undertaken to curb it, led to social upheavals that changed the character of the communities and the social institutions. B.G. Verghese and others have discussed the effects of the village regrouping programmes of the Indian government on the whole social structure of the community: '... it was a painful interlude resulting in an erosion of village institutions, the social fabric and traditional way of life.'[18] These events also accelerated the process of urbanization of the society, thus paving the way for the emergence of a new literature that is now taking shape in Mizoram through the efforts of a host of writers who can handle both their mother tongue as well as the English language with equal confidence and skill.

---

[18] B.G. Verghese, 1996, *India's Northeast Resurgent: Ethnicity, Insurgency, Governance, Development,* New Delhi: Konark Publishers, p. 143.

'The Khasis,' says the Welsh scholar Nigel Jenkins, 'were weaving stories long before the Bible-thumping, hymn-crazy Welsh arrived on the scene.'[19] The same story of a colonial 'civilizing' mission persuading a people to abandon their rich indigenous oral tradition and to adopt an alien way of life which was projected as the only 'universal' civilizational model, was repeated in the Khasi–Jaintia Hills as elsewhere in the region. The Khasi language which belongs to the Mon-Khmer group of languages, was rich in the oral tradition, though in the absence of a script of its own, written literature developed only in the nineteenth century. It was a traditional practice to compose *Phawar*s or rhyming couplets orally to celebrate important social events. In the pre-colonial times, the Khasi rulers used the Assamese, Bengali, Persian, or Devanagari scripts to maintain administrative contact with their neighbours.[20] Significantly, the *New Testament* was translated into the Khasi language at the Serampore Baptist Mission in 1831 and this massive work, running into 898 pages, was in the Bengali script.[21] The Welsh missionaries were the first to introduce the Roman script for giving a written form to the Khasi language and they took the initiative for almost 40 years to publish hymns, moral fables, and Bible stories in the Khasi language. However, 'a great cultural revival' took place in the Khasi Hills towards the end of the nineteenth century when three Khasi writers and a social activist following on the footsteps of S.M. Amjad Ali, a Bengali poet who wrote secular lyrics in Khasi, initiated a new secular trend in Khasi literature and posed 'a purposeful challenge to the influence of Christianity and the missionaries' monopoly over the intellectual and cultural affairs'.[22] The leading personalities in this group who went about in a bold and determined way to create national awakening amongst the Khasis were Rabon Singh, Radhan Singh Berry, Soso Tham, and Jeeban Roy. Soso Tham laid the foundation of a new trend in Khasi poetry by exploring the world of myths, legends, and folklore to find new idioms and subject matter for his poetic creations. The poems included here are written by a new generation of Khasi poets who share a deep sense of cultural loss which came with the conquest

---

[19] Nigel Jenkins (ed.), 1995, *Khasia in Gwalia: Poetry and Prose from the Khasi Hills in North-east India*, Port Talbot: Alun Books, p. 10.
[20] Hamlet Bareh, 2003 [1962], *A Short History of Khasi Literature*, Shillong: Don Bosco Press, p. 13.
[21] Ibid., p. 25.
[22] R.S. Lyngdoh, *Ka Histori ka Thoh ka Tar: Bynta II* (in Khasi), 1983, quoted in Kynpham Sing Nongkynrih, 2004, '*Hiraeth and the Poetry of Soso Tham*', unpublished thesis, p. 37.

of the territory and the mind by waves of colonizers of different hues. While they strive to seek out roots that would firmly bind them to the racial memory of the past, at the same time, they also display an eagerness to master the new modernist poetic idioms that can link them with a global audience.

Tripura's cultural history has been greatly influenced by its long history of close proximity to Bengal. Though the ruling dynasties of this small kingdom had always belonged to one of the indigenous tribal communities of the state, the cultural dominance of the plains by people from the neighbouring Bengal under the patronage of the Tripuri rulers continued to create tension in the region. The unending migration of Bengali-speaking people from the neighbouring districts of eastern Bengal during the colonial period, increased steadily during the pre-Partition days, until the small state became a 'safe haven' for Bengali migrants escaping from communal conflicts in East Bengal.[23] After Partition, the problem of refugee influx took on frightening dimensions, altering the demographic map of the area completely and reducing the local inhabitants to a small minority. At present the Bengali-speaking population constitutes about 70 per cent of the population while only about 900,000 people belonging to the eight indigenous communities speak Kokborok. The inevitable fallout of this was the rise of ethnic mobilization and a long-drawn militant struggle for identity preservation by the tribal groups of the region comprising the five major groups—the Tripuri, Reang, Jamatia, Noatia, and Halam. Since the Bengali language had been receiving royal patronage and it was the language used for administrative purposes, a vibrant tradition of Bengali literature had developed in the region. Rabindranath Tagore was often a royal guest in Tripura and Maharaja Birchandra Manikya Bahadur (r. 1870–96) and his daughter published several books of poetry of their own in Bengali.[24] It was only after the rise of militancy amongst the indigenous groups of Tripura that the Kokborok language attained its status as an official language, and at present conscious attempts are being made to retrieve the rich oral culture of the people which reflects the economic and social life of the communities. It is significant that while the modern Bengali literature from Tripura strives to follow the tradition of mainstream Bengali literature, yet as in the case of the Sylheti writers of the Barak valley in Assam, the writers

---

[23] Ibid., p. 168.

[24] Sisir Sinha, 'The Poetry of Tripura: Past and Present', *Indian Literature*, Vol. 191, New Delhi: Sahitya Akademi.

from Tripura too are struggling to come to terms with their diasporic existence and the need to search for new tap roots for their literature. The modern literature that is taking shape in the Kokborok language, on the other hand, displays a self-confidence and a rootedness in the lived experience of the people. Some of the poems and stories translated from Kokborok which have been included in this collection are refreshingly original, and in their depiction of certain enduring truths about life they defy all stereotypical constructions about notions of mainstream and peripheral culture.

II

A collection of writings which represents a wide variety of cultures, nationalities, and languages cannot be subjected to any accepted notion of compiling an anthology based on similarity of style or content. Considering all the practical limitations mentioned earlier, the present collection like other such existing collections, does not make any claims of comprehensiveness. But at a time when the region is striving to reach out to the rest of the world from its historically and geographically marginalized position, the diverse writings which this anthology has brought together, representing a complex region posited at a historically difficult time, would serve as yet another attempt at the synthesizing of intellectual opinions. The response of the writers to the onslaught of the 'modernity' of the postcolonial state, their negotiations with the idea of the gradual erasure of the notion of community, their understanding of human relationships, especially the complex relationships between communities which had only marginal links with each other in the past, their sensitive approach to the problem of violence and its after-effects—all these could be some of the distinguishable markers that bind together an anthology of this nature.

The stories, extracts from novels, poems, and essays included here are from the post-Independence era. Most of the writers who find a place in this anthology are, in a sense, the children of violence. Many of them have grown up in close contact with people who have memories of the Partition of the Subcontinent and its tragic after-effects in the North-East. Others have experienced at close quarters the violence associated with the insurgent movements in different parts of the region that have changed the very character of the societies in many ways. Still others, including the large influential group of younger writers, are living through the traumatic experience of those daily incidents of violence that disturb the seemingly idyllic surroundings of the region and leave a deep scar on the sensitive mind.

Care has been taken to include some of the representative works in fiction and poetry which have introduced new trends in contemporary literatures from the seven states. Some of the well-known works of an earlier generation of writers have been included not only because they are pioneering works that show a new awareness about the emerging social and intellectual concerns of the post-Independence period, but also because of the evocative power of their language or other finer qualities of style. These are also the resources from which the newer group of writers has drawn inspiration. Many of the new writers whose works find a place in this anthology are perhaps yet to produce their best works, but they hold promise of new possibilities in creative writing from the region. In literary compositions, especially poetry, aesthetic qualities may be considered more valuable than didactic ones. This anthology, however, while endeavouring to follow that ideal, has not lost its focus on the social, political, or moral issues that are of intense concern to contemporary life in the region. It is not merely accidental, therefore, that most of the fiction writings in this volume, and some of the poems too, represent the deep-seated concern of the writers for social issues. While an overwhelming majority of the stories reflect on the theme of violence and peace, yet there are quite a few which deal sensitively with the theme of human endurance and the beauty of relationships in the midst of terror and violence. There are also a few enduring tales on the theme of the growing awareness about the nature–man conflict and the need for conservation of nature which is increasingly being threatened by human rapaciousness. Dissenting voices at the crossroads of history, which question the relevance of cultural practices that are totally at odds with the modern notion of rights of the individual as against communitarian rights, also find a place in this collection.

And finally, it is necessary to mention another departure that this anthology makes in the nature of its collection of fiction. Inclusion of oral literature in an anthology of contemporary writings may be considered unacceptable by some critics because it questions the often implicitly accepted hierarchy between the written and the oral. However, the old definition of folklore as the strange and exotic material produced by a 'primitive, backward' culture no longer holds good after the dissemination of a host of exciting modern ideas about the significance of oral literature as a lens through which to view the negotiations with the various practices of modernity. Traditional myths, in their transmuted form, have often helped modern poets to give shape to their unique visions of the world. They have also continued to exist as a vibrant part of the living present of many cultures, merging with newly created rituals and traditions and giving a new lease of life to the ancient lore. Further, the need to mythologize could also be a response to a sense of loss—subversion as it were—of the changing social order in the region. This could perhaps explain the recovery of orality in recent times by a significant number of writers. Some of the oral narratives selected for this anthology have been retold or 'transcreated' by the modern writers because they are an intrinsic part of the literature from the region. Some of them may be interpreted as civilizational myths that have some relevance to the understanding of the cultural identity of a community. As Esther Syiem discusses in her essay 'Social Identity and the Liminal Character of the Folk', the oral discourse which has always been central to the Khasi society may seem to have shifted to a peripheral space in a more complex modern situation, but it has never ceased to occupy a significant position in the worldview of the community.

The essays included here range from the philosophical to the analytical and the descriptive. There are essays that deal specifically with the literature and culture of particular ethnic or linguistic groups of the North-East, and there are also studies that reflect on the different dimensions of the multi-ethnic and multilingual cultures of the region. In his philosophical essay on the different traditions of spirituality in the West and in India, 'The Spiritual and the Moral', Mrinal Miri comments on the uniqueness of the tribal vision of life which is applicable to the world of the tribesman in the North-East as well. He points out the 'moral lapse' involved in the dismissive tendency amongst many scholars when they judge the concept of self-knowledge amongst the tribesman as 'irretrievably erroneous or lacking in autonomy'. Birendranath Datta, in his discussion of the distinctive features of the culture of the region, highlights the significance of the mixture of 'Hindu-Aryan' and 'Indo-Mongoloid' elements in the culture of the region in relation to what is generally known as the 'mainstream' culture of India. He provides a comprehensive overview of the syncretistic culture of the North-East, highlighting the distinctive features of its 'physical folk-life' as well as the verbal folklore.

The umbrella term 'North-East', which is often used as an emotive connotation for the seven states nestled together in one corner of the country, does not actually denote anything more than a geographical region. But, as it happens elsewhere in the world, geography is history in many ways. The 'seven sisters of the North-East' which had only marginal historical links with each other in the pre-colonial times, had their doors open towards South-East Asia, eastern Bengal, Bhutan, and Tibet—regions with which they shared boundaries and lively commercial and cultural contacts. It was only after the Partition of the Subcontinent that the region became totally landlocked with almost all the doors closed except for a narrow corridor that kept it linked with India. This geographical isolation has led to erasures and marginalization on multiple levels, the effect of which is clearly discernible in the writings from the region.

The creative writers from all the small ethnic communities whose works find a place in this collection, have sought to reach out from the level of the personal to that of the universal. A clear evidence of this may be seen in the flexible attitude of most of the writers towards language. Contrary to the stereotypical notion of the region being prone to chauvinistic, xenophobic tendencies, almost every writer in this anthology is bilingual if not multilingual. Several writers have been writing with equal confidence and facility in both English as well as their mother tongue or in one of the other languages of the region. Boundaries and barriers which hampered an earlier generation of writers are being crossed easily by a new group which believes in sharing of experiences. A tangible evidence of this aspiration is the effort being made in recent years to set up writers' forums which are taking the initiative in translating and publishing literary works from the region.

The task of compiling and editing this anthology has been an immense learning experience for me. Not only have I had the opportunity to interact with writers and translators from all the seven states (and in that process making new friends), but while reading through the stories, poems, and essays I have discovered that in the midst of all the plurality there are certain elements of commonality which give a sense of distinctiveness to the writings from the region. At a point in history when no community can afford to live in isolation despite all the myths that have been circulated about the 'self-sufficiency' of societies geographically isolated from each other and from the rest of the country, the discovery of emerging affinities amongst a new group of creative writers for whom boundaries have ceased to interfere with thought processes is, in itself, a rewarding experience.

October 2010   TILOTTOMA MISRA

POETRY

ARUNACHAL PRADESH

Mamang Dai
The Voice of the Mountain

From where I sit on the high platform
I can see the ferry lights crossing
criss-crossing the big river.

I know the towns, the estuary mouth.
There, beyond the last bank
where the colour drains from heaven
I can outline the chapters of the world.

The other day a young man arrived from the village.
Because he could not speak he brought a gift of fish
from the land of rivers.
It seems such acts are repeated:
We live in territories forever ancient and new,
and as we speak in changing languages
I, also, leave my spear leaning by the tree
and try to make a sign.

The Voice of the Mountain

I am an old man
sipping the breeze that is forever young.
In my life I have lived many lives.
My voice is sea waves and mountain peaks,
In the transfer of symbols
I am the chance syllable that orders the world
instructed with history and miracles.

I am the desert and the rain.
The wild bird that sits in the west.
The past that recreates itself
and particles of life that clutch and cling
for thousands of years—

I know, I know these things
as rocks know, burning in the sun's embrace,
about clouds, and sudden rain;
As I know a cloud is a cloud is a cloud,
A cloud is this uncertain pulse that sits over my heart.
In the end the universe yields nothing
except a dream of permanence.
Peace is a falsity.
A moment of rest comes after long combat:

From the east the warrior returns
with the blood of peonies.
I am the child who died at the edge of the world,
the distance between end and hope.
The star diagram that fell from the sky,
The summer that makes men weep.
I am the woman lost in translation
who survives, with happiness to carry on.

I am the breath that opens the mouth of the canyon,
the sunlight on the tips of trees;
There, where the narrow gorge hastens the wind
I am the place where memory escapes
the myth of time,
I am the sleep in the mind of the mountain.

The Sorrow of Women

They are talking about hunger.
They are saying there is an unquenchable fire
burning in our hearts.
My love, what shall I do?
I am thinking how I may lose you
to war, and big issues
more important than me.

Life is so hard, like this.
Nobody knows why.
It is like fire.
It is like rainwater, sand, glass.
What shall I do, my love,
if my reflection disappears?

They are talking about a place
where rice flows on the streets,
about a place where there is gold
in the leaves of trees.
They are talking about displacement,
when the opium poppy was growing
dizzy in the sun
happy, in a state of believing—

And they are talking about escape,
about liberty, men and guns,
Ah! The urgency for survival.
But what will they do
Not knowing the sorrow of women.

An Obscure Place

The history of our race begins with the place of stories.
We do not know if the language we speak
belongs to a written past.
Nothing is certain.

There are mountains. Oh! There are mountains.
We climbed every slope. We slept by the river.

But do not speak of victory yet

An obscure place haunts the hunter.
The prize slips away.
Yesterday the women hid their faces.
They forbade their children to speak.
Yesterday we gave shelter to men
who climbed over our hills
for glory of a homeland, they said—
those who know what knowing is,
And now the sleeping houses, the men and the villages
have turned to stone.

If there is no death the news is silent.
If there is only silence, we should be disturbed

Listen, the tone of a prayer is hushed:

If a stranger passes this way let him look up to the sky.
A smoke cloud chases the ants.
See! They have slain the wild cat
and buried the hornbill in her maternal sleep.

The words of strangers have led us into a mist
deeper than the one we left behind
weeping, like the waving grassland
where the bones of our fathers are buried
surrounded by thoughts of beauty.

There are mountains. Oh! There are mountains.
We climbed every slope. We slept by the river.
But do not speak of victory yet!

ASSAM

Navakanta Barua
Judas

Murder my death with the weapon of your kisses.
Why do this to life
That has its frontiers on the present?
What is the earthly use, I ask you,
Of stretching and abridging
A few animate moments called life,
With the elasticity of bread and love-making,
Wine and fame?

In your kisses I have not felt a dearth of love;
What inexorable orbiting
Draws in your love into you
Enfolding all planets, stars?
What concentrated emptiness
Where the whirlpool ends!

What is the harm if the flames quivering around you
Be of hell?
Beyond the bounds of space and time
All flames are multidirectional.

Even last night I doled out the bread my body.
Even last night I poured out the wine my blood.
With the weapon of your kisses let my death be murdered;
On the farmyard of blood let there grow as sacred crops
Thirty pieces of silver.

—Translated from Assamese by D.N. Bezboruah

Bats

The inert bats were suspended
Behind the string of grocery shops,
Innocuously blending
With the flaming abundance of yellow cassia—
A multitude of embryonic infants
In the cavernous innards of the sky.

They saw:
The earth strung above the sky,
And the trees that rest on the firmament
Thrusting their roots
Into the hoary darkness of the earth.
Women, their mats pulled over their resilient forms,
Chasing the weary hours of nocturnal ennui,
With a brief midday siesta.
And they saw us boys
Hanging upside down from our kite-strings
Like dubious notes of interrogation …

Then evening.
With the bats' hesitant flight
The perverse trees stand again
On the earth as is their wont;
Women lean on crimsoned portals
Longing anew for the drowsy hour.
And we boys
Inch back our fragile kites

With our reels timidly turning.
Consternation, like a winged missile
Hits them between the eyes:
The sky?
Whence did it rise above our heads?
They kept singing:
Hang on! Cling on!
Hold fast with both feet
To the liquid death that speeds
Through tense electric wires.

And then?
Then the sky will again lie
Recumbent.
The hills will pin it down
Astride in an inverted coital variant;
And under the monstrous mammaries
Of an insatiable witch,
Love will die a shattering death.

—*Translated from Assamese by D.N. Bezboruah*

Silt

The fire of the *palaash*† has gone out now.
In the *saal*‡ and *sotiyaan** woods
Spring-storms of days past—
Days of the Burmese invasion.
How many dreams fell who keeps count?
On the Banks of the Kolong, Kopili, Diju
Grandfather's bones.
The wild lily sprouts through
Grandmother's heart.
What did the clouds say,
Give, give more, give your all,
Plant trees by the road, open a high school,
The dear traveler is always on the road,
Heave a sigh

† A tree bearing reddish flowers.
‡ A timber tree.
* A kind of tree.

Let the water speeding through roofs
Flood out the cells of dead spiders
Let our silt fertilize the banks of the Kolong.
In the furrows of our grandson's new farmstead
We shall wake.
In our fossils they will read
Amusing tales
of those who remember past births.
In the lane where dreams are blind
we stay there. In the gutters
their future.

—Translated from Assamese by Pradip Acharya

Nilmani Phookan
Poem

From here
The waters stretch
Far beyond the horizon

When you reach out
The plantain leaf trembles
When you let fall your hair
The rains descend

In my heart
Sprouts a seed
Left behind by careless men
Who have eaten and
Forgotten

A dove comes flying
A blade of grass in its bill
Or is it a jasmine garland
Now no one is dying anywhere
No child
Nor old man

From here
One sees the sun going down

And
The moon rising

From here
One sees on opening the door
Eternally turning
An earth warm with love

Ageless
Those two women
At the gate of *Da-Parbatiya*†
In a gesture of welcome

From your feet
Stretch the waters
All the way
Far beyond the horizon

—*Translated from Assamese by Hiren Gohain*

After a Couple of Days

After a couple of days
The fog will shroud this city
Even the sewing needle

People will breathe out mist
Like the hills and the river
Yet people will not know it at all

Gazing at the vermilion sun
The ripe oranges will fall off
The fingers of women will go numb with cold

Along the cold deserted path of people's mind
The sad rustle of dry leaves
Will pass by like the footfalls of pallbearers

Flight after flight munias will fly away
Towards eternity
Will silently cruise a spacecraft

† A little-known village near Tezpur on the north bank of the Brahmaputra. The remains of a temple in the Gupta style here contain a relatively undamaged door-frame with two river-goddesses on either side.

And another yellow time will pass by this way
Yet people will not know it at all
Then each of them will change into
A gaunt figure of winter

—*Translated from Assamese by Nirendra Nath Thakuria*

Mating Music

In the woods
Deep in the woods
A crane calls

Open out both your arms
Let a swarm of stars sink
Into the aroma of your hair

In the pond teeming with lotuses
The wind soughs
Deep inside your body
Opens a red bud

The rain pours down
The opening palm frond
The blood of your breasts
Rushes to your lips

Now you are awake
the face of darkness glows
the clouds rumble over the hill

—*Translated from Assamese by Nirendra Nath Thakuria*

Hiren Bhattacharya
The Lone Prayer for Poetry

The poet's voice rebounds from harshness in unrivalled echoes,
On the tip of the pen, the poet's soul,
The promised poem,
The freedom of art,
A hymn of sorrow in the low voice of the starved poet

Imperilled by the burden of nerves.
Let me finish this poem as I would,
Holding the strange banner of the future
The message of blood dies a restless death
At the ungainly naked body.

Grant me the freedom to hammer into pieces
The indifference of these familiar words
Or, the brilliance of the invincible sword
To cut into shreds
This anaemic, moribund, unyielding reality.

—Translated from Assamese by Pradip Acharya

The Earth My Poem

My pen is the hammer in the blacksmith's hands,
I hammer words into shape sharp as the
Farmer's plough-share, the golden Sita on
The furrows, ragged like the carpenter's saw,
I extract from the grains of hard timber,
Words stained by the blood of experience,
Like sure arrows from the Santhal male's bow,
words become ardent in my blood, flesh and desire,
some of them stand high as mountains,
some lie low like rivers,
while others are grave as the lake—
not at anybody's beck and call.

I am a poet of the vast continent
Studded with rivers and mountains,
The earth is my poem.

—Translated from Assamese by Pradip Acharya

Sylvan Song

The naked tree grows stubble of new leaves
someone somewhere lilts a *Bihu*† song
'Blue orchids in your hair'—

† Spring festival of Assam.

beating their drums to a rhythm
drummers of Phoolpanisinga†
throng a path.

These colourful homely village birds
green birds, tailorbirds, woodpeckers romp upon the forest floor
hear the drumbeats vroom away somewhere at once.
The merry chirping of fledglings
traipse all over the forest floor.

—Translated from Assamese by Rupanjali Baruah

Let There be Crop

Let there be crop.
Let them grow vie with the rising water

let rows of paddy furrow my
paddy-field back
my blood turn turbulent run over by twelve
ploughs

let the burden of crop crumble my ever-ready shoulder and
ribcage

let there be crop. Let my mother's tattered drapes flutter in
the wind
with the fragrance of ripening grain

a field full of paddy
a song of plenty
this much of my paddy
challenge water
unfurling the
stalks

—Translated from Assamese by Rupanjali Baruah

† Name of a village.

Harekrishna Deka
Another One

Is this me that I see in the mirror?
With graying hair, elongated chin, knitted brows
And many straight lines drawn across the forehead
Is this the one—
The one who's my very own?
Sometimes I wonder—
I don't know this man:
Whether he's ugly or handsome, straight or knave,
A coward or a brave, spirited man.

O my people, my friends
My wife, daughter, son and brothers,
My masters who sustain me and my loyal co-workers
Whatever you have asked me to be
The same I've sought to become;
But I don't know me
Maybe the image
Getting blurred in the mirror is mine
All of you know him well.

All of you know him
But within his brain an invisible entity called *me*
Shouts out regularly—
It's the fear of being cured by your healthy hands
Have any among you understood this?

—Translated from Assamese by Bibhash Choudhury

A Word for Love

You sought a word from me,
I gave you that word.

I looked at your face,
I called you a flower.

One word leads to another
Flower is a word. Through it our dumbness speaks.

We touch each other
And enthused we are.

Some cruel words can tear a flower apart
Can crush it underneath one's feet, can wipe it away
Just as an infant's neck can be slit open with a knife
And give a sadist pleasure in an anguished cry.

But still there are words like the flower,
It fades, closes upon itself, falls off
But it rests upon your smile and there it lives.

I love such a word
It carries love. A mere black sign,
Yet it touches you, and then touches me.

—*Translated from Assamese by Bibhash Choudhury*

Towards Freedom

You'll come with us. We will take you by the hand.
Don't look at the road. We will cover your eyes.
We will build the road for you. And we will tie up your hands.
We will take you to the freedom ground. And uncover your eyes.
Take you to the freedom ground. And untie your hands.

Don't make a racket. We will give you new table to memorise.
We will give you a new alphabet. Don't make a racket.

We will take you to the freedom ground. We will give you a clear sky.
Freedom showers will welcome you there. Freedom breeze will fan you.

Don't cry in hunger. We will give you sweetmeats of water.
Don't look at the bare boughs. We will give you coloured glasses to see.

We will take you to the freedom ground and tell you to sing our song.
We will make you wear a new mask and teach you a new gait.

You will come with us. You will smile our smile.
You will dance our dance. You will cry our tears.

—*Translated from Assamese by Bibhash Choudhury*

Nilim Kumar
I had Nothing to Offer

There was no
preparation
you had just got up from your poem
and my two hands damp
with sorrow were searching for you

The clouds slowly ran out pouring
rain
I had nothing in my hand to offer you
if there was something on
my lips
it was just one blasted poem.
As a dream comes to an end
I
encircle you
with you

—*Translated from Assamese by Rupanjali Baruah*

To my Son

My child, I will not pull you
backward
at this noon hour, I will not
you scale stairs through the
city's smell of petrol
you race down lifts, handkerchief is sweat
soaked
in the middle of all this if you and your girlfriend
share a
cup of coffee or a cold drink at some place
why should I feel
bad?
That will be a happy thing for me, my child, of happiness

Your
days are difficult than ours

the city is getting tougher
the city bus
conductor, the auto rickshaw driver
the voices of receptionists are
coarse
there is no welcome, my child, no goodwill
they pass overtaking
you, no one is with you on the way

You know better than me, I will
not preach you
and yet let me say this
here in this city do not make
any promise, my child,
do not trust a soul
do not expect someone while
waiting on the footpath
that waiting, in this city may go on for
infinity
do not trust your own self
your words and your deeds
because
your blood may turn against you
time has changed my child!
a
kalapahar of worries sits on your head
in tomorrow's blood-splattered
road, my blinking eyes would see
in the inside of your shoes blood
oozing from your feet
must walk on camouflaging your blistering two
feet
must not limp
wear instead an inconsequential smile on your
lips
must converse with the city
must make your girlfriend laugh
must
sip a steaming cup of tea with your enemy

Your life is awful than
mine
you are paler than me
did you have something for your midday
meal?
Have you lost your comb or why is your hair so unkempt?
Why
those few streaks of gray at this age
because of the kalaphar of
worries?
Your life is full of agony emptier than mine

I will not
pull you backward
forget me my child
those days when I took you to
school riding on a cycle
hand in hand I had taught you to cross the
main street
and the primer's *a aa ka kha, Jyotiprasad's gose gose pati dile*
forget that sweet shiver of sucking on chocolates and ice
creams
while you sat on my lap
forget my child forget
that whole lot
of fathers who is still alive in you.
Because memory comes cheap in
this city

Like Troy, this city too is dead. I, a deceased occupant
I
only follow you about
because I had nurtured a dream in you

but you
too my child
is just somewhat alive!

     —Translated from Assamese by Rupanjali Baruah

Sameer Tanti
The Night of Kadams in Bloom

It's the night of Kadams in bloom
The rain soaks your lips

In your heart is the frangrance of Kadam flowers
O dear, my eyes have lost sleep

Whose heart dies for the luxury of weaver birds
That sway and dance in the wind

Whose whistle beckons me
It's the night of Kadams in bloom

Land is drunk with the wine of rumbling clouds
Come on, kids, come on to my breast

Oh dear, in your navel is the breath of rain
What a night of restless clouds

Fishes play in dream
It's the night of Kadams in bloom

Growing in my body what Kadams are you
The swaying rhythm of *jhumur*

Whose is this laugh, which Kinnari's laugh,
That carries me away to the heart of heaven

Thrilled I trembled and weep
It's the night of Kadams in bloom

—*Translated from Assamese by Nirendra Nath Thakuria*

As the Night Thickens the Stars Nod Off

As the night thickens the stars nod off
And I keep going like an ever watchful boatman
Crossing over current after current
Across the other side of dreams
Around me memories of countless dead people
In their eyes ashes of burnt-out books
Mask within mask behind it

Affection gathered like snow
Unfinished poems of dead poets
Tears of golden tigers
Peculiarities of an unknown jargon
And shadows of butterflies flitting away

I wanted to know all and one day
I forgot her identity
My awakening seemed to be
Close as death yet heartless as night

Nothing was said to me
Nothing at all

—*Translated from Assamese by Nirendra Nath Thakuria*

Anubhav Tulasi
Prodigal

There they say the cow
Disdains the grass in the backyard
Of its owner's cottage
And there I left
Judas's kin
My dear native village long ago
In the prayer of sunflower rain
As the earthworm writhes
Out of its hole in the ground

It was a festive night
With all the banners tranced in a dance
The drum casting a spell
In tune with the beat of the dancer's feet
The owl
Hooting cheerfully
And the ghost of the turbaned old noble
Came on a white charger
And carried away
My horn of plenty

It was in another city
I began a strumpet life
Made of snake's coils
Where the day began
With colourful butterflies
Impaled on the barbed wire
Of trains' shrieks
Long-tailed kites
On blue skies
The humped camel
Among the thorny desert shrubs

The skeleton only
Of the Pushpabhadra river
Left
Under the glare of the Sun-temple[†] of Modhera
Yet the ape gamboled still
In the distance the jacks
Gave their friendly howl
The peacock spread her fan
The nightingale poured her sad melodies
Which reverberated on the ageless rocks
Across the river at Kanai–Barosi–Bowa
And their echoes have hunted me ever since

To solve the riddle
Of ferrying across the stormy river
The tiger, the goat and the bundle of betel-leaves
So that none could prey on the others
Easy enough game for small crooks
But how to jump out of the bed
As the sails go berserk
And leave under the pillow
Blank paper, colour of dreams
With unwritten words gathered

My being
Only a shaft of warm sunlight

[†] This refers to the Sun-temple at Modhera, Gujarat, by the river Pushbhadra, known for its intricate stone-carvings. It was built in AD 1025 by Bhimdeva I, a king of the Solanki dynasty.

That trickled down pink umbrellas
Down a lovely woman's cheeks
A bank of clouds
Like a bunch of juicy flying grapes
A whole grain
Among heaps of empty husks

You gave me a pair of cuckoo's eggs
To smuggle into the crow's nest
I fed them to my master the serpent
And became his court favourite
The Devil gave me a boon
'You will be a poet one day'
And further gave me
A sackful of poison
To mix with honeyed words
Of a party flunkey
And I tumbled
Of high peaks of carefree bliss
Crashed on dreamy rocks
To become a golden bristle
On a grain of wheat in the field

One day that golden fuzz
Grew wings

Beating my wings
A clumsy flier
I hit against the wall of notes
Overturning it
And heard beyond the forest
Unearthly music
Saw lakes of wild flowers
Flocks of magic deer
And purling streamlets
Alive with dragonflies
Where the Devil fancied my shadow
And bestowed on me
An unvalued chain of smoke
And anointed me with molten tar
The Devil showed me the charm
Of hell-fire's flames from afar

And knave that I was
I defied my master's warning
To nestle close to that charm

Only to burn
To cinders

To return
A dead ember
To my old house
On a lonely tired evening
To the sombre beat
Of the prayer-hall's drum

—*Translated from Assamese by Hiren Gohain*

The Infernal Playground

May the morn awaken with light
On the teak sapling's leaf

Flameless darkness smolders
And unbearable the moonlit night
When you lie on that couch of bliss
Seven horses go galloping
Across your dreams

Or is it the burning of the heart
The daybreak still far off
And preparation for the day's awakening
On the teak-leaf a phantom only

Is there no way out of this hell
Are we to rot here without protest
Then why kidnap the obstinate one
Who would not surrender
Or something even more
Inconceivably cruel and monstrous

Does it entertain you
Like a well-plotted dramatic moment
Authored in North Block
Is hell your playground, sirs?

Then why do I suffer page after page
In labour of anxiety and nightmare
To deliver that horror alone

But it's tough to sit unmoved
In a posture of indifference
The gloom of the scenes
Crucifies my conscience
Starts raging forest-fires
Beyond the gnomes in capital

I dip my pen in those flames
And revive the dying breath of the teak leaves

—*Translated from Assamese by Hiren Gohain*

Jiban Narah
Rhythm

Wearied, the fast beats of the *khol* encircle me
And clothe me in a resonant attire

My resonant frame
Paces to and fro through a verse
The feet springs to motion
With the khol's rhythm
The hands flutter as wings
Across the courtyard of the night
Thronged by thousands
I begin a song of lamentation

The river beneath the veils of married women
Sags under the weight of the khol beats
The actors miss their lines as they step with the rhythm
Festivals too have a woe
Amidst all we embrace each other
And return to our dear homes
In a rhythm of our own

—*Translated from Assamese by Krishna Dulal Barua*

Colours

Right after birth
Grandmother had ducked me in the green

My mother picked me up
From among the yellow

The motley threads led me on my path
As the reels gobbled up their length

Till I reached the black

The black soaked through my soles

And now, in the blue
My lips merge with another

Two vital waves

The dappled waves of the threads
Will slowly lead me on to the red

Once I'm ducked in the red
There's no coming back then.

—Translated from Assamese by Pradip Acharya

Mother

Mama, you're drinking more than your need
The grey crop on your head worries you no end
And you drown yourself in the cup
As we are away, you call and holler, pause and wail,
And duck your tears deeper in the pillow.

You're getting on in age, Mama, but don't you cry
Don't you drink more getting mad at what father says
You're addicted, you're hitting it hard
As the night grows you bend over, then sit up again,
You call out to the stars and howl at the moon
You wail, and wailing, burst into song

Don't you wail so hard, Mama
Let the doves'† settle on the boughs
Or their sorrows too might flow wailing,
If they wail your breasts would go dry

A lean river swells again routinely
Your drying breasts wouldn't ever—
It ails all old women
Why would you wail?

—*Translated from Assamese by Pradip Acharya*

The Subaltern

On digging history thousands of villages get ravaged
Under the earth an mingle with the river-water

Some unreal men rise from the water and stare transfixed—
At the historian and the hero of history
Standing across from the shadows of the dead

The historian opens up oddities
Theorises with condensed letters shuffles the past

Learning about it the indigent lot
Burst into laughter years after and sing:

Cunning lads love naïve lasses
History loves the dumb

The lyrics make the unreal men applaud and dip into the river
Immersed under the water they sing:

None can keep count of the current under water
None can keep count of the ripplings of water

And none can close the count of the lies of history

—*Translated from Assamese by Krishna Dulal Barua*

---

† The Mishings believe that after the death of man the soul takes the form of a dove and keeps wailing perched atop a tree-branch near human habitation.

Shaktipada Brahmachari
One Birth of Love, Another of Household Duties

I'm a trivial pebble of love in your cupped palm
If thrown away, it will plunge into the waters, I'll call the sea
To administer me in the gem-bearing darkness
To cause me to dance with its topsy-turvy rumble.
The submissiveness of the foot-soldier is better.

I keep the sound disseminating chariot a thousand miles away
Whether the sound comes along with champagne or instinctively.
Lad, whether the kite in your hand evinces theism or nature-love
There is one birth of Love, another of household duties.

Who administers me, the Goddess or service-maid?
Whether the princess lives in the netherworld?
Whether it's true that by climbing the stairs
One can reach heaven! The camp is captive in the fist
The door will crumble if intended, will fleeing be easier?
Does it mean that throwing away is getting rid of?
Renunciation without least preparation gives room for suspicion,
For one may come back again.
Sound, you've caused internal strife through your song
One birth of love, another of household duties.

—*Translated from Bengali by Kallol Choudhury*

Assassin, Turn Horse

By Sheer coincidence I met on the way.
Redness at the end of *Chaitra*
He had slain the impotent sun
The dusk is gruesome.
Assassin, turn your horse.
Now inheritance has come of age;
There's valid warrant locked in the tresses
For killing.
The neighing is silenced, the axe reddened.
The river of the last dusk;

I'll be sanctified being washed by the blood,
Loosened fingers
If you touch like the mother ...
>   —*Translated from Bengali by Kallol Choudhury*

Anupama Basumatary
Seasons

He came like the first sprout
On the stark, stout tree of winter

As the tree grows green at winter's end
My lonely heart too is green
His coming gives life
Abundant leaves and flowers

And ... for the first time
I too grow green
Winter is so painful
Yet I fall in love with winter today

Because, elbowing through the winter mist
And through the stark trees
He had groped his way to my heart.
>   —*Translated from Assamese by Pradip Acharya*

Earthy

I had entered the clamourless market through the falling rain
Love of life oozed in the laughter of Naga damsels
And in the freshness of perishables
A brimming basket of snails throbbed
With memories of other days
Captive in the ranging varieties of frogs
The possibility of summer songs
In the clusters of mushrooms I saw
A childhood dawn, how, in its light I had picked them
To savour an earthy dish

I sniffed around at the bitter bhekuri
For that familiar smell of yesterday's favourite

And ... the live crabs lay with all ten legs at rest
As if in the throes of a nightmare
Of fire sucking their shells dry

A vigorous earthy smell made redolent
The quiet town shaken by the moist noonday wind.

—*Translated from Assamese by Pradip Acharya*

Aruni Kashyap
Journeys

Trees moved along, clouds too
with the moon, the about-to-drown orange-sun
in sooty hours, slow;
they boiled down to a single feeling:
and I saw markets, old and new
where they sold, the same things—
Flesh of goats, cows, pigs,
hens or roosters,
ducks
and women
    (they wore red, like lipstick
      they wore clothes that failed functions
      like hides, hung
      over bones and clotheslines).
Nothing has changed
like red silk-cotton flowers
on green grass,
they remained
motionless, dead
yet striking
with repugnance,
not beauty.
Sometimes, I saw guns too
and brooms, that cleaned blood
like milk spilled by a cow's hind-legs-kick

from the milk-maid's knee-hold.
The same street, and people
and blood, guns, flesh traded
for money
It all remained the same
like a blood red morning sun
with the newspaper, red
roasted flesh
they still drink tea, brownish red
ginger-flavoured.
Once I saw a river too:
legends flowed on its simmering leaves
carried, with soil and life.
I sat on its bank
and listened.
When they ended, I found myself
on its bank: not in a time beyond
when people were afraid to cross it wearing
gold bracelets, silver toe-rings—
    In case, a stormy wave swallowed them
    a wild wailing wind from the untamed forests
    hit them hard, pushed them into the river.
I felt I was going back.
Just felt.
And I found myself, amidst the river winds,
and legends that its white sands reeked
like rotting fish, jasmines, cow dung,
and rain.
Maybe this road, this journey
tree-crowded, cloud-shaded,
would also end in the same despair
And I would wait, stranded amidst smells
of fish, jasmine, cow-dung.
Though I was moving forward,
continually, I felt
as if I was going back.
Don't know where—
but I knew I would end up
where I started
so I went on.

Me

Flesh, fragrance, jasmine
fish, cow-dung, women
and then the red colour
sometimes sun, sometimes silk-cotton flowers
or the blood which I mistook
for flowers.

Even I have words.
I can clay-mould them
I have languages, literatures
forest songs.
They crawl back centuries,
earthquakes generational.
Grandmas circulated them; with betel nuts
on courtyards under honeyed moons,
like rains, they drench minds, and more—
When first-drenched ones are time-parched,
to the new ones who are parched for stories.
With time, they have descended
Like seasons and mists, to rest with us.
I have tunes too, books
written on bark with earthworm's blood;
they are different,
independent, like these rivers
in my chest, legends-laden
mournful, yet swelling with energy furious
Love-lost like singing spring birds
Anonymous, beyond the hills
Where rivers and rains are born
To flow down as legends, life-blood.
My history is different, defined
by grandmas, rivers, hills,
singing spring birds behind green trees
and seventeen victories.
My words: they have legends in them.
The way tea-leaves run in my veins
instead of blood.

Stories, of new-born speaking from backyard graves
About dogs transforming into man
Man to sheep, goats
And a girl, singing through lime trees,
gourds and lilies from backyards.
And I still wait, for a warm embrace
My throat peacock-parched, in longing
All the rivers from my land
legends, rains weary
Cannot quench my thirst, I need your love
Don't you see,
I'm different?

Even I have words.
Languages, literatures
And stories to tell you
Are you eager to listen, at all?

MANIPUR

Rajkumar Bhubonsana
Should Light be Put Out or Mind Kept in Dark

Should *light*† be put out or *mind* kept in dark
It's government's new notice
Either of the two has to be chosen, it says.

Should the putting out of *light* be chosen
Or the black out of *mind*

All the octogenarians
Ask one another
Whomsoever they come across on the way
Which one would be better this time?
'If it's assured
Letting *light* to be put out

---

† In the original Manipuri poem, light (*mei*) is often used as a synonym of electricity.

And letting *mind* to shine would be better.'
As they relaxed, they answered,
Straightening their bent-backs
After laying down the load of walking sticks.

'This thing about *mind*
We can't understand
When is *now*
When is *tomorrow*
When is what day
If it's possible
When the end is looming large
Make our *minds* shine brightly as we please
Let there be no *light*.'

So a decision is made
Immediately by the government.

Honouring the wish of the elders
The place is kept in darkness
Load-shedding is imposed regularly
Because of the government's inefficiency
It is not that they are resorting to cheating.

Should either *light* be put out or *mind* kept in dark?

News is exchanged
By the middle-aged ones.
Called out with the help of loudspeakers
From their respective houses
Meetings are held
In meadows and at temple-porches
In every neighbourhood
In clubs.

After expressing their individual opinions
A resolution is made.

This thing about *light*
During our childhood days
Also, since the olden days it has always been dark
Even now
It's dark regularly.
The difficult thing is

Mind.
It has been in dark since the day we were born.
Growing up with the *mind* in dark
Half of life has gone.
Mind
Is becoming darker and darker day by day, now.
The remaining few years
Passing away with the *mind* in dark
There won't be any harm.
Instead of that
In the nights
With *light* shining brightly
And after having tasty meals
To be able to sleep soundly
Let *light* shine as we please, so they would say.

They belong to the group with the maximum number of voters
Why shouldn't their opinion be honoured?

Because of this, it is said to have been taken up
By the government
Many new special
Schemes of blacking out the *mind*.
In the examination for the recruitment
Of Manipur's high ranking officers
Marks have been tampered with
Creating scandals
Without rice, from Guwahati
Rice for Manipur had been transported
Without the mechanical parts, from outside
Electrical generators had been purchased
Those entrusted to catch thieves
Were made to smuggle goods
Ministers and MLAs
By crossing the floors often
Have been creating chaos in the state.

Are all these creations of the government
Aren't these the doings of the public, so they say.

Should there be darkness without *light*
Or let our *minds* to black out.

The youths discuss
At street corners
At roadsides
At schools
In groups.

Which one is better?

Decisions are made.

We are youths
The future hope of Manipur
The betterment of Manipur
Would be in our hands
So by compulsion
Let *light* remain put out, *mind* too may stay blacked out
If possible, over and above these
Each of us may be bashed to lose one front tooth, so they say.

For
Light has remained the same
Before Loktak Project came into existence
It's said there was no *light* in Manipur
Even after the commissioning of Loktak Project
There is still no *light*
On the other hand
Loktak Project wastes paddy fields and fishes
Causes submergence under water
Spoils men
Takes away homesteads
Makes unavailable space for working
Causes resentment.
Over and above the unavailability of *light*
It's is better for *mind* to remain blacked out
For
To learn lessons for the development of *mind*
Money is required, time is consumed.
After studying hard, when *mind* is developed
For buying jobs
In search of the required money, the *mind* developed so laboriously
Is lost again, unaware.

Over and above those
Education causes *mind* to develop
If *mind* is developed, one becomes aware of the wrongs
If one is aware of the wrongs, an urge to divulge them is felt
If the wrongs are made public, in our place
One gets bashed up, hip broken.
So it's better to keep *mind* in dark.
And also
Over and above all these
In the place where *light* is not there and *mind* is in dark
What is the use of the facial appearance of a human.
It would be of no use
We the youths, our facial appearances
Would make no difference, it would remain the same
Instead of caring for it
To make it more appealing
Our request would be to lose one front tooth each face.

Good!

It's what the future pillars of the nation say
What they say must be carried out without fail.
So the government as a compulsion
Has made the generators of Loktak fail
To enable the *mind* to remain in the dark
Load-shedding programme has been imposed.
Students and youths
Against their wishes
The extremely annoying
Works, only these have been taken up.
To enable them to lose their front teeth
Whenever strikes and lockouts are called
They are arrested and beaten up
Immediately, it is said.

Thus according to the wish of the masses
Light is put out and *mind* too is kept in the dark
Front teeth are bashed out
In Manipur, the land of jewels.

— *Translated from Manipuri by Tayenjam Bijoykumar Singh*

The Smell of Pomegranate

In dream's meadow
nights
are falling down
as ripe pomegranates.

Wherever one goes,
ripe and cracked pomegranates
lie scattered all around.

In every house
with windows kept ajar,
leaning on the pillars, the stalks of straw left behind after harvest
are drifting downstream
in the sweet smell of pomegranate.

—*Translated from Manipuri by Tayenjam Bijoykumar Singh*

E-nga[†]

Delinquent raindrops
after crossing over the doorstep
teased the room
in their language,
glanced sideways,
pranced around
and ran out again to the courtyard
without paying heed to stop.

The heavily laden
dark hued clouds
moving sluggishly across the sky
laugh aloud heartily
and wink their eyes
at one another
playfully.

—*Translated from Manipuri by Tayenjam Bijoykumar Singh*

[†] A month according to Manipuri calendar falling in June–July.

Robin S. Ngangom
Poetry

What they don't need is poetry,
these gnarled men and wrinkled women
who work on slopes,
swaying in the rain like knotted,
weather-beaten pines, breathing
mountain air, these weavers and herdsmen.

What matters if I can't explain to them
the nuance of an ode or a ghazal,
the iron and flint of a Mayakovsky
or a Guillén, how do I impress upon them
their miserable plight
when all they want to do
is smoke and chatter away time.
When he hears poetry
the peasant will lean on his hoe
in exasperation while his fields lie fallow,
the hunter will return empty-handed with
a sad poem, and if the goatherd listens
to poetry's demented cadences
his goats will not give milk.

Let me explain.

Like the great poets
pardoned by time
I wanted to gather words
from arrows knocked in a turquoise sky.
I wanted to catch words in my embroidered bag,
rainy words spattered, thrown about
by the March wind, I wanted to collect
pebbly words from riverbeds, smooth,
geometrical consonants of primary colours.
I wanted to unearth roots and herbs
and compound a word-salve, I wanted
to forge words on an anvil.
I wanted to be a wordsmith.

The sweeper wakes up the morning without irony.
I want him to burn my anxieties and not
sweep them under the mat as I used to.
I want the carpenter
to fashion me a word-chair
to sit me down and calm me,
I want him to nail me down a poem.
The carpenter has learnt his trade and cannot
waste hours chiselling and planing couplets.
I wanted the mason to lay
the cornerstones of living for me.
The mason awaits cargoes of sand and bricks
on the shores of afternoon and doesn't need
silken rhetoric or spice adjectives.

All I wanted was to sing
with the mystical sparrows,
but only a murder of crows
nest in my throat at dawn.
I wanted to harvest words
which grow on their own, words
which die without tawdry funerals;
of creepers and vines, stars and stone,
wisdom and folly, flowers and moss.

Gangtok, February 1998

(for Guru T. Ladakhi)

Call of faraway snow in the eye of a wish.
When we contemplate your emerald tongue
quivering on pale sand and rock
we grow more weary of striving cities
and desultory roads. But you will
teach us to name the forest and the mountain,
indignant one, who will not wait.
Teesta, tell me the meaning of your name.
Like secretive men impelled by a sinuous love
we follow your scent when the flame of the forest
borrows a monk's robes and something shimmers
beneath the veil of the Himalayan sky

until you lift us on your fraternal lap
of flowers and stone, Gangtok.

II
Who are the artisans of wood that left
no names on the palace gate of the Chogyal?
A misty forest looks up the face of a sheer drop
where the king's men punished hardened criminals
tied up in sacks, by pushing them off this cliff,
so the stories insinuate. The royalty since then
has paid its price to a nation which humbled them
through treachery, so history moralizes. And this
is where a landslide took many by surprise.
A lanky building just slipped off
and lay on its face like a drunk,
and only the prayer flags
stand here to appease the difficult gods.
I look where the mountains keep their enigmatic silence
and climb stairs which lead to the doors of the sky,
and rain entered the afternoon without invitation.

III
5 am one whisky-coated morning
and Khangchendzonga appeared, bust translucent
like a forgotten model, her face quickly
obscured by a cirrus of snow,
provoked by a jealous sunstone
cast on her proud forehead.

In the aquamarine afternoon
Rumtek turns slow prayer wheels
which cuts across the axis of earth
to generate compassion for a cold-blooded world.
The Karmapa who fled Tibet
reconstructed this arabesque seat of learning
from adoration and spotless memory.
We remove shoes and enter a hooded door
to find butter statues meditating
in all the shades of earth.
Thus flesh will melt one day
to yield the running colours of earth.

An intonation of monks
and the deep drone of drums
heighten the mystery of reincarnation each moment.
But what does one seek from the illuminate
if the wayward mind must be conquered first?
A grimy gap-toothed Tibetan comes begging
while young acolytes scurry to fetch water,
as the world of appearance marked time.
Adornment, renunciation, ego, alms,
where is there a life without desire?

IV
5 pm when evenings crumble from Himalayan snow
Gangtok folds us in her breast.
We leave melancholy outside Zam-den,
where positive elements converge,
and song and dance and poetry
find a home.

The First Rain

The first rain like the first letter of May
brings news to the hills.
Perched like the houses on the edge of a cliff
I've lived more days in exile
than my poor childhood.
As a fumbling fifteen-year-old
I abandoned my forward-looking native people
who entrusted terror, drugs and
a civilized plague to children.
Is it better to rejoice and forget
or to remember and be sad?
Only a foolish boy cannot wait to be a man,
adores winter, and leaves home to write poetry.

After the holocaust became a touchstone
it has become possible to convict a people
and make culture and murder co-exist.
If I told you how babies have been shot down
from their mothers' breasts
you would put it down to a poet's overworked heart

but we like to believe in leaders who flock to the capital
only to fly back with spells as latter-day sorcerers.

An animal threatened with extinction
needs a lair for his mate and his young,
I'm not different.
I need the morning for its bright blood
and I need to seize the night.

There was not a day that changed my days.
When I listen to hills
I hear the voices of my faded life.
Whisky and Mehdi Hassan and Billie Holiday
make for strange fruit on nondescript evenings.

They can stop us but not our thoughts
from coming out into the streets,
they can shoot us but cannot kill the air
which carries our voices.

O my love you are still asleep
when the rain carries the night till dawn.
After lying down with dreams of you
I awake in another day of bread and newspapers.

I'm banished to the last outpost of a dying empire
whose keepsakes have become the artefacts of the natives:
necklaces, pianos, lace and tombstones.

I've pursued horoscopes and
only promises and maledictions pursue me.
One day Venus was mine, joy and honey,
another day Saturn would not be propitiated.
I found a moment's peace
in my little daughter's face.
Before I met you
my dreams were limited by ignorance.
Sometimes at night
I put two drops of our past in my eyes
but they refused to close.

Can poetry be smuggled like guns or drugs?
We've drawn our borders with blood.
Even to write in our mother tongue

we cut open veins and our tongues
lick parchments with blood.

I read my smuggled Neruda
and sometimes listen to the fading fiddles
and the mourning voices of my land.

I'm the anguish of slashed roots,
the fear of the homeless,
and the desperation of former kisses.
How much land does my enemy need?

O my love why did you fade
into the obscurity of my life
and left me to look long at the mountain?

I'm the pain of slashed roots
and the last rain is already here.
I'll leave the cracked fields of my land
and its weeping pastures of daybreak.
Let wolves tear our beloved hills.

I'll leave the bamboo flowering
in the groves of my childhood.
Let rats gnaw at the supine map
of what was once my native land.

Everywhere I Go

Everywhere I go
I carry my homeland with me.
I look for it in protest marches on the streets of the capital,
in dark-maned girls of beauty contests
forced to waiting now behind windows.
I harbour the wretchedness of those youths
who do not wish to return
but would rather serve in a city's sordid restaurants
because devils and thieves rule their home.

I often hear about its future
in conflict resolution symposiums
where professors and retired generals
analyze the fate of my people and their misery.

But I can see it returning with women
and water in rural evenings.
And I want to tell my poet-friends
of the twelve mothers who stripped themselves
and asked soldiers to rape them.
In fact, I make imaginary journeys
to its little world every day
and wait for the fog of justice to lift
for a murdered 8-year-old girl.

Those who speak the language of progress
call my homeland a mendicant state
not knowing its landlocked misery,
its odd splendour.
And no one knows who picks up its bodies.

I know I must stop agonizing
(Perhaps I am the only one who broods about his land)
Even if people say
suffering must reach new heights
for a new beginning.
But whenever I touch my homeland's streets
everyone seems happy and have no grouses.
I must stop agonizing or save what I can
Such as the tunes of my homeland
which dance in my blood.

Yumlembam Ibomcha
For the Next Birth

In the next birth
I shall take birth as a bastard
You should also take birth as one
Then let's meet at an ownerless shack of the marketplace
You and I freely.

In that birth
The moment I drop from my mother's womb
I shall stamp on that woman's chest

Then emerge, sprouting wings,
Without drinking a drop of my mother's milk
I shall fly out the house's narrow door.

I shall grow up as a bazaar dog
Walking alone any direction I choose
None feeding me a morsel of rice
None looking at me with loving eyes
I would like to live alone
Then let us meet.

You should also grow up an orphan like me,
The moment she gives birth to you
Let your mother die
Before feeding you a drop of milk;
Let none love you
You should also love none;
Don't eat begging even a grain of rice
Don't eat too what others offer you
You should live—
Grabbing
Snatching
Digging from others' mouths
Then we'll meet, you and I.

Let us only meet
As the price of this birth
Freely, even if only for a few minutes
Let us embrace
For a moment without fear.

—*Translated from Manipuri by Robin S. Ngangom*

Saratchand Thiyam
Shillong

Lifting latches of beauty
one after another
as I neared you
you were weeping

for the tussle between
the house with sculptured features
and the sculpted hills.
As dusk falls
niang kynjah†
wail in all directions.
Why do these quiet ones
shriek and howl
like someone beating bamboo stems?
Do you rouse them
to help you in your sorrow,
to share your dismay
and to support your dissent?
Your mass of hills
leap out with carved features,
drifting through houses
jainsem‡-clad girls saunter
carrying pails of water.
You do shout
no one listens,
you do plead
they are unmoved,
these who walk
along with the spreading light.
Your hill-world's ochre hue
overflows
into your primeval blue tide,
darning needles
stab your twin eyes,
blood runs instead of tears;
the girls learning to wear the jainsem
run in fear
up the steep slopes
thinking ghosts have come
to torment them.

---

† Cricket-like insects.
‡ A traditional Khasi dress for women.

But the all-green *Lawkyntang*[†]
is carefully guarded
by the tiger and the snake
and the forest goddesses.
The little forest trail,
the dependent creeper
play happily inside Lawkyntang.
But your wailing voice
run over by time's wheel
has become hoarse.

—*Translated from Manipuri by Robin S. Ngangom*

Hillworld

On the silently standing hill's broad forehead
Grinds in play the forehead of clouds
Bending down from the sky.

The hill remains asleep though.
Boys and girls of the hillworld
Are eating a picnic meal at the foothill
Dancing
Embracing the loud songs of a tape recorder.

On the hilltop's broad helipad
When the helicopter lands roaring
The girls of the hillworld who were bathing
Ran for their homes
Panting.
The hill remains asleep though.

Boys who wear chains made out of thread
Are playing hill-climbing.

The hillworld's mothers stand
Holding torches throughout the night
Facing the glaring lights of the power station.
The hill remains asleep though.

—*Translated from Manipuri by Robin S. Ngangom*

[†] A sanctified grove of the Khasis.

Hill

You remain standing and
Don't speak at all.
You can suffer too, neither denying nor affirming,
Wearing a shawl of fire you can stand quietly.
When it's evening your picture
Can be seen lucidly,
Standing with a clean shaven head.

The hill tracks that go bursting through
Amidst forest once green
Are gradually becoming red
With a group of people
Searching for a crown of laurel leaves.

This long road
Connecting Wordsworth to Eliot
Is being measured today with a yardstick.
You must know, having lived for centuries,
You who have been wallowing in time's tide.
Even if speechlessness
For you is a matter of poise
But for the blame of generations
It has become fearsome war.

You could remain looking silently at
Two hands that shake happily,
Two cheeks that are kissed affectionately
Turning into thorns nonetheless.

Raising its head
Today's generation is looking at today's sky
If those white pigeons
Reared by majestic you come flying at all.

—Translated from Manipuri by Robin S. Ngangom

Pokhran, Kargil, Gaisal

Desert
so vast, huge, faint, sweeping
flaunted might
signified courage
powerful, very powerful without equal
surpassing everyone, above everyone.
A land of sand, of drops of sand
a land of sand, made up of grains of sand
we know, we've been briefed
it has been demonstrated—
that power.

Snow
thick, layer upon layer,
covering every hill
having become colourless water
when it flows as liquid
it has become blood again.

The bullet holes dwelling on icy slopes
are carefully guarded by globs of blood night and day.

Empty land
completely barren, uninhabited, absolutely quiet
dawn about to break
death wiping softly, lovingly
sweat from the forehead
torn bodies
amid morning's beaming rays,
among stinking organs
crisp fresh dolls are bathing.
Statues of stone
flowers made of paper
birds composed of glass
come to frolic bloom sing in this wilderness
happily, freely.

—Translated from Manipuri by Robin S. Ngangom

Gambhini Devi

Hansapadika

Hansapadika! I want to look at your dead face
Hansapadika, stop your singing
Even though not much of a song
What men recognize as ditty nowadays.
Before those who have interpreted
Your discontented soul's lament as song
In the morning itself tomorrow
Wait, hanging like a bat
On the electric wire.
Rotting, crumble piece by piece
On the heads
Of those who think that your lament
Is song,
Hansapadika!
Stop your singing Hansapadika!
I want
To look at your dead face.

—Translated from Manipuri by Robin S. Ngangom

A Village Girl

I will not unfasten my hair
I am a village girl
Village girls do not unfasten their hair
Not a single strand of our hair
Is tossed by the wind.

I do not look
Towards the golden star
Of the dark sky.
I am a village girl.
Village girls
Do not look up towards the sky
For our sake
Not a single star would fall.

On the pasture wet with morning dew
I do not walk around
For our sake
Not one drop of dew would fall.
We are village girls.
At our feet
Not one morning flower would drop down.
That is why we
Do not laugh when we smell a blooming flower.
We are laughing heartily—
When we smell golden paddy and the soil,
Colouring our mother's hair
With charcoal from the hearth.
We are village girls.

—Translated from Manipuri by Robin S. Ngangom

Memchoubi
Red Chingthrao[†]

On Echai bank stood benumbed
An empty church, its doors shut
And the bell tolled for no one.
Standing secluded and hushed
The deserted village's
Little scorched bamboo huts' courtyards
Were bestrewn with red roses.
In the empty breeze there bloomed
The black cotton flower dejectedly,
Forcibly disrobed by
Deities guarding the directions.
In the distant terrace fields
Ears of mountain rice yet to be harvested
Were braving the torments of wild boars and monkeys.
Then the budding red *Chingthrao*[†]
Smiled unexpectedly like before
Emerging from green leaves

[†] Orchid tree (*Bauhinia*); *Bauhinia* flower.

In that innocent endearing smile of former times.
But they fell on the ground one by one suddenly
Without number, all in red
On floral stalks not fully bloomed.
Where's life, where's dream.
At the foot of the Chingthrao
Mother in her highland dress
Was sitting quietly alone
Spreading her loom in front
The *sanam*† strapped to her waist
Picking up the fallen red Chingthrao
She continued weaving it into the fabric
Her left hand lifting the *suna*‡
Her left hand beating the *tem** with a thud.
Upon looking again I saw
A red bloodstream of tears
Shedding from mother's eyes too ceaselessly.
Echai's thin red flow
Carried away the gushing blood with heavy tread
The charred hillocks in the surroundings
Stood sorrowfully with their heads bowed
Unable to console their beloved Echai.

—*Translated from the Manipuri by Tayenjam Bijoykumar Singh*

The Goddess of Lightning

Even if your soul listens or not,
Even if you agree or not,
I am
The answer to your age-old question.
Did you think of me as
The skylark floating in moonlight
Or the dewdrop clinging
To the soft petal

---

† A flat piece of wood forming an integral part of a back-strap loom, worn by a weaver by strapping it on the waist.
‡ Rows of loops through which yarn is passed.
* A thick wooden or bamboo blade used for beating in lattice-yarn to tighten, while weaving cloth in a back-strap loom.

Of a rose blooming at dawn.
No, I am none of these.
I am the goddess of lightning,
The goddess of lightning, do you know.
At my harsh, strident voice
The old world will crumble.
You who preserved
After smearing with new colours
Your two rotten arms outstretched,
Standing bravely
At the threshold of a new history.
With the thousand-fold sparks
Reflected from my eyes
I shall burn them,
The mouldering burden of ideas
You've carried for centuries,
While you endure with closed eyes
My misshapen form,
The renewed creation of earth
Shall be complete.

—*Translated from Manipuri by Tayenjam Bijoykumar Singh*

Thangjam Ibopishak
I Want to be Killed by an Indian Bullet

I heard the news long ago that they were looking for me; in the morning in the afternoon at night. My children told me; my wife told me.

One morning they entered my drawing room, the five of them. Fire, water, air, earth, sky—are the names of these five. They can create men; also destroy men at whim. They do whatever they fancy. The very avatar of might.

I ask them: 'When will you kill me?'

The leader replied: 'Now. We'll kill you right now. Today is very auspicious. Say your prayers. Have you bathed? Have you had your meal?'

'Why will you kill me? What is my crime? What evil deed have I done?' I asked them again.

'Are you a poet who pens gobbledygook and drivel? Or do you consider yourself a seer with oracular powers? Or are you a madman?' asked the leader.

'I know that I'm not one of the first two beings. I cannot tell you about the last one. How can I myself tell whether I'm deranged or not?'

The leader said: 'You can be whatever you would like to be. We are not concerned about this or that. We will kill you now. Our mission is to kill men.'

I ask: 'In what manner will you kill me? Will you cut me with a knife? Will you shoot me? Will you club me to death?'

'We will shoot you.'

'With which gun will you shoot me then? Made in India, or made in another country?'

'Foreign made. All of them made in Germany, made in Russia, or made in China. We don't use guns made in India. Let alone good guns, India cannot even make plastic flowers. When asked to make plastic flowers India can only produce toothbrushes.'

I said: 'That's a good thing. Of what use are plastic flowers without any fragrance?'

The leader said: 'No one keeps toothbrushes in vases to do up a room. In life a little embellishment has its part.'

'Whatever it may be, if you must shoot me please shoot me with a gun made in India. I don't want to die from a foreign bullet. You see, I love India very much.'

'That can never be. Your wish cannot be granted. Don't ever mention Bharat to us.'

Saying this they left without killing me; as if they didn't do anything at all. Being fastidious about death I escaped with my life.

—*Translated from the Manipuri by Robin S. Ngangom*

Gandhi and Robot

A long time ago
Nehruji owned a robot sent by Russia,
Which could chant a thousand 'Hare Ramas'
From its mouth in a minute.
Ballabhaiji possessed a Gandhi borrowed from Birla,
Which could spin ten balls of thread
On the charkha within an hour.

Vikram Sarabhai declared on Republic Day:
I'll create a new pilgrimage site for science at Trombay.

In Delhi's Red Fort donkeys bray
On empty stomachs and parched throats;
The dhobis who rear them feed them
Old copies of the newspaper 'Harijan'
By tearing them up into pieces.

Today the sadhus proclaim:
We will construct a pagoda at Pokhran
To keep the 'New Buddha'.
Elated, I cried:
'Bravo, Bharat, bravo!'

— *Translated from Manipuri by Robin S. Ngangom*

MEGHALAYA

Desmond Kharmawphlang
Letter from Pahambir

At sundown we set out in a car,
Past silent, dark huts,
Cicadas buzzing the dusk.

We have left the church far behind,
Glowing strangely in pallid
Arrogance, through the dust kicked up
By our passing.
Village curs turn quarrelsome
As we city men await
The verdict of reception, smoking uneasily
Outside the village Chief's abode.

'We come,' I plead, 'to learn, not to teach.
We come with longing, we are the
Forgetful generation, our hearts tapping
A rhythm spawned in shame, a shame

That splits our present from our past.
We have suckled for so long
On a wisdom of falsehood—we ourselves
our own worst enemies.'

A fire dances crazily, throwing
Shadows on the hard mud floor, and good
Laughter swells like moonlight
Someone breaks out in song
And hardened feet tap unsteady punctuations
Around the weird tune.
Voices intone, hands fashion leaf plates
To hold food for the men
From the big city. I shove more brushwood
into the fire.

Poems during November

The boundless plains unfold
Its glassy rivers
Printed along with the early stars.

There is a hint of salty air,
Like a remembered past of trade routes,
Criss-crossing the giant curve
Of a heel, rimmed by mountains,
Thrashed by untold tragedy at
The sea's straying ways.

Earlier in the day,
We stood and watched
The transparency of the air,
Of silent conflict with ghosts,
Inhabiting every living memory.
We shuffle along dried river beds,
Scarred with colourful stones,
The sun trailing, my dark shadow
Brokenly thrown to one side.
At Kshaid Dain Thlen, the clear
Waters make the heart weep

And, like an ancient call, a drama reenacts on
This great
Table of beaten rock.

Forgetfulness spawns a curse
Carried far across the eyes,
Linked like a coil of fear.

II
This is a strange trip, taking us
To track down private wars waged
In the territories of mind.

There is a changeless smell here
Although we could not refuse
The visit of religion, and the
Recorded centuries of an empire rests
Mutely in graves and monuments.

The rains still weep on these hills,
Filling the thin air with softness,
Sending a fox howling halfway down
The ravines.

The Conquest

I never get tired of talking about my
Hometown
In summer the sky is pregnant,
Swollen with unborn rain.
Winter arrives, with a tepid sun
Touching the frozen hills, the dream-
Boats on lakes.

Long ago, the men went beyond the
Surma
To trade, to bring home women
To nurture their seed

Later came the British
With gifts of bullets, blood-money

And religion
A steady conquest to the sound of
Guns began

Quite suddenly, the British left.
There was peace, the sweet
Smell of wet leaves again

But in the wavering walk of time
There came those from the sweltering
Plains,
From everywhere.

You stricken Land, how they love
Your teeming soil, your bruised children.
One of them told me, 'You know,
Yours is a truly metropolitan city.'

—Translated from Khasi by the author

Esther Syiem
Retelling Nam's Tale

The tales they tell about me, redundancies.
Of meek subservience,
acceptance of marriage,
I repudiate them all, I repudiate them all.

If in the fitness of things
I reach the heavens
atop the branches of my sister-trees
can I say that I have won?

San ko kong A pat ko kong Ri

I am dogged by feline speed
and memories brewed in the shock
of recent discoveries
of a mother who gave me up
to a pungent, avaricious tiger
whom I then believed was my own.

San ko kong Ri pat ko Kong A

Am I running away from them
or away from myself?
disguised in loathsome toad-skin hide
my identity: hidden from even myself
my mother: rodent or human?

San ko kong A pat ko kong Ri

You rat, whom I now call mother
you saved me from adversaries:
the tiger—father who plotted to seal my fate
and the human mother
who auctioned me
and abandoned me to fetters of her making;

San ko kong Ri pat ko kong A

Am I pushing on, of my own accord,
or am I being taken
to the heavens to seek more
than what my future holds?

San ko kong A pat ko kong Ri

I ascend
on the relentless upswing
of trees shooting skywards,
from ignorance to experience
from simplicity to complexities
ferried upwards
as if on a draught that pulls me away
from you,
mother rat.
Must I turn to myself only,
(your imprint on me)
even in this short length of time
that I have put between you
standing firmly on earth
and me
borne skywards alone?

San ko kong Ri pat ko kong A

I am halfway up,
within the embalming silence
encircling me.
It is not the silence of the tiger-jungle that I once knew,
in my ignorance taunting me,
where I yearned for voices that would speak;
it is the silence of an untasted world
neither giving nor receiving

San ko kong A pat ko kong Ri

that resists me
but compels me to itself.
Will I meet like or unlike others?
Empty, my mind; unsteady, my heart;
in this unlike sphere.

San ko kong Ri pat ko kong A

Only this morning, in a fragile space,
in a known garb, in a known setting,
in a known world,
in a relationship with a tiger-father
that I thought was known.

San ko kong A pat ko kong Ri

My memories, shards that cut deep.
Always on my own
Always alone.

San ko Kong Ri pat ko Kong A
San ko Kong A pat ko Kong Ri

When I reach the heavens
who knows
what will be?

San ko kong Ri pat ko Kong A

2
The bewitching chants that drew my sister-helpers out
to grow unceasingly till they touch the heavens

can charm them no more. Sister-trees
you've delivered me safe.
I now strike out on my own
to patch words to life, life to words
to form a convincing tale to my listening ears.

Within the folds of an aloneness
that few understand,
repeated in the aloneness
of those whose lives
have never been tabled by habit
or the expectations of others,
I shall only say what I know
with words
that will alchemise the words
that have been told of me.

So
in transcribing my life,
I refuse to marry the son of the celestial mother.
I refuse
a strangled future.

I feel
more alone
more vulnerable
to unborn challenges

I call upon my sisters,
my helpers,
but they no longer hear me
they no longer come—
This heaven
the unmatchable suitor
promises me,

has never been mine,
will never be mine.

Ko Kong A ko Kong Ri

Kynpham Sing Nongkynrih
The Colours of Truth

A siesta phone call
oozes friendly warnings.

Insurgents have grown
incredibly urbane, these days.
The question is, must we subterfuge
to shield a pedagogic stooge?

I close my eyes
turn towards the sun.

The colour I see is
disgorging blood.
I close my eyes
shade them with my palms.

the colour I see is
life-erasing black.

These are the colours of destiny
of immutable truth
and the colours also
with which warring pawns
are daily decorating our towns.

The Ancient Rocks of Cherra

(For Nigel, who questioned)

This land is old, too old
and withered for life to be easy.

Poverty eats into the hills and squeezes
a living from stones and caterpillars
gathered for out-of-town drunks
each market day.

Where the serpent's death throes[†]
cut deep wounds into the land
lie deep gorges like fiendish mouths
yawning for desperate victims.

There is nothing remarkable here
only this incredible barrenness.

Men and trees have left their habitats
to a crude and lowly breed like brush,
but the sight of dark grey rocks like sages
spells home to me.

A Day in Sohra[‡]

Dressed for the warm April,
the cool blasts of Sohra
cut through my thin clothes.
But I could feel gentle autumn in the sun
and there's no dust in the wind.
The wind rules the land
howling like a maniac,
for where are the trees
to temper its wild laughter
into romantic wooing?

I could see old trees like old men
die off every winter.
Young ones are put to the flame,
or are not troubled to be born.

Yet the rivers and the creeks
slapping music on stone drums,
are full and clear as ever.
The waterfalls are as glorious

[†] Legend has it that the immense gorges of Sohra (or Cherrapunjee), the wettest place on earth, were caused by the death throes of the Thlen, a gigantic man-eating serpent that once supposedly stalked its wilderness.
[‡] Cherrapunjee.

and Likai,[†] wild with suicidal fury,
still plunges into its cerulean pool,
forever fleeing from a destiny
of beast-men and a wounded conscience.
But then comes summer.
The sky is now blue,
in a wink it is black.
The wind is now joined by the rain,
blazing and thundering as it comes.

This is the famed rain,
making a fool of sorry umbrellas!
Zooming in like swarms of fighter planes!
Bouncing back metres high to the sky!
Now it sprints with the wind!
Now it turns waltzing round!
Now it's a million whips
for the gale to lash at pretty legs!
And now, it's a violent downpour
to whitewash the ditches and the roads,
till at last, the fog comes cloaking all.

This is a day in Sohra,
come to Sohra and get wet,
unbothered by the stains of mud.

A Farewell Letter of Cherries

(For Professor MB)

Dear friend, this is a letter
of cherries, this is a poem
born of cherries and my affection
when the town is pink
with their blush.

[†] Noh-ka-Likai Falls in Sohra, named after the woman, Ka Likai, who was tricked by her second husband into eating the curried flesh of her only daughter. Mad with grief and rage, she flung herself into the falls where she died.

This is a poem
born when summer greets winter
under a compassionate sky
like two old-timers
like you and me
before we go our separate ways.

This is a poem
born of sadness
for the cherries will yield
to a blasé green
and the cold will finally conquer.
This is a poem
born of consolation
for the business of man
is not to possess
and the only part you can keep
of things that come and go
is that which you have photographed
with your mind.

Dear brother, we live in our memory
in the memory of the world:
stoking that memory with fondness
is all that we can do.
We can do no more
we can do no less.

MIZORAM

Mona Zote
What Poetry Means to Ernestina in Peril

What should poetry mean to a woman in the hills
as she sits one long sloping summer evening
in Patria, Aizawl, her head crammed with contrary winds,
pistolling the clever stars that seem to say:
Ignoring the problem will not make it go away.
So what if Ernestina is not a name at all,
not even a corruption, less than a monument. She will sit
pulling on one thin cigarillo after another, will lift her tea cup
in friendly greeting to the hills and loquacious stars
and the music will comb on through her hair,
telling her: *Poetry must be raw like a side of beef,*
should drip blood, remind you of sweat
and dusty slaughter and the epidermal crunch
and the sudden bullet to the head.
The sudden bullet in the head. Thus she sits, calmly gathered.

The lizard in her blinks and thinks. She will answer:
*The dog was mad that bit me. Later, they cut out my third eye
and left it in a jar on a hospital shelf. That was when the drums began.
Since then I have met the patron saint of sots and cirrhosis who used
   to stand
in every corner until the police chased her down. She jumped into a taxi.
Now I have turned into the girl with the black guitar
and it was the dog who died. Such is blood.*
The rustle of Ernestina's skirt will not reveal the sinful vine
or the cicada crumbling to a pair of wings at her feet.
She will smile and say: *I like a land where babies
are ripped out of their graves, where the church
leads to practical results like illegitimate children and bad marriages
quite out of proportion to the current population, and your neighbour
is kidnapped by demons and the young wither without complaint
and pious women know the sexual ecstasy of dance and peace is kept
by short men with a Bible and five big knuckles on their righteous hands.
Religion has made drunks of us all. The old goat bleats.
We are killing ourselves. I like an incestuous land.* Stars, be silent.
Let Ernestina speak.
So what if the roses are in disarray? She will rise
with a look of terror too real to be comical.
The conspiracy in the greenhouse the committee of good women
They have marked her down
They are coming the dead dogs the yellow popes
They are coming the choristers of stone
We have been bombed silly out of our minds.

Waiter, bring me something cold and hard to drink.
Somewhere there is a desert waiting for me
and someday I will walk into it.

Girl with Black Guitar and Blue Hibiscus

The reality of music is a problem
waiting to be solved by the black guitar,
not the girl, nor the jug of blue hibiscus
The pigeons are insane with grief because you left them
The clouds will be noble and distant as always

The scent of citrus flowers will fade in soft explosions
And the girl will put a blue hibiscus in her hair
And the computer will speak in flawless Japanese
Talking of the elegant instant and how the quasars are forever
    expanding
How the jealousy of common stuff finds itself fully
in an uncommon criminal act. In the red earth lay her like a seed.
The sad subterranean gong will go on accusing
Until it becomes the black guitar and music becomes
A cleft of a certain colour waiting for the first quiver of strings,
until the gong is quiet and the woman in the earth goes to sleep

Cherrie L. Chhangte
Rain

Rain washes my window pane
Like the tears that bathe my face;
The muted rhythm of raindrops falling
Only echoes the half-forgotten music
Playing in my mind,
Music I never heard
Except deep within my heart,
Yet my every waking moment
Is haunted by those notes.
I see you, an ephemeral shadow,
Sitting by the piano,
Lost in the symphony of timeless Time.
The soft breeze caresses your hair
While you play for no audience
But the velvet blackness of night.
Clear, pure, like the tinkle of glass
Your notes fill my silence,
And the rain merges with your music
To heal my soul once more.
I become the keys your fingers awaken,
I am the rain that dances with life.

Night

Poetry is
This Rock.
Your sacred Space.
Suspended between
Heaven and Earth.
Above, the sky
A black blanket
Patterned with stars;
Below, an inky darkness
And village lights twinkling
In the horizon.

Music is
The low resonance
Of your voice
Blending perfectly
With the quiet night.
Words are beautiful
When they come together
The way they do
On your lips
And a voice
Can drown one's senses.

Peace is
Knowing I matter
Enough to be shown
This haven.
An unworthy devotee, perhaps,
Yet my breath is taken
Captive, by the sheer majesty
Of the shrine, and You.
Made heady by moonlight,
I spin round and round:
I think I catch a falling star.

Awe is
Lying on this flat bed,
Feasting on the vista

And the magnificence of Night.
I realize this is a piece of Heaven
A rare taste of things unseen.
And then I shatter the peace.
My query is like a pinprick
That disturbs the solitude.
Your eyes become black, blank
Empty pools of disquiet.

Plea

Demystify me.
I would rather be woman
Than shadow or idol.
Flesh and blood
With human failings,
As also human feelings.

Demythologize me,
I would rather be a person
Than a representative of my tribe;
Individualistic and selfish
With personal quirks,
But also personal needs.

Disenchant yourself.
I would rather be an open book
Than an intriguing enigma,
If that entails your refusal
To reach across the chasm
That separates you and I.

Disorient yourself.
Discard the prejudices and assumptions,
Delink the past from the present,
The legacy of customs, tradition and learning,
I would rather be a temporal reality
Than an intangible wisp of memory.

What does an Indian Look Like

Celebrated land of diversity,
Tourist brochures, colourful and vibrant.
Rich hues, striking costumes,
Interesting faces—a veritable Benetton ad.
Differences, in theory, are appreciated;
Make a good topic for the politicians' speech.
Are we as proud of our unity
As we are of our diversity?

The 'largest democracy in the world'.
Sounds good on paper; not too good
For those who, in a land that professes
To deny the presence of a mainstream,
Still has little rivulets and brooks
Furiously trying to keep pace with the river,
Sidelined, side-tracked, side-stepped,
A minority in a majority world.

You look at me, and you see
My eyes, my skin, my language, my faith.
You dissect my past, analyse my present
Predict my future and build my profile.
I am a curiosity, an 'ethnic' specimen.
Politics, history, anthropology, your impressive learning,
All unable to answer the fundamental question—
'What does an Indian look like?'
—An Indian looks like me, an Indian is Me.

Lalrinmawii Khiangte
Betrayal

Warm tears freeze into icicles at the 'injustice'
The heart of flesh turns into stone at the 'betrayal'.
Traitor! Heart of Judas! Betrayer!
Away with you—do not pollute me thus!
What was once lovely, clean, sweet and pure
Like discarded empty beer tin canisters

Rattle and roll on the graffiti-chequered streets.
Passing snickered feet strike and kick them
With ruthless force: seeking gratification;
The burdened, bitter heart of stone wants to avenge.
The taps of high heeled stilettos echo in the alley.
The hungry rats hide in fright in the dirt-filled crevices.
Only the sun can melt the ice ...
... and the hammer break the stone.
Where is the Hammer? Where is the Sun?
One has only to 'want' to seek—then find!
One has only to 'want' to forgive—then heal!
'Seek and ye shall find'
'Forgive us our trespasses as we forgive them who trespass
against us'.
In apathy—it hurts to seek.
In hurt—it is agony to forgive.

For a Better Tomorrow

We are besieged ... internally ... we don't resist ...
a society fragmented ... torn at the seams ... instability ...
inability ... invisible chains ... we need a captain ...
an able captain ... to guide us through ... the stormy ...
murky waters ... surely there is among us ... a Moses ...
... a Gandhi ... a Nelson ... a Lincoln ... a somebody!
Courage ... moral courage ... physical courage ...
mental courage ... discernment ... for withstanding ...
complacency ... conformity ... yet censoring glare ...
of ... associations in community ... church ...
government ... double standards rampant everywhere!
Morals and ethics ... codes of conduct ... all flown
away ... or are they still there? ... we spot out a lot ...
... sermonize a lot ... values ... principles ... honour ...
we all mean well ... but we're divided!
Globalization ... the world's a small village ...
Commercialization ... collaboration ... i-tech ...
hi-tech ... the latest science-engineered gadgets ...
genetic mutation ... many streaks of fashion ...
many kinds of music ... hip-hop ... rap-rock ... east-west

fusion ... lots and lots ... of competition ... a mad
mad race ... to reach the stars?
Many religions ... physics and formulae ... new age
philosophy ... modern theology ... history ... psychology ...
sociology ... 'education for all' in SSA mantras ...
reforms in economy ... many more re-forms ...
dispersion of knowledge ... but where is stability?
The Mizo community ... unprecedented growth ... a search
for identity ... a quest for roots ... Chhinlung? ... Ephraim?
... Manase? ... we don't 'have' to be ... a victim of
the media ... a painful forced accelerated growth ...
like expecting a child to run ... before it even
learns to walk!
Beautiful buildings ... nice furnishings ...
yet ... rot and decay ... indiscernible ... abound in
plenty ... in self destruction ... and ... other's destruction!
Side by side ... in co-existence ... ill-ventilated ...
ill-lit drudgery ... deprived of basics ... can the
voice of poverty ... not be heard?
It's not a shame to be poor in honesty ... or
be rich by hard work ... but ... let's not be poor ...
because of laziness ... or ... be rich by corruption ...
remember ... it's not a sin to be rich though ...
... just not let the means be questionable!
There's got to be ... a morning ... after ... the night ...
... for a better tomorrow!

L. Biakliana
Cry of Mizo Women

Raising my voice in my own way,
To speak out about wretched life of women,
I'll always wonder at the ultimate goal,
Of perceiving our Heavenly King face to face.
Bowed down and suffering ...
We have borne long,
Our expectations here on earth
Expecting thus our joys amidst our Heavenly Abode.

Let us rise up with justice,
Let us act together jointly,
Let the Kingdom's value be known,
On earth and reap the fruits.

—*Translated from Mizo by Laltluangliana Khiangte*

True Love

The long dark night is past!
All the gloom and labour
Like a cloud of exhaust vapour,
Are cleared away at last!
In the eastern region,
Lo, the sun is rising;
With it, joyance comes creeping,
From our hearts' horizon.
Are you sore and distressed my friend?
Never bemoan your fate;
To suffer now for true love's sake,
Is to be happy in the end.

—*Translated from Mizo by Laltluangliana Khiangte*

NAGALAND

Temsula Ao
Blood of Others

In the bygone days of the other life
Before the advent of the WORD
Spilling the blood of foes
Was the honour-code

Head-takers became acclaimed
Tribal heroes, earning the merit
To wear special cloths and ornaments
And live in grand houses.

We believed that our gods lived
In the various forms of nature
Whom we worshipped
With unquestioning faith.

Then came a tribe of strangers
Into our primordial territories

Armed with only a Book and
Promises of a land called Heaven.

Declaring that our Trees and Mountains
Rocks and Rivers were no Gods
And that our songs and stories
Nothing but tedious primitive nonsense.

We listened in confusion
To the new stories and too soon
Allowed our knowledge of other days
To be trivialized into taboo.

We no longer dared to sing
Our old songs in worship
To familiar spirits of the land
Or in praise to our legendary heroes.

And if we ever told stories it was
To the silent forests and our songs
Were heard only by the passing wind
In a land swept clean of ancient gods.

Stripped of all our basic certainties
We strayed from our old ways
And let our soul-mountain recede
Into a tiny ant-hill and we

Schooled our minds to become
The ideal *tabula rasa*
On which the strange intruders
Began scripting a new history.

We stifled our natural articulations
Turned away from our ancestral gods
And abandoned accustomed rituals
Beguiled by the promise of a new heaven.

We borrowed their minds,
Aped their manners,
Adopted their gods
And became perfect mimics.

Discarded our ancient practice
Of etching on wood and stone

And learned instead to scratch on paper
In premature tryst with the magic Script

But a mere century of negation
Proved inadequate to erase
The imprints of intrinsic identities
Stamped on minds since time began

The suppressed resonance of old songs
And the insight of primitive stories
Resurface to accuse leased-out minds
Of treason against the essential self.

In the re-awakened songs and stories
A new breed of cultural heroes
Articulate a different discourse
And re-designate new enemies

Demanding reinstatement
Of customary identity
And restoration of ancestral ground
As a belligerent postscript to recent history.

In the agony of the re-birth
Our hills and valleys reverberate
With death-dealing shrieks of unfamiliar arms
As the throw-back generation resurrects

The Old Story Teller

I have lived my life believing
Storytelling was my proud legacy.

The ones I inherited
From grandfather became
My primary treasure
And the ones I garnered
From other chroniclers
Added to the lore.

When my time came I told stories

As though they ran in my blood
Because each telling revitalized

My life-force
And each story reinforced
My racial reminiscence.

The stories told of the moment
When we broke into being
From the six stones and
How the first fathers founded
Our ancient villages and
Worshipped the forces of nature.

Warriors and were-tigers
Came alive through the tales
As did the various animals
Who were once our brothers
Until we invented human language
And began calling them savage.

Grandfather constantly warned
That forgetting the stories
Would be catastrophic:
We would lose our history,
Territory, and most certainly
Our intrinsic identity.

So I told stories
As my racial responsibility
To instill in the young
The art of perpetuating
Existential history and essential tradition
To be passed on to the next generation.

But now a new era has dawned.
Insidiously displacing the old.

My own grandsons dismiss
Our stories as ancient gibberish
From the dark ages, outmoded
In the present times and ask
Who needs rambling stories
When books will do just fine?

The rejection from my own
Has stemmed the flow

And the stories seem to regress
Into un-reachable recesses
Of a mind once vibrant with stories
Now reduced to un-imaginable stillness.

So when memory fails and words falter
I am overcome by a bestial craving
To wrench the thieving guts
Out of that Original Dog[1]
And consign all my stories
To the script in his ancient entrails.

The Spear

It was the spear that started it all.

I had to go back for it
To the shed in the jhum
And when I regained the main path
The others were long gone.

At the stream I stood hesitant
On the tree-trunk lying across,
But its cool waters inviting, I waded in
For a quick soak in its wet fold
Before the long trek home.

In the embrace of the soothing fluid
Weariness left my tired limbs
And I came out a new man
My mind bent on home and
The one waiting there.

The shadows were lengthening
As the rays of the fading sun
Sped through bushes and shrubs
Along the rough-hewn jungle path.

---

[1] The Ao-Nagas say that they once had a script which was inscribed on a hide, and hung on a wall for all to see and learn. But one day a dog pulled it down and ate it up. Since then, the people say that every aspect of their life, social, political, historical, and religious has been retained in the memory of the people through the oral tradition.

With the spear as my only companion
I hurried my pace
When suddenly a low bark
Stopped me in my track.

Another low moan and a blurry flight
Across the path and my spear fled
With lightning speed.
No volition, only instinct accelerating
Deadly aim towards the shapely silhouette

A thud and a crash in the shrubs
And afterwards, a great stillness.

I crept forward and gasped at the sight
Of a writhing doe, my spear firmly
Impaled in her wounded bigness.
Her life ebbing away

She exhaled with a last moaning heave
Expelling new life from her dying frame
Wrapped in her guts and the birthing blood.
She tried to free her new-born
From its watery fold
But my spear stood unyielding in its hold

Grief engulfing my suddenly
Tired body, I stood there numb,
A mute witness to my own crime
Until, the evening shadows urged for safety.

Hurriedly gathering some wild grass
I covered her unseeing teary eyes
To mark my shame and invoke
Nature's forgiveness.

Next I erected the circle of *genna*[2]
Around the still and bloody duo
Praying fervently that other predators

---

[2] It is a word which may mean several things: unclean, sacred, as well as taboo, all meanings indicating prohibition of some sort. The practice of 'genna' has been a part of Naga rituals observed on many different occasions.

Would know the sign and steer
Clear of the spear-blighted spot.

Leaving my accursed weapon where it stood,
I ran and stumbled.
Fearful of other demons stalking me
I ran faster, bleeding and weeping
Until I stumbled into the waiting arms
Sitting by the roaring hearth.

As she cradled my tortured self
In the stillness of the night,
I caressed her rounded fullness
Praying to the gods

To protect my seed
From mindless stalkers
Such as me
For now I knew
It was not the spear alone
That caused it all.

Easterine Iralu
Genesis

Keviselie speaks of a time
When her hills were untamed
Her soil young and virgin
And her warriors, worthy
The earth had felt good
And full and rich and kind to his touch.

Her daughters were seven,
With the mountain air in their breaths
And hair the colour of soft summer nights
Every evening they would return
Their baskets overflowing
With the yield of the land
Then they would gather round
And their songs filled all the earth.

Till one called Plague, a sojourner
Grudged them their plenty
And, wielding her terrible scythe
Reaped premature harvests of fields and men
Laying waste her young, her song, her hills.

The seven grew weary and worn
Their soft, summer night locks
Grew lank and were shorn;
Their music, dead notes
Scratched at parched throats
And turned them heavily away
From the dry, the dead earth.

Ah Kelhoukevira,
Keviselie knows you better than you know yourself.

He speaks of another moon
When she will be made whole
Restored to herself again
But until such a time
Yea, until winter come
Stay, stay the songs of Kelhoukevira.

Monalisa Changkija
Mist over Brahmaputra

From the silence of my
Air-conditioned hotel room
I flow with the currents
And coherence of Brahma's Son,
Sometimes filthy with human inadequacies,
Other times chaste in spiritual serenity.
And in moments such as these
I will myself to breathe
The perseverance of Brahma's Son
And disintegrate
Into the shapes, colours and volume
Of water—untouched and unscarred
By time, space and the elements.

...in moments such as these
I will myself to emulate Brahma's Son
To celebrate the sights, scents and sounds
And the strength in my solitary self,
And allow time to heal
These self-destructive tendencies
That sometimes buzz around my head,
As they do over Brahma's Son.
And like Brahma's Son, I wait
For the serenades of the Sun,
To soak up the mist over Brahmaptura.

One of these Decades

One of these decades when our dreams
Become as real as the nightmare now
We will gather around the fire
On moonlit nights as did our forefathers
Before strangers traversed across
Our strong and secure hills
And kept us chained to be tamed
To keep their date with destiny.

One of these decades when our dreams
Become as real as our nightmare now
We will gather around the fire
On moonlit nights as did our forefathers
Before we fall prey
To the lure of riches and glory
Walked into slavery
And missed our date with destiny.

One of these decades when our dreams
Become as real as the nightmare now
We will gather around the fire
On moonlit nights as did our forefathers
Before our land became a battle field
Of conflicting dreams and designs
Drowning our songs in the din of gunfire
Changing the colour of our destiny.

One of these decades when our dreams
Become as real as the nightmare now
We will gather around the fire
On moonlit nights as did our forefathers
And silence the gunfire with our songs
Loud and clear across our green hills
In rhythm with all humanity
To keep our date with destiny.

Shoot

Go ahead, shoot and blast us to eternity
I give you my word, we will not move
Neither from our stand nor to distract your aim
Shoot, what's stopping you?
What's making you tremble?
Shoot, I give you my word, we will not move
Shoot, you, all of you who have us covered from your sides
You have us now the way you want, so shoot.
Shoot and claim victory, it's all yours
We will stand firm and not move
From our dreams of brotherhood
Shoot, you have the guns.
Surely you are confident of world opinion?
Surely you are convinced you are right?
So shoot, I give you my word, we will not move
Shoot, after all we are only an inconvenience of a few lakh souls
So go ahead, shoot, blast us to eternity
I give you my word, we will not move
Neither from our stand nor to distract your aim.
Shoot, wipe us out from the face of the earth
You, all of you, who swear by Christ or the Mahatma
Shoot, don't stop now, pull those triggers
Shoot surely you have the courage of conviction
Of the rightness of your causes?
Go ahead then, shoot, blast us to eternity
I give you my word, we will not move
Neither from our stand nor to distract your aim
Shoot, we will stand firm and not move
From our dreams of brotherhood.

Nini Lungalang
Mirror

They say I look a lot like mother:
I do not think this pleases her.
It cannot please her.
I do not blame her,
But we've learnt, she and I,
To live with our mirror.

I know why I look like a lot like my mother:
She's put much of herself into my making.
After my birth, as well as before;
More after my birth, because,
Before my birth,
When I was just a nebulous wish in her,
Then, a tangible hope, then a palpable joy,
Then she'd stroke me gently through her flesh
And she'd see me,
In her day dreams, she'd see me,
She'd see me the way she wanted to see me.

Sometimes I'd see that phantom child
And it would anger me to unreasoning hatred,
I'd see it in the things she'd say
'Why aren't you? Why can't you?
Why do you always …? Why do you never …?'
And I would weep in wild frustration,
Weep hot and helpless, hopeless tears;
Hopeless, because I'd recognized, even then,
My invulnerable rival, my little enemy:
What I had never been,
And could not hope to be,
And did not want to be.

So you see, I look a lot like my mother.
She's stamped herself soul-deep in me
With things that are of hers
And things that are of hers
And did not want to be …

Yes, I look a lot like my mother
And my daughter looks
A lot like me.

I Will Be

If someone should render
My body, after death,
To its barest elements,
I'm told I'd be worth
A bucket of water
A couple of iron nails
A handful of various salts
And a few sticks of chalk
At most.

But it isn't just these things
That make of me 'myself'—
It's some magic alchemy—
With these, and time and space,
That run around, between
The molecules and cells of me
That give me weight and heft and height
And some relevance at least
To those who know and love me.
And time and space are simply not
Empty abstract things ... after all,
It's the pauses the nuances
And the silences
That give my words
Meaning, music, matter.
Beethoven was deaf and knew this,
And Homer, blind, saw
The wine-dark Aegean sea.
And when I 'am' no more
I will be the echo that you hear
In songs of joy or lament,
I will be the growth that surges
In your children's limbs,
I will be the glinting thought

That you try to pin down
Like a butterfly,
I will be the dust that tints
And gilds your dusk and dawn,
I will be ...
I will ...
I ...
...

Rock

My father slipped away in sleep;
He'd never agreed to die,
So he never knew he'd died.
For me, grief came late—
Long after the burial—
And I wept at last
For the bitter defiance
That refused to concede
The authority he'd claimed—
Something I would not yield—

And love's no substitute.
For we were both hewn,
He and I, of the same
Rock.
Flint strikes flint,
Anger seeks anger,
Ignites—
Burns, Burns, Burns.
But he slipped away
So I remain
Rock.
Unforgiven, unforgiving.

I see his stern face
In death-sculpted
Austere waiting.
Wait, my father; let
Your rage of living
Sear and scorch my heart

Till we wear down
Rock,
Erode time itself
Become an instant
Of flaming vapour
Stardust of eternity
Formless. Forgiving. Forgiven.

TRIPURA

Chandrakanta Murasingh
O Poor Hachukrai

Hachukrai, do you hear
The blind man mouth a harangue?
At every pause he knocks
His head against the ground
Kisses the dust and sings—
O, my brothers and sisters
Come to me, come by my side
Let's touch our beloved soil.

Hachukrai, how would you touch the soil
And swear by it?
You don't have an inch of land left,
All is lost bit by bit
In a distress sale to pay
For the cure of this man's myopic vision.
You are anaemic now

You don't have strength
Left in your hands,
Your smile has lost its lustre,
O, Hachukrai, your eyes are now dazed with sleep.
The flag waves atop the tree.
Do you see—
The flag that has been coloured
By the blind!

    —*Translated from Kokborok by Bamapada Mukherjee*

Of a Minister

There are times I get weary of talking;
Words, sounds and echoes whirl within.
At such times I wish I were a minister.
The best way to relieve the heavy winding entrails.
The minister has so much to say,
He never suffers from pent-up words.

There are times when I find all roads blocked,
The threatening *Ker*-bows aiming from all sides.
At such times I wish I were a minister.
The ministers know and show a thousand roads,
They live on crossroads at a million juncture.

The day comes with the colour of monsoon winds
And gets lost on the sandbanks of the dried river-bed.
We sit sad and quiet and look outside,
And think, if I were a minister.

The minister has neither inside, nor outside,
No air, no fertile soil on a sandbank.
There are only words, call of a hundred open roads,
Pulling at the sleeves day and night.

    —*Translated from Kokborok by Saroj Chowdhury*

The Python's Call from the Deserted Tong

A *chong* ful of fish for Totema to bring,
Days on end did I spend

Gazing into the water of the spring
Getting used to a life by the waterside.
A chongful of fish for Tote to bring
Through streams and creeks
Long did I wade
My feet finally touching the river-bed.
No one tells me
Where the river ends.
Only tales of the other bank
Does the boatman deliver.
I know all the stories
That the forest tongs harbour.
Thy python of fairy tales
That presently in the deserted jhum-tong dwells
Beckons me,
O how incessantly
Whenever I call the boatman now
From the other side of the hill
The python calls me
Little knows he, I'm not his fiancé.

—Translated from Kokborok by Bamapada Mukherjee

Your Dreams

You saw in a dream
That our mother was smiling
Your dreams hover like clouds
That gather at times, darkening the sky
And at other times sail gently on
With its golden lace.
But from up above the clouds
Running over the shoulder of Longtarai hill
Down, deeper down
Like the currents of Holong Cherra
Whispering secrets of the heart
Through darkness
And the white elephants of legend thunder
Will you make us hear
The sound of our mother's laughter?

You have taken up the gun
To kindle a fire—
But our jhum is not aglow
The flash of guns is scorching our eyes.
Are you the one
Who will show the blind his path?

— *Translated from Kokborok by Udayan Ghosh*

Pijush Raut
Feelings

Unearthly detachment gives
A poet Chaitra's wail,
Gives ashy solitude of a dead valley.
Unearthly detachment gives a poet the power of the divine Sound.
The moonlit hills, the village meadows
Get washed by that sound.
In an aquarium, the realm of fishes underneath the sea,
The beauty of colours on the body of fishes
Makes the poet yearn for ocean-adventure.
It gives a feeling to the poet
More than what is needed.

— *Translated from Bengali by Kallol Choudhury*

Picnic

Those fifteen revellers who went to the forest
For a picnic, thinking the minibus to be a Boeing,
Of them only two returned home,
Unconscious, in the dead of night.
It wasn't possible for the parents to identify them instantly
The accidents which occur sometimes in picnics,
In this case, nothing of the sort happened.
The bus didn't fall into ditches.
There was not food poisoning even.
Nobody drank overmuch, yet the accident occurred.

People did not tread for about a decade
Where those fifteen went.
They were also indomitable.
Poet Nazrul, despite your praise for youth,
Thirteen of them didn't return home.
When they will, in lieu of what,
Whether they'll return at all or not,
Nobody knows.
Who knows, maybe the life-savings
Of thirteen fathers will be bartered.
The wrath of insurgents will present
Thirteen fathers with thirteen fresh corpses.

—Translated from Bengali by Kallol Choudhury

Bijoy Kumar Debbarma
Eklavya of the Longtarai

The Arjuns will never let you climb the *chhatim* tree,
Lest you touch the sky
And lest their heads bow down
If you achieve a dexterity in archery,
Absorbed in meditation the seed of creation
From the formless,
From the void,
From inert things,
However complete you become,
the Arjuns will always cut off your thumb,
Dronacharyas being behind them
The moonlight spreads better
over the courtyard of the Arjuns
The fat of the sun falls on them.
Laxmi empties her wicker-basket?
at the doors of the Arjuns
for them Saraswati plays on her Veena
Ekalavya, you are like Abhimanyu.
There is 'Chakrabyuha' around you
To defeat you the Yudhisthras and the Duryodhanas

forget their enmity
and spread for you a death-trap.

Ekalavya, why do you want to climb atop the Longtarai
Where in a bamboo pipe wine has been kept for you?
If you can take a sip of it
You will feel a dream settle on your eyes
and will desire to see the sunrise
and the tiger-hill and the Kanchanjanga of that moment.
Overhead across the sky there will be an intermingling of clouds and
    colours
in a desire to build a Khajuraho
to see Ajanta and Ellora
represented in your sculpture
the jealous Arjuns are veritable chameleons
and wear a variety of clothes
at every crossing and every traffic point.
In alleys and on table and chair,
in corridors and in red tape
when you climb atop the Longtarai
tree Arjuns, Duryodhans and the Dronacharya
will waylay you
to cut off your thumb.

—*Translated from Kokborok by Bhaskar Roy Burman*

Jogmaya Chakma
The Martyr's Altar

On the martyr's altar!
With face covered in black cloth
wished to sleep with you.
On your chest I wanted to sleep eternally.
In brutal torture
in the pulsating last drop of my blood,
standing on the earth itself I asked you
to break the sky in fragments
I wanted to sleep by your side
with my face veiled in black
wanted to lie for all time to come.

You did not allow me to sleep
making me a witness of the difficult time,
filling my inkpot with your blood
You left me
under the blood-stained tricolour.
With the last throbbing of your blood
you placed your hand on my breast and said—
in the perilous beast-infested way of the world
when all the din and bustle come to a dead halt
you remain alive in
the undying flames of the torch.
Blooming by the side of my grave
in all the barren lands
strewn with fragrance-less fallen flowers.

—Translated from Chakma by Mihir Deb

Narendra Debbarma
The Border

By the lake at Kasba we stood,
When my daughter, seven years old
said—
'See dad there stands
the railway train.
Let's go and get into it.'

'No,' said I,
'This far is our limit
we can't cross the border
and go to the other side.'
The little daughter of mine didn't understand.
Baffled, she asked, 'Where's the border?
Only this patch of land stretches itself there.
Why can't we go there?'

The more I laboured to make her realize the barrier
the more she, too, tried to convince me of the point.
In no way she was to be convinced
in no way she was prepared to accept.

In my mind, I said,
You're an innocent child
and that's why, alas,
you know not
where the border does exist!
Had you been a grown-up you'd have seen—
The posts that mark the border
lie not so visibly without
as within the minds of men
hidden.

—Translated from Kokborok by Bamapada Mukharjee

ESSAYS

Mrinal Miri
The Spiritual and the Moral[†]

There are several 'received' views about spirituality. One of them is that spirituality is primarily an epistemic notion—that it is concerned with knowledge of oneself, or, quite simply, knowledge of the self, and that achieving such knowledge requires efforts of very special kinds. Another received view of spirituality is that it has to do with knowledge and techniques of dealing with the presence of 'spirits' in the material world—'spirits' which intervene in our day to day life with erratic regularity and unpredictability. 'Phenomena' such as these and others, e.g., telepathy, a person's capacity to tell accurately, or even relatively accurately, what is happening somewhere at a great distance from where she is located and similar others used to be the subject of both conceptual and empirical enquiry of the discipline named, 'Extra-sensory Perception' (ESP), fairly popular in the west in the

---

[†] A version of this paper was delivered as the Ramchandra Gandhi Memorial Lecture at University of Hyderabad on 14 February 2008.

early part of twentieth century. Techniques were also developed to 'communicate' with 'spirits' of dead persons, which, although devoid of physical bodies, were thought to be somehow entrapped in the physical world—a subject which also featured in fictional writings of various kinds. In this lecture, I shall not be concerned with this second view of spirituality, although, perhaps it still has an interesting presence in some of our religious thoughts and practices.

I should, however, say right at the beginning, that the second view of spirituality must be distinguished from the view, which is prevalent among many tribes of India—and elsewhere—that the entire world of nature and even artifacts are permeated by an intangible 'force' (for want of a better word) with which it is possible to communicate—or be at least in 'touch'. I shall have something to say about spirituality of this kind. The most important thing about this view, to my mind, is that it is based, unlike some other revered traditional views, on an emphatic acceptance of the reality of the day to day mundane material world.

The view that self-knowledge requires efforts of a special kind, that it is a matter of achievement, implies that the self is not transparently, self-evidently, available to us. Within many religious traditions, the assumption is that the original, unknown or epistemically beclouded self is *given* and stands apart from the physical world with which we human beings are willy-nilly engaged. It is, however, precisely this engagement with the physical world that is the stumbling block to achieving authentic self-knowledge. There are many traditionally prescribed practices aimed at removing this stumbling block: some kinds of meditations, yogic exercises, the idea of a spiritual retreat away from the entanglements of everyday life, performance of various kinds and degrees of austerities and so on.

In her excellent paper, 'Love and Attention',[1] Janet Martin Soskice puts the view of one of the traditional Christian conceptions of 'the spiritual life' that still enjoys great respectability and reverence as follows:

For each of us, no doubt, a vision is conjured up by the phrase, 'spiritual life' and for most... in our personal lives at least this is an eschatological vision—something to be piously hoped for in the future, but far from our daily lives where, spiritually, we just 'bump along'... In its Catholic Christian form it might involve long periods of quiet, focused reflections, dark churches and

---

[1] In Michael Mcghee (ed.), 1992, *Philosophy Religion and the Spiritual Life*, Cambridge University Press.

dignified liturgies. In its higher reaches it involves time spent in contemplative prayer, guided or solitary retreats, and sometimes the painful wrestlings with God so beautifully portrayed by the Metaphysical Poets. Above all it involves solitude and collectedness. It does not involve looking after small children.[2]

Or take the great Sufi tradition. True self-knowledge which is also necessarily knowledge of God, involves deliberate 'uprooting' of what we call sensory knowledge and complete rejection of knowledge based on argumentation, scholarship and study. In the Sufi tradition this is called *fana*—annihilation. And it is fana that finally leads to *baqua*—permanence in God. The role of music in the movement from fana to baqua is absolutely crucial (at least in the Chisti tradition). A verse extolling the two is introduced by a *quwwal* (musical performer), then it is highlighted by a prominent master or senior devotee, then it becomes the focus of constant repetition to the point of transforming both consciousness and physical existence, and then in some cases the result is a shift from ritual engagement to mortal disengagement. The verse, the music, the mood render the listener/devotee blank to any mood save that of the calling, and the call, once heeded, leads to death. To outsiders, it appears as suicide, but to insiders it is surrender to love. The death of the second major Chisti master, Shaykh Qutb ad-din Bakhtiyar Kaki is attributed to such a verse and music.[3] Within the high Hindu Brahmanical tradition too the spiritual life is frequently seen as demanding complete 'detachment' from the life of the world—*samsara*—and being firmly established in this detached consciousness—*sthitaprajna*. Sometimes, the original, detached self, which the life of spirituality endeavours to 'recover', is also called the 'witness' consciousness or self—the self as the disengaged witness to samsaric life. One difficulty with such views of the original self and self-knowledge is that if life begins with complete ignorance of this self, then how do we know that the spiritual practices that we devise will lead to its knowledge? Must the story rather not be something like the following: we begin with self-knowledge; somewhere, along the way, we lose it or almost lose it, and then devise ways of recovering it? That is frequently, within such traditions of spirituality, the language of 'forgetfulness' and 'remembering' has a central significance. There is, therefore, self-knowledge before spirituality; but how do we know

---

[2] Ibid., p. 61.

[3] C.W. Ernst and B.B. Lawrence, 1994, *Sufi Martyrs of Love*, New York: Palgrave, pp. 16–17.

that the self-knowledge that the spiritual life generates is the same as the self-knowledge that such a life is directed at achieving? The idea of 'forgetfulness' does not help, because even if we allow that we did forget how do we now know that we remember correctly?

This may sound like logic chopping, and in a way it is. But a more serious difficulty for me with this view of spirituality is that the disengaged self must also be disengaged from the life of morality, because the arena of the moral life is the mundane world of samsaric human relationships. The original self is as disengaged from the life of the virtues and vices as it is from all other aspects of the ordinary world of sense perception, of desires and emotions. My present self is shaped by the contingencies of my engagement with the world around me—my specific location in it, the language that I learn to wield which I cannot do except in and through relationships with the other, my memories and the human practices in which I willy-nilly get caught up, e.g., the games that I play, the books that I read, the conversations I have, the life within and outside my family, my professional commitments, my friendships and so on. It is in this arena of the contingencies that the so-called virtues and vices—qualities of character such as honesty, courage, justice, love, generosity, jealousy, greed, cowardice, deceitfulness, etc.—come necessarily into play; these qualities of character are the very stuff of the moral life—without them the moral/immoral distinction disappears; and therefore morality itself disappears.

Self-knowledge is crucial to the life of morality. Is my honesty genuine? Is my courage not really a cover for my deep-seated cowardice? Is my generosity not really self-seeking by other means? To seek and find authentic answers to questions such as these is an integral part of the life of morality. Self-deceit and self-ignorance are, as it were, constituent hurdles to the life of the virtues, and the ego is their impeccable ally—the 'big fat ego', as someone calls it. The overcoming of the ego is a necessary step in the battle against the 'cunning' of self-deceit. The spiritual 'discovery' of the self can be given an intelligible, significant content at all only if it is seen as the overcoming of the ego that leads to a knowledge of the true springs of our actions of our historically and contingently constituted being. Overcoming of the ego also must mean moral transformation, and it is my contention that moral transformation and spiritual self-discovery are of a piece.

One way of showing this may begin with the realization that the reality which we human beings—or indeed all living beings inhabit—is a reality that is necessarily laden with value. Reality must be something that either *ought* to be or *ought not* to be—it is, therefore, seen as something that must remain as it is, or something that must be changed. In the case of animals and plants this aspect of reality is manifest in what has been called their 'instinct' for adaptation. In the case of human beings, it becomes evident through our sense of obligation. Devoid of the sense of obligation, one might indeed still be aware of a world, but it will be a world in which there will be no such thing as human *agency*. Human freedom is inalienably connected with the idea of human agency. If—to put it in the language of modern Anglo-Saxon philosophy—the 'is' is no longer permeated by the 'ought', then human reality will no more be *human* reality.

Given that the sense of obligation is embedded in us, the important question for us is: what is special about *moral obligation* or, why should one be moral? The question arises against the background of the fact that one of the most profound predicaments of human life is the difficulty of cultivating the moral motive. The difficulty springs from the fact that to be established in the moral form of life requires what Kierkeggard calls the 'transformation of our whole subjectivity'. To be morally motivated is not just to do the right thing in a given situation, but to be settled in a state of mind such that the right conduct simply flows from it. One of Wittgenstein's aphorisms in *Culture and Value* runs as follows: 'No one can speak the truth, if he has still not mastered himself. He *cannot speak* it—not because he is not clever enough yet. The truth can be spoken only by someone who is clearly *at home in* it.' One can achieve such a settled state of mind or a state of being at home only by undertaking an arduous internal journey into the 'springs of action, to root attitudes, thence to their expression in conduct'. Such a journey frequently involves the dismantling of whole forms of life before a settled state of moral 'purity' is achieved. This is primarily an epistemic journey—a journey of self-discovery overcoming self-deception, self-knowledge overcoming self-ignorance. The assumption is that the possibility of the moral motive is conditional upon the possibility of achieving lucidity, utter clarity about oneself. It is sometimes suggested that the latter achievement is really at the hands of Providence. I shall leave this suggestion aside, and, instead say something about the suggestion that self-discovery is a matter of self-education.

The aim of moral self-education is to overcome the powerful impulses towards self-deception and self-ignorance, which tend always to entrench us in forms of life which are devoid of the moral motive. These impulses are powerful because they emanate from the ego. The first step towards overcoming the ego is to develop a form of attention, a concentration of epistemic energy, which will enable us to counter the benighting force of the ego, and, as it were, afford a glimpse beyond the ego into the self. An example of such a form of attention is perhaps aesthetic perception. Kant said about aesthetic perception that it quickens our cognitive faculties, and induces much thought. In other words, in aesthetic perception, as Mcghee has pointed out, 'there is a receptivity in which ordinary perceptual experience becomes *perceptiveness*—a perceptiveness which reveals to us, through the concrete object of perception a general truth about reality... thus we may see in the fading of a flower impermanence-in-itself, and in the moment of seeing discover an attitude to it.'[4] Kant also said that an aesthetic judgment—judgment of taste—is grounded in a delight in the object that does not owe its origin to any representation of some prior interest that we judge the object to further. Many eyebrows may be raised by the invocation of Kant here. But all that needs to be admitted is the *possibility* of such receptivity and such disinterested delight. When Swaminathan, the powerful Indian painter says, 'I paint because I cannot keep away from it, and it takes me away from myself', he affirms, at least in part, the possibility for himself. In the case of moral perception the receptivity and attention produces insights into moral truths: 'true *ahimsa* (love) drives out all fear', 'the power of ahimsa is incomparably superior to that of violence', 'true humility is the other side of true dignity'. An important aspect of such insight, such quickening of awareness, is that it bears upon one's experience of the world and thence on one's conduct, so that one acts differently from how one would have done otherwise.

To my mind, spirituality is another name for the kind of attentiveness or sensibility that I have talked about and the concentration and gathering of energy that is associated with it. I would also like to think that at least part of the aim of spiritual practices, e.g., meditation is to achieve the stability of such attentiveness. I take here the example of Gandhi, and consider very briefly, the curious notion of 'experiments with truth'.

The truth that Gandhi was concerned with, was the truth (the real as opposed to the Illusory) of the moral life. He believed that there is an 'interior route' to moral truths just as there is an exterior route to the truths of the natural sciences. His experiments consisted in traversing this interior route until the possibility of the moral life is established.

---

[4] Michael Mcghee, ibid., p. 235.

They were, as it were, purificatory exercises, which took him to the roots of the matter to what I have called 'springs of action' resulting in 'transformation of subjectivity', and subsequent pulling down of a form of life and founding another. Gandhi's fasts were an instrument of this experimentation; and there were several occasions in his life—in the early years, while in London, in South Africa and back in India—when dismantling of a form of life and establishing another took place. The journey is far from easy. As Gandhi puts it: 'it may entail continuous suffering and the cultivating of endless patience. Thus step by step we learn to make friends with all the world: we realize the greatness of God or Truth. Our peace of mind increases in spite of suffering, we become braver and more enterprising... our pride melts away, and we become humble... the evil within us diminish[es] from day to day.'

The use of the word 'experiment' is also suggestive of the fact that the moral quest—the traversing of the interior route—is not just a psychological journey, but an epistemic one—a journey which yields at once self-knowledge, and a knowledge of moral truths, such as the ones I mentioned a little earlier on. To achieve such self-knowledge, such quickening of awareness, is also to attain true freedom, *swaraj*—a state where one's actions flow with utter spontaneity from one's knowledge. Freedom is not the capacity to choose at random between alternative courses of action, but to act from an integral moral-epistemic stance.

For Gandhi, as for many others, the religious vision is inseparable from spiritual experience and the authenticity of the latter is guaranteed by the moral transformation that ensues. Morality, religion and mysticism are of a piece. The crucial difference between the Gandhian vision of spiritual life and some of what I have called the 'received' versions of such a life is that for Gandhi, an active, total (that is, with one's entire being) engagement with ordinary life—being 'fully there', imaginatively present to that which concerns us—can be informed by the most profound spirituality; spiritual pursuit does not require disengagement from samsaric life. To be spiritual and to be moral is to respond with utter ahimsa to what requires our response:

> My countrymen are my nearest neighbours. They have become so helpless, so resourceless, so inert that I must concentrate myself on serving them. If I could persuade myself that I should find Him in a Himalayan cave, I would proceed there immediately. But I know that I cannot find Him apart from humanity. I do not believe that the spiritual law works on a field of its own. On the contrary, it expresses itself only through the ordinary activities of life.

Working on the spinning wheel, looking after an injured calf, being engaged in *satyagraha* for a particular end, keeping one's own home clean and tidy—each one of these activities can be touched by a joyous spirituality, a sense of being in touch with the real order of things.

It would be interesting to compare the account of spirituality as knowledge of the self that is rooted in historical contingencies with the modern—rather post-modern—discourse of the politics and knowledge of 'identity', the anti-colonial nationalist discourse of Indian identity, the black movement, feminism, ethnicity, subalternity, the dalit movement in India and many others. Self-knowledge is the central concern of these discourses and the aim of such self-knowledge, as in the case of spirituality, is freedom. But one crucial difference between the idea of freedom that is part of the concept of spirituality and the notion of freedom that is embedded in the various discourses of identity is that while the latter is also seen as freedom from deception, here the deception has not so much to do with the self-aggrandizing strategies of the ego as with the relationships of power between the dominating other and the dominated self. These discourses are, therefore, necessarily also political discourses.

But, of course, the two discourses are importantly connected. Take, for example, the discourse of feminism. The politics of self-knowledge here can lead, and frequently has led, to a deepening perceptiveness and sensibility within an area of moral darkness created and sustained for centuries by the visible and invisible strategies of the 'will to power'. And it is in such unsuspected corners of darkness that the ego thrives and exercises its powers of self-deception. A community's will to power provides a fertile ground for the cunning of the ego to devise its own schemes of self-deception. In the domain of politics the feminist discourse, with all its internal differences and occasionally serious self-questionings, has been a formidable weapon in the 'game' of power; in the moral domain, it can be a source of spiritual renewal of the kind that I have talked about. And, of course, for someone like Gandhi, politics *is* the proper arena of moral agency.

Connected with the politics of self-knowledge that I have just talked about is the question of diversity of cultures and civilizations in the world and the possibility or otherwise of intercultural understanding and knowledge. One way of making clear the idea of modernity is to see it as centrally motivated by the idea of epistemological unity as embodied in the natural sciences. If cultural diversity is a fact of life, then modernity's definition of culture must desist from any reference to the unitary idea of knowledge and truth. Universal, overarching epistemology must not be seen as overriding cultural diversity. Take the following typically modern 'definition' of culture: 'a culture is a way of life of a people, including their attitudes, beliefs, values, arts, science, modes of perception and habits of thought and activity.'[5] Armed with this definition, we might think nothing of going forth into the world individuating cultures and distinguishing them one from another. But it is not quite that easy. Each of the identifying marks mentioned above is a potential source of problems. Apart from any specific problems that we might have in determining an entire people's [and what for that matter is a *people*] attitudes etc. there is one general problem that I would like to mention. This is as follows: If concepts such as 'attitudes', 'values', 'arts', 'science', etc. are to be cross-culturally available—which they must if they are to perform the function envisaged for them by the definition—then, they must be independent of any particular culture, i.e., they must be capable of being wielded and understood independently of reference to any particular culture. This, of course, immediately brings up the question of a core—a decisive core— of human consciousness which must be culturally uncontaminated—which must be available in a culture-transcending pristine form. And this question has not only been answered affirmatively in the modern west, but this answer and its ramifications are, as it were, the defining character of western modernity. A major part of the west's intellectual energy has been devoted to an ever more complex articulation of this culture-free pristine core of human consciousness—the core whose substance is universal, unitary epistemology. It is also informed by the conviction that only the clearest possible grasp of this core can afford the correct vision of the multiplicity of cultures in the world. This is the vision of Thomas Nagel's famous 'view-from-no-where' man. Armed with the resolute grasp of the all important core of human consciousness the viewer 'from no-where' stands outside the world of cultures, or culture-worlds and judges the worth and place of such worlds from its uncontaminated view point. There is, of course, great poignancy in this, but such is the fate of western modernity that having cast itself in the role of supreme judge, it must inevitably deprive itself of the solace of belonging to *a* world. But the rewards of this sacrifice are enormous. The no-where-man not only knows the truth about himself; he knows the truth, or at least is

---

[5] Simon Blackburn, 1996, *Oxford Dictionary of Philosophy*, Oxford: Oxford University Press.

in a position to know the truth about all others; he also knows the true meaning of 'right' and 'wrong', of 'moral' and 'immoral'; he, therefore, occupies the unique vantage point from where he can tell the illusory from the real; the better from the worse; the more developed from the less; the beautiful from the ugly; and, in principle, can find the just place for each culture of the world in the community of cultures. No wonder, therefore, the idea of the no-where-man is a compelling idea. Ironical as it may sound, it replaces in western modernity, the traditional idea of God or the received idea of the original, disengaged self that we talked about at the beginning of this paper. It is also a very close cousin of the idea of Cosmic Exile introduced (though not subscribed to) by W.V. Quine. The Cosmic Exile, like the no-where-man, does not belong to any world; he stands outside all worlds. But how does one attain such a position? I find Ernest Gellner's answer to this question the best:

> A most favoured recipe for attaining this is the following: clear your mind of all conceptions, or rather perceptions, which your education, culture, background, what-have-you, have instilled in you, and which evidently carry their bias with them. Instead attend carefully only to what is inescapably *given*, that which imposes itself on you whether you wish it or not, whether it fits in with your perceptions or not. This purified residue, independent of your will, wishes, prejudices and training, constitutes the raw data of this world, as they would appear to a newly arrived Visitor from the Outside. We were not born yesterday. We are not such new arrivals, but we can simulate such an innocent, conceptually original state of mind; and that which will be or remain before us when we have done so, is untainted by prejudice, and can be used to judge the rival, radically distinct opposed visions.[6]

But neither the no-where-man, nor the Cosmic Exile is a real possibility. To think otherwise is to be self-deceived. For the nowhere-man the common core of human consciousness which is his only resource is too meagre for it to generate a *vision* for him. The candidates for culture-free concepts mentioned in the definition of culture are in fact saturated in culture and are, therefore, linked to a point of view whatever the nature of this link may eventually turn out to be. Deprived of these concepts and other comparable concepts the nowhere-man fails to form *any* vision at all, and therefore, is incapable of making any judgments. About the Cosmic Exile, I quote Gellner again: 'It is not possible for us to

---

[6] Ernest Gellner, 1985, *Relativism and the Social Sciences*, Cambridge: Cambridge University Press, p. 87.

carry out a total conceptual strip-tease and face bare data in total nudity. We cannot, as Marx put it, divide society in two halves, endowing one with the capacity to judge the other. We can only exchange one set of assumptions for another.'[7]

Cultural diversity and the related diversity of visions, including, of course, diversity of epistemic visions, is an inalienable fact of human life. What, then, about self-knowledge which we have claimed to be embedded in the idea of spirituality. I do not here wish to go into questions of incommensurability of visions and relativism that have been raised in the recent debate in the west about the issues of diversity. I shall limit myself to making just the following point: Although the view that a language embodies a form of life or culture is misleading in many ways, there is an element of truth in it. It is misleading because there are many identifiable cultures in the world, which are naturally multilingual. Take, for instance, the culture of the part of India that I come from: Assam. There are many native languages spoken here—with varying degrees of differences between them. While some of them might, linguistically speaking, be members of a *family* of languages, others may belong to different 'families' altogether. However, it will be a grave mistake to split the culture of Assam up into different cultures along linguistic lines. Multilingualism is a part of this culture: people move from one language to another or from one 'dialect' of a particular language to another with a natural ease that is hardly like a schizophrenic jump from one world to another, or from one vision to another. The culture, as it were, includes difference or multiplicity within itself. The element of truth in the idea that language is constitutive of a form of life can be stated as follows: Language is a *gift* that, as St Augustine might have said, lights up the world for us. It is a *gift* because of its *givenness*. We cannot set out to invent language, because in order to invent language we must already have a language to invent it in. But every language is a distinct way of lighting up the world. Self-knowledge of the kind that we have talked about is necessarily articulated in language and every language has built into it the possibility of an articulation specific to it. In a multilingual culture such articulation might take an interestingly variegated form. But even if articulation of self-knowledge is presumed to require singularity of language—it will be wildly false to think that this will rule out the possibility of conversations between different articulations and transformations as a result of such conversations. There are traditions of

[7] Ibid., p. 89.

spirituality which are distinct, but which can yet talk meaningfully with each other. A most powerful validation of the truth of this is the utter authenticity of the life and thought of Gandhi.

I would like to add here a word about tribal cultures, particularly about the tribal cultures of India. Of course, we have used all kinds of unfortunate adjectives in describing our tribes, e.g., 'primitive', 'prehistoric', 'savage', 'uncivilized' and so on. In this, the nineteenth and early twentieth century nationalist anticolonial discourse in India is not much different from the European discourse of the non-European other in the era of European expansion into the so-called 'new' and the 'old' worlds. The central European preoccupation with reference to the possible other in the age of colonial expansion was whether he was within the threshold of salvation, conversion, or whether he was irretrievably established in the domain of the Devil. If the former, then, in essence, he is the same as the European although the road to realizing this essence could indeed be hard and arduous; if the latter, then he was beyond hope just like his counterpart in Europe. The anticolonial, nationalist history and anthropology of colonial India substantially retained this distinction between the self and the other—the self in this case being the self of the great Indian civilization. It will be an extremely interesting and instructive exercise to locate the place of tribal India in the intellectual history of nineteenth and early twentieth century India. This will, however, take me too far a field in the context of the present paper.

If, however, my view about the 'ought' determining the 'is' is correct, then the world that the tribes inhabit are as real and as capable of transformation from within, as the world constituted by the language of modernity. One thing that can certainly be said in favour of the tribal vision is that the disjunction between the disengaged original self and the samsaric world of the received view of spirituality that we discussed at the beginning of the paper does not exist in this vision. The world of the tribesman is seamlessly continuous between the inanimate, the animate and the human; she/he is ensconced in the contingencies of time and space as anything else in the world. Self-knowledge for the tribesman, therefore, must be bound by these contingencies. The episteme of the tribal vision is similarly continuous between the natural, the moral and the spiritual. To dismiss this espiteme as either irretrievably erroneous or lacking in autonomy is, to my mind, as much of a moral lapse as an intellectual one.

Let me at the end briefly address the question of the place of spirituality in the age of digital utilitarianism and virtual reality. Digital language is incapable of the following: lying and pretending, of artifice (therefore, also of telling the truth or of sincerity). It is also incapable of expressing the exercise of virtues such as courage, generosity and unselfish attention to the other; the great subtleties of emotions such as love, jealousy, hatred and joy. The great—often-unstated—desire of humans today is to be able to imitate the machine as much as possible, in fact to become it, if possible. To the extent that humans succeed in imitating the machine, they are in danger of becoming intractably forgetful of their self; and in the eventuality of their *becoming* machines, they will also cease to be humans. We are heading perhaps towards a different kind of civilization altogether where questions, which were crucial to the ones we have known so far, will become pointless. Facets of what we consider humanity, self-knowledge, spirituality and the moral life might still remain, but only as simulacra of their original. Our capabilities and powers of manipulation will increase no doubt to an unimaginable extent, but the transformations that humans shall undergo with this enhancement of their capabilities and powers are also equally unimaginable.

Birendranath Datta
North-East India and its Socio-Cultural Milieu[†]

An apprisement of the role of the Mongoloid peoples in the development of the composite Hindu or Indian culture, the peculiar line of development of this culture in its expansion in North-Eastern and Eastern India through Mongoloid contact or participation—should be looked upon as an important line of enquiry tracing the history of Indian civilization.[1]

North-East India has been, and still remains, the traditional homeland of the Indo-Mongoloid population of India. But neither the region nor the contribution of its people to the culture and civilization of India has received adequate notice, much less appreciation. Rather it is not

---

[†] Birendranath Datta, N.C. Sharma, P.C. Das, and Anundaram Barua (eds), 1994, *A Handbook of Folklore Material of North-East India*, Guwahati: Anundaram Barua Institute of Language, Art and Culture.

[1] S.K. Chatterji, 1974, *Kirata-jana-krti*, p. 18.

unusual to hear it suggested, both overtly and covertly, at different times and in different contexts, that the north-eastern region is removed from the Indian mainstream. If we leave aside the political implications of such suggestions (which, when applied indiscriminately to the people of this region at large, is open to serious challenge), and confine ourselves to the socio-cultural ones, we might as well agree that they somehow reflect shades of historical and contemporary reality. The north-eastern region does have a special character of its own: the socio-cultural milieu of this region holds up in the present day, as it has done in the past, a picture that somehow distinguishes it from the rest of India. As such, this special character cannot be understood, much less assessed, in terms of the commonly accepted standards of what is believed to constitute the Indian mainstream.

What we want to suggest is that the socio-cultural pattern of the north-eastern region should be studied in frame of reference which is specific for this region and which, although not being in full conformity with the all-India frame of reference, need not be considered un-Indian or even less Indian than the other one. This is true as much of the general character of the population of the region as of the social and cultural traditions which include the folklore material. There is so much here that is obviously of all-India affiliation and perhaps so much more that is peculiarly North-East Indian.

One of the outstanding peculiarities is the fact that the process of assimilation and absorption of tribal communities into the Hindu fold, which had stopped working in other parts of India quite some time ago, has been operative in this region till comparatively recent times and cannot be said to have completely ceased to work even today.[2]

Another significant fact is that almost the entire tribal population of the region and a very sizeable proportion of the population absorbed into the non-tribal society through Sanskritization (or otherwise detribalized) are drawn from the Indo-Mongoloid or Kirata stock, making for a kind of homogeneity in the midst of the apparent heterogeneity. True, the Kiratas have been relatively late arrivals in the Indian scene—some hordes coming in the recent centuries (although the earliest arrivals date back to the Vedic times); but that cannot mean that they have been cut off from the main currents of Indian history and culture. Concentrated in the eastern and particularly the north-eastern peripheries of the sub-continent, they have participated in the course of

[2] Ibid., p. 52.

Indian history and contributed to the evolution of Indian culture in no small measure.[3]

While the Hindu-Aryan element is fairly strong in certain sectors and traces of the Austric and Dravidian element linger on from a remoter past, the dominant presence of the Indo-Mongoloid element in the culture of the north-eastern region is a reality that cannot be brushed aside easily.

From the cultural point of view, the population of this region could be divided into three categories:

1. Those tribal communities living in the rather distant hills, more or less isolated and free from the impact of 'Sanskritic' or other 'organized' cultures (except in the case of tribes with Buddhistic connections).
2. Those tribal groups, both in the hills and the plains, who have retained their tribal group identity but who have been acculturated in various degrees as a result of living in close proximity or contact with the 'non-tribal' Sanskritized majority, or through the impact of Buddhism or Christianity or Islam.
3. Those societies which are more or less fully Sanskritized, where the population is wholly (as in case of the Meiteis) or substantially (as in the case of the Assamese) made up of erstwhile Indo-Mongoloid stocks. Local Muslims of this region, although not Sanskritized from the religious point of view, are culturally a part of this milieu.

In the process of Sanskritization of the latest category of the population two agencies have been at work: the Hindu religion and an Indo-Aryan language (chiefly Assamese, and to a lesser degree, Bengali). While in the case of Assamese society both the Hindu religion and the Assamese language have worked simultaneously, in the case of the Meiteis it is almost entirely the religion that has been responsible for this transformation, their language continuing to be of the Kuki-Chin group of the Tibeto-Burman family. The Bishnupriyas stand midway between the two: religion-wise they are Sanskritized and at the same time their language contains elements both of the Indo-Aryan Kamrupi and Kuki-Chin Meitei.

---

[3] Ibid., pp. 52–7.

Even the Sanskritized Hindu communities of this region retain elements which according to orthodox standards are patently tribal. For example, the caste system in the Assamese society is flexible and fairly liberal. While Brahmins (and one or two other castes) do occupy a higher position in the society, they do not dominate the scene. All non-Brahmins are lumped together as *sudir*s (Shudras), among whom there is considerable inter-caste mobility, and there are practically no untouchables. Castes are not profession-oriented and caste-based disabilities are few. In the Meitei society also there are just two broad caste divisions—the Brahmins and the Kshatriyas; and Brahmins can take non-Brahmin brides and vice versa. Although there are trades and professions traditionally practised by particular family groups, such functional specialization is not integral to the caste system. In both the societies, far from being a degrading occupation, weaving is a most honoured and desired skill for women of all categories, unlike in any other part of India. Similarly in the matter of food, not to speak of non-Brahmins and non-Vaishnavas, even the purest Assamese Brahmin has no scruples about eating both fish and meat, while the Meitei Brahmin would restrict himself to fish.

In the field of religion, side by side with the Brahminical gods and goddesses of pan-Indian affiliation, hosts of pre-Brahminic deities continue to receive veneration and propitiation. While in the Assamese society belief in, and worship of, such deities are more or less confined to the semi-Sanskritized peripheral communities, in the Meitei society Sanamahi, Pakhangba and a very big number of other *lais* (gods) are still intimately associated with the Sanskritized core—the best evidence being provided by the famous Lai-Haraoba festival. Non-Brahmin priests and spiritual mediums (*deodha* and *deodhani* in Assamese, and *maiba* and *maibi* in Manipuri) and their shamanistic dances and other activities are met with in both the Assamese and Manipuri societies.

Again, although Vaishnavism has deeply touched both the societies, Saktism and more particularly Saivism continue to prevail in different forms. Apart from Bathou–Brai and Mouthansri of the Bodos, Gira–Girasi of the Deuris, Pha-Mahadeo and his consort of the Tiwas, and so on, which are original tribal versions of Siva–Parvati, the influence of Siva–Parvati on the Assamese society is evidenced by the big number of Siva temples and the innumerable Bura–Buri shrines scattered all over rural Assam, whereas in the Manipuri society it is discernible through such myths and legends as the story of Nongpokningthou–Panthoit and that of the origin of the Rasa dance.[4] Thus Hinduism has assumed in this region some peculiar feature through the processes of syncretism.

The process of 'universalization' and to a certain extent that of 'parochialization' have also been at work. What is important is that such processes are still operating, however imperceptibly in certain fields. It may be pointed out that in this region even Islam and Christianity have taken characters which have local flavours.

In the field of material culture—which in folkloristic parlance is 'physical folklife'[5]—there are certain distinctive peculiarities. Much of the traditional pattern of life in the hills centre round jhuming or shifting cultivation which at best makes for a bare subsistence economy, gradually giving over to settled cultivation in the plains, even where the indigenous economy is hardly above subsistence level, professionalism and trade-mindedness not being the strong points of the local population. Weaving of exquisitely coloured and designed textiles by the womenfolk in their indigenous looms is a distinctive feature common to the lives of all the communities of the region, including the 'Sanskritized'. What is more, even the dress worn by the women has a basic similiarity—the Assamese *mekhela*, the Manipuri *phanek*, the Karbi *pini*, the Bodo *dakhna*, the Rabha *ruphan*, the Mising *gaseng* the Adi *gale*, the Mizo *puan*, and so on, are practically variations of the same basic format.

All this—and many other traits—make the distinction between the tribal and the non-tribal lose much of its relevance in the context of the socio-cultural milieu of the north-eastern region.[6] And from the midst of the seemingly incompatible diversities there emerges a pattern that is characterized by a certain 'commonness' and 'togetherness'.

It is against this background of commonness and togetherness in the midst of variations and distances that we have to study the folklore material of the north-eastern region—without, of course, losing sight of the broader of all-India backdrop. Although many of the items cited above themselves constitute folklore material highlighting the common perspective for the north-eastern region, we shall take some random examples from verbal folklore items to illustrate the points we have made above.

[4] J. Roy, 1973, *History of Manipur*, pp. 3, 10–11.
[5] R.M. Dorson, 1972, *Folklore and Folklife: An Introduction*, pp. 2–3.
[6] B. Datta, 'The Tribal and the Non-Tribal in the Context of Assamese Society and Culture', *Journal of North-East Council for Social Science Research*, Vol. II, No. 11.

A big number of tales and other narratives available among the different communities in this region are found to have identical types and motifs. The tiger being scared by an imaginary dreadful thing (*Dighal-thengiya* in Assamese and *Tapta* in Manipuri), the old man and the old woman being cheated by the cunning animal (the jackal in Assamese and a number of tribal versions and the monkey in the Manipuri version), the simpleton who is plotted against by jealous relatives and who successfully turns the table against them (Assamese, Karbi, Naga and other versions), the step-mother's ill-treatment of the step-children and the ultimate prevalence of justice (Assamese, Manipuri and various tribal versions) are just a few cases in point.[7]

It is true that the existence of tales and other narratives with identical types and motifs even among widely separated communities is the rule rather than the exception. However, certain cases of the appearance of some particular types in a few communities of this very region to the exclusion of others calls for some special attention. For example, the story of Harata Kuwar[8] of the Karbis has an almost exact parallel among the Bodos (Alsiya Kowar),[9] but the type has not been noticed elsewhere. Again, the story of the brother's incestuous infatuation with his sister has been found in three communities—the Bodos (Raona Raoni),[10] the Misings (Bijuli Aru Dherekani),[11] and the Bishnupriya (the story of Pani and her brother). The Bishnupriya tale starts with the same motif as the Mising tale but ends in a different note. Incidentally, a Mising mythical story about how the sky, once very low, happened to go high up being hit by a rice-pounding flail[12] has an exact parallel amongst the Bishnupriyas while the Assamese version has it that a broom, and not a flail, was used.

Speaking of myths, it may be pointed out that there is a remarkable similarity in the patterns of stories about the creation of the world as obtaining among the various groups of the region, both tribal and 'unofficial' Hindu: the world arising from a primeval ocean, the world coming from a great personage of a tree, the world directly created by a

[7] J. Borooah, 1954, *Folk Tales of Assam*; S.N. Barkataki, 1972, *Tribal Folktales of Assam*; P. Goswami, 1970, *Ballads and Tales of Assam*; 1976, *Songs and Tales of North-Eastern India*; 1980, *Tales of Assam*; T.C. Hudson, 1908, *The Meitheis*; and Y.K. Singh, 1963, *The Folk Tales of Manipur*.

[8] C. Lyall and E. Stack, 1908, *The Mikirs*, pp. 55–69.

[9] B.K. Das, 1977, *Boro Sadhu*, pp. 6–17.

[10] P. Goswami, 1980, *Tales of Assam*, pp. 16–17.

[11] T.C. Pamegam, 1980, *Missing Sadhu*, pp. 20–1.

[12] Ibid., pp. 55–6.

heavenly being, creation coming out of a cosmic egg and earth and sky being born of a universal mother, etc. As has been brilliantly brought out by Verrier Elwin, 'such traditions can be paralleled in both the classical and the tribal literature in India'.[13]

But apart from such examples of 'commonness', what is interesting is that many myths and legends examplify the idea of 'togetherness' that we spoke of earlier. Quite a number of tribal myths about the creation of man are concerned not only with the coming of the first progenitors of the respective communities but of those of neighbouring communities as were not excluding the 'non-tribals' in the plains. For example, Karbi myths speaks of the eggs laid by the mythical bird *plakpi*, out of which come the first men—a Naga (Naka), Kachari (Ramsa), a Khasi (Chomang), an Assamese (Aham) and of course a Karbi. There is a Bugun (Khowa) creation in which a Bugun marries a girl from the Assam plains;[14] in a Dhammai (Miji) tale where one of the their earliest progenitors becomes the Raja of Assam;[15] a Taraon (Digaru) Mishmi tale speaks of how the first human children were carried by water to the plains and how all others except the oldest son remained in the plains to become the Assamese.[16] There is a Singpho tale about how the different races including the Assamese came down by ladders made of different materials.[17] The Hrussos have a similar but more elaborate story.[18] According to one Wancho tale: 'At first there were no different clans or tribes. But at that time a great flood poured over the hills of Assam and levelled some of them and the land became flat. Since there was not enough water in the hills, some of the children of Wanchos went down to the plains and became the Assamese.'[19] The Taraon Mishmis have a tale about the first human who got from the tusk of his elephant father his wife and many soldiers from whom came the Assamese, the Aka, Daflas, the Miris and the Mikirs.[20]

A story very widely distributed among the tribes of this region 'attempts to explain how it is that the tribes are illiterate, and the plains people, though not such talkers, can read and write'. According to this

---

[13] Verrier, Elwin, 1958, *Myths of the North-East Frontier of India*, p. 1.
[14] Ibid., pp. 100–1.
[15] Ibid., pp. 105–7.
[16] Ibid., pp. 133–4.
[17] Ibid., pp. 126–7.
[18] Ibid., p. 27.
[19] Ibid., p. 136.
[20] Ibid, pp. 133–4

story, all knowledge was at first written on animal skins which were distributed among all communities. While the plainsmen preserved their skins and so the knowledge of reading and writing, the hungry tribesmen boiled and ate their skins resulting in their illiteracy.[21] There are also various traditions current among the different tribes of Manipur about the common origin of, or close connections between, the tribals of the hills and the non-tribals of the valley.[22]

Some myths, legends and tales certainly point to the awareness of the tribal people of the region about the 'togetherness' we have been talking about. There are also many tales which reflect on the 'peculiar' socio-cultural standards of the Sanskritized people.

For example, in many Assamese tales (and folk-songs) the Brahmin is the butt of ridicule, showing that his position is not all that sacrosanct. In one such tale the Brahmin and his low-caste (often a tribal) attendant sit for their meals in the same room, only a little apart. Piqued at being given only one fish while the Brahmin has the rest of the score of the fishes, the attendant throws the one fish of his lot to the Brahmin's dish. His food thus defiled, the Brahmin leaves everything and the attendant has a hearty meal.[23] There are many other specimens in which the attendant scores over his Brahmin master. In one such story the attendant even marries the daughter of the Brahmin's brother.[24] Apart from providing humour, such tales also highlight the fact of the absence of caste-ridden rigidity and the looseness of food taboos here. It can be said that even the famous Sorarel story of the Manipuris, in which the human wife of god Sorarel comes down to her father's house and partakes of forbidden food and drink,[25] represents a sense of loss of a community with a tradition of meat-eating and liquor-drinking passing into a stage where the consumption of such food and drink is prohibited. A Bishnupriya tale which speaks of the daughter of a non-tribal family being married to a Kuku man and proving to be a better devotee of God than the father himself despite the 'impure' ways seems to contain a tacit admission of the fallacy of non-tribal superiority.

There are other tales in which the physical folk-life of the people is faithfully represented. Jhuming is central to many of them. Many others

---

[21] Ibid., p. 99.
[22] T.C. Hudson, 1911, *The Naga Tribes of Manipur*, pp. 8–17; 1908, *The Meitheis*, pp. 4–10.
[23] P. Goswami, 1980, *Tales of Assam*, p. 70.
[24] J.D. Anderson, 1895, *Kachari Folktales and Rhymes*, pp. 34–8.
[25] Y.K. Singh, 1963, *The Folktales of Manipur*, pp. 36–7.

are connected with weaving. There are many etiological tales in which the bright plumage of birds is explained in terms of brightly coloured textiles. For example, a beautiful tale current among the Garos,[26] the Rabhas[27] and the Bodos[28] tells how the peacock and the peahen got their colourful plumage. The Tangkhuls have a tradition involving the cicada.[29]

A very interesting example of narratives reflecting the physical folk-life of the region is provided by the *Sabin Alun*, the Karbi version of the Ramayana. In this folk epic king Janaka works in his jhum farm; Sita carries rice and rice-beer to him in a basket slung across her head; guests are served betel-nut and rice-beer; being a good weaver, Sita wants the golden deer killed as its skin would make a good seat while weaving; and Rama dries the deer meat for future consumption, and so on.[30] Further, the Misings have tales recounting their descent into the valley from their original home in the Adi country.[31] Karbis have vivid legends about their heroine Rangpharpi and hero Thong Nokbe highlighting their traumatic experiences under the Kacharis and the Khasis respectively. One song contains a fervent appeal to Karbis to rise against the Ahoms—representing their frantic reaction about the earliest encounter with that mighty power.[32] There are also Naga legends centering round hills–plains relations.[33]

True, such material makes up only folk history or ethno-history and cannot be accepted as history proper; but they can certainly supply useful raw ingredients and provide clues to missing links.

There is another class of legends—drawing heavily from the epics and the Puranas—with the instrumentality of which Sanskritized and semi-Sanskritized groups have sought to establish their linkage either with pure Aryan lineage or with one or more Hindu gods or goddesses. One of their best examples of such a legend is linked with the Meitei tradition that they are related to Babhrubahana born through the

---

[26] D.S. Rongmuthu, 1960, *Garo Folktales*.

[27] R. Rabha, 1977, *Rabha Sadhu*, pp. 51–8.

[28] P. Goswami, 1980, pp. 19–22.

[29] Y.K. Shimray, 1982, 'Legacy in Songs' (Tangkhul Tribe), unpublished paper read at a seminar in Imphal.

[30] B. Datta, 1982, 'The Karbi Ramayana: An Overview', *The Assam Tribune*, 25 April.

[31] T.C. Pamegam, 1980, pp. 288–90.

[32] S.K. Chatterji, 1974, p. 125.

[33] B. Datta, 1982, 'Karbi Folklore: A Few Observations', *The Assam Tribune*, 13 September.

union of the Mahabharata hero Arjuna with Chitrangada, a princess of their land. The Kacharis claim their descent from Bhima through Ghatotkacha who is believed to have been the former's son through his Kirata wife Hidimba. Then there is the tradition prevailing in Assam that the Mishmis are the same people whose princess Rukmini was in the remote past married by Krishna himself. The Rajbanshi-Koch people consider themselves to be progenies of 'pure Kshatriyas' who had 'lost their caste' to Mech (Bodo) women while hiding themselves from the wrath of Parashurama. Examples could be multiplied. The stories linking non-Hindu kings or royal lines directly with particular gods of the Hindu pantheon and those identifying local deities with Hindu gods and goddesses are of a piece. They are as much the result of the eagerness of newly Sanskritized groups to be ranked high in the Hindu-Aryan hierarchy as the product of the ingenuity of the Brahmin priests. All these clearly have a common pattern.

This is the overall socio-cultural background against which we have to view the folklore material of the north-eastern region. It is in this broader cultural context that the various folklore material of the region—even individual items belonging to particular groups—can be seen in their proper perspective. As such, the approach in the study of such material should be an integrated one in keeping with the 'special character' of the region.

Esther Syiem
Social Identity and the Liminal Character of the Folk
A Study in the Khasi Context

In an age when small narratives and counter-discourses legitimise reality, the folk becomes a forked weapon of assimilation and dissemination. In its intersection with the living it is a changing and evolving phenomenon. It has garnered a rationale that places it apart from other knowledge systems. It may thus in the Khasi context be viewed as a powerful identity-giver, identity-shaper and identity-promoter, the lifeline that, whilst manifesting old identities also revamps them.

One begins with a common form of greeting in the Khasi language, which has common usage in everyday life, which, by virtue of its ordinariness as being a common linguistic tool, gives it the nature of the folk; as a culture-bearer of the community. Hence, the common Khasi word *khublei* (God speed), a counterpart of the Hindi *namaste*, and of several other such greetings around the world, is at face level, only a greeting. This greeting, however, carries with it the social and cultural weightage that particularises a group of people who have placed importance upon the spoken word, who have prided themselves in their oral networking[1] and who wield their khubleis differently from their counterparts elsewhere. The word khublei is characteristically multi-dimensional and culturally non-interchangeable, for it presents a way of life that has been primarily God-centred. Khublei as it is still being used, is connotative of the inward and outward looking make-up of people who have had to make the best of a cultural and a religious onslaught that swept them at the beginning of the nineteenth century. Whether they have at all weathered it well, is debatable, but like all colonised subjects the linguistic stratagem of subterfuge, begins with one word: khublei, which is a confirmation of one's social identity. It is a unit of culture and social practice that has been existentially proved. It has fortified the Khasis and kept them strong within its ramparts. Khublei as it has always been understood to mean, is a way of life, a circumscribing reality that has an inbuilt system of values that have given a particular group, social credence. Creation and birth signifies gratitude to God: khublei; a greeting called out to another: khublei; the signifying reality of worship is, khublei; death brings forth affirmation of the journey towards an after life: khublei; work as worship: khublei; forgiveness or the need to be forgiven expresses itself as khublei. It is central to life and has remained wholly undefeated.

It has formed the basis for the construction of Khasi identity in the link that it has had with the orality that is synonymous with society. Khublei contains within its contours the face of a community that has striven to organise itself around a body of philosophical, socio-cultural and folk discourses (that also employ diverse mediums) that have never actually been classified in writing. They have been re-constructed several times over by word of mouth but as they contend with an increasingly complex world, they have dissolved their boundaries, shifted from the centre and occupy a space that, on the face of it, may seem to be a liminal one, as they exist on the peripheries of everyday life. This liminality must not, however, be misjudged or misunderstood as being indicative of inevitable erasure. In fact, this has proved to be a vantage point; an area rich in the psychical reserves of society, an unnamed area, milling over with significances, nuances and challenges striving to be heard and

---

[1] Esther Syiem, 2005, 'Folk Networking the *U Hynñiew Trep* Way', *Laiphew NaAr Jingmut* (Thup 1).

to be taken up all over again. It is against this background that the folk must be understood in its relation to Khasi consciousness.

The inevitable moulding of identity that it was actively engaged in, began to take a back-turn in the mid-nineteenth century when the Western missionary gave a new direction to Khasi identity. When the colonisation process started, it claimed the faith and imagination of the many but left in its wake a society that was no different from other societies which endured similar forces of subjugation. The unavoidable backlash took place, several decades later,[2] in the form of some re-converted intellectuals who sang paeans in honour of the re-discovered beliefs of their ancestors. They re-established their faith in the values that the world of their ancestors represented when they revived it in the scheme of their re-discovered beliefs. This has been viewed by some as a revivalism[3] of sorts that produced a network of social and religious activities that countered the backsliding of the indigenous faith. Community meetings of religious and cultural significance are now being regularly held in many villages in Mawphlang, Sohra, Pynursla and in the Bhoi areas where the politics of identity stem from the forces that counter what is now considered to be mainstream culture—emulation of the erstwhile alien faith and attitudes of the Western world. Even amongst the Christianised section of the community, this imitation of Western cultural practices has been looked upon as being slavish and unthinking. Churches like the Presbyterian Church and especially the Roman Catholic Church have striven to inject a degree of home-grown culture in their worship services through the use of indigenous musical instruments and the adaptation of local tunes to some hymns.

The oral nature of Khasi society has never completely broken down even in the face of the cultural and religious invasions that brought with them the power of the written script. One notes that beneath the veneer of a Western imbibed education, there has always been one side of the face turned towards a hidden self. This is the self residing in shadowy darkness, invisible to the rest of the world. The invisible protagonist of Ralph Ellison's book *Invisible Man*[4] refers to this hidden area of darkness as being a productive area seething with the creative consciousness of an entire race. It is to this undefined darkness that

---

[2] These refer to intellectuals like B.M. Pugh and O.H. Mawrie.

[3] H. Kelian Synrem, 1992, *Revivalism in Khasi Society*, New Delhi: Sterling Publishers.

[4] Ralph Ellison, 1995, *Invisible Man*, 2nd Edition, New York: Vintage International.

the protagonist finally realises that he owes much to; and to which he must turn in order to find himself. Similarly, the Khasi writer Bevan Swer, talks about the aliveness of the folk in his book, *Ka Matïong Ki Khanatang*. He describes the folk as being a living entity, tenaciously involved in finding creative expression for the Khasi community. It spills over with tremendous vitality.[5] The protagonist of *Invisible Man* draws upon the resources that are to be found in this region; but he can only do so when he has exhausted all other probable but inauthentic means of finding himself. The folk diffuses itself in multiple ways in the book. Thus the blues, jazz, Black American folk tricksters like Brer Rabbit and other folk motifs provide the necessary tools for regeneration and survival. To a great extent too, suspended on the fringes of life in Khasi society is this living body of folk knowledge that has always had a dialogic interchange with its closest associate, society itself. But it now faces a challenge of another kind; the kind that, as mentioned earlier stems from the inevitable cosmopolitanism that, in its negative aspect, tends to trivialise and reduce the folk to a one-dimensional entity, flat and nondescript.

Although the folk may seem to have been side tracked from its original position of centrality, it can never be recanted, never erased. If at all it has now assumed a position of potent 'invisibility', a hidden strata of creativity mirroring the compulsions of a community. This is a term that has been borrowed from the protagonist of *Invisible Man*, which signifies a hidden area of darkness, heady with energy; distinctively its own. Withdrawing into this underground region, it has simultaneously exerted pressure upon society as it waits to be disseminated amongst those who are still alive to its multi-layered existence. Hence its liminality has become its strength and it is from this region of partial shadows that it waits to re-emerge in its new avatar, equipped to take on the challenges of a complicated age.

This is an age that, in an increasingly globalised ethos would seem to be coercing the individual to adopt a standard norm of existence. At first sight there are no exceptions to the orientations of this common culture reflected as it is in popular tastes for fashion and food. But on further scrutiny, there are a host of exceptions to the general consensus over lifestyle and existence. These are the exceptions that 'hibernate'[6] in the unlikely spaces between the conformities of transculturalism,

---

[5] Bevan Swer, 1995, *Ka Matïong ki Khanatang*, Shillong: Ri Lum Offset Printing Press.

[6] *Invisible Man*, p. 6.

globalisation and transnationalism.[7] They are rooted in a life that signifies meaning away from these conformities. They form a cohesive counter-force of energy taut with the potential that remains 'invisible' to the indifferent or to the uninitiated.

In the context of this structural reversal, the folk may also be understood to be, the 'pre-text' or the 'sub-text' of society, assuming a concurrent existence with the lived reality. It has allowed itself to be heard, to be read, to be dismantled altogether, or to be re-visited by the changing sensibilities of an existing generation; or alternatively, existing as it used to in an unchanging substratum of tradition and habit; or maneuvering itself through a dialogue with its audience. Above all, it continues to aerate the channels of communication with a community's inner sense of self. It fulfills the criterion for its continued existence, in providing a multilateral scaffold for the constructs of the racial imagination. It is in this manner that the folk has been understood and assimilated, in order to find within it that indestructible grain of life that has refuted suppression, especially in an age teeming with urban compulsions.

The figure of Ka Nam[8] may be taken to be a fossilised character of no real significance, a paltry figment of the imagination; or, she may

---

[7] Frank J. Korom, 'Uncharted Waters of Folklore Scholarship', *NEHU News*, Vol. 7, No. 1, January–March 2006. (Paper presented during a seminar on Folklore Studies organized by USEFI, Kolkata in collaboration with the Dept. of English, NEHU, Shillong on 11 March 2005).

[8] Briefly told, the tale is as follows: There was once a woman who, heavy with child, saw a cluster of fruit trees upon which grew the luscious *sohphi nam* fruit. She wailed aloud to herself at the misfortune that had brought her there with no one to pluck the fruit for her. Unknown to her a tiger sitting high on the branches, overheard her and volunteered to pluck the fruit for her. He, however, stipulated that, as a reward, he wanted the unborn child for himself. But if the child were a boy she could keep him for herself. She promised her child to the tiger and greedily ate the fruit that he gave her.

When the child was born, the tiger received the news from the fox. He went to the village and crouched under the floor of the house, the *khrum*, only to hear the contradictory cries of, *it's a girl, a girl, a girl, no a boy, a boy, a boy*, being repeated over and over again until he had to leave in disgust. The child whose name was Ka Nam, grew up quickly. Her mother, however, never let her out of sight and never told Ka Nam of her broken promise, until one day when Ka Nam insisted that she accompany her friends to the well. What could her mother do but allow her to go only to be informed later that the tiger had kidnapped her child.

Unknown to all, Ka Nam was brought up as the tiger's daughter performing household chores for him. When he saw that she was old enough to be eaten, he left one morning, instructing her to cook a basketsful of rice. There was no curry, however, and this she puzzled over aloud as she was busy preparing the rice, until a be perceived to have multiple relevance to a society that has begun to document the significance of gender relationships and gendered responsibilities in a matrilineal society. Her role in the story is, on the one hand, as a woman victimised by circumstance: the circumstances of her birth, her abduction by the tiger, her consequent escape into another world and her marriage to the sun's son. On the other hand she is an image of survival. Deprived of the sustaining culture of home Ka Nam emerges strong within herself. In the unfamiliar environment of, firstly the tiger's home, which she takes to be her foster father's home, and secondly, of an extra-terrestrial planet where the heavenly bodies reside; she lives out her resistance through sheer grit and later on, through disguise, camouflaging herself in a toad-skin. Abandoned and left alone from early childhood, the resources that she displays speak much of a character who could have easily surrendered to a hopeless sense of fate. She has the ability, however, to draw strength from the myriad resources that surround her.

In the episode where the tiger goes off to round up his friends for the kill when they would feast upon her, she is left alone in his house, in a limbo of un-knowing. But she rises above her situation in her responsiveness to the rat that emerges from her hole. This is the rat that would initiate her into an existentialist world full of the choices that she would ultimately have to make alone. For the moment, however, in a life that has been deprived of any other normal relationship, except

---

rat darted out of its hole to speak to her. Great was her joy when she found that the rat could talk to her. But her joy was short lived when she heard what the rat had to tell her about the tiger's murderous intentions. However, the rat promised to help her since she had always been kind to her in the past. Hurriedly then, Ka Nam ran off with the rat to the obdurate toad's house, *ka hynroh*, to seek for help. The toad gave her a discarded toad skin to disguise herself with, after which the rat took her to two trees growing close to each other. She told her to climb onto the branches of one and to repeat a chant after her. The trees would then quickly grow upwards to reach the heavens.

Once in heaven, Ka Nam went looking for a job as a menial. Finally the sun took her in and permitted her to stay in a dilapidated shack a little away from the house. Thus did Ka Nam work for the sun disguised in the toad skin. At night, however, she would take off the skin in order to bathe and to comb her luxuriant hair. One night the sun's son U 'Lur Mangkara heard her soft humming and peeped in. The sight that met his eyes was of a beautiful maid busy at her toilette. One night, unknown to her when she was still at her bath, he snatched the toad skin away and threw it into the fire. The result was that Ka Nam had to marry U 'Lur Mangkara. [Reference may also be made to K.S. Nongkynrih's recently published book, *Around the Hearth: Khasi Legends* (2007), New Delhi: Penguin Books India.]

for the one shared with the tiger, everything rests upon her ability to make the best of an unusual encounter. She establishes the required connection with the rat who has watched her, unknown to her, several times from her hiding place and, who now comes out into the open to find out if she really is what she seems to be. Ka Nam is an image of the resourceful, though inexperienced, woman. She communicates with ease, with a creature which is not of human stock; and displays remarkable humility in her deference to a creature which has always been considered to be several rungs lower than humans. Consequently she is assisted by all of nature when she has to make a hasty flight from the tiger. This emanates from a world-view that has upheld the sanctity of created life, but which also understands that humankind's superiority rests upon the power of the human word as a constructive tool that may be wielded over other living creatures.

After the rat tells her of the tiger's plans of eating her up, Ka Nam places herself at the mercy of the four-legged creature who undergoes a symbolic transformation when she initiates action for Ka Nam. Thus she is no longer simply, rat, *ka khnai*, but *ka mei 'nai*, mother rat, a common phenomenon in the world of the folk where animals take on human proportions to facilitate or de-facilitate life for the protagonists. The contradictory dimensions of the rat's personality, that of being small and devoid of physical strength, yet possessing the cunning and shrewdness of a seasoned matriarch, brings into focus the conflict of the sexes: rat versus tiger; female tenacity versus male power. Within the parameters of the larger conflict, that of the tiger as antagonist to Ka Nam, who now works in collusion with mother rat, are embedded many smaller conflicts that erode Ka Nam's base on earth.

Thus mother rat takes Ka Nam to the toad's or Ka Hynroh's doorstep seeking for help from a creature known for her obduracy. The next episode echoes with the verbal exchanges that take place between mother rat and toad; one, protecting the rights of the human protagonist, and the other, unwillingly drawn to assist in facilitating escape for her. Ka Nam's timely discernment of her peculiar situation is the only solution for her at the moment. There are no ready answers available to her for the time being, but her willingness to act in order to preserve herself opens many doors for her. Hence the toad-skin that she is forced to wear in order to hide her identity from the tiger, who might also be in pursuit of her, may seem to be a deterrent to her freedom. But it is only in disguise that she can leave the earth to look for a future elsewhere.

The ultimate assistance that mother rat renders her, is to enable her to reach the heavens, far away from the tiger, through the help of two trees growing close together. Significantly, in an all women's tale where the antagonists belong to the opposite sex, the trees are also female. In common parlance trees as a species, are masculine in gender. There are some individual types that are, however, female. Ka Nam is aided in her flight by two female trees who respond to her chanting call to them:

San ko kong Ri, pat ko kong A, san ko kong A, pat ko kong Ri

symbolically repeated until she reaches the heavens. Once there, she is left to the mercy of those around her but manages to find suitable employment in the Sun's house, still disguised in the toad-skin.

The penultimate episode tells of her attempts to hide herself from discovery. At night under cover of darkness, she takes off her toad-skin in order to wash herself and comb her hair. When U 'Lur Mangkara, the sun's son, discovers her at her toilette, combing her hair by the flickering light of the kitchen-hearth, he keeps watch over her, until the right moment comes. Several nights later when it does come, he snatches the toad-skin away from her while she is having a bath late in the night, secure in the knowledge that she is all alone. She marries him when her identity is inadvertently revealed.

The marriage that takes place at the end of the story may be understood to be the final vindication for the aggrieved one, but for the contemporary woman, marriage no longer becomes the desired end. The story delves into the complexities of womanhood within a matrilineal society and, for many women in Khasi society, there are familiar situations in the life of Ka Nam that reverberates with equally insurmountable situations. The rat is a figure of weakness as well as of strength. Despite her puny size she has been able to outwit the hostile forces that threaten the very existence of Ka Nam. She is the polarised opposite of Ka Nam's biological mother, who, at the beginning of the story, pregnant with the child to be later called Ka Nam, promises the tiger anything that he desires if only he would quench her craving for the fruit, that he could so easily pluck for her. With cunning alacrity, sitting high on the branches of the fruit tree, he humours her in the hope of obtaining the child that she is carrying. He makes his desire known to her, but states his explicit preference for a girl-child. Ironically, a boy-child would be unacceptable to him. Later in the story the mother refuses to keep her promise to him. But he is ultimately able to capture the girl and raise her for his own selfish purposes. The sexual innuendo is very strong; as are the counterpointing forces of innocence and experience, of dominance and subjugation. The story plays upon the conflicts that are inbuilt in gender relationships that are unbalanced by mis-understandings and/or, absence of mutual give and take.

At face level this is a story that imaginatively postulates greener pastures for women victims of all societies. Notwithstanding her ill fortune at having a mother who abandons her, the story presses on to show how help may be obtained from the same sex, the male sex, that has also given her a raw deal. The story portrays at one end, the male predator, the tiger; and at the other end, the besotted lover, U 'Lur Mangkara. At the same time, the image of woman maybe drawn from Ka Nam, Ka Nam's mother, the rat, the toad and the sun, who in Khasi folklore is female.

The tale springs deep from the Khasi imagination. But where once it would have been spun several times over within the story-telling paradigm, now, it is only to those who are interested in safeguarding what it says, that it makes itself accessible. Hence, the significance of Ka Nam in an electronic age, is to a large extent dependant upon stalwarts like the invisible protagonist in *Invisible Man*, who refuses to surrender completely to the infiltrations of a digitalised culture. They wield their authority through an articulating self-consciousness, to stay the threat of, influences that would make the Khasi imagination completely porous. The image of Ka Nam has, therefore, withstood the alternative images of womanhood brought in by the pluralistic environment that surrounds society. She remains steadfast as an image of life, an unrelenting figure of womanhood that has had a tenacious hold upon the Khasi imagination, exerting a seminal influence upon the idea of woman as being participatory to the making or unmaking of her future. Strangely enough, Ka Nam's flight from earth finds parallels in the lives of many other women who also take flight from their homes, for some reason or the other: from abusive husbands or lovers; conversion to Christianity in the early nineteenth century and therefore, recourse to flight; or elopement with a lover; or for several other unnamed reasons. The move away for Ka Nam was a move that took her out of herself into an unknown future amongst alien beings. Yet she manifests courage and quick-wittedness in her attempts to ward off danger to herself. Many women in Khasi folktales show unexpected initiative in handling difficult situations. This maybe understood to be a telling observation on the character of the Khasi woman, who has been entrusted by man, as told in another folktale,[9] to take over the responsibilities of the clan and to carry on the clan name.

In a supposedly egalitarian set-up, men as well as women share a symbiotic relationship where gender roles are clearly defined, though the gap between what is and what should be, has always been obvious. The non-sexist point of view that reveals itself in the telling of the story of Ka Nam commiserates with her plight in the simple language of the discerning. That she marries an alien being clinches her fate, but her experiences cannot be cancelled-off. They form an integral part of a woman's experience even in the present system. The original telling by a male elder,[10] of such tales classified as *ki khanatang*, reflects upon a sexually unbiased perspective that provides its own comment upon the society from which it comes.

The story of *Ka Nam* has echoes in several other stories, such as *Ka Noh Ka Likai*, *Ka Lang Byrku Sang Khyndew* or *Ka Sohlyngngem* that speak of the plight of women and their relationships with men. Historically, Khasi women have been free of the kind of oppression that patriarchal societies have forced upon their women. But discrimination, however, does show itself in many ways; reflected as it is in the way in which women have been defined as being of single strength, rather than possessing the many-layered strengths of men—*ka kynthei shibor* compared to *u shynrang khadar bor*. This has inculcated unhealthy prejudice in men who wish to take advantage of women but it has also brought out an ideal gallantry in others. Nevertheless, the experiences of *Ka Nam*, speak audibly for women who have had to battle similar circumstances of fate. The one factor that the tale focuses upon in the course of the telling and corroborated by facts of everyday reality is, the help that women extend to one another in a community of shared experiences. In her book, *In Search of Our Mother's Garden*,[11] Alice Walker, a black, American novelist who is also a social activist, speaks of the link that all women have with others who have lived before them. This is the tie of the matrilineal that Khasi women feel no necessity to make too much about because it is taken for granted by all. The rat, Ka Nam herself, the toad, the sun who allows her son to marry Ka Nam, even the erring woman, Ka Nam's mother, belong to a community of women who are

---

[9] Donbok T. Laloo, 1970, *Ki Paju Lyngkot*, Shillong:Don Bosco Press.
[10] W.R. Laitphlang, *Katto Katne Shaphang ki Katto Katne*, Shillong.
[11] Alice Walker, 1983, *In Search of Our Mother's Garden*, London: Orion Pub. Gp. Ltd.

after all, able to initiate action on their own. Ka Nam's identity, before her marriage to U 'Lur Mangkara cannot simply be relegated to irredeemable oblivion. Within the logistics of the folktale, she does deserve a better future and this is dispensed with by her fortunate marriage to U 'Lur Mangkara. But the transcripts of her life before her marriage has had more takers than the marriage itself, and the significance of the tale for many lies in its ability to impart a sense of life in the single-mindedness with which she struggles to conquer her situation.

Despite the attempts by several creatures to possess Ka Nam, she manages to keep them away and to move on without them. The main contention of the argument is not whether she succeeds in outwitting them. It lies in the fact that she is still relevant to society. She is a figure of survival that continues to exist in the liminal spaces of the imagination; just within reach of a society that is attempting to finetune identity for itself, in terms of the negotiations that it has had to make with other cultural images impinging upon its consciousness. Ka Nam is not a lone icon in the Khasi cultural framework. She exists surrounded by other equally potent figures of life, such as the ones mentioned before. Together they exert an influence that has impacted Khasi identity in more ways than one.

In a similar way, when one looks at the monoliths and megaliths that dot the Khasi countryside one observes tangible evidence of an identifiable way of life and thought. These are the stones that have been hewn out of solid rock. They bear witness to the binary opposites of male and female upon which Khasi society was founded. The belief was that when these stones were erected, the strength of Khasi men was legendary. Apart from other symbolic significances that are associated with the monoliths, the utilitarian uses to which they were put were for purposes of rest for travellers, or for the benefit of the *Syiem* when he visited his people in distant regions. They bear stolid witness to a remote past; inerasable monuments that are inextricable from the Khasi sense of self, inscrutable mystiques of society. They belong to a past that can only be observed from a distance in time. The combined power of the mental and the physical had to be invoked for the erection of these stones. For, when the monoliths were erected it is said that the spoken word (*ka ktien*) still wielded its mystical power in smoothening obstacles and facilitating the work of erecting them in their appropriate places. The supremacy of mind over matter which constitutes the core of Khasi thought played the most significant role in the work of putting up these stones. These monoliths bring up the inevitable comparison with a past that challenges the competence and integrity of a present that has been dwarfed by its own iniquities, especially with respect to the spoken word. Hence, there is always an inevitable feeling of inadequacy on the part of every Khasi when he/she relates himself/herself to his/her past.

This is related to the origin myth that tells of the tragic consequences that befell the Khasis when they broke off ties with their Maker. The accompanying sense of loss and exile[12] that resulted from this, has been traumatic for the entire race. It sees itself living in a dislocated present cut off from the munificence of its Creator, by its own willfulness. The rest of the story is fuelled by an obligatory sense of setting things right with one's Maker through the judicious power of the spoken word. This has been the central focus of life for the Khasi. The orality that defines it stems from the internalisation of this loss which in turn has driven the Khasi to articulate about it, to rationalise it, to attempt to understand it or to justify existence for himself/herself. The other oral discourses form a crucial extension of this narrative.

In the same way in which these monoliths serve as a point of reference for the understanding of Khasi identity, so do the narratives provide the logistics for an understanding of who the Khasi are. Their roots are sunk deep into a past that provides a linkage with the future, re-making or re-defining identity in a fluid present. The narratives are culture specific fraught with the experiences of people who are still caught between the pull of the present and the call of the past. In a community as small and as close-knit as the Khasis where development at the grass root level was suddenly abandoned with the coming of the British,[13] these narratives form one of the primary sources of information, defining knowledge and existence for everyone. The telling of them cannot, however, be interchangeable with the reading of them in the newly found,[14] comparatively speaking, and medium of the written word. Although there are also the never-ending possibilities of preserving these narratives within a digital space, this too would never replace the art of telling. In the telling lies the mystery of grassroot editing where the narrative passes through several re-makes of the original and though the storyline

---

[12] Jawaharlal Handoo, D. Kharmawphlang, and S. Som (eds), 2003, *Folklore in the Changing Times*, Bhopal: IGRMS Publications.

[13] Helen Giri, 1998, *The Khasis under British Rule 1824–1947*, New Delhi: Regency Publications, p. 57.

[14] Emory Elliot (ed.), 1988, *Columbia History of the United States*, New York: Columbia University Press, p. 6.

remains unchanged the texture waxes and wanes with each telling, thereby adding to, subtracting from, dividing and multiplying the Khasi sense of self. These narratives have survived on the strength of the oral tradition. This is a tradition that, in the words of the American Indian writer N. Scott Momaday, stands in a special relation to language, where words are 'intrinsically powerful' capable of transforming life itself: 'By means of words one can bring about physical change in the universe ... can one quiet a raging weather, bring forth the harvest, ward off evil, rid the body of sickness and pain, ... live in the proper way and venture beyond death. Indeed there is nothing more powerful.'[15]

Within the Khasi context, the telling is sacred, a compelling habit that tames reality and shapes destinies. In its less formal aspect it may be compared to the compulsive Khasi custom of *kwai* eating and kwai sharing. This in itself calls up an entire world-view, that explains the philosophy of Khasi hospitality and the rules of friendship. This is a tradition that has another oral tale[16] supporting its customary existence in a society that endorses the habit as a cementing factor of goodwill.

Within the ambit of the oral, there are endless possibilities of relocating identity in newer spaces and contexts. Although many of these narrative discourses have now been given a written form, yet no written version can claim itself to be the authentic one. Even in the writing, the rationale of the oral prevails over the written and their acceptability becomes questionable to the transcriber who is always aware of other existing versions. Realistically speaking, in an age that has lost touch with the colossal vitality of the spoken word, this is the only way in which to preserve many of them from being erased. However, the fact is, that though neglected by some, others are there who labour hard to keep it alive and constant. These are those who empower it through the active medium of the self. This is the self that defines itself in relation to a community of other selves who see themselves as the message bearers of society. These individual 'selves', profile the import that Khasi society still places upon those who are the village elders, with whom rests the wisdom of society. They form an important segment of intellectual aliveness where, ironically however, women, though allowed in, cannot

---

[15] Ibid., p.7.
[16] Kynpham Sing Nongkynrih, 2001, 'Death in a Hut', *Indian Literature*, Vol. XLV, No.1, January–February.

claim equal status.[17] Folk sayings, *ki phawar*, or chants and aphorisms are other important adjuncts apart from many others, of this living network of intelligence that surrounds the individual within an informal ambience of folk culture never to be ruled out from any society; least of all from the miniscule societies of the world who are still anchored to their roots in a very basic way.

The enunciation of identity in the Khasi context, stems from the liminal regions of an imagination that has preserved the folk in a critical way: through its oral tradition. As pointed out earlier, this orality no longer manifests itself in the consistent ways of the past because it has merely gone underground, but never overboard; and in the Preface to his book *Katto Katne Shaphang ki Katto Katne*, W.R. Laitphlang, comments upon the contradictions that civilisation has brought with it to a society such as the Khasis. In places where roads and communication are almost non-existent and where life flows on undisturbed by the turbulence of material development, Khasi thought exists in its pristine form. In other regions where development has been comparatively more progressive, there has been a lopping off not only of verdant forests and a plundering not only of the land, but of a dimension of society that has affected it in many uncountable ways.[18] The threat is as always to a certain way of life and its preservation lies within the hearts of, amongst many others, individuals such as W.R. Laitphlang. Their answer to the challenge is an aggressive wielding of the pen that draws inspiration from an orality as inerasable as it is well seasoned. The individual efforts of people like W.R. Laitphlang, Hipshon Roy and H. Elias have succeeded in documenting the oral in a way that solicits its aura even within the pages of their manuscripts. Though not as obvious as it used to be, the oral tradition lives on through individuals whose foundation for living is rooted in the folk wisdom that they have inherited from their ancestors. Hence, Ka Nam comes through to us as a symbolic figure of the Khasi woman deeply entrenched in the grain of the telling, transforming herself through the changing avatars of the oral as it continues to infuse life into its own.

---

[17] In many ways the Christian church has replaced these village elders with church elders. Women too are being given identity within the church. But respect for society's elders, whether Christian or Non-Christian is an ingrained habit in society. Ironically, many of these church elders are also well-versed in the ways of their ancestors.

[18] W.R. Laitphlang, p. ii.

Thingnam Kishan Singh
Encounters and Literary Engagements
A Critique of History and Literature in Manipur

The development of a historical sense of tradition is underlined with an intrinsic logic of understanding difference between what may be collectively conceptualized as an established order and the emerging changes in a society. Juxtaposed with the term 'modern', tradition in a commendatory sense invokes an associated reference to the past. Reference to 'the tradition' or 'a tradition' along with a qualitative sense of being 'traditional' necessarily underscores the inherent sense of difference with the 'modern'. Debates on modernity in human history have generated a broad-based understanding and perception of certain values responsible for phenomenal changes in society. These values emerged historically in Western Europe with the onset of Renaissance which was basically a resurgence of Graeco-Roman spirit of scientific curiosity and of humanism in the arts and learning.[1] Along with the

---
[1] B.V. Rao, 1978, *History of the World*, New Delhi: Sterling, p. 124.

Renaissance major developments like the reformation, geographical discoveries and subsequent colonization of the American continents and parts of Asia and Africa and the advancement in science and technology altered the contours of life in western Europe significantly. Disintegration of the feudal system and the emergence of industrial capitalism eroded those aspects of life associated with tradition in those parts of Europe. Reinhard Bendix sees debates during the early nineteenth century drawing contrasts between tradition and modernity as an ideological projection of industrialization.[2] Broadly speaking, modernity as a cultural order arising from the developments in the West implies certain values. In the words of Marion J. Levy, 'the structures of all relatively modernized societies reflect an increasing emphasis on rationality, universalism, functional specificity, and emotional neutrality or avoidance (objectivity)'.[3]

History bears testimony to the travails of a civilization running through a course of two thousand years as the people inhabiting what is presently called Manipur experienced numerous upheavals subsequent to clashes with different cultures and powers. Known as *Kathe* to the Burmese, *Meklee* to the Assamese, *Mooglie* to the Cacharies, *Cassey* to the Shans, the people of this ancient Asiatic kingdom have witnessed three major epoch-making encounters in the vicissitudes of its history. The first has been the contact with Hinduism, which in so many ways brought a massive cultural displacement in terms of religious and collective consciousness.[4] Even though traces of Manipur's contact with Hinduism can be traced to King Charairongba's reign in the seventeenth century, it was with King Pamheiba's ascension to the throne in 1709 that saw the brutal imposition of the alien faith.[5] Apart from the historical importance of this clash between the indigenous Meetei faith and the alien Hindu faith, the nature of its impact on the collective experience of the people and its culture needs careful scrutiny, as it was not actually an encounter in terms of tradition and modernity. It was

---

[2] Reinhard Bendix, 1964, *Nation Building and Citizenship: Studies of our Changing Social Order*, New York: John Wiley & Sons.

[3] Marion J. Levy, Jr., 1966, *Modernization and the Structure of Society*, Princeton, New Jersey: Princeton University Press, p. 62.

[4] For a detailed account of the indigenous Meetei faith and belief, see Saroj Nalini Parrat, 1980, *The Religion of Manipur: Beliefs, Rituals and Historical Development*, Kolkata: Firma KLM.

[5] Penetrating study of Hindu missionary activities and proselytization is provided in Gangumei Kabui, 1991, *History of Manipur, Vol. I: Pre-Colonial Period*, New Delhi: National Publishers.

essentially an encounter between two pre-modern, traditional cultures, two traditional world-views. The second has been the encounter with the Western civilization vis-à-vis the British conquest of Manipur in 1891. Here also, contact with the British was established much earlier. Viewed from a cultural perspective, it was historically an encounter between a traditional and a modern culture system. It was all the more accentuated by the Second World War, which suddenly exposed the Manipuri people to the undercurrents sweeping across the globe. The impact was substantial as it not only brought about a massive change in the collective experience and consciousness reflected in terms of cultural values being rendered more open, liberal, egalitarian and humanistic but also far reaching political changes vis-à-vis the swelling tide of decolonization that swept Asia, Africa and Latin America. Manipur eventually became free from British control in 1947 and remained a sovereign democratic state till its 'integration' with the newly independent state of India on 15 October 1949. The third comes with this contact with India in 1949. It presented a queer picture of an encounter with another not too dissimilar entity, as it was also much on the same path towards modernization. With its own logic the society and culture of this ancient Asiatic land has experienced the dynamics of the encounters. The paper seeks to foreground the essential nature and dynamics of these encounters by scrutinizing certain aspects of Manipuri literature as it unfolds during the travails of its growth and development. It aims to assess the nature of the encounters vis-à-vis Manipuri literature's engagements with the changing realities.

Prior to its encounter with Hinduism, Manipuri literature till the seventeenth century has been said to constitute its early period. Ritual songs and hymns composed before the advent of the Manipuri script[6] form part of the corpus of the literature of the early period. These songs and hymns are not treated as folk songs or part of folklore as they were not widespread amongst the people. Neither were they handed orally through successive generations. They were confined to a certain erudite section of performers whose performances were again limited to 'particular ceremonial functions, ritual observance and festive occasions'.[7]

[6] Historical research provides evidence of the advent of the Manipuri script at the close of the 12th century. See Wahengbam Ibohal Singh, 1991, *The History of Manipur: Early Period*, Imphal: Manipur Commercial Co. and W. Yumjao, 1935, 'Report on Archaeological Studies in Manipur', *Bulletin No. 1*.

[7] Chongtham Manihar Singh, 1966, *A History of Manipuri Literature*, New Delhi: Sahitya Akademi, p. 12.

The manuscript *Panthoibi Khongkul* gives an account of the religious and social festival known as the Lai Haraoba where the Khaba community paid homage to the deity Nongpok Ningthou and his consort Panthoibi. This festival believed by scholars to be part of the cosmological theory of creation in Meetei myth, is a repository of numerous songs. Significant amongst these Lai Haraoba songs found in the *Panthoibi Khongkul* text are the *Ougri, Khencho, Anoirol* and *Lairemma Paosa*. *Ougri* and *Khencho* are much more archaic in diction and steeped in historical allusions. They are considered to be composed earlier than the rest. *Ougri* is also mentioned in the manuscript *Laishra Pham* as a coronation song on the occasion of the ascension of Nongda Lairen Pakhangba in AD 33, which marks the uninterrupted reign of Meetei King till British conquest in 1891. The royal chronicle known as *Cheitharol Kumbaba* begins with Nongda Lairen Pakhangba's ascension to the throne in AD 33. Another manuscript titled *Naothingkhong Phambal Kaba* refers to the *Ougri* as an important aspect of Meetei culture and tradition. The lines of the first part of *Ougri* comprise of six syllables each while those in the second part comprise of eight syllables. Noted for its cadentic quality, *Khencho* remains as an obscure and unintelligible literary piece to the modern generation. Still considered as one of the most important component of the Lai Haraoba festival, this immensely rhythmic song is characterized by its archaic diction. It consists of lines of six syllables each. *Lairemma Paosa* and *Anoirol* are based on the theme of love. Diction appears to be comparatively simple in these songs with a lyrical flow created through alliteration and rhythm. Another song associated with the festival is the *Hijan Hirao*, a long narrative poem extremely lyrical and sentimental. Some other prominent songs associated with rituals are *Ahonglon, Yakeiba, Pakhangba Langyensei, Langmailon* and *Kumdamsei*. *Ahonglon* is important as it is mentioned in the manuscript *Loyumba Sinyen*, a written codification of laws and customs dating back to the twelfth century described by modern jurists as a treatise on legal jurisprudence and statecraft resembling a modern constitution.

Another important aspect of the literature of the early period was the treatment of heroism. Rivalry and clashes between the clans resulted in the development of martial skills. Bravery and courage remained central to the numerous conflicts that created a martial culture. This cultural trend predominates the spirit of the society till the late nineteenth century. Anonymous writers of the early period dealt with the saga of heroism in numerous works like *Chengleiron, Tutenglon, Numit Kappa,*

Thawanthaba Hiran, *Chainarol* and *Nongsamei*. *Chengleiron* stands as one of the earliest known text in Manipur literature whose style has been followed widely. Opening with a dedication to the patron king, the writer points out that it is meant to be recited or sung. It is a narrative that spans three generation of kings of the Chenglei clan. Particularly interesting is *Numit Kappa*, an allegory with strong political overtone. However, the first work to register the note of realism is *Thawanthaba Hiran*, a tragedy based on a crime story. Departing drastically from the legendary nature of stories in the other works, it was based on historical events. Closely aligned with history, it grapples with the violent and bloody conflicts between the Khuman and Meetei clans. The horrific violence that characterized the work makes it distinct. *Chainarol* is an account of combats based on the feuds of the clans. There are twenty-seven stories based on real-life incidents.

Besides the numerous literary tracts on the cult of heroism and bravery, the theme of romance and love found abundant expression in the literature of the early period. During this time we find works, which can be classified as pure fiction, in clear distinction from those fictions based on historical realities. Many of these fictions were based on mythical legends. *Nungpan Ponpi Luwaopa* narrates the romantic saga of Luwang Prince Luwaopa and Koubru Namoinee, the adopted daughter of the Koubru King. Myth and legend fuse together with divine intervention playing an important role in the narrative. After a series of mishaps and torturous ordeals the two lovers are finally united. Fate emerges as the overarching power dominating human lives in the tragic story of *Naothikhong Phambal Kaba*. Human actions and human characters are helpless in the sweeping changes brought by the elements of fate and destiny.

Panthoibi Khongkul is one of the most esteemed literary works in Manipur. It is, perhaps, the most, critically assessed work of Manipuri literature of the early period. As the title suggests, the story deals with the trial or footsteps left by Panthoibi after she leaves the house of her husband. The narrative highlights the rigorous hardships faced by individuals in love in the face of severe odds posed by social barriers, tradition and custom. Panthoibi, the Meetei Princess, is described as a maiden of rare beauty. Eagerly sought by many powerful kings and princes, she is portrayed as an extremely independent character. Her spirit is symbolic of a natural zest for life. Spurning many proposals for marriage, she is finally persuaded to marry Taram Khoinucha, the

Khaba Prince born of Khaba Sokchrongba, king of the Khaba dynasty and the queen Teknga. The marriage ceremony finds elaborate description, as it was a matter of great rejoicing and celebration. With great pomp and grandeur, the bride was received in her new household. However, Panthoibi still retained her zest for freedom and independence. She never took to married life as a married woman was meant to. Instead of keeping indoors, she roamed the countryside alone, wandering among the running rivers, streams, trees and open fields. It was fate, which took her to a chance meeting with Angoupa Kainou Chingsompa, the lord of the Langmei hills. Instantly they were attracted to each other. The lovelorn couple decided to break all traditional social barriers by running away. Angoupa wanted to take her to his land. After some dramatic twists and turns, the lovers finally manage to elope. The Khaba warriors led by their king gave pursuit to the couple but eventually failed in their task to capture them. Thus united, the two lovers were received by the Langmai people with dance and music. Apart from several other works based on the theme of love, mention may be made of the literature coming from the culture of the Moirang region of Manipur. Many scholars of history, culture and literature have noted a civilization based on the magnificent Loktak Lake, the culture of the Moirang clan. One of the most popular stories refers to the seven pairs of lovers who are regarded as incarnations of the same souls in different generations or ages. The seven cycles are:

a. *Pouoibi amasung Akongjamba*
b. *Henjunaha amasung Leima Lairuklembi*
c. *Khuyol Haoba amasung Yaithing Konu*
d. *Kadeng Thangjahanba amasung Tonu Laijinglembi*
e. *Ura naha Khongjomba amasung Pidonnu*
f. *Wanglen Pungdingheiba amasung sappa chanu Silheibi*
g. *Khamba amasung Thoibi*

It may be noted that literature of the early period is deeply rooted in the indigenous culture of the people of this ancient civilization. Even though development of this literature in its written form may be traced to the twelfth century with the widespread usage and popularity of the Meetei script, the oral tradition had existed much earlier as indicated clearly by the chronicles. The literary tradition that prevailed till the encounter with Hinduism was rooted in the indigenous script, language, culture and social milieus. A pertinent aspect of this literature of the early period is its distinct character vis-à-vis its development on its own sans any outside influence. This remained a characteristic feature till the dawn of the eighteenth century.[8]

The close of the seventeenth century and the beginning of the eighteenth century mark a turning point in the history of Manipur. Much as the name Manipur itself suggests its recent origin, the first epoch making encounter or clash with an alien entity takes place at this juncture. The year 1709 witnessed the ascension of Pamheiba to the throne of Manipur after the death of his father King Charairongba. Rechristening himself Maharaja Garibniwaz, he was responsible for an upheaval that leaves colossal implications for a society's identity. Deeply influenced by the teachings of the Bengali Vaishnavite Shantidas Goswami, a preacher on a proselytizing mission along with the prevailing socio-political circumstances, Garibniwaz lived to the true ideals of a tyrannical despot when he issued a diktat pronouncing Hinduism as the new religion of Manipur. Opposition and resistance to this autocratic move to obliterate the traditional faith and culture were brutally repressed. The king and his Bengali mentor left no stone unturned to erase traces of the indigenous faith. Places of worship were destroyed, worship of traditional and local ancestral deities, traditional rituals and rites, Lai Haraoba festivals, eating of meat, drinking of liquor and burial of the dead were immediately banned. Burial was replaced by cremation. Edicts were proclaimed to bring about these changes with severe consequences for disobedience. Along with the imposition of Hinduism, the manuscripts and texts in the indigenous script were confiscated and burnt in full public view in officially sanctioned events known as the Puya Meithaba. Use of the indigenous script was banned with dire consequences for those attempting to resist. It was to be replaced by the Bengali script. Shantidas Goswami composed an entirely different chronicle known as *Vijay Panchali*, which was a deliberate attempt to efface the history and culture of the people. It projected the land as the Manipur in the Hindu epic Mahabarata and traced the lineage and genealogy of the first King of Manipur to Chandrabhanu whose daughter Chitrangada was married to Arjuna, the great Pandava archer. Brabrubahana was the son born of this wedlock. His son Yavistha was then identified with Nongda Lairen Pakhangba who first ascended the throne at Kangla in AD 33. Imported art forms like the Natya Sankirtan actively encouraged by the royal power gained popularity. Corruption in language became the

---

[8] Ibid., 105–6.

order of the day as the elite and aristocratic class got increasing exposure to Indo-Aryan languages like Sanskrit and Bengali. Manipuri vocabulary witnessed introduction of many new words from these languages.

Literature as a social entity conditioned by historico-political, material circumstances naturally did not remain unaffected by these drastic changes. With the restrictions on practice of the indigenous faith and the widespread patronage to the newly imported alien faith, writers experienced a sudden influence of literatures in the Indo-Aryan language especially Sanskrit and Bengali. Apart from the changes that can be seen in the formalistic domain of writing, the new religion and its associated cultural aspects heavily influenced thematic engagements. The two Hindu epics, the Ramayana and the Mahabharata, became central in many aspects of Manipuri literature of the period. Garibniwaz patronized one Kshema Singh Moiramba to compose the Ramayana in Manipuri. Five young scholars were engaged in the project—Pramananda Nongyai Khumanthem, Mukundaram Khoisnam, Laxmi Narayan Soiba, Ramcharan Nongthomba and Lakhmi Narayan Saikhuba. *Parikshit*, a part of the Mahabharata was translated by one of the king's Vaishnavite teacher, Gopaldas. *Virat Santhuplon* was another work from the Mahabharata produced by crown prince Nabananda. He associated with two eminent writers Wahengbam Madhabram and Mayengbam Brindavan to produce this work. In the sphere of fiction writing, contact with Indian culture brought about new trends in themes and narration. Mention can be made of Wahengbam Madhabram's *Sanamanik* and *Dhruba Charit*, Ananda Pukhrambam's *Dhanajoy Laibu Ningba*, the anonymous *Rupaban* and Labananda Das's *Bhakta Gunamirta*. Translations of the *Bhagavad Gita* are also a notable feature of this period.

Repressed and marginalized, people who retained the traditional indigenous faith also worked hard to produce some remarkable literary works. In the face of severe constraints, they had to retain anonymity while producing these works. After having witnessed the brutal attempts to efface any existing trace of the indigenous faith, these writers had no choice but to retain their anonymity. Several manuscripts of this period extol the need to protect and nurture the indigenous faith, culture and works of the pre-Hindu period. A text known as *Sanamahi Laikan* stands out distinctly with its rich historical, legendary and mythological references woven in an intricate narrative pattern. Many critics have noted the poetic quality of this work. The other great works of this strand are *Khagemba Langjei, Sanamahei Laihul* and *Chingoiron*.

The close of the nineteenth century marks another significant turning point in the history of Manipur, as the Anglo-Manipuri War of 1891 altered the political contours of the land. It is crucial to note that Manipur's political interaction with the British had started quite some time back as a result of constant conflicts with the Burmese along with fratricidal tussles for the throne.[9] The British were also looking forward to build alliances in the region to check growing French influence in the east especially in Indo-China that could well threaten their Indian empire.[10] British conquest and subsequent control of Manipur result in the introduction of foreign rule for the first time in the history of this land. The British were not only responsible for introducing a new administrative system but also other things like new roads, new judicial system, new modes of trade, schools based on Western system of education etc. Apart from the technological changes brought by them, the British also made inroads in the social landscape of the land with their religion. Christian missionaries played a crucial role in proselytizing the non-Meetei people living in the hills. Encounter with the British is significant in terms of the traditional Manipuri society establishing contact with a modern imperialist power. Rapid changes could be seen in every aspect of life as forces of modernity in the wake of British rule ruptured the traditional fabric.

In the literary domain, the moment of British colonial intrusion remain conspicuously silent as mainstream Manipuri consciousness was steeped in Vaishnavite Hinduism and its art forms that evolved in Manipur. The majority largely intoxicated by the rhapsody of *Sankirtan* and *Raslila*, there was a lull in creative and critical efforts in the field of writing altogether as dance and music enthralled and captivated the collective consciousness and mindset. An important literary personality of this transition period, Haodijamba Chaitanya, published four significant works that, however, appears to be traditional in its essence: *Khamba Thoibi Warini* (1899), *Khagi Ngamba* (1900), *Takhel Ngamba* (1902) and *Chingthangkhomba* (1902). Except for the first one, which is based on the romantic saga of Khamba, the orphan, and Thoibi, the

---

[9] Alexander Mackenzie, 1884, *History of the Relations of the Government with the Hill Tribes of the North-East Frontier of Bengal*, Calcutta: Office of the Superintendent of Printing.

[10] Sanjeev Thingnam, 2006, 'Redefining Frontier through LEP: A Colonial Articulation of Manipur', *Alternative Frames*, Vol. I, Issue III, April–June, Imphal, pp. 4–19.

princess of Moirang, the remaining three are based on the historical significance of three great kings of Manipur.

Engagement with the changing realities by the thrust of modernity did not take long to emerge. The literary landscape witnessed a dramatic upheaval in the early part of the twentieth century with the entry of three overarching figures—Khwairakpam Chaoba, Lamabam Kamal and Hijam Angahal. New consciousness shaped by forces of modernity imprinted clearly in their works herald the advent of modern Manipuri literature. Prolific as they were in terms of literary expression, they made a sudden impact on the collective Manipuri consciousness by interrogating several assumptions and notions of received ideas and practices. Their literary works deeply assuaged the need for the Manipuri people to resurge and recover the richness of their culture, language and history. Literatures written in grass-root Manipuri language with an explicit attempt to foreground its strength and vitality marked their writings. Their versatility made them foray into different genres—poetry, drama, novel, short story, essay, epic and criticism. Rightly called the founding fathers of modern Manipuri literature, they paved the path of modern sensibility in literary expression. A serious poet, Khwairakpam Chaoba never fails to use a word with optimum effect. His collection of poems *Thainagi Leirang* (1933) bears the hallmark of effective choice of words. In prose also, he was equally prolific. His prose work *Chhatra Macha* was prescribed by Calcutta University in 1942. The historical novel *Labanga Lata* (1940) also remains as a work of distinction. As a poet, Lamabam Kamal laments the debility and neglect of the rich Manipuri cultural heritage. He calls forth with a vision to reinvigorate the rich traditional culture. Influenced by Western Romanticism, his appeal for nature's beauty and harmony is striking. Nature and rural landscape emerge as important aspects of his creative impulse. As a novelist, Lamabam Kamal is credited for giving Manipuri literature one of its greatest classics *Madhabi* (1930)—a story of love and sacrifice. Hijam Angahal, inspite of poverty compelling him to drop school at an early age, gave Manipuri literature some of its most remarkable poems and fiction. Of his works, *Shingel Indu* stands out along with *Khamba Thoibi Seireng*, his magnum opus, which is a true classical epic in about 37,000 lines. His lone fiction *Jahera* has continued to exercise a grip on the minds of the people till today. Based on a love story between a Muslim girl and a Meetei boy, it has remained popular. It weaves a powerful narrative of the complex and intricate patterns of interactions between the two communities in Manipur based on their belief systems and lifestyles. His plays *Thabal*

Chongbi, *Nimai Sanyas*, *Ibemma* and *Poktabi* performed by the Manipur Dramatic Union, one of the premier theatre organizations in the land, make him a rare genius gifted with great literary skills and imagination. Other literary figures like Hawaibam Nabadwipchandra, Ashangbam Minaketan and R.K. Shiltaljit made significant impact on the Manipuri literary landscape.

Hijam Irabot emerges as a towering personality whose overarching presence was felt in almost all aspects of life and consciousness in contemporary Manipur. His radical vision and activities left an indelible mark in the collective psyche of the Manipuri people. Apart from being the most charismatic and visionary leader in contemporary political history of Manipur, his contribution to Manipuri literature has been immense. A pervasive legacy of marginalizing and obscuring this great personality from the Manipuri mind-frame in the interest of the prevailing power structures, from the colonial and feudal period till today, can be seen clearly. Hailed as the first truly modern poet of Manipur, many of his works were published posthumously. Some have not been published even today.[11] A pioneer in different spheres of life, he was the first to start a literary journal in Manipuri. Titled *Meitei Chanu*, the first volume appeared in 1922 with contributions from great poets like Lamabam Kamal. His early work titled *Seidam Seireng* (1924), a collection of poems was prescribed as a text for schools in Manipur. He wrote the first proper travelogue in Manipuri, titled *Mandalay Khongchat*.

As a radical revolutionary leader spearheading organized political resistance against feudalism and British colonial imperialism, his life was a memorable saga filled with imprisonment, deportation, banishment and exile. An interface between Irabot and history took place during his imprisonment in Sylhet Jail (now in Bangladesh) in 1941.[12] It resulted in the production of some of the finest poems in Manipuri literature—titled *Imagee Pujah*,[13] the poems Hijam Irabot wrote during his imprisonment in Sylhet were published posthumously only in 1987. A first glance at these poems immediately strikes the reader with its profound engagement on varied themes like identity, nationhood, nationality, patriotism, human struggles against injustice, emancipation

---

[11] Soyam Chatradhari, 1966, *Hijam Irabot*, Imphal: Soyam Publication.

[12] Soyam Lokendraji, 1997, 'Irabot Ki Seireng', *Ritu*, Imphal: Manipuri Sahitya Parishad.

[13] Hijam Irabot, 1987, *Imagee Pujah*, Imphal: Irabot Leirak Phongba Lup. A revised and enlarged version of this collection has been published by Langol Publications, Imphal in June 2005.

of the exploited, gender issues, etc. The bitter struggle against brutal colonial oppression reinforces the need to envisage a concrete framework of the motherland in the poet's imagination.

The desire to liberate his motherland makes him lament the loss of historical consciousness in the collective mindset of the Manipuri people—'Oblivious of our mother, hardships are here.' Atrocities committed by the colonial apparatus in its brutal attempt to repress popular uprisings such as the Second Manipuri Women's War (*Nupi Lal*) in 1939 against massive rice exports and artificial scarcity make Hijam Irabot resolute when he writes, 'For a handful of rice, blood had to be given.' His poems in this collection attempt to capture a historical picture of Manipur since the pre-colonial era to the grim realities of contemporary Manipur. He also visualizes the need for an emancipatory struggle of the exploited peasants and labourers. A commonly held view amongst critics of Manipuri literature is that if his poetry saw the light of publication during the colonial period, it would have made substantial impact on the revolutionary tendencies of the day.[14] However, some of these poems were immensely popular as songs on the lips of the people whose consciousness was given a new direction in the urge to struggle against inhuman colonial exploitation. As songs they were used by Hijam Irabot to generate a radical consciousness especially in rural Manipur amongst the peasants who constituted the base of his political radicalism.

Post-Second World War Manipur, ravaged and battered in the conflict between Allied and Axis forces, painfully tries to comprehend the reality of a changing world order amidst the traumatic memories of death, destruction and devastation left by the War. Literary expression scaled new heights with the sudden exposure of Manipur to the outside world as a battlefront during the war. Dramatists picked up the threads of literary expression pulling the public away from the vagaries of dance and music. Haobam Tomba and Sarangthem Bormani heralded a new beginning with their vibrant plays that draw from the rich ballads and legends associated with Moirang. *Tama Salon Saphaba, Pidonnu, Thainagi Leirang, Sajik Thaba* and *Thaja Thaba* by Haobam

---

[14] Soyam Lokendrajit, Ibid. Also, Elangbam Nilkanta, 1996, 'Irabot and Social and Cultural Awakening in Manipur', in *Ningsing Chephong*, Imphal; Hemango Biswas, 1996, 'Irawat Singh: The Artist in Arms', in *Ningsing Chephong*, Imphal; and L. Damodar, 1998, 'Irabot ki Kavita: Anouba Yening Hunbagi Lambida', *Ritu*, Imphal: Manipuri Sahitya Parishad.

Tomba, and *Kege Lamja, Tonnu Laijinglembi, Nura Santhlembi* and *Haorang Leisang Saphabi* by Sarangthem Bormani are notable works. G.C. Tongbra is another literary figure whose plays created ripples in the literary landscape for a long period. With his first published work *Mani Mamou* he went on depicting the menaces of life in its various shades and colours. In the field of poetry Ashangbam Minaketan and R.K. Shitaljit continue to carry out their literary mission.

The rapidly changing political configurations in the post-Second World War era vis-à-vis the swelling tide of decolonization that hits the Indian subcontinent with the departure of the British in 1947 marks a new signpost in Manipur's history too. The British Union Jack was taken away from Kangla—the historical seat of power in Manipur—and the Manipuri National flag depicting seven colours was hoisted, thus marking the end of colonial rule and the beginning of a free independent Manipur. The polity was soon transformed into a democratic one with elections based on universal adult franchise under the Manipur State Constitution Act, 1947. Fifty-three legislators were elected to exercise the governance of independent Manipur. Another epoch making encounter takes place at this juncture. The ancient Asiatic kingdom newly transformed into a democratic political structure in the postcolonial period was 'merged' with the newly independent State of India on 15 October 1949 in pursuance of a treaty of accession. It is this crucial encounter with India that people largely perceive has produced highly conflicting tendencies in terms of explicit moves to impose a homogenizing framework which operates at every level of existence—social, political, cultural, legal, economic, etc. Contest at the political level with the emergence of armed resistance against the 'merger' with India has profusely created the articulation of a conflict at various levels of existence.[15]

One may perhaps look at Elangbam Nilkanta's first published poem 'Manipur' (1949) as a pointer towards the future course of events. It indeed raises fundamental questions that suggest the shape of things to come in the not too distant future:

O Mother Manipur, one day your children
will trace you
Like Dushyanta, with eyes bathed in tears,

---

[15] K. Hemchandra, 2005, 'Houjikki Manipuri Sahityagi Khongchat: Sheireng', Seminar paper, Imphal: Manipuri Sahitya Parishad.

But by that time where shall they find you?
Where shall they find you?[16]

Intensification of the armed struggle, ensuing conflict and the endless battles fought all over the land of Manipur have made profound impact on contemporary literature.[17] Poetry especially has plunged deep into this conflict and the experience it has produced over the years. Laishram Samarendra, Yumlembam Ibomcha, Thangjam Ibopishak, Sri Biren are notable names associated with the expression of a sordid reality—a reality filled with the bitter experiences of an ugly and shattered society. *Apaiba Thawai* (1969), Ibopishak's collection of poems, has been hailed by critics as a trendsetter for a new wave of poetry that grapples with the rising tide of conflicts emerging from the crucial encounter in 1949. A growing sense of dissent and anger at the degeneration, debility and recalcitrance in society can be discerned clearly. Sri Biren's 'Asibagi Lamdamda' ('In the Land of Death') aptly captures the decadence that has eroded the social fabric. Yumlembam Ibomcha's 'Shingnaba' (1947) documents the extreme note of anger in contemporary Manipuri society. R.K. Bhubansana's 'Marup Ani' in his collection titled *Mei Mamgera Budhi Mamgera*, expresses the stark and sordid reality of life under draconian laws like the Armed Forces Special Power Act 1958.

Women poets have attempted to scrutinize contemporary life and society in a radical tone. Questions of identity, freedom and status figure prominently in many of these poets whose female sensibilities offer another dimension of social analysis and critique. Arambam Memchoubi's *Androgi Mei*, Borkanya's *Mongphamgi Meenok* and Pukhrambam Urmila's *Ashibagi Marakta* are notable works that capture the stark social realities.

Different genres like the drama, the novel and the short story share similar concerns. Writers in these genres write in the same vein. In drama, mention can be made of writers like Arambam Somorendra, Brajachand Khundrakpam and Kanhailal whose literary engagements are shot through with stark social realities. In the realm of novels mention can be made of writers like M.K. Binodini, Aribam Chitreshwar, Elangbam Sonamani, Arambam Biren, Loitongbam Pacha Meitei, B.M. Maishnamba, Hijam Guna and M. Borkanya. The short story

---

[16] Quoted in Chongtham Manihar Singh, p. 256.
[17] K. Hemchandra, Ibid.

has emerged as a powerful mode of literary expression with writers like M.K. Binodini, N. Kunjamohon, Kh. Prakash, Shri Biren, Hijam Guna, Keisham Priyokumar, Yumlembam Ibomcha, Sudhir Naoroibam and others.[18]

A more detailed study and analysis of Manipuri literature can provide crucial insights of the encounters and contests in the socio-political history of Manipur. The upheavals in the civilizational ontology of the Manipuri people, as seen in this limited attempt, raise fundamental questions regarding the nature of identity, culture and modernity as experienced in contemporary Manipur. Assuaging an analytical framework through the contours of Manipuri literature through the ages, one indeed feels the need to address crucial debates on the society's attempt to come to terms with modern values sans the material aspects of modernity. Material reality as opposed to value based reality in terms of a society's ontological experience can be a source of tension and contests as seen in Manipur.

---

[18] Thokchom Ibohanbi, 2005, 'Manipurda Houjikki Manipuri Sahitya-Wari macha', Seminar paper, Imphal: Manipuri Sahitya Parishad.

Sanjoy Hazarika
There Are No Shangri-Las Left[†]

India's Northeast, home to seven states and many more insurgencies, is part of a great tropical rainforest that stretches from the foothills of the Himalayas to the tip of the Malaysian Peninsula and the mouth of the Mekong river as it flows into the Gulf of Tonkin.

As the crow flies, it is closer to Hanoi than to New Delhi.

For me, as for millions of others, it also is home and sanctuary, where I grew up and which holds a special, magical attraction with its mist-clad hills, lush green forests and smooth valleys, the bewildering range of its languages and the rich, colourful mix of its people, ranging from former head-hunters to city slickers.

All this has changed in my lifetime. At times, dramatically; and other moments, covertly.

It has changed in every way: the shape of the Northeast—or rather its shape on the maps of the world—has been altered with new lines drawn

---

[†] Sanjoy Hazarika, 1994, 'Note from the Author', *Strangers of the Mist: Tales of War and Peace from India's Northeast*, New Delhi: Pengiun-Viking.

to recognize new political and administrative realities. The names of these units have changed: the Naga Hills became Nagaland, the Lushai Hills changed to Mizoram and the North Eastern Frontier Agency, still known to many simply as NEFA, was converted to Arunachal Pradesh, the Land of the Rising Sun. I am sure that those who coined the last title meant no offence to Japan.

And if these frontiers have changed, so have attitudes among its people so have the skylines of its cities and towns. So has the way people talk to each other, the things they talk about and in which they involve themselves and one another.

Its forests of pine, teak, sal and mangrove swamps are being maimed by plunderers. Yet, thick bamboo, coconut and banana groves, rubber and tea plantations, clusters of frangipani and bougainvillaea still dot the countryside. Its hills are terraced with rice fields. So are its steamy plains.

One image that endures is of wiry farmers with Mongolian features, balancing bamboo poles across their shoulders with cane baskets filled with vegetables, chickens or eggs at either end, walking jerkily to market.

Another image is of naked, cheerful children on water buffaloes, prodding the animals along narrow village tracks.

These images could be true of any part of this belt, which comprises a single geographical entity. Yet, under this postcard-like facade of calm and exotic locales, smiling faces and lushness lie deeper emotions: grief, terror, war and all the torments, tragedies and gore that accompany them. For decades, this jungle has seethed with unrest, rebellion and violence.

The jungles of Southeast Asia sweep down from Bhutan and Arunachal Pradesh across seven other nations—Bangladesh, Myanmar, Thailand, Laos, Kampuchea, Malaysia and Vietnam—spanning political boundaries, irreverential even of physical frontiers. Ethnic coalitions, oral traditions and lifestyles based on respect for nature have mattered more in these regions than frontiers. Here men and women, with common origins but different nationalities, share a racial, historic, anthropoligical and linguistic kinship with each other that is more vital than their links with the mainstream political centres, especially at Delhi, Dhaka and Rangoon.

It is this affinity that has played a role in the unrest and insurgencies that have long troubled the Northeast of India. The embattled communities have been bonded by suffering and opposition to the brutality of government crackdowns against militancy and revolts.

Affinity and Identity. These, more than any other factors, represented the principal compulsions that triggered the Naga, Mizo, Meitei, Tripuri and Assamese affirmation of separateness from the non-Mongolian communities that dominate the Indian subcontinent.

India's Northeast is a misshapen strip of land, linked to the rest of the country by a narrow corridor just twenty kilometres wide at its slimmest which is referred to as the Chicken's Neck. The region has been the battleground for generations of sub-national identities confronting insensitive nation-states and their bureaucracies as well as of internecine strife. It is a battle that continues, of ideas and arms, new concepts and old traditions, of power, bitterness and compassion.

Yet, it also holds warm memories.

Some of these are of the years in school: crisp mornings, the joy of friends and St. Edmund's School, run by largely-cheerful, occasionally sherry-laden Irish missionaries from the Christian Brothers. Cramming for exams, lunches from tiffin boxes brought by servants and served in the Great Hall (where exams were held three times a year for senior classes), cricket on the playing fields on Sundays and on the back lawn of the sprawling bungalow where we lived during my father's tenure as head of the Reid Chest Hospital, a treatment centre for tuberculosis patients. We broke more windows with our home cricket than I care to remember. There were picnics in the hills among pine trees and streams with relatives and school friends. Above all, the fresh aroma of pine in the air, the sight of golden and pink flowering orchids growing wild.

And the rains: steam rising from smartly macadamized roads with the first sharp showers of early summer, the wet, warm, sensuous smell of fresh earth washed by rain, so fresh that you could almost taste it.

In winter we gathered in one main bedroom around a crackling fire where we dozed in our chairs, munching on sweet oranges, throwing pips into the fire and listening to their sputter as they exploded in the heat. The fire also slowly baked the large sweet potatoes, placed under the iron grate, with a mixture of heat, embers and ash.

We were exposed too, to the power of nature. I remember watching with awe as a thunderstorm slammed into Shillong and crumpled our garage like a piece of paper. Then, as if in slow motion, the wind picked up the heavy asbestos roof and hurled it 100 feet away, spinning above the servant's outhouse into a vegetable patch.

In many ways, it was a carefree existence. But we were also aware of the turbulence around us.

During the 1965 war with Pakistan, all the windows of our home and of every home in Shillong, the capital of undivided Assam and located nearly 5,000 feet above sea level, were plastered with blackened paper to prevent any light from escaping and indicating our presence to the enemy (A flight of planes? A spy, perhaps?)

We went through air raid drills at school, flinging ourselves enthusiastically at the red, wet earth by the playing fields, ruining our sparkling, starched white shirts and grey flannels. There were mock drills but there was one which came late at night when we were at home.

'Out', snapped Father, as he switched the lights off and opened the front door. We dashed to the nearby khud, flung ourselves face down on the grass and covered our heads with our hands as we had been trained to do. I was frightened and excited. And before the All Clear sounded, I broke discipline: I looked up.

Moving noiselessly and gently against the starlit sky, a small band of planes flew above us, their lights twinkling peacefully until they swept out of sight.

The Northeast has been described as Asia in miniature, a place where the brown and yellow races meet and mingle. The oral history of the tribes of Mizoram, Nagaland, Manipur and other areas tell of ancestors from the shadowy past, from mountains steeped in mist and romance, from lands far away, of snake gods and princesses, epic battles and great warriors.

Its people have a fear of being swamped by 'outsiders', of lifestyles and histories being destroyed by modern nation-states that bother little about small communities but pay more attention to 'strategic' considerations such as the natural resources of the area, their exploitation for the national 'good' and the region's proximity to a friendly or inimical neighbour. Decisions for the little peoples of such regions—the historian Amalendu Guha describes as 'sub-nationalities'—are made by bureaucratic and political mandarins in national and state capitals, far removed from the realities of the customs and beliefs that govern the thoughts and lives of the indigenous peoples.

The women are pretty, the men handsome. The girls of Imphal in Manipur who ride cycles and scooters, resemble their Thai and Lao counterparts. They could easily be placed either in Bangkok or Vientiane. The seductively swaying Manipuri dances are similar to the gentle rhythms of the Khmers and Laotians as well as the Thais and Indonesians. The distinctive shawls of Nagaland, Manipur and Mizoram, each colourful strand proclaiming a tribe, a lifestyle and an identity, share a commonality with communities across the borders in Myanmar and Thailand.

That diversity was seen every day at school, located on a series of gentle hills several of which had been flattened to make space for playing fields, tennis and squash courts, and buildings. To them came Khasis and Garos, Assamese and Punjabis, Bengalis and Anglo-Indians, Bodos and Garhwalis; we were Christians, Hindus, Sikhs and Muslims and we were not infected by the viciousness of today's society.

Our friends, especially the Khasis, had delightful names. Parents gave their children the names of their favourite rock star or any other name that caught their fancy: there was Elvis Presley Lyngdoh, North Star Diengdoh and a politician named Hopingstone Lyngdoh.

The buildings were of sturdy wood, and had a rough-hewn attractiveness about them. The best classroom was the Senior Cambridge room, located above a stone porch and looking out over the front lawn. These days, the buildings are of ugly concrete; the senior classroom has been pulled down, the solitary date palm tree has gone too. Those days a businessman, old man Goenka, would chug in every afternoon in his 1926 model Ford, lovingly polished and cleaned, to pick up his grandchildren. Now the narrow road leading to the school is packed with Marutis, jeeps and outsized Contessa cars as school ends to the clanging of the great bell, located above the water tower in the old wing. The bell has remained constant in the midst of these frantic changes.

The physical transformation to the school reflects the larger changes in Shillong where pretty bungalows of wood and plaster are giving way to concrete and brick monsters, faceless, heartless, ugly and symbolic of the devastation that easy money and irresponsibility have wrought on the place.

These days, it is easier to walk from my mother's home, on the hill above the Fire Brigade, to Police Bazar, a distance of about three kilometres, than to travel by taxi or bus. The reason lies in the traffic of buses, trucks, taxis, private and government vehicles that swamp the roads.

Every winter, we travelled to Nowgong, home of our grandparents and lazy days of cricket, films, playing with the dogs, cycling and picnics. We would race our dogs and plunge in together into the smooth and gently flowing Kolong river, scrub the animals with soap and brushes, towel them down. Then would come the best part: as all of us, wet and happy, would sprint along the sandbanks, over the narrow lane home, each trying to outrush the other.

Home here was where my grandfather and his younger brother, a doctor, whom we affectionately called Da, lived. And it was at Da's clinic where my brother and I learned of the kaleidoscopic sweep of the ethnic mosaic of that little town: Muslim Mymensinghias, who seemed to complain the loudest, came to him; so did Lalungs, a major tribe, Kacharis and Assamese and Bengali Hindus. Da is a figure that perhaps exists in every family around the world: selfless, always prepared to attend to a call at any time of the day or night and ever patient with questions that all children ask. His sturdy Austin 16 car was a landmark in the district, the only one of its kind at the time.

But there was an anger below this placid surface of a society apparently at peace with itself that was always trying to get out.

My first glimpse of public anger was in my father's company one day, when while returning from school, we were suddenly confronted by a furious mob, waving clenched fists, shouting something incomprehensible. As we watched, the mob surrounded a city bus, forced all the passengers out and then with a great surge sent the vehicle toppling on its side. The bus was then set on fire.

'Go away from here,' said a bystander. As he spoke, my father swerved the car and took a safer route home.

The people of the Northeast are the guardians of its most precious asset: its uniqueness. Which other area has such beauty among its people and its environment? Which sees such a range of religions, creeds, communities, lifestyles and traditions? Which other area can match it in the sheer raw power of nature: whether it is the Brahmaputra that resembles a great sea during its rain-swollen, flood-hungry days; or the force of its gales and the grace of its waterfalls, the lushness of its forests and bamboo thickets. And the solitude of its spirit, found in the mist of the mountains.

But these days, those of the area are grappling with the changes that the modern age relentlessly brings. And it is these changes and alienation that are at the root of the militancy, the insurgencies, the desperation and the growing violence.

This book does not purport to be an analytical treatise on insurgency and the superiority of the political wing over the military arm. Far from it. It is largely a look at how little men and women have reacted to imperial, insensitive administrations, politicians and policies through their eyes and mine.

There are no Shangri-Las left. Perhaps it is just as well for the people of the region—ranging from Bhutan to Bangladesh and Nagaland to Nepal—as they confront each other and India, strangers in the mist, and span a thousand years in a lifetime.

Udayon Misra
Peasant Consciousness as Reflected in the Oral Literature of Assam
A Study of Two Assamese Ballads[†]

Assam possesses a vibrant tradition of peasant resistance and rebellion, with *Raij Mels* and *Krishak Sabhas* acting as major planks in the growth and consolidation of Assamese national consciousness. This tradition, from which the Assamese middle class derives much of its tap-roots, has been amply reflected in the oral literature of the region. This study will concentrate on two Assamese folk ballads, *Barphukanar Geet* and *Maniram Dewanar Geet*, which deal with two important periods in the nineteenth century history of Assam. The first deals with the last days of the six-hundred-year-old Ahom rule when palace intrigues and rivalries helped the Burmese to ravage the kingdom, thereby paving the way

---

[†] An earlier version of this paper was first published in 2005 in *Man and Society*, Vol. II, No. I, Shillong: ICSSR, North Eastern Regional Centre.

for British intervention.¹ The second ballad is set in the eighteen-fifties when Maniram Dewan,² unhappy at British efforts to erase the power

---

¹ The last decades of the eighteenth century saw the disintegration of Ahom rule following a series of revolts by the Moamarias, which began in 1769 and continued intermittently till 1805. The Moamaria Revolt, which was in effect a civil war of grave dimensions, seriously depleted the province's population and upset the social structure based on *paiks* and *khels* which had been developed by the Ahoms and which was predominantly dependant on the peasantry. Even as the Ahom administration tottered, the plight of the Assamese peasant became pitiable with thousands being reduced to virtual penury in a resource-rich land. The damage done by the Moamaria Revolt to the social structure based on paiks and khels was aggravated by the Burmese invasion and occupation of the province (1817; 1819–25) which led to further depopulation and the total collapse of trade and agriculture. It was British intervention as sought by the then Ahom King was resulted in the defeat of the Burmese in June 1825 followed by the Treaty of Yandabo of February 1826 which virtually formalised the British occupation of Assam. The Moamarias were largely peasants, initially belonging to the Moran tribe of upper Assam. They followed the teachings of Anniruddhadeva (1553–1624) who preached a neo-Vaishnavism which questioned the authority of the upper-caste Gosains and Mahantas of the *satras* or Vaishnava monasteries which were very influential in Assam. The Moamarias did not worship idols or acknowledge the supremacy of the Brahmins or the upper castes. The Moamarias fell out with the Ahom rulers who ruthlessly persecuted their religious heads. The struggle of the Moamarias was directed against the feudal structure of Ahom rule and, with it, began a series of civil wars which eventually accelerated the downfall of the Ahom monarchy.

² Maniram Dutta Baruah (Maniram Dewan) had, in the initial years of the Company's rule in Assam, been of great help to the British. He came into contact with David Scott while he was staying as a fugitive in the Rangpur district of Bengal during the Burmese occupation of Assam. He entered Assam along with Scott's army and was actively involved with the anti-Burmese campaigns. Maniram was made Sheristadar-Tahsildar of upper Assam in 1828 and he successfully organised the khels so that the revenue picked up. He did not have any sympathy for the uprisings by the Khamptis and the Singphos or the revolt of Peali Phukan. Rather, he helped the British in suppressing these. Maniram was made a Dewan of the Assam Company in 1839. When upper Assam was taken over by the British after Purandhar Singha failed to pay the promised annual tribute of Rs 50,000, Maniram was divested of most of his powers and eventually all the *mauzas* under him were taken away. He resigned from the Dewnaship in 1845 and opened two tea gardens despite obstruction by the British administration which refused to give him land at concessional rates as was given to European planters under the wasteland regulations. Deprived of power and privilege, it was but natural that Maniram Dewan thought of restoring Ahom rule. The British were obviously apprehensive of Maniram's actions because they knew his sharpness of intellect and his capacity to organise things. Maniram was arrested for his alleged conspiracy to restore the Ahom monarchy during the Revolt of 1857. He was executed after a highly partisan trial on 26 February 1858. His tea gardens were confiscated by the British after his death.

of the Ahom nobility, tried to join hands with the anti-British forces of 1857 and restore Ahom rule in Assam.

The old Ahom aristocracy's resentment against British rule reached its culmination in the rebellions of Gomadhar Konwar and Rupchand Konwar in 1828 and 1829. Though these revolts might have had some degree of popular sympathy, yet this was never translated into support and the British quickly suppressed them. Peali Phukan, son of Badanchandra Barphukan, former Ahom Governor of Guwahati, and Jeuram Dihingia Baruah were hanged by the British for their involvement in the rebellion. But Peali Barphukan's attempt to dislodge the British, though seen by many as an attempt at a palace revolution by the pretenders to the Ahom throne, made the British panicky because they feared it could inspire other revolts among the different nationalities of the region. But the mass of the Assamese peasantry did not sympathize with the rebels. On the contrary, the peasantry largely welcomed the advent of the British because it had resulted in some return to normality and the rule of law after the spell of Burmese occupation. However, it did not take long for the peasantry to discover that the main aim of the new masters was the maximum possible extortion of land revenue and that they weren't particularly interested in the people's welfare.[3] The burden of increased taxation and the disastrous impact of the monetization process on the peasantry would ultimately find expression in revolts like the Phulaguri Dhewa of 1861 and the more organized peasant revolt of 1894 known as the Battle of Patharughat. Meanwhile, the rumblings of the Revolt of 1857 could be heard in Assam. Led primarily by the pro-feudal, upper-class elements, the attempted revolt in the province was aimed at restoring the Ahom scion, Kandarpeswar Singha, to the throne. Maniram, the rich, powerful and highly intelligent Dewan of the Company, was the person who co-ordinated the moves aimed at starting an armed uprising against the British. In this, he was helped by a wide section of people belonging to different ethnic groups as also by some of his friends in Bengal. Maniram Dewan had, in 1853, submitted a memorial to A.J. Moffatt-Mills, judge of the Sadar Dewani Adalat, who was visiting Assam to enquire into the state of the administration in the province. In the memorandum, Maniram prayed that the monarchy as well as the lost privileges of the Ahom nobility and the upper classes

---

[3] The revenue policy of the British drove the peasants to a point of desperation because they were unaccustomed to pay their taxes in cash, there being little monetization during the Ahom period. S.K. Bhuyan (ed.), 1951 [1924], *Barphukanar Geet*, Guwahati, pp. 564–5.

be restored. It was Maniram who had helped the British during the early years of the consolidation of their rule in Assam and he had been amply rewarded by being made a Sheristadar-Tahsildar of the Company in Upper Assam. He had been an indispensable ally of the British. But he had seen through the British game of virtually pauperizing the peasantry and reducing the erstwhile nobility to the position of ordinary folk. Having failed to convince Mills, Maniram went to Calcutta in the early part of 1857 to represent the cause of both the young prince and the people of Assam to the Lieutenant-Governor of Bengal. It was in Calcutta that he came to know of the revolt of the sepoys in Kanpur, Meerut and Lucknow. This inspired Maniram to draw up plans to drive the British out of Assam and he wrote several letters to Kandarpeswar Singha asking him to rise in revolt with the aid of the sepoys who were stationed in the province.[4] Some consultations did take place at the king's residence in Jorhat and a section of the sepoys stationed at Golaghat is said to have offered their support to the Kandarpeswar. On finding out about the correspondence between Maniram and the king, the British rulers panicked, arrested the subedar and some other sepoys and court-martialled them. Maniram was arrested at Calcutta and brought to Jorhat. Subsequently, after a hurried and highly partisan trial,[5] Maniram and Peyali Baruah were hanged in February 1858 and the rest of his associates transported for life.

The revolt of Maniram was quite different from that of Peali Phukan's. Maniram did have a considerable degree of people's sympathy, though there was no chance of this being translated into active support. His death was widely mourned by the people and ballads were sung to remember the incident. These ballads are known as *Maniram Dewanar Geet.* and they continued to be sung even after a century of his death. Maniram's trial had its repercussions and Assamese villagers working in the newly planted tea gardens struck work to express their solidarity with those who were against the British. Amalendu Guha refers to this and say that Madhuram Koch who was one of the leaders of the strikers, was sent to prison for seven years.[6] However, another leading historian of Assam, H.K. Barpujari, does not share Guha's view and blames the failure of the planned revolt on the lack of unity amongst the nobility and the indifference of the common people, especially the peasantry,

[4] Barpujari, pp. 69–70.
[5] K.N. Dutta, 1969, *Landmarks in the Freedom Struggle in Assam*, Gauhati, pp. 21–2.
[6] Guha, 1977, pp. 4–5.

towards the cause espoused by Maniram and his comrades.⁷ While one tends to agree with Barpujari on this point, yet it must be said that there was a distinct difference between the revolt of Peali Barphukan and that of Maniram because unlike the former, the Dewan did not represent just the feudal forces. He himself was keeping pace with the times by organizing his own business and had successfully set up two medium-sized tea gardens without any support from the British. It has been rightly observed that there are some signs of capitalist enthusiasm and efficiency in Maniram's efforts.⁸ But the average peasant of Maniram's own times was obviously not prepared to put his fate into the hands of someone whom they viewed as primarily a representative of the feudal nobility.

Maniram Dewan may not have been able to carry the people with him, for that would have given a completely different shape to his efforts. But it would be wrong to suggest that he did not feel the plight of the peasantry overburdened with fresh taxes. This, despite the fact that during the initial years of British rule, it was Maniram who had been an active partner of the British in working out the land taxation plans. Nevertheless, he became a rallying point of the nationalist forces and acquired the halo of a martyr.⁹ But, it is interesting to note that in the popular ballads on Maniram, there is a sharp degree of criticism about his role under the British and of how he died because of excess of ambition. It is interesting that the popular image of Maniram as presented in the ballads is at variance with that projected by representatives of the emerging Assamese middle class. We shall have occasion to reflect on this when we take up the ballad, *Maniram Dewanar Geet* for discussion.

With the consolidation of language-based Assamese nationalism in the first decades of the twentieth century and the gradual involvement of the Assamese masses in the national struggle against the British, the revolts of Peali Phukan and Maniram Dewan came to be viewed as part of the overall struggle of the Assamese to free themselves from the foreign yoke. The peasant uprisings of the eighteen-sixties and the eighteen-nineties were also projected as 'people's wars' against the colonial rulers. Maniram and Peali were turned into symbols of Assamese nationalist aspirations and their deaths commemorated as days of national remembrance. It was part of the glorification of the past which constituted

---

⁷ Barpujari, pp. 77–9.

⁸ Hiren Gohain, 1991, 'Asamiya Madhyabitta Samajar Itihas', *Sahitya Aru Chetana*, Guwahati, p. 25.

⁹ Benudhar Sharma, 1950, *Maniram Dewan*, Gauhati, p. ix.

the rise and consolidation of Assamese nationalism.[10] The valorization of Peali Phukan and Maniram Dewan was part of the nationalist construct, although neither of the struggles could be viewed as 'national' struggles against the British. Similarly, attempts were made by nationalist historians to show that the peasant uprisings in Assam were part of a wider struggle to free Assam from British rule. However, the fact remains that these peasant uprisings were directed against the British government in a bid to force it to change its uxorious taxation laws. At no stage of the struggle is there any evidence to suggest that the peasants thought of launching a movement aimed at making the British quit the province. These were essentially movements aimed at securing immediate economic relief in the form of reduction of land revenue and were in no way linked with other forms of struggle. But given the relatively egalitarian nature of Assamese society, the participation in the struggle of different segments of the population was ensured. Rather, the peasant resistance movements of the eighteen-sixties and the eighteen-nineties in Assam were similar to peasant movements in other parts of British India. Hardiman, for instance, writes:

British rule led to an extreme disruption of rural relationships throughout India. In the late eighteenth and the early nineteenth centuries, the peasantry had been impoverished through extremely high rates of land tax levied by the East India Company. After the taxes were lowered, new forms of expropriating the surplus of the peasants through intermediaries such as landlords, merchant money lenders and British planters, were evolved.[11]

What happened in the rest of British India in the late eighteenth and early nineteenth centuries took place in Assam towards the end of the nineteenth century. Though these movements had distinctly local characteristics, yet they conformed to the all-India pattern as mass movements aimed at redressal of particular grievances.[12] There is no evidence to suggest that there were any efforts to co-ordinate these movements in order to put up a joint resistance to British rule.[13] Just as nationalist historians tried to give their own interpretations of the peasant uprisings, similarly British official accounts too suffered from partisan positioning.

[10] Tilottoma Misra, 1987, *Literature and Society in Assam*, Guwahati, pp. 215–17.
[11] David Hardiman (ed.), 1992, *Peasant Resistance in India: 1858–1914*, Delhi, p. 6.
[12] Kathleen Gough, 1974, 'Indian Peasant Uprisings', *Economic and Political Weekly*, Special Number (August), Bombay; David Hardiman, p. 6.
[13] David Hardiman, p. 11.

British officials constructed their accounts of peasants revolts as historical narratives. Colonialism needed such narratives to continue its hold over its subjects as also to know the situation better so as to handle it more effectively.[14] Ranajit Guha argues that the security of the colonial state becomes the 'central problematic' in all accounts about peasant insurgency, that the peasant himself is not given his rights as a subject of history. He becomes just an 'element' in the career of colonialism. If the peasant is to be seen and accepted as a maker of his own rebellion, then one must attribute a consciousness to him and not view peasant acts of revolt merely as expressions of spontaneous outpourings. It is here that the question of the conscious leadership and action comes in and one learns to accept peasant struggles not as unstructured movements but as organized ones. As Ranajit Guha says, it is important to accept the fact that:

there was nothing spontaneous about all this in the sense of being unthinking and wanting in deliberation. The peasant obviously knew what he was doing when rising in revolt. The fact that this was designed primarily to destroy the authority of the the superordinate elite and carried no elaborate blueprint for its replacement, does not put it outside the realm of politics. On the contrary, insurgency affirmed its political character precisely by its negative and inversive procedure.[15]

The experience of the peasant struggles in Assam towards the end of the nineteenth and the early part of the twentieth century bears ample evidence of a collective consciousness being at work. But in most cases, the voice of the peasant is not at all there. We have no chance of listening to the peasants' version of the events in which they were the principal actors. And the evidence on which one has to rely on is not at all free from bias.[16]

Therefore, it appears that whatever be the source of the accounts about peasants uprisings, the question of bias would always continue to plague them. Even in accounts that are apparently sympathetic to the cause of the peasants, an elitist bias is bound to be evident. The only way to tackle such a bias is to bring into play the voice of the common people which is expressed in both oral and written folklore. But here too a problem arises. With the overwhelming majority of the peasants being illiterate, it was inevitable that most of those who recorded the

[14] Ranajit Guha, p. 3.
[15] Ibid., p. 9.
[16] Ibid., p. 14.

events in the form of ballads and folk-songs would have little sympathy with the peasants. Moreover, despite such shortcomings, even in the form of government notes and documents and there are almost no known non-governmental written accounts by of the peasants struggles of referred to in this study, it becomes all the more imperative to search for the subaltern voice in the oral tradition. Moreover, even if the folklore discourse appears somewhat elitist, there is still scope to recover the peasant's viewpoint from these. Thus, the importance of the oral tradition becomes all the more clear. As Jan Vansena says,

> Oral traditions make an appearance only when they are told. For fleeting moments they can be heard, but most of the time they dwell in the minds of the people. The utterance is transitory, but the memories are not. No one in oral societies doubts that memories can be faithful repositories which contain the sum total of past human experience and explain the how and why of present-day conditions... whether memory changes or not, culture is reproduced by remembrance put into words and deeds. The mind through memory carries culture from generation to generation.[17]

This is true of the folk-songs and ballads in Assamese which relate to the peasant uprisings and major political events of the late nineteenth and early twentieth centuries. The revolt of Peali Phukan, the events leading to the execution of Maniram Dewan, the peasant uprisings of Phulaguri and Patharughat have become so etched in the collective memory of the Assamese people that the memory of these events has been carried from generation to generation and has found expression in folk ballads and songs like the ones sung mainly by the peasantry. For instance, the *Doli Puran* made up of songs about the Battle of Patharughat gives an entirely new dimension to one's understanding of the history of the period and the role played by the peasantry. Therefore, in order to build up interpretation from inside, one would have to depend a lot on the oral tradition. Thus, as a source it is quite unique. Notwithstanding the fact that compared to the mass of official documents, folk songs and ballads as sources are rather few, yet they are important tools in our effort to understand our past.[18] Although songs and ballads as repositories of the peasant consciousness in Assam are rather few in number, yet the importance of this source cannot but be stressed. Given the fact that almost all the records that are available are in the form of official records or elitist accounts, the dependence on the oral tradition to retrieve the

---

[17] Jan Vansena, 1985, *Oral Tradition as History*, London, p. xi.
[18] Ibid.

voice of the subaltern becomes all the more important. Even then, one has to be careful in the use of the oral tradition because that too is often part of the overall intellectual tradition of a community and could suffer from an intellectual or elitist bias.[19]

Despite such limitations, folk-songs and ballads which form part of the cultural tradition of a people or a community act as a major supplement to traditional historical sources and help us greatly to get an inside view of certain historical events where the common people played the major or pivotal role. For, such narratives often tell of protest 'in a manner that reflects the ideological stance of their audience'.[20] In the following pages we shall take up for discussion two of the major ballads of Assam, viz., *Barphukanar Geet* and *Maniram Dewanar Geet* and shall try to analyse how these ballads reflect the peasant consciousness of their times and help us to gain a view from a different angle about the certain historical characters and events. Nationalist historians, trying to relate these characters and events to their own interpretation of history, have often neglected the voice from below and created constructs meant to suit the national struggle. Hence, Badanchandra has been continuously seen as a traitor and Maniram valorized as the greatest freedom fighter the province has produced. The importance of the subaltern voice makes itself felt when we realize that such positionings could give us only one aspect of a region's history and could often smother the 'history from below'. These two ballads are central to our understanding the subaltern voice in Assam's history. We shall also have occasion to refer to some other relevant folk-songs and ballads which could help us to have an insider's view of the history of Assam from the early part of the nineteenth century till its closing years.

Barphukanar Geet

This ballad sung by village minstrels for well over a century is one of the typical Assamese ballads and deals with the events during one of the most difficult periods in the region's history. Set against the happenings of the early period of the nineteenth century, sometime between 1810 and 1820, the ballad tells us of the plight of the common people during

---

[19] Ibid., p. 198.
[20] Anne Walthall, 1983, 'Narratives of Peasant Uprisings in Japan', *Journal of Asian Studies*, Vol. XLII (May).

the Burmese invasion of Assam, the role played by Badanchandra Barphukan, Purnananda Buragohain, the king Chandrakanta Singha and that of his mother, and the conspiracies and rivalries which marked the world of the nobility. No one is certain about the exact date of composition of *Barphukanar Geet*. But there is common agreement among historians that the period of composition of the popular ballad must have been in the years immediately following the Burmese occupation of the province and the subsequent take-over by the British. Discussing this, S.K. Bhuyan says that since the feelings and emotions of the Assamese people who suffered untold miseries in the hands of the Burmese forces appear very fresh in the ballad, this must have been composed in the early part of the nineteenth century, i.e., during the initial years of the British rule of the province.[21] The memory of Burmese occupation and its terrible impact on Assamese society is sketched in clear detail in the ballad. There must have been several versions of the ballad, but the version that is today commonly referred to is the one sung by Bhakatram Mistri of North Lakhimpur. S.K. Bhuyan recorded the song from Bhakatram Mistri in 1923.[22] Like folk-songs and ballads, it is impossible to say as to when it was composed and who sang it first. Moreover, as time passed, the ballad was bound to take on new meanings and additions, thereby expanding its base. But, on the whole, the central meaning of the piece centred around a very crucial period in the life of Badanchandra Barphukan, remains intact. Assam has had a strong and vibrant tradition of folk-songs and rhymes in the form of *Bia-Naam, Husari*, nursery rhymes, *Aii-Naam*, etc. and *Barphukanar Geet* is part of this tradition which has been expressing itself over the ages as the spontaneous expression of the life-spirit of a people. It deftly sums up the events of a particular period of Assam's history and, in doing so, gives a viewpoint which is that of the common peasant who sees the happenings from an angle quite different from that of the administrator or the traditional record-keeper. *Barphukanar Geet* is easily one of the more important of Assamese historical ballads.

Barphukanar Geet takes its name from Badanchandra Barphukan, the *Barphukan* or governor of lower Assam and deals chiefly with his rivalry with Purnananda Buragohain who was the prime minister under Chandrakanta Singha. Buragohain, who was the most influential minister of the king and who virtually ruled the province, was suspicious of the

---

[21] S.K. Bhuyan (ed.), 1951 [1924], p. 28.
[22] Ibid., p. 1.

moves of Badanchandra who was accused of running an authoritarian administration from Guwahati. Among the many allegations brought against Badanchandra by Purnananda Buragohain was his association with the Charingia Phukan named Satram who had conspired against Purnananda. Badanchandra was also accused of allowing his sons, Peali and Janmi, to terrorize the common people. These allegations, however, appeared to have been built up with the intention of curtailing the powers of Badanchandra Barphukan with whom Purnananda Buragohain had a deep-seated rivalry and whom he looked upon as one of his major opponents. Purnananda's son had married the only daughter of Badanchandra, Pijou Aideo and it was she who ultimately warned her father of the danger of arrest. When Purnananda sent Maheswar Parbatiya Phukan to Guwahati to arrest and bring Badanchandra to the Ahom capital, it was clearly with the intention of eliminating his main rival. In this, Purnananda had the full support of the king-mother who was deeply indebted to the former for a variety of reasons. On being warned of his possible arrest by his daughter, who sent messenger to Guwahati from the Ahom capital, Badanchandra fled from Guwahati on the night of 18th October,1815, accompanied by a Hindustani soldier, Udaysingh Subedar. When the East India Company refused him help, Badanchandra went to Myanmar where its king, Badowpaya (1782–1819) welcomed him. The Burmese king helped Badanchandra with a force of several thousand soldiers so that he could return to Assam and regain his rights. In his efforts, an Assamese princess of the Burmese king, Rangili, actively aided the Barphukan. (Rangili belonged to the Ahom nobility and was given off to the Burmese king as part of a peace treaty that the Ahoms had entered with the Burmese who had come to aid the Singhphos and the Khamtis during the Moamaria Revolt.) Badanchandra came back to Assam with the Burmese troops and as he was about to enter Sivasagar, Purnananda Buragohian died. That was in March 1817.[23] Though Purnananada died a natural death, the minstrel of *Barphukanar Geet* shows him as having committed suicide. We shall discuss this later when we take up the subaltern's voice and opinions as expressed in the ballad. The Burmese did not interfere with the king's position and Badanchandra became the prime minister.

The arrangement approved of by the Burmese did not last long because of the machinations of the king, his mother and some of the

---

[23] Praphulladatta Goswami, 1960, *Ballads and Tales of Assam*, Gauhati University, p. 18.

nobles. Within a few months Badanchandra was murdered. The king whose complicity in the murder was suspected, was soon replaced by Purandhar Singha. When the Burmese king came to know of these developments, he sent some thirty thousand troops under Ala Mingi. The Burmese forces overran the country and reinstated Chandrakanta to the throne. Soon another Burmese army under Mingimaha Tilua invaded Assam and met with little resistance from the Ahoms, with their king Chandrakanta having retreated to Guwahati. What followed was widescale destruction of life and property and the ushering in of one of the darkest periods in Assam's history. Efforts by Chandrakanta to resist and drive out the invaders were unsuccessful and the common people were left at the total mercy of the Burmese. Only when the Burmese started encroaching upon British territory, did the latter finally declare war and the Anglo-Burmese War began. This ended in the defeat of the Burmese and the Treaty of Yandabo of 1826 by which the Burmese withdrew from Assam, thereby leaving the path open for the British to enter and occupy the region.

The wide-scale and unprecedented human tragedy that was unleashed by the Burmese occupation covered a period of just ten years or so. Within this relatively short span of time, the Assamese peasant suffered so much in the hands of the Burmese invaders that this experience came to be permanently etched in the memory of the people. Anything associated with anarchy, lawlessness and extreme forms of cruelty came to be associated with the Burmese in such a manner that the period of Burmese rule became synonymous with all that is evil in the Assamese mind. But the debate was there even during the composition of *Barphukanar Geet* as to whether it was the Barphukan alone who was responsible for the people's sufferings because he 'invited' the Burmese over, or was he just made into a scapegoat to cover up the misdeeds of people like Purandhar Buragohain and the Rajmau. It is interesting to note that the mainstream Assamese historians led by stalwarts like S.K. Bhuyan have always held Badanchandra responsible for the Burmese occupation of Assam and have seen him as a traitor. In his rather self-contradictory preface to the first edition of *Barphukanar Geet* written in 1924, S.K. Bhuyan details the different faults and misdeeds of Badanchandra and justifies Purnananda's action in trying to get him arrested.[24] Bhuyan quickly comes to the conclusion that in bringing the Burmese into Assam, Badanchandra was acting the traitor to Assam, her

---

[24] S.K. Bhuyan (ed.), 1951 [1924], pp. 2–4.

king and its people.²⁵ But Bhuyan does not deal with the Purnananda-Badanchandra rivalry or with the role of the King Chandrakanta vis-à-vis the Burmese. He also tries to overlook the fact that Chandrakanta was during the initial period, quite friendly with the Burmese and depended upon them for retaining his kingship. Also that Badanchandra had successfully kept the Burmese in control and that, only after his being treacherously killed, did things go out of control and the Ahom administration collapsed totally, leaving the Assamese peasant fully at the mercy of the Burmese invaders and other marauders. It is these aspects of the history of the period that seem to come to light in *Barphukanar Geet*. The folk-consciousness revealed in *Barphukanar Geet* opens up new possibilities in our understanding of not only a particular period of the region's history but also helps us to re-assess the role of personalities like Badanchandra Barphukan who have been summarily dismissed as traitors.

The ballad opens with an invocation to the goddess Saraswati,²⁶ and quickly moves on to the events surrounding the rivalry between the Buragohain and Badanchandra. It narrates how, when Assam had a dearth of ministers, the Buragohain came unto the scene; of how there was no one to challenge his position, except, of course, Badanchandra who was the viceroy of lower Assam. The Buragohian looks in all directions and sees no enemy except Badanchandra. The Buragohian realizes that there was none who could kill him except Badanchandra.²⁷ Realizing the danger posed to him by Badanchandra, Purnananda sends the Parbatitya Phukan to arrest Badanchandra at Guwahati and then bring him over to the Ahom capital. But there is one interesting line which suggests that Purnananda is not too sure of the Prabatiya Phukan's loyalty. For, he cautions him by saying: 'Don't you accept money and let the Phukan (Badanchandra) go' (*'Dhan khai Phukanak nahibi eri'*)²⁸ This one line sums up the climate of distrust that prevailed among the Ahom nobility during the closing decades of Ahom rule in Assam. The prime minister cannot trust one of his senior-most officials, the Parbatiya Phukan, and knows that he too could be won over with money by Badanchandra. As such, Purnananda tempts the Phukan by saying that if he succeeded in capturing Badanchandra, then he would

---

²⁵ Ibid., pp. 8–10.
²⁶ *Barphukanar Geet*, lines 1–36.
²⁷ Ibid., lines 39–48.
²⁸ Ibid., line 156.

be made the viceroy.²⁹ The subaltern voice helps us to see into the inner conflicts and contradictions within the Ahom aristocracy which eventually brought about the inglorious end to six hundred years of uninterrupted Ahom rule of the province.

The ballad narrates the story of how Barphukan's daughter, Pijau, who was the daughter-in-law of Purnananda Buragohain, came to know of the conspiracy and sent a messenger to warn her father. The Parbatiya Phukan too seemed to have willingly taken things easy and made no haste to apprehend Badanchandra. In fact, he virtually gave enough time to Badanchandra to escape from Guwahati. This becomes clear from the words of the ballad which seems to have a deep sympathy for Badanchandra and his family. The ballad describes in detail the feelings of Badanchandra's wife when she is about to be left behind by her husband. The minstrel's sympathies are obviously for the lady in distress and he refers to the plight of Guwahati which is now without its master—'The dogs bite, the children throw stones/Nowhere is there any happiness.'³⁰ The story takes us through Badanchandra's voyage to Calcutta and his eventual escape to Burma, of his being received warmly by the Assamese princess of the Burmese king and how he secured Burmese help to come back to Assam and seek his revenge. Although the ballad records the promises made by Badanchandra to the Burmese king in return for his help, such as giving him plenty of gold and the choicest Assamese girls,³¹ yet the minstrel seems to be quite tolerant of Badanchandra. Rather, it is Purnananda Buragohian who is shown to be without either the support of his nobles or of the people.³² Moreover, the ballad shows that when, during their first entry into Assam, the Burmese forces advanced upon Jorhat, the 'devilish' or 'satanic' Buragohain commits suicide by poisoning himself. Though this is not historically true, the Buragohain having died a natural death, yet it reveals the attitude of the common people towards the prime minister who had appropriated all the powers of the king. It is clear from the ballad, that the Buragohain, all his administrative powers notwithstanding, had alienated large segments of the nobility and officials as well as the common people. Otherwise, the use of the word *narakiya*, a loose translation of which could be 'devilish' or 'satanic' would not have been

---

²⁹ Ibid., line 60.
³⁰ Praphulladatta Goswami, pp. 20–1; *Barphukanar Geet*, lines 248–49.
³¹ *Barphukanar Geet*, lines 437–40.
³² Ibid., lines 469–72.

used by the minstrel to describe the Buragohain. This interpretation of the Burgohain's character runs counter to most of the accounts of him which one comes across in Assam history. For instance, S.K. Bhuyan in his introduction to *Barphukanar Geet*, refutes the argument which tries to evaluate the Buragohain as a power-thirsty unscrupulous individual and says that 'if one goes by the facts of history, then such a view is not acceptable'.[33] He refers to those lines of the *Barphukanar Geet* which say that at a time when Assam did not have any *mantris*, the Buragohain came to the scene and he did not have any enemies anywhere but for Badanchandra. This was but natural especially after the Buragohain had played such an effective role in containing the Moamaria Revolt and in restoring law and order under the Ahom monarch. There was no one in the Ahom state who could challenge the position of the Buragohain. However, seen from another angle, this could mean that Badanchandra was the only individual at that time who could stand up to the whims of Purnananda Buragohain who had assumed almost unlimited powers under a weak king. At least, the slant of the lines in the ballad point in that direction. Praphulladatta Goswami, while discussing the account given in the ballad of the Buragohain's death and the use of the suffix narakiya, says: 'The minstrel rather unexpectedly calls the Buragohain "devilish" when the latter—rather unhistorically—is made to commit suicide.' Why should the minstrel who is expressing the popular voice in his ballad, 'unexpectedly' call the Buragohain 'devilish'? The minstrel must have been giving voice to what the common people felt about the Buragohain and his role in trying to corner Badanchandra Barphukan. Nowhere in the ballad do we come across any lines which refer to the inefficiency or corruption of Badanchandra. And, it is here that *Barphukanar Geet* helps one to have a different look at certain events which changed the course of Assam's history. One is left with the impression that the Buragohain's hatred of Badanchandra and his conspiracy to have him arrested and tried on certain charges framed exclusively by the prime minister, drove Badanchandra into the hands of the Burmese. But before going to Burma and seeking help from the king of that country, Badanchandra did try to secure help from the British who refused. This is recorded in the ballad.

Apart from the Buragohain's hatred, Badanchandra was also the target of ire of the Rajmau, the king's mother. The Rajmau conspired with Dhani Barbaruah to eliminate Badanchandra whom she could never

[33] See S.K. Bhuyan's Introduction to *Barphukanar Geet*, pp. 11–12.

accept in his new position of the Mantri-Phukan after Purnananda's death. On his part, Badanchandra was not apprehensive or suspicious of the Rajmau who happened to be his aunt. The ballad shows how the Rajmau calls Badanchandra and asks him to narrate his adventures in the foreign lands. She also asks him about the secret of his successes and Badanchandra tells her of the charm or amulet which saves him from all dangers.[34] The minstrel shows that Badanchandra has full trust in the Rajmau and does not hesitate to share his most precious secret with her. It can't be said how far this is historically true. Nonetheless, it shows the positive side of Badanchandra's character who has the confidence to trust others. On the contrary, it is the king-mother who draws up the plan to kill Badanchandra and asks Rupsingh Bangal to strike him when he is most vulnerable. Rupsingh kills Badanchandra when he having a bath.[35] The minstrel expresses his sympathy for Badanchandra's wife and children and refers to the attempt by the Rajmau to have the three sons of Badanchandra executed. It is the king's interference which saves their lives and all this is narrated very plaintively in the ballad.[36] It is but natural that the common people's sympathies were with Badanchandra who was killed in a treacherous manner. This is exactly why the minstrel refers to the Rajmau as 'Rajmau Pakhari', a highly uncomplimentary term to use for the king's mother. Praphulladatta Goswami, for instance, cannot accept the fact that the minstrel of *Barphukanar Geet,* calls the Rajmau 'notorious', while all the while being aware that 'the Barphukan was a traitor'.[37] But it appears clear from this reference that the common people viewed the Rajmau as a notorious character who got Badanchandra killed in a very mean manner. Moreover, the Rajmau and Rupsingh Bangal were the first to flee the country once the Burmese came. They were also aware of the fact that but for the murder of Badanchandra, the Burmese perhaps would not have come to Assam a second time. It was during this second invasion that the Burmese troops carried out the most inhuman of atrocities on the Assamese people. When they came with Badanchandra, the latter ultimately persuaded them to leave. But it was after Badanachandra's death, that the Burmese came with the clear intention of seeking revenge and ravaging the land. Thus, in the popular mind, people like Purnananda and the Rajmau were seen to be responsible in many ways for the misery of the common man

---

[34] *Barphukanar Geet,* lines 616–40.
[35] Ibid., lines 689–96.
[36] Ibid., lines 724–42.
[37] Praphulladatta Goswami, p. 25.

under Burmese occupation. It would not do just to put all the blame on Badanchandra, for he was in many ways a victim of circumstances. And, this is what comes out in *Barphukanar Geet*. Thus, *Barphukanar Geet* decidedly helps us to have a more comprehensive view of the events in Assam's history in the closing years of Ahom rule.

Maniram Dewanar Geet

Maniram Dewanar Geet refers to all those folk-songs and ballads which deal with the life of Maniram Dewan and his execution in the hands of the British, on the 26th of February, 1858. Maniram, was a charismatic personality and during the initial days of British rule in Assam, he had, along with several others belonging to the Ahom nobility, welcomed the Company's rule. In him the British found a highly intelligent and well-informed friend and he was soon made the Dewan of the Company. It was primarily because of Maniram's efforts that the Company's revenue collection in upper Assam went up considerably and measures were taken to introduce the cultivation of tea into the region. Even as the British consolidated their hold over the province, they started depending more on their chosen set of officials and the power of the Ahom nobility was increasingly marginalized. Maniram's efforts to start his own tea gardens and chart an independent course was looked upon by the British with suspicion, for they saw him as a possible business rival who could eventually upset their plans of turning Assam into a profitable colony. Maniram too, after his initial stint with the British, fell out with them and started espousing the cause of the Ahom monarch and the nobility. Modern political consciousness in Assam may be said to have commenced from around the year 1853 when Maniram Dewan and Anandaram Dhekiyal Phukan submitted their memorials to Moffatt Mills. In his petition, Maniram had asked for the restoration of the rights and privileges of the monarch and his nobility. Apart from this, the memorial gives one an idea of the deep knowledge which Maniram had about the region and its inhabitants. The British knew that such an intelligent and independent-minded person could not be their friend for long and that eventually he would pose a threat to their presence. Therefore, they took the first opportunity to eliminate him. They got their chance when, against the backdrop of the events of 1857, Maniram tried to organize the discontented nobles and men of the upper classes in favour of the Ahom king and against the British. On the basis of rather flimsy evidence and through a hurried and highly partisan trial, the British sentenced Maniram and his associate, Peyali Baruah, to death by hanging. The execution of Maniram Dewan sent the signal to all the opponents of the British that they would be dealt with harshly, irrespective of social status. It is true that Maniram's efforts to restore the monarchy (which many in his time viewed as an attempt to make him all-powerful) did not have the backing either of the upper classes or of the people in general. Years of Burmese occupation had wrought havoc on the social fabric of the region and the people welcomed the peace and stability that came with colonial rule. Nevertheless, the public hanging of a person of Maniram's standing sent shock waves throughout the province and people reacted in spontaneous grief. It did not take too long for Maniram to become a national icon of resistance to the British and with the beginning of the nationalist struggle against the British, Maniram became the most important Assamese martyr in the cause of independence. Nationalist historians like Benudhar Sharma have carved a niche for Maniram in the freedom struggle of the Assamese people and he has been turned into a symbol of people's resistance to foreign occupation.[38]

But, how did the common people of his own times view Maniram Dewan? It is for this that we have to go to ballads like *Maniram Dewanar Geet*. Composed during the period immediately following the execution of Maniram Dewan and Peyali Baruah, these are songs dealing with the life and times of Maniram and sung by different people with slight variations in the content. But, when all the songs that are available to us are analysed, what appears is not just an adulatory picture of Maniram Dewan. Unlike the valorization of Maniram indulged in by the nationalist historians of Assam during the anti-British struggle, the different *geets* or songs which make up the corpus of *Maniram Dewanar Geet* are quite critical of Maniram's role under the British as also of his vaulting ambition. This, however, does not stand in the way of the minstrel expressing his feelings of sorrow and outrage at the execution of this highly talented man. One thing is, however, clear. The people as a whole were deeply affected by the manner in which the British did away with Maniram. His execution also showed the final fall of the Ahom nobility and the upper classes because the common man could never imagine that someone of the stature of Maniram could be tried and hanged in public. The people had been accustomed to

---

[38] Benudhar Sharma, 1966 [1950], *Maniram Dewan*, Guwahati.

murders within the royal family or its nobility; but to see someone who they held in such high esteem that to be hanged in public was bound to leave a deep scar in the collective consciousness of the people. There was bound to be a lot of contradictory feelings about Maniram. And, all these are expressed in the songs which make up the ballad, *Maniram Dewanar Geet*.

Like other Assamese ballads, *Maniram Dewanar Geet* also begins with an invocation to the goddess Saraswati and then moves on to describe the coming of the British into Assam. It narrates as to how David Scott befriended Maniram during the initial days of British rule in Assam and of how eventually Maniram became a Dewan of the Company; of how, because of his ambition, he fell out with the British and, betrayed by those very people whom he trusted, met his final end. The songs refer to the different periods in the life of Maniram and how from being a loyal supporter of the British, he eventually became the leader of a small group which planned to overthrow the British. Although the central content and tone of the songs relates to the feelings of the people consequent to the execution of Maniram, yet there are several portions of the ballad which reveal different aspects of the Dewan's personality which are not necessarily complementary. For instance, Maniram's death is bewailed in the following lines:

> *Sonar Dhowakhowat Khali oi Maniram,/Rupar Dhowakhowat Khali.*
> *Raja Hoboloi Ulali Maniram,/Dingit Sipejari Lali*
> *Sonar Dhowakhuat Khali Oi Maniram,/Rupar Dhowakhuat Khali*
> *Ati Tajbajia Hoisili Maniram/Barasi Akura Pali.*
> *Rupar Dhowakhuat Khali Oi Maniram/Sonar Dhowakhuat Khali*
> *Atikoi Sara Holi Oi Maniram Bangalar Sipjari Loli.*[39]

In these lines the balladeer sings about the luxurious lifestyle of Maniram Dewan and how his excess of ambition led to his tragic end. Maniram wanted to be the king and that brought about his fall, says the people's poet. There are several more stanzas where Maniram's over-zealousness in supporting British rule is referred to and how he was instrumental in fleecing the common people by helping the British with their new revenue rules.

> *Bamune Ganake Paik Kaktiye/Lalbandi Karile Raj;*
> *Bangale Kangale Deshkhan Bharale/Barbaruak Karale Baaj.*

---

[39] Lila Gogoi, 1976, *Maniram Dewanar Geet*, Calcutta, pp. 34, 36.

Maniram Hole Oi Uthi Bahi Raja/Dah Bulile Hoi Pachi;
Fauzdari Dewani Adalat Patile/Raijak Nile Oi Susi.[40]

The above lines also refer to the bartering away of the country by its own people, of how it was being filled up by foreigners and how the officials appointed by the Ahom rulers were being replaced. The following stanza reveal the collaborationist role of Maniram Dewan and bemoan the fact that he ended up siding with the British at a very early stage of their rule:

Keloi Enekua Holi Oi Maniram/Keloi Enekua Holi,
Desh Patibor Nohol Sari Din/Raijar Dorohi Holi.

Thus, while there is a sense of deep sorrow at the hanging of Maniram Dewan, yet there are several stanzas which are quite critical of his collaborationist role. These particular stanzas also show the Dewan as not being particularly sympathetic towards the common man. There is also an interesting reference to the hanging of Peyali Baruah by the British. Peyali Baruah, known as Maheshchandra Gabharumelia Baruah, was known to have actively sided with the Dewan in his efforts to bring an end to British rule. But one particular stanza of *Maniram Dewanar Geet* seems to give a different view. It gives the impression that the common man somehow held Maniram Dewan responsible for getting Peyali Baruah involved in the conspiracy against the British:

Maniramak Marili Bhalake Karili/Piyalik Marili Kia,
Seinu Katha Suni Rangpurar Amolar/Akase Uri Gol Jiva.[41]

Here the balladeer expresses surprise at the hanging of Peyali Baruah and says that the officials of the Ahom capital, Rangpur, are all stunned by it. By contrast, there isn't much of an outrage at Maniram's execution. Discussing these lines, Lila Gogoi feels that maybe the minstrel who composed this portion had some grudge against Maniram.[42] But, this could also be seen from another angle. Could it be that the people's sympathies were more for Peyali Baruah who was seen as a pawn in the hands of Maniram. While Maniram was seen as bringing about his death through excess of ambition, the death of Peyali Baruah because of his association with Maniram might have evoked a different sort of feeling among the people. Thus, it is interesting to find that, the two men who

---

[40] Ibid., p. 23.
[41] Ibid., p. 35.
[42] Ibid., pp. 23–4.

were hanged for the same reason by the British, were seen differently at the popular level. It couldn't have been, as Lila Gogoi suggests, just a case of ill-feelings on the part of the minstrel towards Maniram.

Interestingly, there is a reference in the songs to Maniram's visit to Calcutta to pay the revenue which the Ahom king had promised to pay the British after the Treaty with Purandhar Singha.[43] According to some historians, Maniram along with two other Ahom officials had gone to Calcutta in 1838 to pay the one lakh and fifty thousand rupees as three years revenue to the British. But, these three officials misappropriated the huge sum and, as a result of this, Purandhar Singha lost his kingdom to the British. It is not known as to how true this story actually is. But, Lila Gogoi says that the three officials were Kashinath Tamuly Phukan, Lathou Khargharia Baruah and Maniram Barbhandar Baruah.[44] Following the take over of upper Assam by the British, Maniram became the Dewan of the Assam Tea Company and in this position he became very powerful. But within a few years, Maniram fell out with the British and made enemies of the top Company's officials in Assam. He resigned from the Dewanship in the year 1844 and set out to establish his own tea gardens at Cinnamora and Chenglung. For about ten years from 1844, Maniram steered an independent course and established himself in his own right. But, It was during this period that Maniram grew increasingly anti-British and finally got involved in the attempt to restore the Ahom monarchy in 1857. The treatment meted out to the former Dewan of the Company by the British had a far-reaching effect on the minds of the people and they tried to forget Maniram's earlier role as a collaborator of the British. And, once he was hanged after a trial which the people saw as highly partisan and unjust, popular sympathy swerved towards Maniram and he gradually got the halo of a martyr for freedom. The minstrel who sang about Maniram fleecing the people in order to augment the revenue collection of the British, sings now about how taxes increased after Maniram was executed:[45] 'Ever since Maniram died/The taxes have increased'. Maniram after death emerges as a hero who is mourned by every section of society as also by nature.[46] He is credited with having introduced tea cultivation in Assam—something which changed the province's economy. This change in the image of Maniram from that of a collaborator to a patriot

[43] Ibid., p. 42.
[44] Ibid., p. 11.
[45] Ibid., pp. 22, 45.
[46] Ibid., pp. 576–7.

as may be seen in the different songs of *Maniram Dewanar Geet* is quite significant and points to the possibility of the songs having been composed and sung at different periods. Those that were composed and sung immediately after his death appear to be quite critical of Maniram's role; whereas, those composed and sung after some time has elapsed since his execution seem to concentrate only on his heroic qualities. Transmission by word of mouth over a long period brought about these changes and this is quite natural as far as the oral tradition is concerned. Along with the change of the levels of perception and consciousness of the common people, most of whom were wedded to the soil, the image of the central character of the ballad is also bound to change—so that it fits in with contemporary ideas of dedication, sacrifice, patriotism, etc. Discussing this, Vansena observes:

> The first and the simplest model supposes that an observer reported his experience orally, casting it as an initial message. A second party heard it and passed It on. From party to party It was passed on until the last performer acting as informant told It to the tape-recorder. A chain of transmission exists in which each is of the parties is a link... the truly distinctive characteristic of the oral tradition is its transmission by word of mouth over a period longer than the contemporary generation.[47]

This could perhaps explain the apparently contradictory responses to Maniram shown in *Maniram Dewanar Geet*. But, it also shows that unlike those historians who often reflected the class or community or nationalistic viewpoint, the response of the peasant was quite different. There was deep sorrow and outrage over the manner in which Maniram was killed; but, that does not prevent the village minstrel from singing about the limitations of this great personality, of how, like so many other human heroes, he too was a prey to excess of ambition and opportunism. This decidedly adds a tragic note to the character of Maniram Dewan and enhances the aesthetic beauty of the ballads.

---

[47] Vansena, p. 29.

Moushumi Kandali
The Colonial Impression on Vaishnavite Art Form of Assam
A Study of the Sculptural Reliefs of the Srihati Satra†

Art mediates, maps, reflects, records its time-space—sometimes with bold letters, at times with indecipherable scribbles that call for decoding. Art has been playing this role, even within tethered restrictions and bindings. For instance, religious art which acts as one of the medium for propagating the canonical truths and mythical narratives of certain religions through symbolic depictions or realistic illustrations, also at times sparks off a glimmer of political reflexivity in the guise of the spiritual. The Srihati Satra of Assam, which is an important site of Vaishnavite art form, can come across as an amazing example of this. During a visit to this monastery in the year 2000, I was enthralled by some of

† An earlier version of this article was published in *Yaatra*, Vol. 2, No. 2, 2006, Guwahati.

the wooden sculptural reliefs on the walls of this satra that seemed to whisper of something political in the tune of the mythological. In a humble attempt to listen to and capture that whisper, we shall proceed by delving into the background and origin of the art form and mapping its evolution at first.

The Background and Origin

The neo-Vaishnavite Bhakti movement of medieval India was a religio-cultural upheaval of an unprecedented kind. It was in fact a cultural renaissance manifested in literature and art forms in its diverse expressions that transported the Bhakti movement to its all encompassing magnitude. Alongside certain regions in the south, the entire North India from Assam to Rajasthan was inundated by this wave. A host of literature—poetics, verse plays, as well as the theaters such as Jaya Deva's *Geeta Govinda* and Bihari's *Satsai* sprang up simultaneously carving out the space for a repertoire of multiple art forms like manuscript painting, fresco, sculpture/sculptural relief, wood carving, dance, drama, music, recitals and other minor art forms which acted as an illustrative media for the religious/philosophical/literary expressions of this movement. The class of artists who played the major role of illustration of narratives not only depicted the text but also added new dimensions with their imagination, visual perception and experimentations to explore and render a high aesthetic order within the visual semiotics.

In Assam, Srimanta Shankardeva (AD 1449–AD 1568), the Bhakti saint-artist-poet-social reformer who propounded the Vaishnavite movement, established the first *satra*—a medieval monastery, a forerunner of about two hundred and fifty six such existing satras of today.[1] Satras are wonderhouses that nurture and unfold a vast spectacle of cloistered art forms such as *Borgeet* (raga based Bhakti music), *Satriya Nritya* (classical dance form), *Bhaona* (theatre performance), manuscript painting, sculpture, wood carving/sculptural reliefs (on the walls of satra structures) and other associated art forms such as mask making, costume designing, and production of artifacts like the votive wooden structures (*asana, sim-hasana*), *thogi* (book rests), decorated pleasure boats (*khel-nao*), *dola* (litter), etc. Some satra-associated ritual enactments such

---

[1] As reported in Dr Nirupoma Mahanta, 2001, *Satriya Sanskritir Rupsayan: Achar, Riti aru Utsav-Anusthan*, Guwahati: New Print.

as the erection of a*kash banti* (massive sky lanterns made of bamboo) in Kamalabari Satra of Majuli would remind one to the contemporary art of installations.

Manuscript painting is the major narrative form of visual art of Vaishnavite traditions that grew under the satra patronage. This school comprising of the refined and sophisticated works such as the *Chitra Bhagavata* (tentatively dated AD 1539), *Geeta Govinda* (Assamese translation datable to late 17th to early 18th century) and others bears a distinct stylistic idiom. It is characterized by an admixture of classical/elitist and folk-tribal elements—a fusion of specific indigenous locale and broader pan-Indian features. A range of scholars like Nandalal Bose, Dr Suniti Kr. Chatterjee, Asit Kr. Haldar, Basil Gray, Moti Chandra, Rajatananda Dasgupta, Dr Maheshwar Neog, Jugal Das Dr Biren Dutta, Nilamoni Phukan, Dr Naren Kalita and others have attributed different stylistic influences and resemblances to other traditions of Indian manuscript and miniature painting. According to them, influences of Mewari, Rajasthani, Jaina miniatures, Buddhist Pala tradition, Indo-Persian/Mughal, Pahari, Deccani styles along with the characteristic elements of the South East Asian visual traditions are evident in these paintings. Scholars have discerned elements of indigenous folk–tribal traditions such as Tai-Buddhist manuscripts of the Monpas, Sherdukpens (tribes of Arunachal), Bhutiyas and others. Though manuscript paintings sprang up as the major narrative tradition in Vaishnavite culture, the wood carvings/sculptural relief (occasionally done on mud plastered surfaces) used in satra architecture form an equally significant visual tradition. The significance of this genre of art lies in the fact that unlike manuscript painting which gradually dwindled at the advent of colonialism, wood carving/sculptural relief has continued as a living tradition till date. This is a visual tradition which has mediated it's immediate spacio-temporal changes and has been adaptive/reflexive of the socio-political-economic-cultural environments. It has been enduring itself by an ongoing process of appropriation/re-appropriations, both in the stylistic and technical levels. This is evident in uses of new medium, material and executional methods and techniques of composition, treatment of space-time, typology of figurations, architectural settings, costumes and apparel and other such pictorial or formal elements. The observed deviations from conformity with the standardized canons of visual narratives is probably due to exposure to and encounter with other parallel art forms, along with the spacio-temporal changes. There is a possibility that this genre of art can be seen as a link phase between the traditional mode of visual narrative and the modern westernized mode of narration which emerged in Assam during the third decade of the twentieth century. Of course this is not to claim that modernism (in Assam) is a natural descendant of this phase; but is rather a re-fabrication/re-construction of western idioms and ideologies in the Indian context. Whenever the phasing out of the rich and vibrant tradition of manuscript paintings by the modern art of western orientation is examined, one often tends to disregard the living tradition of wood carving/sculptural relief which has had a continuous and unbroken existence right from the origin of Vaishnavite visual art to contemporary times. Sustaining on an endeavor of assimilations of traditional manuscript painting and indigenous folk traditions with the new forms of European academic realism and popular art forms like the calendar art, bazaar paintings, modern iconography of idol making etc. has given it a distinct narrative form which at times unfolds a mosaic of multiple intersection and juxtaposition of the sacred/secular; classical/folk and the traditional/contemporary. Hence it is necessary to re-evaluate and reclaim a place for this tradition within the art historical paradigm.

As we have already observed, though manuscript painting has drawn the attention of scores of scholars, the art of wood carving and sculptural relief has not been examined in depth except by a few scholars such as Jugal Das, Nilomoni Phukan and Dr Birendranath Dutta. Nilomoni Phukan in his book *Loka Kalpa Drishti* (1987)[2] has made a noteworthy appraisal of this art from an aesthetic standpoint. Considered from an art historical perspective, a seminal observation is made by Dr Birendranath Dutta in Chapter III of his book *Folk Painting in Assam* (1998).[3] In his formulation, this genre is clubbed with other related art forms in what he has named the khanikar style, after the versatile traditional artists/artisans who displayed expertise in all forms of art—painting, wood carving, idol making, mask making, costume designing, stage setting and drop scene painting, props making, theatrical make up and artifacts of religious and everyday use. As a class (not a caste), Khanikars received enduring patronage both from the satras and the royal court of Ahoms before colonial rule and perhaps formed a kind of guild. It would not

[2] Nilomoni Phukan, 1987, *Loka Kalpa Drishti*, Guwahati: Asom Prakshon Parishad.
[3] Birendranath Dutta, 1998, *Folk Painting in Assam*, Tezpur: Tezpur University Publications

be irrelevant here to discuss this formulation in some details. Dr Dutta observes that

> the painting done by them on the carved panels and figures—in conjunction with the forms carved or modeled—incorporates a distinctive style, and it manifests itself in the making out of the forms, the drawing of the lines, the choice and combination of colours and particularly in the application of the paints consisting of such traditional materials as vermilion (*hengul*) yellow ochre (*haital*), indigo (*nil*), chalk (*dhal*), lamp black (*kajol*) etc. which stand out both for the brightness of their hues as well as for their durability and capacity to retain the freshness for years. This particular style, which may be called the khanikar style, has some affinity with what Das Gupta designates as the Satriya style of manuscript painting. Considering the fact that in spite of Satra-oriented refinement, the art of the *khanikars* is not confined to the Satras but extends to the decoration of such objects as musical instruments and household appliances like weaving accessories, the *khanikar* style of painting has the essentials of a folk art genre.[4]

However, in this context the term 'khanikar' style appears to carry an element of ambiguity as the illustrators of manuscripts were also known as khanikars. In fact, whoever would sculpt, paint, model and fashion artifacts are known as khanikar in Assam. It is not known whether any distinctions hierarchical or otherwise, existed between those who illustrated the manuscript paintings and those who carried out wood carvings/sculptural relief and other art activities of the satras. Hence to name one of the two parallel visual traditions after the artists who were associated with both the styles seems somewhat ambiguous. It may be that the author wanted to emphasise the point that whereas in several cases, the illustrator-painter cum calligrapher of the manuscript paintings have been traced to their individual identities (like the Ghanashyam Kharghoria Phukan, Sri Sashadhar Aata of *Parijat Haran* fame or Sri Durga Panchanan or Durgadas Dwij of *Karna Parba* and others), the artists or khanikars of wood carving/paintings of the satra architecture are all anonymous without decipherable names. Hence all the art forms done by the anonymous khanikars are clubbed together to give a common name after the artists may be seen as a tribute to them. Or perhaps the author wanted to emphasize the fact that one of the art forms is abandoned while the other is still a living tradition. Still, it might be more convenient if the style is named after its medium in analogy with manuscript painting. Further, a question can be raised

[4] Ibid., p. 21.

here as to whether it would be appropriate to incorporate khanikar style of painting and wood carvings within the category of folk art. The visual narratives are regional manifestations of classical artistic expressions and cannot be viewed in isolation from the high art tradition of local culture. On the other hand, indigenous elements have been amalgamated into the stylistics of this art form to give it a culture-specific folk form/look. It is often observed that the realm of the secular gets permeated within the confined thematic of the sacred. As pointed out by Nilomoni Phukan, common humane concern has been reflected in the artist's imagination in guise of the depictions of the supra-human/divine as in the picture of Jasoda caning child Krishna painted on a *Sim-hasana* in Bholaguri Satra.[5] In this context, it must be pointed out that the wall paintings and sculptural reliefs were more integral part of common life as they were accessible to the common masses unlike the illustrated manuscripts which were exclusive in nature, kept in the secluded sacred interior of satra premises to be accessed only by a selected few like the satra dignitaries and privileged literati. Wood carvings and sculptural relief's painted on the walls had a definite functional objective to serve. Apart from being used as decorative embellishments of the satra architecture, they played a role similar to the fresco paintings of the medieval European church by acting as the vehicle for the spread of the gospel message amongst the masses. Thus this art form came up as a visual medium within the distinct indigenous traditions to become an integral part of folk-life. To quote Dr Dutta again,

The khanikar style of carving, modeling and painting, both in form and technique appears to be the result of fusion of the neo-Vaishnavite spiritual and artistic ideals with one or more earlier indigenous artistic traditions of this region. One such tradition that readily comes to mind is the one still flourishing among some of the Buddhistic communities, particularly the Monpas, the Sherdukpens and the Bhutiyas living north of Assam proper. Painting is a living tradition with the Monpas and Sherdukpens who have links with Tibet and Bhutan. They execute carvings and paintings on their houses and fashion wooden masks, mostly in conventional local Bhuddhistic design. There are reasons to believe that the khanikar style of wood carving and painting has some sort of connection with this particular style and its technique. The dragon-like forms of some khanikar models and designs speak out in favour of this conjecture. Some elements of this style seem to have entered even into the Satriya School of manuscript painting.[6]

---

[5] In his book *Lok Kalpa Drishti*, p. 25.
[6] Birendranath Dutta, *Folk Painting of Assam*, footnote of pp. 22–3.

Going by this formulation of 'khanikar style', it appears that a definite stylistic distinction has been established between the manuscript painting and the art of wood carving/sculptural relief. That there is a mediumistic difference between the two art forms is self-evident. Manuscript paintings were done on *saachipaat* folios prepared from the bark of Agor tree, indigenous paper called *tulaapaat* and occasionally on muga silk, palm leaves and even on woven bamboo strips, whereas the carved and painted panels on the walls of a satra were mostly done on wooden surface and occasionally on mud plaster. Obvious differences are seen in the size of the two genres where the typical manuscript painting medium dimensions being say 10" × 4" while a carved panel would cover several square feet. The mediumistic difference also leads to the difference in technical and execution methods. However, apart from these mediumistic/technical differences the two are quite similar at stylistic level. The pictorial elements such as the rendering of the narratives, style and typology of figuration, treatment of space—time, architectural settings and designs, costumes and apparel, flora and fauna, decorative motifs and patterns, etc. are strikingly analogous. Of course the manuscripts seem to be more refined and sophisticated with free flowing delineations, and exhibit finer handling of other pictorial elements as compared to the wood carvings and sculptural reliefs. However this can be attributed to the fact that the smaller medium of manuscript painting has inherent advantages in these aspects. This is also the reason why the carved and painted panels are mostly simple, direct, and comprehensible which enacts a crucial moment of a narration rather than the entire sequence of events. The task becomes more challenging as one has to execute the narration within the limited space available conforming to the pre-determined architectural set up. (The most imaginative and appealing capability of these artists is evident in the technique of utilizing the negative spaces of the pictorial design to carve out decorative windows which serve the dual purpose of admitting light and air besides enhancing the aesthetics of the structure/design.) Therefore taking the foregoing into account, the art of wood carving/sculptural relief may be considered as an extended form of manuscript painting in spite of the visible mediumistic/technical differences between the two. While the manuscript paintings can be assigned approximate dates, the reliefs carry no such obvious information. In many cases, there are controversies as to when a particular satra was established. Also it is quite possible that the decoration in the form of sculptural reliefs were carried much after the construction of the architecture. Therefore there is no direct evidence to substantiate the claim that the art of wood carving/sculptural relief is an extended form of manuscript paintings. (However, by using radioactive techniques it is possible to assign definite dates to them; but to our knowledge, no such exercise has been carried out till date in Assam.) But from a technical standpoint, it may be stated that manuscript painting predates decorative wood carvings/sculptural reliefs since it is logical to execute a concept on a smaller scale and subsequently scale it up in size.

The Evolution: History of Appropriation and Assimilation

Be it as it may, the two related art forms thrived side by side till early nineteenth century. However after the decline of the Ahom Kingdom and advent of colonialism, the genre of manuscript painting lost its patronage and gradually faded out. Wood carvings and sculptural reliefs on the other hand continued to thrive as a vehicle of popularizing traditional Vaishnavite sermons. Reaching the masses was all the more important after the coming of the Baptist missionaries who tried to woo the masses from the grasp of pagan deities with missionary zeal. The satras were competing with the missionaries to retain their disciples whose relation with the satras was not only spiritual but also material since it was they who provided the tributes that a satra needed to survive. Communications and inter-regional interactions underwent a quantum change after the advent of the British. With the coming of railways it became possible for even a relatively less wealthy person to visit other parts of the country especially for religious, educational and commercial purposes. Cheap rail travel made it possible for an *Adhikar* of even a minor satra to visit Calcutta with his entourage for *Ganga snan*. In lower Assam, it was quite common for a Brahmin to have several disciples amongst the landed gentry of East Bengal and Cooch Bihar. They would undertake an annual visit to these disciples for carrying out puja and also to collect tributes. Brahmins were also engaged as priests in satras especially those belonging to the *Brahma Sanghati* where idol worship was practiced. Thus the people, both social elite and commoners had encountered the sweeping changes both in the realm of life as well as of art, either first or second hand. On a broader context, Victorian illusionist art, naturalism/academic realism and the notion of artistic progress took root in India around this time and new genres such as oil paintings were introduced. The artist began to lose his previous faceless character and gained a new status as an individual 'gentleman artist'. The first of the gentleman artists Raja Ravi Varma whose particular adaptations of western techniques—using European perspective and figure-modelling, with Hindu and nationalist imagery—evolved into India's ubiquitous, gaudy, glossy painted pictures of gods and goddesses, called 'calendar-art'. His oleograph prints were spread all over the country thanks to the advent of printing presses. (An examples of which reached even the remote town of Margherita in the eastern corner of Assam.) Calendar art began to play a major role in the lives of average Indians as objects of devotion, advertisement (in the form of business giveaways) and as an affordable decorative essential. Besides portraying the mundane concepts of love, romance, devotion, etc., they continue as reflections of significant temporal events, ideas and personalities, from the rise of nationalism to the Kargil War. The emergence of bazaar paintings was another significant phenomenon of the Raj. *Patua*s migrating from rural Bengal to Calcutta to set up their practice around the Kalighat temple created a new school of art where from mythological depiction to the impressions of dynamic social environment of urban Calcutta and its Babu culture were recorded. Being mass produced and affordable, these were prized by the low and middle-income groups as objects d' art. All these along with the media of theatre and newly introduced bioscopes contributed to the growth of a popular culture whose form continues to be transformed over time till today. No wonder that these changes would have repercussion in the living art traditions of the country. Thus the changing socio-political and cultural arena brought about by colonialism also began to get reflected even in the satra related art praxis, especially the living art form of decorative sculptural relief, registering a deviation from the standardized canons of visual narrative. New assimilations/departures further heightened its hybrid folk–classical–popular character. The foremost change was in the material, wood and mud plasters at places replaced by cement, as concrete buildings began to replace thatched construction and synthetic dyes taking the place of hengul and haital. The sculptural relief on the walls of the Srihati Satra of Suwalkuchi is a witness to these changes which we propose to discuss below.

The 'Political' in Religious: The Sculptural Reliefs in Srihati Satra

There is no definite date as to when Srihati Satra, a *udasin* satra of Suwalkuchi, was established. According to the *Burha Satradhikar* Sri Madhav Chandra Mahanta, Kanu Burha Thakur who is believed to be a relative of Sri Sri Madhav Dev established the satra where Sri Ram Nidhi Prabhu was the first satradhikar. There have been eleven satradhikars till date, some of whom are Sri Nakul Atoi, Gokul Atoi, Manmath Atoi, Harijay Mahanta, Baksiddha Purush Bood Ram Mahanta, etc. The satradhikar, *bhakat*s and nearby residents claim that the satra is about 400–450 years old whereas the *Deka* Satradhikar Sri Dipak Ch. Mahanta opines that the satra is about 250–300 years old. The later claim however appears more plausible. Satra structure of the Srihati Satra is adorned by wood carvings and paintings on all sides except the rear side of the *Manikut*. The right wall (as we enter the premises) is adorned by a panel of wall paintings on the uppermost portions, below which are several curved windows bearing rectangular frames of wood carvings. The lintel below the window is decorated in *lataakta* style with *jalikata* panels below. Most of the carved panels are of high relief pattern. The subjects are drawn from Vaishnavite religious texts—Vishnu in his various incarnations, various mythological characters from *Bhagavat Purana* and other religious texts. Artistic playfulness in the form of incorporations of some neutral subjects such as two cavorting monkeys (Is it Bali and Sugriva or just an ordinary pair of the Rhesus variety?) is an interesting sidelight. The uppermost panel depicts the scenes of *Yama–Yatana*, the sinners being punished in the kingdom of Yama, a scene which is reminiscent of one in the Barpeta *Kirtan Ghar*. Though scholars have doubts whether the Yama Patika tradition prevalent in ancient and medieval India really existed in Assam, it is interesting to see some of the satras, mostly from the lower Assam region depicting the scenes of *Yama Puri*. Perhaps the most refined and highly aesthetical rendering of the iconographies depicted with high craftsmanship, artistic sensibility and skill are to be found in the two doors—the main door and the one on the left wall. Metallic plates are stuck over the wooden plank of the doors with compartmentalized multiple niches within each of which an icon is placed. Nilomoni Phukan in his book has commended the artistic excellence of some of them. According to the Burha Satradhikar, the doors are made in the style of those in Old

Kamalabari Satra and Titabor Satra and were part of the old satra architecture, which was demolished in the earthquake of 1897. The panel on the right of the sculptural relief conforms to the style of Satriya manuscript painting—from the standardized figurations to the placement of icons in the niches, which is a distinctive style of manuscript painting having resemblance to the Buddhist Pala manuscripts. (It is worth mentioning that this feature is evident in numerous decorative relief panels in the various temple architecture of the Ahom period.) Some of the figures in the panels on the right wall clearly follow a typical *oda bhangi* or the stance of standing with feet apart and bent a little at the knees during a Satriya dance recital, which is a distinct feature of Satriya manuscript painting. The costumes and apparel, the floral patterns and the rich palette fairly conform to the manuscript painting. But as we move to the panels on the left, we come across a shift in the narrative style. This is where our main concern lies and the focus will primarily rest on the visuals of this left side wall. According to the Burha Satradhikar, who is in the mid fifties, these panels were in existence since his birth. The paints used in the panels appear bright and gaudy and appear to be of commercial origin and definitely not hengul–haital of yore. The primary colours are mostly used in contesting juxtaposition. The empty and uncluttered backgrounds of most frames are painted monochromatic like the manuscript paintings but are azure coloured. The themes of the narratives are mostly centred around Krishna Leela and one or two from the Ramayana. The panel is divided into various rectangular compartments/niches adorned by connecting *toranas* and each depicts an abbreviated narration of an incident in its crucial moment. Like the Kalighat paintings, here also the sequential narration is abandoned to give place for the abbreviated expression. Now let us review some of the salient picture frames of various panels in detail. To start with, in Plate 1, Kamsa is shown sitting on a *sim-hasan* to the left wearing a waistcoat, trousers and shoes. The guard standing nearby is also similarly attired whose headgear looks like the *pugree* of a police constable. In the back ground, Vasudeva stealthily spirits away infant Krishna. The next frame shows Kamsa about to smash Yoga Maya while two guards witness the scene. One of the guards shown standing on top of the prison, points to the deficient sense of proportion on the part of the artist. Kamsa is now on a more traditional attire—barefoot and dhoti, while the guard on top is attired in western clothes. The way the guards are carrying clubs is also more akin to the posture of European soldiers trained in shouldering arms rather than the strong men of

Hindu mythology carrying war maces. The apparel in both the frames are clear deviation from tradition and show the influence of colonial times. Of course, conformity to the traditional style of composition is maintained. In Assamese tradition of manuscript painting, within the same picture plane several simultaneous events are depicted. A certain pictorial strategy is applied to create a connecting link among the different spaces within one picture frame. At times the figures are placed either in convergence or divergence to distinguish between two different events. The narrative placed within a niche under an arch or torana is a distinct feature of manuscript painting where the connecting link composition is manifested. In the connecting link composition, a common object connects the different spaces, and the space division is done either by torana or pillars, trees, etc. These features have been conformed to in most of the narrative frames. In the middle frame of Plate 2, Krishna and Balram are shown walking along the streets of Mathura followed by two of the townsfolk. One is wearing a Gandhi cap and both wear Jawahar coats over dhotis. The man wearing the Gandhi cap resembles the image of a Satyagrahi seen in the popular art and theatre of those times. Though such topis or caps were pretty common in the western part of India, it was not much seen in the north eastern part until the advent of twentieth century, when the freedom movement spread like wild fire to all parts of India. A rare spectacle is seen on the background where two of the three women are shown baring their breasts, something not visible elsewhere in this genre—perhaps a faint echo of the images of fallen women in bazaar paintings and calendar art. The right frame of the third plate also shows a guard clad in trousers and boots in a soldierly posture. In the right frame of Plate 4, the guards are again attired in European style, this time wearing knee boots and red police caps. Even Chanuka (Chanoor?) and Muristhaka (Mustika?) the wrestlers assigned by Kamsa to slay Krishna and Balaram bear striking resemblance to Europeans in facial features as well as dress in Plate 5. In the narratives of these panels, Kamsa is often depicted as a monumental iconic figure dwarfing other figures in the frame in order to show his power and position. As we have already seen that there is conformity to certain standardized norms as the connecting link composition, placement of icons within the niche, there are also stark deviations as illustrated above. There are further deviations in the mode of figuration and the gesture/posture of the characters. The conventional figuration in profile with the oda bhangi posture is now mutated to frontal postures with a forward-looking gaze. The typology of figures also has undergone much change into a rounder and plumper shape like that of the popular calendar art figures and the figures of 'modern day' idols such as seen in Durga Puja. It is worth mentioning here that the popular 'modern' iconography of the Kumartuli tradition of idol making was popularized in Assam on a mass scale during the mid part of nineteenth century with the influx of Bengali babus who migrated to serve in the state. In the fairs and *haat*s associated with various festivals like Raas, scenes of Krishna Leela were presented as puppet shows and idols. The similarity of the figuration of Satriya sculptural relief to these popular art forms may be traceable to such cultural developments. Nilomoni Phukan mentions about a babu smoking hookah in the style of Kalighat painting in another satra of Suwalkuchi.[7] The Pith-*pat*, *Maju* paintings of Goalpara/Dhubri region, *Bishohari* pats of Gauripur–Golokganj–Bilasipara area—shows a clear connectivity to the bazaar paintings of Kalighat. Hence their reflection in sculptural relief of Srihati Satra cannot be a far-fetched concept. To carry the study further, European optical perspective and the elements of foreshortening which were not to be seen in traditional renderings are also visible here. A fine example of this is the picture of Sita sitting in the Ashok Vatika with Sarama and Trijatayu (Trijata?) in Plate 6. All the four figures are placed in different positions and spaces with a balanced use of space and optical perspective. It is a clear evidence of British academic realism being appropriated within a local tradition and of stark deviation from the overall earlier look of this art form. Such developments are also evident in the picture frame of Krishna Balarama and Sudama (left part of Plate 3) and the one where Garga Rishi is sitting in the background while Nanda Jasoda and a Dasi are seen discussing (the juxtaposition of some local artifacts and household appliances are noteworthy) in Plate 7. Of course the artist still seems to grapple with the perspectives and proportion of the figures which at times appear crude and comical. A few reflections of change can be seen in minor details such as the shape of the asana, which resembles a chair. It is not that there are no references to the European costumes, apparel and persona in the manuscript paintings. In a plate of *Brahmabaibarta Purana* written in the nineteenth century (British Library Collection) four British officers are shown seated on chairs in the court of King Purandar Singha.[8] But whereas the Britishers of *Brahmabaibarta Purana* were an authentic naturalistic

---

[7] Nilomoni Phukon, *Loka Kalpa Drishti*, p. 25.
[8] Kakoli Borkakoty, 2001, *Cinha,* Silver Jubilee Volume, p. 70.

representation, depiction of Kamsa and his gang of villains in European apparel seems like an interesting subversion. The devotees of Mathura in Satygrahi's dress and the oppressors as Europeans are a subtle pointer to the ideological fervour and the socio-political climate of the times. Thus it seems that even costumes and apparel become a signifier to the social and economic realities as well as the reflection of current ideological perception.

Any study of changing style of a visual tradition involves primarily three factors—the organization of artistic production confined to a specific historical period and its relation to socio-economic situation, the ideologies which determine them and the formal changes that accrued therefrom. In our present study of changing style of sculptural relief panels of Srihati Satra, we can infer the socio-economic-cultural changes related to a specific historical time inversely, through the stylistic and formal changes. As already stated, there is no available means of precisely dating the production but through the stylistic changes, we can assume the time frame and the socio-political environ that gets mediated and reflected therein. In a genre of art form, which is essentially a means of religious representation, it is the circuitous and subtle suggestions through which such things are reflected and one has to unearth the nuances hidden below the surface. Though the khanikars could not afford to be as sharp and direct as the Kalighat and bazaar painters, they too in their own way have been the recorders of their time. Their roles were different; whereas the bazaar or calendar artists had thematic liberation with a huge market and the advantage of mass production, for the khanikars it was a limited arena, a job of once or twice in a lifetime. Even then despite all adversities, the khanikar's art survived and continues to pulsate.

Tayenjam Bijoykumar Singh
'Kurukshetragi Peeraang'—
Ratan Thiyam's Gift to Mothers

'War' and 'Peace', two terms carrying strikingly opposite meanings, are the mainstay of many of Chorus Repertory Theatre's plays. Their latest production, *Kurukshetragi Peeraang*, a Manipuri adaptation of Kanthi Tripathy's script in English (*Crying for Kurukshetra*) is no exception. With each new play Ratan Thiyam's obsession with peace becomes louder and clearer.

Obviously a deviation from Chorus Repertory Theatre's earlier productions, in this play scintillating lights, dance movements, martial arts steps, lyrical songs, folk elements and special sound effects are conspicuously absent. The cast itself is small by Chorus Repertory Theatre's standard. Another marked difference is the use of permanent stage props. The duration of the play is eighty minutes. It comprises of a single scene with two flashbacks superimposed.

Nevertheless, *Kurukshetragi Peeraang* highlights all aspects of drama with profound impact—the whole aesthetic of drama consisting of

Bhava and *Rasa* is present. The actors project and communicate the meaning of the play through *Abhinaya* (histrionic representation). All the actors are well versed in *Angika* (physical representation through the movement of hands, fingers, lips, neck and feet), *Vacika* (communication through speech), *Aharya* (representation through costume and make-up) and *Sattvika* (communication through the entire psychological resources of the actor).

This play is an all women's play, or almost so. Except for a minor role played by a male actor all the others are female actors. The story is adapted from a tale, which everyone knows—an excerpt from the great Indian epic, the Mahabharata. The scenes are set in Hastinapur in the aftermath of the great battle of Kurukshetra fought between cousins, the Kauravas and the Pandavas, with close relatives and their friends taking sides. The characters in the play are Gandhari, Kunti, Panchali, Yudhistira and two maids in the palace of the Kauravas, Sevika and Kinkari.

Words may fail to describe the anguish of a mother and the fire burning in her heart at the tragic death of her precious son. But the actors, personifying the bereaved mothers, have brought it out live on stage to pinch the hearts of the spectators. A restless Kunti, in search of solace, comes to meet her forlorn sister-in-law, Gandhari, and tries to console her. Kunti has lost only one son, Karna, whom she had refused to overtly accept as her son. She still has her five sons, the Pandavas, alive. Gandhari has lost all her hundred sons, the Kauravas. The two sisters-in-law talk about leaving Hastinapur and head for the forest to retire along with Gandhari's blind husband, Dhritarashtra. Kunti reminisces fondly how she had fondled Karna as a newborn baby, embracing him tightly in her bosom, only to discard him for fear of being disgraced. Sevika finds it implausible that Kunti still loves Karna whom she had refused to accept as her son while he was alive. Kinkari too finds it disgusting.

A highly charged Panchali, another bereaved woman, daughter-in-law of Kunti, makes a regal entry and a verbal battle soon starts. Overcome with anguish at having lost all her sons, brother and father in the battle, she accuses the Kauravas for starting the devastating war. She holds Gandhari responsible as their mother. Kunti tries to intervene and cool down Panchali. The tempo slowly picks up and reaches a crescendo with a flashback—humiliation of Panchali in public.

The mother's heart in Pancahli softens down. Roughly translated, she says, 'I had cried for blood of those who had humiliated me. I wanted to wash my hair with their blood as revenge. I was overwhelmed with joy to see their blood. I had thirst for blood, only blood. But, when I saw my own sons' blood I could not stand the sight—it was so appalling.' Panchali's sarcastic remarks, charged with emotion on learning that both Gandhari and Kunti are planning to leave Hastinapur to retire in forests, also carry a lot of meaning. Putting it in English roughly, she says, 'I'll not stop you from leaving Hastinapur; never again shall I stop you. If you don't want to stay and work to undo the devastating effects of the war, why don't you leave? I request you to leave. Never again, shall I request you to stay.'

Both, Sevika and Kinkari have also lost their husbands and dear ones in the battle. They represent the common folks, the ultimate sufferers of the war. They cannot fathom the ways and thinking of the royalty—they had started a war in which multitudes of braves had been killed and now they are talking of retiring to the forests.

Panchali goes on to sermon on 'Dharma' or righteousness. Her duty is to undo the devastating effects of the war and wash away the blood from the soil of Hastinapur.

It is not known how far the original play in English could convey the intricacies of the story. English, a foreign language, in its entirety may fail to express the subtleness and nuances of Indian culture and traditions without bending to blend Indian ethics. Indian tradition demands that a daughter-in-law should never refer to her husband or mother-in-law by his or her name. But, in English one is free to refer to anyone by name irrespective of his or her age or relationship, of course with a suffix put to the name.

While rendering the play in Manipuri, many options are available. Manipuri, an archaic language, has developed several intricate systems or codes over the centuries. The language spoken in the royal household is quite different from the one used by the commoner. Anyone who wishes to serve in the palace or attend the *Durbar* has to learn the appropriate language. For instance, an altogether different form of address is used while referring to a member of the *cheirap* or a magistrate having civil powers. A cultured person has to use different forms of addresses and appropriate language while speaking to dignitaries, friends and servants. Care also has to be taken while addressing or referring to any stranger according to the age of the person.

After Manipur joined the Indian Union in 1949, the distinction between the royalty and the commoner has waned and it is not so clearly marked, now. The language spoken in the royal household has almost become obsolete.

Since the play is enacted in the royal household, the dialogues must be in the appropriate language to keep the old world charm intact. But not many people of the present generation will be able to follow the dialogues entirely. To keep the old world charm intact as well as to make the dialogues clear to everyone a balance has to be struck somewhere by taking certain liberties. Here lies the difficulty. R.K. Bhogendra has done a commendable job of translation. He has struck the right balance.

Ratan Thiyam's mastery over theatrical arts is evident everywhere. He has strived neither to be prodigal nor niggardly but to strike the right note. And, he is overwhelmingly successful in the venture. The precise moment at which the characters enter the stage, the point of entry, the movement of the characters on the stage, positioning of the characters while delivering dialogues—everything has been meticulously planned. No space of the vast stage is left unused. Nor a single dead moment is allowed. Blindfolded Gandhari's movement is thoughtfully restricted while agile Panchali walks all over the stage. Two arches, both facing the sides, one placed at centre stage down and another at up stage right, give immense depth to the setting of the stage. Background music has been scored with utmost care—melodious sound of *veena* for the opening scene and a soul-searching *raga* in vocals while Panchali is being humiliated in public. The story is taken from the Mahabharata, the theme is universal, the dialogues are in Manipuri and the costume is again undoubtedly Manipuri.

The play ends with the lighting of oil lamps. Sevika and Kinkari light the numerous oil lamps one by one. Panchali lends a hand. 'Lighting oil lamps'; what does it mean? Well, it signifies enlightenment. Wars bring only destruction, *Dharma* or 'righteousness' is the only weapon with which one can undo the devastating effects of wars and re-build the society anew. An enlightened Panchali vows to arm herself with Dharma and wipe away tears from the eyes of the multitude of anguished mothers whose valiant sons had been felled in the battlefield of Kurukshetra.

Though the story is taken from the great epic, the Mahabhrata, it has a strong relevance to the present. Many scenes of the play draw a parallel between the bereaved mothers, particularly of Manipur today whose sons had to give up their lives at a tender age, and the bereaved mothers of Hastinapur. Everyday news about the killings of youths in various circumstances flashes in the headlines of local newspapers at Imphal. Is it a prelude to peace and prosperity of Manipur? Has anyone ever bothered to think about the woes of the bereaved mothers?

No wonder, Ratan Thiyam has dedicated his latest production to the mothers of Manipur: 'Bringing an end to the killings'—the message is loud and clear. War and hatred should be done away with. Only when peace prevails, can a society progress.

Margaret Ch. Zama
Mizo Literature
An Overview

The corpus of Mizo literature as it stands today is decidedly limited in scope and volume when compared with some sister states of the North-East region. Much of their oral narratives and traditional practices still require more detailed documentation, not to speak of translation efforts for wider readership. One major consideration here no doubt is the fact that the transition from a pre-literate to a literate culture came much later for them.

If legend is to be believed, the Mizo ancestors claimed to have once possessed a leather scroll wherein lay ancient records presumably in their own script. But at some point the guardians of this scroll grew careless and was unfortunately eaten up by stray dogs. The Mizo fondness for a good joke and tall tales make it difficult for most to take this story seriously. It was thanks to the efforts of the two English pioneer missionaries, J.H. Lorrain and F.W. Savidge that the Mizo got their present Roman script in the year 1894. Amongst the first great literature to have been written in this new script were the translation of the Holy Bible initiated by the two missionaries. They completed the gospels of St Luke and St John as well as the Acts of the Apostles in 1897; the two gospels were published in 1898 by the British and Foreign Bible Society. Again, Lorrain's great work, *Grammar and Dictionary of the Lushai Language*, was published by the Assam Government in 1889.

An interesting fact emerges when the topic of the first Mizo script is mentioned. This is because historically, the first attempts at putting the Mizo language into the Roman script took place 25 years prior to 1894, by Lt. Col. Thomas Herbert Lewin, who was Deputy Commissioner at the time, fondly christened Thangliana, by the Mizos. His book *Wild Races of South Eastern India* (1870) contain some 27 pages about the Mizo tribe including a number of Mizo words in the Roman script.[1] This was followed, more significantly, by his book entitled *Progressive Colloquial Exercises in the Lushai Dialect of the Dzo or Kuki languages with Vocabularies and Popular Tales* (1874). Another historic book in this connection was *A Grammar of the Lushai Language*, to which are appended a few illustrations of the Zou or Lushai popular songs and translations from *Aesop's Fables* (1884) written by Brojo Nath Shaha. These earliest exercises in the language became useful primers for the two English missionaries before they entered the then Lushai Hills.[2] Meanwhile, it is interesting to note that the Meiteis of Manipur trace the existence of their script back to the 8th century in the inscriptions found in 10 bronze coins issued by King Khongtekcha (763–773).[3]

The above summation is not an attempt to justify the present literary output of the Mizo but rather to highlight the many areas, yet unexplored, which are now ripe and ready for intensive research. As a case in point, in the course of writing this paper, I realize that my scope will be limited to Mizo literature of the state of Mizoram, and not necessarily the literature of *Zo hnahthlak* or descendants sharing common Zo ancestry, such as the Hmar, Kuki and Gangte of Manipur, the Biahte of North Cachar and Meghalaya, the Hrangkhawl and Langrawng of Tripura and Cachar, nor even the Lai (Pawis) and Mara (Lakhers) of southern Mizoram. Scholarly research is yet to make headway in efforts to compile, document and initiate critical studies

---

[1] Laltluangliana Khiangte (ed.), 2006, *Thuhlaril*, 4th edition, College Text Book (Mizo) Editorial Board, p. 127.

[2] B. Lalthangliana, 1993, *Mizo Literature*, Aizwal: RTM Press, p. 85.

[3] T. Bijoykumar Singh, 2002, 'Fiction in Manipur', *New Frontiers* (Journal of the North-East Writers' Forum), Vol. V, Guwahati, p. 74.

of this collective literary trove, not to mention the dearth of translated works. There are a number of well-known composers and writers amongst these tribal communities making rich contribution. Mention may be made of Hnialum and V. Lalchhawna of the Lai community, Hrachu and Kauva of the Mara community and Laldena of the Hmar community amongst many more.

Mizo literature like many others, first emerged out of ancient folk songs and narratives that generated besides the chants and songs, their many ballads, proverbs and narratives (tales, legends, myths). This oral tradition has also proved to be an invaluable source of data for the tracing of their culture and structuring of their history, in the absence of written historical records. They help throw light on their long migration trail from Central Asia, their way of life, important events like wars and famines, while at the same time expressing their deepest sentiments and aspirations. Their early songs and chants, seemingly a natural outcome of their poetic and nostalgic nature, first originated as couplets which later developed into longer, more complicated forms. They seem to have emerged not out of a conscious effort to compose but rather out of a spontaneous need. The first chants called *thruthmum zai*, literally meaning 'song sung in one place', were in fact dirges expressing grief at the loss of lives brought on by the famine known as *thingpui tram*. Other song chants of this early period of 1300–1450 approx.,[4] include lullabies, *hlado* and *bawhhla* of hunters and warriors, the first to celebrate game killed during a hunt, the latter for enemies killed in battle.

As the Mizo progressed in dress, food habits and lifestyle, so too did their songs. Both the *Chawngchen zai* and *Chai zai* were celebratory in nature and sung by the community. The latter was mostly performed during the Chapchar Kut festival when all men and women came out together in a clearing to dance, and celebrate the completion of their jhums for rice cultivation. More complex songs of later period reveal a unique feature, which is, that the original composers of these folk songs are identified, and happen to be women, and the later songs composed in the same tradition continued to bear their names. Thus we have *Pi Hmuaki zai, Lianchhiari zai, Laltheri zai, Darpawngi zai* and *Saikuti zai*, among others.

Pi Hmuaki was the first known composer and legend has it that the chief and village elders finally had her buried alive for fear she would finish composing all the songs and leave nothing for posterity. Her

---

[4] B. Lalthangliana, 1993.

singing accompanied by her gong was heard for seven days before it finally stilled. Numerous stories have been woven around the love story of Lianchhiari (1760 approx.) a chief's daughter, and Chawngfianga, a commoner. Their thwarted love provoked her into composing some of the most touching and enduring love songs.

The songs of Laltheri (1850–1860 approx) and Darpawngi (1880–1890 approx.)[5] may be said to be revolutionary in nature for they were amongst the first to have brought about social change of some significance in Mizo history. Laltheri was the daughter of a Sailo chief who fell in love with, and became pregnant by a commoner named Chalthanga. He was killed at the order of her father for this was a right they claimed over a layman who dared to be the lover of their women. In her grief Laltheri stripped herself naked and refused to eat, using her shame and humiliation as weapons to defy her family. Her songs tell of her great sorrow yet defied and mocked the vanity of the Sailo clan of whom it was said that 'they walked between the sun and the moon'—such was their absolute sovereignty in their heyday. Her songs had the desired impact and is believed to have brought about a gradual change in the relation between chiefs and their subjects. *Darpawngi zai* came to prominence for two reasons. She was the first to compose *Lusun zai* or songs of lamentation brought on by her intense grief at the death of her three-year old son, and more importantly, she was the first commoner to dare, rebel and challenge through her songs, the injustice she suffered under her chief, songs that had the power to move the institution of the chieftainship.

The oral narrative genre of myths, legends and tales bear witness to the fact that the Mizo had a rich and fantastic imagination. This is borne out by the thematically rich tales of etiology; tales of the existence of a path between heaven and earth where young men go courting their beloved into the other world; tales of metamorphosis like *keimi* or 'tiger-man', and stories like *Tlingi and Ngama* which reveal the belief of Mizo ancestors in the journey into afterlife, passing through *Rih dil,* a lake, and onto *mitthi khua,* the abode of the dead.

With the passing of time, the themes become more daring and indicative of the progress that was made not only in the expression of their creativity, but also in the development of form and technique. The concept of reincarnation especially of lovers, into creatures such as the butterfly, cicada, a bird, or even a star, becomes a common theme. Some

[5] B. Lalthangliana, 1993, pp. 77–8.

tales also show brave men and women not afraid to challenge and overcome fearsome creatures such as the ogress. Mizo folk literature is also enriched by a unique collection of tales associated with the legendary Chhura who runs the gamut of roles from brother, husband, fool and trickster, to culture hero. In him is fused both positive and negative traits, and is in many ways a reflection of the various aspects of the native Mizo character itself.

That an overview of Mizo literature should dwell at some length on the oral tradition is significant. The later predominance of religious and secular songs or 'poems with tunes' of various hues composed throughout the twentieth century, and the parallel dismal output of poetry genre as we understand it in literature today, is a point worth pondering upon. The Mizo may be said to have an innate musical talent and love for singing, and it is the early chants, songs and narratives that root them in a culture that otherwise would have been lost without record, and is recognized as the cornerstone of their past and present creative output. But if being musically gifted is reason enough to be more prone to express emotions and sentiments through songs, and if proximity to, and love for, nature be another reason, the same may be said of many others, not only the Mizo.

This issue has of late, prompted an academic debate of sorts as to whether or not the syllabus at college and post-graduate level should now consider excluding the 'song poems', be they secular or religious, and include only poetry. Though the output of the new crop of talented Mizo poets is encouraging, it might still take awhile for the poetry genre to truly come of age. Meanwhile, it would be unreasonable to abruptly exclude the very same 'song poems' taught and studied over the decades, on the grounds that they are now no longer deemed to be true poetry. They should be replaced gradually and judiciously.

Ever since the arrival of the two Christian missionaries mentioned earlier, in 1894, and the key role that they played in ushering literacy to 'this bloodthirsty race',[6] followed by the conversion of the Mizo to Christianity, literary output till date, continues to be influenced to a great extent by a non-secular mindset. Leaving aside the body of writings of religious content and the composition of numerous hymns of the period spanning the decades from the 1920s and 1930s onwards, prose writing also began to make its mark with essayists like C. Thuamluaia,

---

[6] Mangkhosat Kipgen, 1997, *Christianity and the Mizo Culture*, Aizwal: Mizo Theological Conference, p. 193.

Kaphleia, Zikpuii pa, Thanpuii pa and Rev. Zairema. A huge body of songs was also composed during this period on themes of love, nature and patriotism, spanning the traditional to modern. Names of some well-known composers that come to mind are Awithangpa (1887–1965), Hrawva (1893–1956), Rokunga (1914–1969), Vankhama (1906–1971), Lalzova (1924–1945) and P.S. Chawngthu (1922–2005). Mizo literature saw the birth of the first Mizo novel in *Hawilopari* (1936) by Biakliana, quickly followed by the short stories *Lali* (1937) by the same author and *Chhingpuii* (1938) by Kaphleia. Lalzuithanga whose creative works were printed long after he died in 1950, followed with *Thlahrang* (1977) and *Phira leh Ngurthanpari* (1994). The novel has since continued to enrich the Mizo literary corpus immensely.

Drama writing as a full-fledged genre had a late start. In fact, the first published drama was *Sangi Inleng* by Lalthangfala Sailo, written in 1959 but published five years later in 1963. There is something to be said though, about the Mizo society's initial encounter with drama which to me, has a significance all its own. The earliest skits were prepared purely for staging to celebrate the special occasion of Christmas, and had strong entertainment value which revealed Mizo satirical wit and humour. The first audiences were a people undergoing the initial and very significant transition from an isolated pre-literate tribal society, to one which adopted in a very short span of time, a foreign religion from the West, and whose new mindset was being moulded totally by the white man from across the sea. The Mizo alienation from mainstream India, already nursed and facilitated by the British occupation since 1890, was continued by the white missionaries and accepted without question by the people. To state that the colonization of the Mizo land, soul and mind was hence synchronized effortlessly and changed the dynamics of a whole society, would be no exaggeration.

The year of the first annual Christmas celebration recorded as 1912 by Lianhmingthanga[7] was a pot-pourri of various items and skits that portrayed encounters between an elderly Englishman and a 'Mosolman', a 'Khasi Dialoch', dialogue between a Christian and a non-Christian, the explanation of the Christmas story, song presented by a 30 member choir and so on, though not necessarily in this order. That this provided good opportunity to spread the Gospel was obvious while also catering to the audience's thirst for entertainment through skits riddled with comic situations. The most notable skit of this first concert was believed

---

[7] Laltluangliana, pp. 222–3.

to be *Borsap lem leh thu chhia nei tu leh rasi lem chang be*, a hilarious court case brought before the Superintendent. The next Christmas concert of 1913 witnessed, amongst other items, a choir Christmas carol rendition in English called *Oh Merry, merry, merry, Christmas chime*. The third religious revival of 1919 supposedly affected a temporary lull, though staged plays continued sporadically elsewhere and gradually took on the garb of a more secular nature.

Satirical songs that provoke and lampoon individuals or groups, though not necessarily unique to the Mizo, makes interesting study, for apart from the creativity and way with words, they reflect the social, religious and political turmoil that the tribe underwent even as it found itself caught up in events beyond their control and sometimes, beyond their understanding. What may be termed as 'war of songs' between villages under different chiefs used to eventually provoke brutal raids on each other that did not spare even the women and children. The famous 'Chhim leh Hmar Indo' (war of south and north), 1849–1856, between the descendants of Chief Rolura of the south and those of Chief Lallula of the north was over territorial rights, while 'Chhak leh Thlang Indo' (war of east and west), 1877–1880, between the descendants of Chief Lalsavunga of the east and those of Chief Manga of the west, was believed to have been originally provoked by broken vows over a maiden involving the sons of two chiefs. It was the numerous 'war of songs' which first built up resentment and enmity that finally resulted in the outbreak of these famous wars in the history of the Mizo. Such is the power of words, whether sung or put down in print.

This is not all. Even the revered white missionary was not spared. Though conversion to Christianity had a relatively smooth passage, it was not without its detractors who not only refused to convert but poked fun at the new believers. There were satiric songs that echoed their resentment at the banning of the traditional rice beer or *zu* for the new converts, while others scoffed at the practice of *buhfai tham*, wherein a handful of rice before cooking of meals in Christian homes, was put aside for the church. One such song mocks this by asking whether the saviour is starving, and the composer goes on to sing that he does not believe this is so when he sees the huge amount of collected foodgrain on Sunday evenings!

Such provocative and satirical 'war of songs' have today evolved into powerful election weapons for political parties. It was the Mizo Union party born in 1946, and incidentally the first political party of Mizoram, which started the trend way back in 1947 when a split occurred and the conflict was given vent to in songs composed by both the quarrelling sides. But this took on more spiteful and provocative overtones with the electioneering songs of the 1980s and 1990s.

The present day literary output continues the trend of the previous decades with its new crop of writers and composers, but rather than dwell on enumerating names and book titles, an attempt is made here to highlight some new trends that have emerged with the years to enrich Mizo literature. The underground movement of Mizoram (1966–1986) has now begun to generate fictional and non-fictional writings which one may term 'conflict or insurgency literature/writings'. There was no spurt of such writings at the height of the actual uprising. Fictional works such as *Silaimu Ngaihawm* (1992)[8] and *Rinawmin* (1970) by James Dokhuma, and *Nunna Kawngthuam Puiah* (1989) by Zikpuii Pa are the few but noteworthy novels which use the period and incidents of the rebellion as setting for their novels.

However, the literary output based on this dark period obviously still has a long way to go. There is to me, a niggling suspicion of the presence of a certain reluctance to delve, and portray experiences while the repositories are still alive. But the unlocking of memories has begun and the genre is likely to recreate and deal with highly sensitive, complex and controversial themes in the years to come. A case in point was the release of a non-fiction book entitled *Zofate Zinkawngah: Zalenna Mei a Mit Tur a Ni Lo* (2006) by R. Zamawia, ex-defence minister and army chief of the erstwhile Mizo National Front (MNF) underground. This book is an insider's version of the inside story, considered by many to be a crucial future reference for the rewriting of the history of the MNF movement.

Because creative writing did not flourish at the height of the underground movement, the creative role of giving vent to sentiments of nostalgia, anger, frustration and patriotism, seem to have been taken on by song writers. True that some noted patriotic songs such as *Zoram nuam* (1937) and *Zoram ka ram* (1939) had been earlier composed by Kaphleia, and several others by Rokunga, the most noted with political overtones being *Harh la*, which appeared in the third edition (1962) of a collection of songs for the youth called *Thalai Hlabu*.[9] But credit for composing songs with direct bearing on the movement goes to

---

[8] James Dokhuma, 1992, *Silaimu Ngaihawm*, 1st edition, J.D. Publication. (This fiction has been translated into English by Margaret Ch. Zama and published in *Fresh Fictions* (2005), New Delhi: Katha.

[9] B. Lalthangliana, 1993, pp. 364–5.

Laltanpuia of Sialsuk village who in 1964 composed two songs *Zoram hi kan ram ani* and *Independent kan Zoram tan,* the former still popularly sung whenever election fever hits the state.

The outbreak of armed conflict between the Indian Army and the insurgents in early March 1966 was followed by untold misery for the people, particularly those of the rural areas. One of the resultant tragedies faced by numerous villages was their forced 'grouping' to a selected village, while burning down the rest, for security and administrative convenience as well as to stem underground infiltration. James Dokhuma has poignantly described this draconian practice in his fiction *Silaimu Ngaihawm,* where the reader is informed that though such grouped villages were called Protected Progressive Village or PPV, the victimized Mizo populace angrily and derisively subverted the PPV as Public Punishment Village, and even referred to them as 'concentration camps', an obvious reference to Hitler and the Holocaust of World War II.[10] Their misery found voice in several *khawkhawm hla,* or 'songs of village groupings' and again, reflected in songs such as the two with the same title *Sialsuk khaw kan hla* composed by Laltanpuia in 1966 on the burning of his native village. The sentiments of nostalgia and sadness continues in the same vein in *Curfew kara suihlunglen* by K. Rammawia, which enlightens us to another evil of insurgency, the freedom denying curfew.

This overview of Mizo literature shows several socio-cultural-political trends and movements that have impacted the growth and evolution of this young literature. Though Mizoram has 89 per cent literacy, the second highest in the country, literacy alone does not denote nor produce rich literature per se. In order for Mizo literature to make headway meaningfully, the inhibitions that still shackle Mizo creativity must be transcended. The influence of the Church is pervasive and has not spared the thought process of the writer or composer. Literary output has to now strive to be more flexible and broad, and realize that a moralistic tone or theme is not necessarily an essential. Wider exposure to literatures of other cultures need to be encouraged even as we encourage and appreciate the creative efforts of our own. Most importantly, Mizo literature needs to address the long overdue development and application, of critical and analytical interpretation of texts to theorize, and learn how to place one's literature on an equal playing field with others. Only then will Mizo literature develop its full potential; for literature, like people, cannot flourish or bloom in isolation.

---

[10] James Dokhuma, 1992, p. 42.

Tilottoma Misra
Crossing Linguistic Boundaries
Two Arunachali Writers in Search of Readers†

The artifacts of imagination which are today recognized as important indices to the understanding of the relationship between the individual self and the public world have been given little space in most recent studies on the tribal societies of India. The focus of most of the studies on the languages of the smaller ethnic communities has been on questions of bi-lingualism, language-shift, language maintenance and on language as a rallying point of autonomy movements in the tribal areas. But the problem of language as a vehicle for articulating the growing crisis in an underdeveloped society which is trying to evolve ways to cope with the demands of modernism, has not been sufficiently researched. This paper proposes to highlight how the politics of speech has interfered with the relationship between the writer and the reading public and

---

† This article was originally published in the *Economic and Political Weekly*, Vol. XLII, No. 36, 8 September 2007.

has threatened the reception of a text in the very region which forms the material basis of its composition. While the influence of linguistic colonialism in the framing of educational policies by the successive governments which have ruled over the tribal regions of India since the British days had been detrimental to the production of creative literature in the tribal languages, the more pragmatic approach to the politics of speech adopted by the tribal leadership in the hill states of north-east India also has not been very conducive to the growth of such literature. For, language cannot be separated from the material lives of the people and from the culture which it reflects. 'Reality for each society,' says Stephen Greenblatt, 'is constructed to a significant degree out of the specific qualities of its language and symbols.'[1] A writer who tries to depict that reality in a language other than his/her own, is faced with the difficulties of translating the images, symbols and idioms of his/her native speech into a new language and in that process he/she often fails to grasp the reality. 'Discard the particular words and you have discarded the particular men', says Greenblatt.

The tribal people of north-east India came into the fold of nationalist politics only after Independence. In Nagaland and Arunachal Pradesh, for instance, where people speak a variety of languages not intelligible to each other, the process of nation-building has of necessity pushed language politics to the back seat and a more pragmatic attitude towards speech has been adopted. Perhaps the emerging nationalist politics in these regions have set a new trend by rejecting language as an important marker of the cultural identity of a people and people now prefer to remember their past in an acquired language which can bind communities together.

When Yeshe Dorje Thongchi[2] and Lummer Dai[3] write in Asamiya, they create a new tradition in Arunachali writing as well as in Asamiya

---

[1] Stephen J. Greenblatt, 1992, 'Learning to Curse: Aspects of Linguistic Colonialism in the Sixteenth Century', in *Leaning to Curse: Essays in Early Modern Culture*, Routledge, p. 32.

[2] Yeshe Dorje Thongchi (1952) belongs to the West Kameng district of Arunachal Pradesh. Educated at the Bomdila H.E. School. He graduated with Honours in Assamese literature from Cotton College, Guwahati. He holds a postgraduate degree in Assamese Literature from the Guwahati University. At present a senior IAS officer in Arunachal Pradesh, he is the author of several novels and short stories in Asamiya and is a recipient of the Sahitya Akademi award for his novel *Mouna Ounth Mukhar Hriday*.

[3] Lummer Dai (1941–2002), was born in Pasighat in the Siang district of Arunachal Pradesh. After completing his school education at Pasighat, he graduated

writing. When Mamang Dai records the ancient legends of the Adis preserved in the collective memory of the people, she uses the English language with the lyrical softness of an Adi rhapsodist chanting his songs amidst the hidden mountains.[4] Her rich and vibrant language may not be her mother tongue, but she has made it her own in the most convincing manner. The following passage, describing the haunting melodies of the rhapsodist and the rhythmic movements of the *ponung* dancers, convey an idea of a new literary tradition that has been born in Arunachali literature as well as in Indian English fiction:

They have not slept for many nights. If they close their eyes for a minute, if their souls stray, if they miss a step, then the journey will be over before its time and they will return to the present overwhelmed with a sorrow that will haunt them to an early death. The man who leads them is dressed in a woman's ga-le and wears the dumling, an intricate hair ornament that swings with the rhythm of his chanting. He is the miri, the shaman and the rhapsodist. Tonight the dancers have arrived at the crucial point in the narration of their history where they will 'travel the road'.[5]

The writers from Arunachal Pradesh have crossed the linguistic barriers decisively in order to create a literature of their own. Their fictional works can claim a double parentage and are 'twice-born' (to borrow a term from Meenakshi Mukherjee)[6] in the true sense of the term because they belong both to the tradition of Arunachali literature as well as to the literatures of the native speakers of the languages which they have chosen to make the vehicles of their own thoughts. A writer's works do not cease to be defined by the region with which he/she is identified and which has shaped his/her sensibilities in the first place only because his/her chosen medium is not the mother tongue but an acquired language. At the same time, the acquired languages may create a distance between the writer and her world because there would always be the native speakers of those languages who would claim that the languages were theirs before they were acquired by the others. For the writers too, the distant lands from where the languages came would always remain the ultimate 'repository of the word' with which they

---

from Cotton College, Guwahati and served as an officer in the Arunachal Pradesh Government. He has authored several novels in Asamiya.

[4] Mamang Dai, a former civil servant, was born in Pasighat in the East Siang District of Arunachal Pradesh. She is a journalist, a poet and a fiction writer.

[5] Mamang Dai, 2006, *The Legends of Pensam*, New Delhi: Penguin, p. 50.

[6] Meenakshi Mukherjee, 1971, *The Twice Born Fiction: Themes and Techniques of the Indian Novel in English*, Heinemann.

would continue to struggle to express their ideas or feelings.[7] For many writers, the decision to write in an acquired language is also based on the desire to target a readership which is wider than the limited one available in one's own native tongue. The writers from many of the smaller ethnic communities of northeastern India whose native languages do not have a script of their own or are spoken by only a handful of people have, however, adopted English as their acquired speech not merely out of choice but because the policy decisions of the state governments in these regions have favoured English above other languages as the medium of instruction in schools. Even in Arunachal Pradesh, Hindi which had once eased out Asamiya from the schools, has now been replaced by English and this decision was not propelled by any imperialistic design of a foreign power but as a measure taken by the post-colonial state to set the wheels of 'progress' rolling. It would be necessary to locate the linguistic situation of the present-day Arunachal Pradesh in its historical context in order to understand the effect of the past on the present.

The long tract of hilly country bordering Bhutan, Tibet, China and Burma was historically almost a virgin land largely undisturbed by the succession of Ahom rulers in the Brahmaputra valley and by the later colonial projects of exploitation which often go by the name of development. Myths, however, continue to speak of contacts between rulers from the Brahmaputra valley establishing kingdoms in the fringes of the hills at some mythological period. The stories of Parasuram's journey to the source of the Brahmaputra, of the legendary king Bhismak and his daughter Rukmini who was carried away by Krishna, of Bana's grandson Bhaluk who set up his capital at Bhalukpung, of the fugitive Kalita king Ramchandra who built a brick fort near the present-day capital of Arunachal Pradesh, have often been cited as instances of mythical connection between the hills and the plains.[8] Historical records tell us however that the powerful Ahom kings of Assam followed a policy of non-interference in the affairs of the hill people except to carry out punitive raids in response to occasional raids and encroachment into Ahom territories by the different tribes inhabiting the surrounding hills. The British when they took over the administration of Assam in the early nineteenth century, continued the

---

[7] Edward Said, in *Culture and Imperialism* (London: Verso 1994), uses this argument to describe the relationship between the educated native bourgeoisie of the colonies and the languages of the white men which they have acquired and made their own (p. 270).

[8] Verrier Elwin, 1964 [1957], *A Philosophy for NEFA*, Shillong, pp. 1–2.

same policy of non-interference towards the hill people of the frontier regions. They kept up a rudimentary semblance of administration in the region through their political officer stationed at Sadiya on the bank of the Brahmaputra in the northeastern corner of Assam. Occasionally, punitive raids were carried out in the surrounding hills to ward off any possible threat to the colonial projects in the valley.[9] But, the imperial zeal to map, control and possess territories of strategic importance, did not fail to motivate the British to work through organizations like the Topographical Survey which undertook hazardous expeditions into the interior regions of the area identified as the North East Frontier Agency (NEFA). These expeditions were primarily aimed at discovering alternate trade routes to Tibet and China.[10]

The government of independent India did not consider it expedient to abandon the British policy at one stroke and strike out in a completely new direction. On the contrary it followed in the lines of the colonial administration which was only discreetly modified to accommodate developmental projects without disturbing the existing tribal structures. The 'Nehru Plan' which was largely an endorsement of Verrier Elwin's vision for administering the NEFA as set out in his book *A Philosophy for NEFA* (1959), followed a policy of not 'over-administering' these regions, but to bring in new ideas slowly. Nehru's clear directive in this mater has been succinctly put forward in the following words: 'We cannot allow matters to drift in the tribal areas or just not take interest in them. In the world of today that is not possible or desirable. At the same time we should avoid over-administering these areas and, in particular, sending too many outsiders into tribal territory.'[11]

---

[9] T.T. Cooper refers to the attack on the British garrison at Sadiya by the Khamtis resulting in the death of Lt. Col. White. He also gives an account of the careful policy of conciliation followed by the British in that area after the incident: 'Some of the tribes such as the Abors, Dufflahs, Nagas and others had levied tribute from the people of the plains from time immemorial, and were accustomed to receive it as a right. When the Indian Government interfered with their privileges in this respect, the hill tribes resorted to these predatory visits... And a knowledge of this fact induced the Government to enter into an arrangement with the different tribes, by which each should receive a yearly present of cloth, beads etc., as an equivalent for the former tribute... this policy was found to succeed most admirably, and predatory incursions of late years have been few and far between' (*The Mishmee Hills: An account of the journey made in an attempt to penetrate Tibet from Assam to open new routes for commerce*, 1995 [1873], rpt., New Delhi, p. 131).

[10] See Cooper, Chapter 1.

[11] Jawaharlal Nehru, 1959, 'Foreword to the Second Edition', in Verrier Elwin, *A Philosophy for NEFA*, Shillong.

The Nehru Plan sought to take up development projects to improve roads and communication, education and medical facilities as well as to introduce better agricultural techniques. But all these steps were to be initiated keeping in view the primary concern that 'people should develop along the lines of their own genius and we should avoid imposing anything on them'. Whether this policy was actually followed in the letter and spirit, especially in the matter of adopting a medium of instruction in the schools, would be discussed below.

Amongst the projects that were taken up most vigorously in the post-Independence NEFA were establishment of schools in the interior regions and building of new roads to connect the hills with the plains. The early pioneers in both these fields were a band of enthusiastic school teachers and engineers from Assam who went into the most inaccessible areas to set up government schools and to assist in the road-building projects. The zeal and earnestness of some of the Assamese school teachers of those days has left their indelible marks on a whole generation of educated people in Arunachal today who had their initial education through the medium of the Asamiya language.[12] Many of those early writers and intellectuals from NEFA acquired such fluency and skill in handling the language that without being their mother-tongue it became their 'own tongue' which enabled them to use it for creative purposes.

Before entering into the fictional worlds of two of the writers from Arunachal Pradesh, Lummer Dai and Yeshe Dorje Thongchi, it is necessary to go into the historical context of the language situation in the Arunachal Pradesh and the response of the writers to the situation. Arunachal Pradesh is a state composed of heterogeneous linguistic and cultural groups. There are at least 25 major tribes speaking as many languages which are mutually unintelligible. The situation is similar in Nagaland too. As is common in such situations elsewhere, local pidgins or creolized languages have developed over the years for inter-group communication. These languages have become de facto lingua franca

---

[12] The autobiography of one such teacher, Annada Prasad Borthakur, provides valuable insight into the changes in the educational scenario in NEFA which took place between the forties and the eighties of the last century and the groundwork done by the Assamese teachers and educationists for the spread of primary and secondary education in the hills. See Annada Prasad Borthakur, 2004, *Chan Poharat Arunachal*, Moranhat.

of the people.[13] In Nagaland and Arunachal Pradesh varieties of pidgin languages with Asamiya as a superstrate, known as Nagamese and Nefamese, are still being widely used for oral communication. These languages are also languages of the marketplace because local traders in the various rural markets bordering the hills communicate with each other in these tongues. But, in recent years there has been a marked change in the attitude of the tribal people towards these contact languages. After the introduction of Hindi as the official language and the medium of instruction in the secondary schools of NEFA in 1956, and of English as the official language of Nagaland after it attained statehood, the status of the link-languages has undergone a drastic change. As the census figures of the two states show, people are generally reluctant to admit bilingualism and the young, educated sections are especially averse to admitting the pidgin languages as their lingua franca. This is a general tendency noticeable in other tribal regions of the country as well.[14]

This tendency is the outcome of the process of identity assertion as well as that of a major political decision of the government of India in the post-Independence era. The policy of faster and more effective 'integration' of the tribals into the Indian 'mainstream' saw the vigorous pursuit of the policy of spreading the use of Hindi in NEFA, a policy that went against the so-called Nehru Plan of trusting the 'natural genius of the people'. According to some analysts, the motive force behind this political decision to integrate the region with the mainland India rather than with Assam was the impending threat of Chinese

---

[13] Linguists have offered different definitions of 'pidgins' and 'Creole' languages. Though many believe that creoles developed out of pidgins in some parts of the world, others hold that each has an independent existence. Pidgin languages are simple modes of communication without complex grammatical rules, between two groups of people who speak different languages but who need to communicate with each other for trade and other reasons. Pidgins do not attain the status of the mother tongue and it is usually learnt as a second language by the people who use them. According to some linguists, pidgins are generally created out of three different languages of which one is the superstrate or the dominant tongue. Creoles also are mixed languages; but they are used as vernaculars by the speakers. Creole languages, like the race denoted by the term, have strong colonial connotations because they usually developed in the European colonies where the speech of the native speakers of the European language (usually the indentured workers) would be heavily influenced by the language of the local people.

[14] L.M. Khubchandani, 1993, 'Tribal Identity in Plurilingual Milieu', in M. Miri (ed.), *Continuity and Change in Tribal Society*, Shimla: IIAS, p. 539.

attack in the late fifties[15]. This political decision has played a crucial role in deciding the fate of the new generation of tribal students who are forced to adapt themselves to a situation where they can no longer cultivate a literal form of their oral contact-language for more sophisticated forms of communication. Tribal children were compelled to familiarize themselves with the Devnagri script and the alien sounds of the Hindi language. R.S. Rangila has pointed out the effect of such political decisions regarding language on the lives of the tribal people elsewhere in India. His focus is on the Wagri areas of Rajasthan where the decision to promote Hindi in the tribal areas has been guided more by political considerations than by a genuine concern for the progress of education.[16]

The case of the Arunachali people is however more problematic. Here Hindi was totally unfamiliar to the people at the time of its introduction, though the situation has changed considerably after the invasion of the Indian market, especially in the form of the Bombay films and the TV. When the NEFA administration which was manned by representatives of the central government from the Hindi 'heartland' (NEFA at that time being under the Ministry of External Affairs, with the Governor of Assam acting as the agent of the President of India) took the decision to remove Asamiya from the post-elementary stage of education, there was considerable bewilderment amongst the tribal people. This was reflected in the contents of the two memoranda submitted by them to the government pleading for the retention of Asamiya at the primary level in schools because it was the natural language for inter-tribal communication.[17] When the Asamiya language was ultimately replaced by Hindi in all schools of NEFA, a major rift was created between the hills and the plains because the Assamese teachers were gradually replaced by a new set of teachers who, like the administrators and the army personnel whose presence was considerable in the region, had little or no contact with the distinct history and culture of the hill people.

The relationship between the people of the Brahmaputra valley and those of the hills was, on the other hand, based on common memories

[15] See B.G. Verghese, 1996, *India's Northeast Resurgent; Ethnicity, Insurgency, Governance, Development*, Delhi, Chapter 11.

[16] R.S. Rangila, 'Pressure of Change on Language and Ecology in Indian Tribal Society', in Mrinal Miri (ed.), *Continuity and Change*, p. 514.

[17] One of these was signed by 'the tribal students of NEFA' and the other by the tribal people of Lohit Frontier Division. See Parag Chaliha (ed.), 1958, *The Outlook on NEFA*, Jorhat: Assam Sahitya Sabha.

of shared historical experiences and cultural practices. Despite the peripheral nature of the contact, there were many points of cultural similarity in dress, food habits, music, dance and folk festivals between the people of the valley and the hills. Language was only one of the natural manifestations of these cultural ties. This tradition of 'mutual friendliness between the tribes of the foothills and people of the Brahmaputra valley' has been commented upon by Verrier Elwin who had carried out extensive studies on the culture of the northeastern region. He has also observed the fact that 'many of the leading tribal people, and particularly those along the foothills speak Assamese and they are now learning Hindi as well'.[18] But, when it came to the problem of 'integration' of the tribes with India, Elwin's views corroborated those of the policy makers at the Centre who had their own rigid views about the 'mainstream' and the 'periphery'. The following words of Elwin defending the Government of India's policy smack of that prejudicial notion:

The NEFA administration has been accused of isolating the hill people from the plains, the most curious charge being that they are doing this by stressing the national language in schools. This, of course is nonsense. The Administration is not isolating the tribal people at all. Indeed, if it is to be criticized, it might rather be on the ground that it is bringing them a little too quickly into the main stream of modern life... It is encouraging both the national language and Assamese to help the tribesmen to communicate more readily with the outside world; it takes schoolboys on tours round India and sends parties regularly to New Delhi on great occasions... its officers are penetrating into the wildest regions with the message that beyond the hills there is a friendly world with a desire to help and serve.[19]

The policy of 'integrating' the tribal people with the 'mainstream' through exposure to the 'national culture', however, ironically backfired in later times. Almost every tribal state of the region—Meghalaya, Mizoram, Nagaland and Arunachal Pradesh—virtually rejected Hindi as the medium of instruction and introduced English which subsequently became the official language of the state. In their 'march towards modernity', the tribal leaders did not waste precious time bickering over the suitability of one or the other tribal language or Hindi as the medium of instruction in schools, but opted for a language that would put them at par with the ruling elite of the 'mainstream'. The newly emerging

---

[18] Verrier Elwin, *A Philosophy for NEFA*, p. 4.
[19] Ibid., p. 47.

tribal elite in these states had realized that in modern India no matter how emotional one might get about one's mother tongue, no regional language can empower the people as much as the English language can. The contribution of the English language in creating a divide between the powerful elite and the powerless Other, irrespective of caste or race, has been commented upon perceptively by Madhu Kishwar in a recently published article: 'The English-speaking pan-Indian elite [which] is entrenched in the higher echelons of bureaucracy, politics, the armed forces, corporate business and diverse professions... act as though they alone have a national perspective on vital issues of national importance and the regional language elites represent narrow sectarian and divisive tendencies.'[20]

The tribal elite of the northeastern states have unambiguously taken up a stand in favour of joining the ever-growing 'New Brahmin' class of India which is at home with the English language rather than being left behind with the 'New Dalits' who speak and write in the regional languages. Historical factors like the activities of the Christian missionaries in the region have also contributed to the strengthening of such an attitude. Most tribal leaders of the region today assert unambiguously that it is more in their advantage to opt for a 'useful' language as the medium for school education rather than languages which are merely spoken by the people. A Naga intellectual has posed a series of questions in a recent article: 'How useful is Bengali to the tribals of Tripura? How useful is Assamese to the tribals of Assam? And how useful is Meiteilon to the tribals of Manipur? For that matter, how useful is any regional or state language to the tribals of that region or state anywhere?'[21]

The pidgin languages (called Nagamese in Nagaland and Nefamese in Arunachal Pradesh) which have served as the link languages in some of the multilingual hill states have also failed to acquire the status of a 'useful' regional language because, as a Naga politician has pointed out, these languages do not have 'native' roots. But, elaborating this point further, he comes to the more significant argument that these languages are not 'respectable' enough:

---

[20] Madhu Purnima Kishwar, 2006, 'Diagnosing and Remedying Backwardness: English Education Defines the New Brahmins and the New Dalits in India', *Manushi*, No. 154, May–June.

[21] T.A. Shishak, 2001, 'North East Tribals and the Language Issue', in R. Sachdeva (ed.), *Language Education in Nagaland*, New Delhi, p. 29.

As a lingua franca Nagamese is O.K. But it would be unwise to make it a common written language—I think that's the way in the present situation Nagas would feel—the situation can change, but it must change with the will of the people, and Nagamese may be difficult to accept. Nagamese is not based on any of our Naga Languages, its roots are not 'native', and it is not a Naga language—not a marker of Naga Identity. It is a borrowed languge and people don't want to give it a place in their culture. Personally, I'd rather speak Hindi, which is much more respectable and useful.[22]

The regional languages in India today seem to be fighting a losing battle everywhere in the country and the future of creative literature in these languages hangs in the balance. The two Arunachali writers whose works had created a new tradition in Arunachali literature as well as in Asamiya literature have become representatives of a tragic generation of creative writers whose works are no longer read by their own people because they are written in a language that is not 'useful' to the new generation. Lummer Dai accepted his death as a writer long before death actually snatched him away. This reticent, introvert writer once shared his painful thoughts with a fellow writer, Yeshe Dorje Thongchi who was still treading the thorny path. 'Writers like you and me,' he said, 'have no place in Arunachal Pradesh. In fact, people ridicule us because we write in Asamiya. When I sit down to write, these thoughts trouble me and I say to myself, for whom should I write and what? Is there any use in writing? And then my pen stands still, my words dry up.'[23]

These words reflect an unfortunate situation when authors feel that their readers have been alienated from their works. Yet, there was a time, as Thongchi reminisces nostalgically, when young students of Arunachal who aspired to become writers themselves, read the novels of Dai with enthusiasm. The novels of Dai and Thongchi, which are sensitive representations of the lives of the people in the Arunachal hills, will perhaps have to reach their own people in translations before they are recognized as pioneers in creating a literature of Arunachal Pradesh.

---

[22] 'A View from he Top: A Dialogue with Shri Imkong, Ex-Minister of School Education, Government of Nagaland', in R. Sachdev (ed.), *Language Education in Nagaland*, p. 13.
[23] Yeshe Dorje Thongchi, 2003, 'Lummer Kakaideu' [Elder Brother Lummer], in *Ajir Asom*, Rangali Bihu Special Issue, Guwahati. [Translation mine]

II

In the Asamiya literature of the colonial period, the tribesman was represented either in accordance with the pattern set in the English literature of the nineteenth century or as he/she had been depicted in the emerging colonial discipline of anthropology. The tribal characters in the works of Lakshminath Bezbarua, Padmanath Gohainbarua or Jyotiprasad Agarwala are the 'noble savages' of an idyllic world, a world that had been idealized in English Romantic literature. The most memorable of these characters are the female characters who epitomize innocence, natural grace and simplicity. Significantly they all bear typically Assamese pet names (such as Dalimi, Chinu, Jinu, Runuk, Junuk, Thunuk). A new trend was set by Rajanikanta Bordoloi (1869–1939) in his novel *Miri Jiyori* (1894) where he attempted to combine the idyllic mode with the method of ethnographical documentation generally adopted by anthropologists. This novel, like most of his other historical novels, was based on the historical and ethnographic material collected by him as a part of his duties as a civil servant, for Sir Edward Gait's monumental work, *A History of Assam* (1905). The story of the pair of star-crossed lovers, Jonki and Panei, afforded Bordoloi the imaginative space to depict the inner workings of a tribal society where individual rights are cruelly suppressed in the interest of community rights. This theme again becomes the main focus of the novels of Dai and Thongchi, but, from a completely different perspective. Bordoloi's representation of the tribal life of the Mishing (Miri) folk was partly idyllic, focusing on the innocence, beauty and simplicity of these people living on the banks of the great river, and partly ethnographic, with details about their customs, traditional laws and religious practices. Bordoloi, however, failed to effectively integrate the two visions because he was bound by the limited perspective of an outsider for whom, despite all the sympathies of a liberal intellectual, the tribal folk remained the reified 'other'. As a narrator, he adopted the stance of the colonial ethnographer for whom the Other was always fixed in a timeless present. The tribal people, in such representations, are always referred to as a '*sui generis* configuration, often only a list of features set in a temporal order different from that of the perceiving and speaking subject.'[24] The following generalization of the Mishing people, which attempts to create a clear

---

[24] Mary Louis Pratt, 1985, 'Scratches on the Face of the Earth', *Critical Enquiry*, Antumn, p. 49.

distinction between the perception of the narrator and that of the tribal folk would adequately support this argument:

> Readers! These people came to testify as witnesses in the case, though in an unintelligible manner. None of them would concede his rigid stand on the matter. We have already stated earlier that these Miris are a secretive race. They would keep their own purpose concealed in their tummies and go around the world with an innocent face. They would never come forward to tell you the truth.[25]

The author–narrator here includes the reader in the intimate circle of 'us' who are judging and critically evaluating the other as a generic category. At one point in the same novel, even the central character, Panei, is made to recede into that mass of others when the author abandons his earlier perspective of the sympathetic observer and adopts the viewing angle of the Assamese babus who are the probable readers of his novel. The author joins them in gazing dispassionately at the inhuman scene of a tribal girl being dragged away from the District Court by her kinsmen in assertion of their traditional custom, while the British Magistrate refuses to interfere in what he perceives as the sphere of 'customary' law.

The problem of gazing at another with the purpose of wielding power over her or him has attained great significance in modern postcolonial studies. The imperial gaze, according to this view, involves how the oppressor defines the mode by which the oppressed are to be seen and also how the oppressed people are to look at themselves.[26] An even more significant aspect of this theme is the one of resistance by the Other which is expressed in the form of what, in postcolonial language, is known as 'returning the gaze'. How an apparently illiterate, powerless people, gazes back boldly at the oppressor determines the status of the people in relation to the others. In Lummer Dai's *Prithibir Hanhi* (1963) there is a brief moment of such a returned gaze when two Adi men come down to the town of Dibrugarh to sell their shawls and encounter the curious gaze of the plains people. Kardug is cunning enough to take things in his stride. But, Libo, the village idiot, is bewildered by this experience of being gazed at and innocently gazes back at them, assessing the urban culture of the plains in its true colours as inhuman and uncharitable compared to his own. In Thongchi's *Mouna Ounth Mukhar Hriday*,

---

[25] Rajanikanta Bordoloi, 1993, *Miri Jiyori*, Guwahati, p. 49.
[26] Jeremy Hawthorn, 2006, 'Theories of the Gaze', in Patricia Waugh (ed.), *Literary Theory and Criticism*, New York: Oxford University Press.

there is an even more interesting description of returning the gaze. Dilip, a man from the plains, has his first uncomfortable experience of being gazed at and assessed critically when he first encounters a tribal group in the hills: 'As soon as Dilip sat down on the blanket spread out near the fire, the people surrounded him. Their inquisitive eyes seemed to lick him up—every limb of his body. He felt like an animal in a zoo.'[27]

Lummer Dai and Yeshe Thongchi deal with the problem of defining the private space in a pre-modern community where individuals do not exist as separate units but as part of a closely knit family. Researchers of folk societies have observed that 'behaviour in the folk society is traditional, spontaneous and uncritical' and there is little scope for critical objectivity or for abstract thinking in such a society.[28] Dai and Thongchi, however, have effectively portrayed tribal characters who are questioning the validity of customs that have become inimical to a changing world. Though the revolt is not always forcefully staged, the very fact that individuals are expressing their dissent against the established norms of the tribal society, gives these novels and stories a historic status in Arunachali literature. The perceiving subject in these fictional works is not an outsider but one who is intimately a part of the tribal world. 'All these people [in my novels],' says Dai, 'are people I knew well. But, they did not come to me. I went to them on my own. I did not have any plans of writing a great novel. I merely wanted to paint a picture of these people exactly as I saw them. I got their permission to paint them. So, I drew the picture and printed it in the pages of this book.'[29] The difference in perspective of Bordoloi and the Arunachali writers becomes at once evident if one examines the following passages from their novels. Bordoloi describes a meeting of the village council of the Hill Miris who were the traditional enemies of the Mishings of the valley, in the harsh language of the imperial subject:

It is the day of the village council meeting amongst of the Hill Miris. About three scores of these Gassis have assembled. They are all wearing bamboo hats with cane belts around their waists. Each savage is carrying a *dao* in his hand and each has between his lips, a pipe made of bamboo, brass or some alloy.

---

[27] Yeshe Dorje Thongchi, 2001, *Mouna Ounth Mukhar Hriday* [Silent Lips, Resonant Heart], Guwahati, p. 10. [Translation mine]

[28] Robert Redfield, 1947, 'The Folk Society', *American Journal of Sociology*, Vol. 52, No. 4, pp. 293–308.

[29] Lummer Dai, 1963, *Prithibir Hanhi* [The Smile of the Earth], Tinsukia, Preface. [Translation mine]

They are smoking those pipes with dry leaves stuffed into them. Two pigs have been killed with iron spikes thrust through their bodies. Then the pigs were roasted whole in the fire and with blood still oozing out of them, pieces of meat were chopped off and consumed. When those demons had gorged on the meat, then each sat with his legs spread out, like real animals. Today is their big meeting. The Baregam[the headman] has made his appearance. Something important is going to be decided here. It seems as if these beasts are holding their Sessions Court![30]

The narrative stance here is one that is typically adopted by the colonial ethnographers whose accounts of the northeastern tribes often tend to deny even the basic human attributes to the tribesmen.[31] Bordoloi's wry humour in the last line, comparing the proceedings of a *kebang* to a colonial Sessions Court, seeks to project the indigenous institutions of the pre-colonial times as 'savage' and 'unjust'. Most of the writers and intellectuals of the nineteenth century had taken up such a stand in support of the colonial agenda to project the British system of governance as the best and most suitable for the Indian people. A refreshingly new stance is visible in another description of a *kebang* in Dai's *Prithibir Hanhi*. Dai too is capable of adopting a critical attitude towards the tribal institutions, but his narrative stance is free from the superior attitude of the outsider who has never lived the life of a tribesman:

A kebang is being held at the village *munsup* [a bachelor's dormitory] today. All the people have gathered there. The meting is about to begin now. Both the parties, the accused and the complainant, have brought *apang* [a drink] for all the members of the *kebang*. The village elders have come in large numbers. So, the supply of *apang* from both the parties is also proportionately plentiful.[32]

Dai and Thongchi belong to a completely different tradition of writers writing in Asamiya. They were educated in a post-colonial set-up where they never had to read textbooks that 're-presented' the indigenous people variously as 'natives', 'savages' or 'brutes'. They were the first generation of educated elite in NEFA who responded sensitively and

---

[30] Rajanikanta Bordoloi, 1993, *Miri Jiyori*, Guwahati, p. 68. [Translation mine]

[31] See, for example, T.T. Cooper's description of the Abors in *The Mishmee Hills*: '... two of the *dirty savages* put their arms in mine, while the others followed, still laughing like *fiends*, and in this order of procession we marched into the porch of the house. Here the fellows squatted themselves on their *hams* and lighted their pipes, of which each man carried one of Chinese make, purchased during their visits to the Thibetan outposts beyond the Abor hills (p. 127).' [Emphases mine]

[32] *Prithibir Hanhi*, p. 181. [Translation mine]

enthusiastically to the new programme of development and opening up of the region which was being initiated by the government of independent India. They were intensely aware of the customs and beliefs which they considered to be obstacles for progress of their societies and often severely critiqued them. The strong element of social activism in their writings with the focus on women's emancipation makes the novels of Dai and Thongchi even more powerful than some of the nineteenth century 'Renaissance' texts in Indian languages. The following dialogue between an educated Adi girl and her father who had 'sold' her in her infancy for a bride-price, is an instance of such a powerful statement:

'Marriage of an infant?' Gumba laughed aloud in mockery of the whole idea. 'An infant falling in love in her mother's womb!' The very idea was hilarious for her.
Her parents looked at her questioningly.
'Father, I am asking you. When did you sell me? At what price? Answer me.'
'Keep quiet, Yaba!' Kargum said menacingly.
'But, I must know! I should know when I was married!' Gumba replied.
'Yaba, will you be silent?' This time Kargum spoke more harshly.
'Father, I *ought* to know when and how I was sold in marriage!'
'You have been sold, that's all and you should have nothing to say on that.'
'So, I am someone else's slave, isn't it?'
'So what?'
'Father, can't you see that if I am a slave of somebody then your own blood is also a part of that slavery? And if your blood is enslaved then you too are enslaved?'[33]

The voice of protest and resistance heard in Gumba's words is the voice of the enlightened opinion that is rapidly becoming audible everywhere in the tribal societies of northeastern India. In Arunachal Pradesh, in particular, the 'great leap forward' from a primitive lifestyle to a modern one which has wrought corresponding upheavals in the sphere of ideas, has been spectacular. Social analysts have pointed out that in those remote hills, people who had never set their eyes on a simple potter's wheel or a cart wheel have suddenly been exposed to the wheels of an aircraft. How the tribal societies would adjust their existing structures to accommodate the changes would remain to be seen in the years to come. But, in the novels of Lummer Dai and Yeshe Dorje Thongchi the society is presented as amenable to change and adjustment. The demand for change comes from within and it is heard in the dissenting voice of

[33] Lummer Dai, 1982, *Koinar Mulya* [Bride Price], Tinsukia, p. 15. [Translation mine]

the younger generation of educated people. In the village kebang which is traditionally dominated by the elder males, women being in a marginalized position, the voice of the youth gradually makes itself heard. This is the message that comes through loud and clear in the last chapter of Dai's *Koinar Mulya*. There is a long and sustained debate between the two voices, of rigidity and change, in this scene. Unlike *Miri Jiyori*, the kebang in this novel is respectful of democratic norms. The opinion of the youth, including that of the women, is not suppressed, but allowed articulation. The sane, balanced views of Minjup, an educated young man of the community, is ultimately shown to turn the tide of the whole debate in favour of change. Minjup speaks patiently and reasonably without giving in to anger and passion. He even allows the right to freedom of expression to his opponent, in the true democratic spirit: 'Yejam is only expressing his opinion. Everyone has a right to speak up here. Otherwise this institution called the *kebang* will not survive.'

Minjup's long speech in support of women's emancipation from patriarchal oppression ends with a plea for a humane approach to the problem:

Why don't we understand that by adopting such a cruel attitude towards our own daughters we are only deceiving ourselves? We do not realize that by practising such an inhuman custom we are turning ourselves into creatures worst than animals. When we claim to be human beings, we are actually being more shameless than the worst of the creatures![34]

The story of Gumba's resistance, the support she receives from the educated youth of her tribe and the ultimate defeat of the forces of orthodoxy in the hands of the organized opinion of the progressive elements in the society, reads almost like some of the early Indian novels of the 'Renaissance' period. Lummer Dai, uses the novel as a vehicle for social reform and his plea for the transformation of the traditional institutions is based on rational principles. 'What is a social custom?' asks Borgan Gaken in *Koinar Mulya*. 'Should we accept as our social laws today those customs which have been practised since the time of Abotani?[35] No, I do not think so. Although our Adi society has been ruled by laws prevalent since the days of Abotani, yet, these customs have changed a thousand times in accordance with the needs of the times....' [translation mine] Dai questions the central role of the kebang in the

---

[34] *Koinar Mulya*, p. 135.
[35] The first human being according to Adi belief.

lives of the tribal people and pleads for the need for a change in these powerful traditional institutions in order to accommodate the claims of individual freedom.

At the end of *Koinar Mulya*, the opinion of the new generation prevails over that of the old and Gumba breathes in the sweet air of this newfound freedom. The loud clapping of hands from the young audience in support of the new order resounds through the hills. The sound of this clapping is almost as momentous for the future of the community as the sound of the banging door at the end of Ibsen's *Doll's House*. It registers the triumphant assertion of ideas that would change the opinion of the society regarding the status of women. Significantly, Dai's earlier novel, *Prithibir Hanhi* (1963) also ends with a kebang scene where a girl is being tried for alleged infidelity towards her husband. The novel concludes with the courageous self-sacrifice of a young girl, Liyi, in the hands of brutal patriarchal power. She speaks out defiantly in front of the elders of the kebang against the injustice and corruption of this institution. Her voice represents the voice of modernity which holds everyone spellbound in this small tribal community. But in that novel, written more than two decades before *Koinar Mulya*, the organized voice of resistance was not yet audible. The kebang, representing brute patriarchal force remains a silent spectator to the oppression of women. Perhaps, at that point of time it was not possible for Dai to visualize a more forceful ending for the novel because in the early sixties the other voice representing the modern subject who is alone capable of exercising reason and critical opinion to empathize with others beyond one's immediate family, had not yet emerged in Arunachal Pradesh.

Prithibir Hanhi is rich in intimate details about tribal life. The later novel, *Koinar Mulya*, is however more infused with an 'idea' which makes its action more concentrated and focussed. In the earlier novel, the action moves at a slower pace and the details about Adi life, as it is lived by the people, are worked out in a more leisurely manner. No writer before Lummer Dai had portrayed the inside of a bachelor's dormitory [musup] or of a family dormitory [*chang*] in such authentic colours. The strengthening of the bonds of kinship that goes with the sharing of sleeping space and the problems of the individual who betrays those bonds, are very sensitively depicted in Dai's novel. Dai looks at those secluded spaces of tribal life not with the inquisitive gaze of the anthropologist who violates the privacy of their inner spaces, but with the sympathetic eyes of someone who has lived and shared that life intimately. The almost modernist situation where a character shares his living space with others and yet feels alienated because of his mental state, has been effectively portrayed in the following passage describing the interiors of a tribal home where the son-in-law shares the sleeping space with his wife's family:

Kardug sighed deeply. He straightened his legs on the floor and looked around. It was quite dark and he could not see anything. But, every object in that room was so clearly etched in his mind that he could almost see them. On the left, in the corner near the door, was the water-rack. Near it was the place where they made the *apong* [a home-made beer]. Move a little west from there, about fifteen paces south of the hearth, was the door to the pig-sty. Southwest again, about ten paces from the hearth, was the big pestle. Next to that, hanging on the wall, were the bamboo baskets and trays...[36]

In this authentic delineation of a tribal home there is no self-consciousness of a modern individual who is jealously possessive of his 'privacy'. If Kardug is unhappy in this shared space, it is because he suspects that his wife has admitted someone else into her heart, which implies that he is ousted from her hearth. Such a unique way of presenting complex relationships between the public and the private is, one may say, a feature of Dai and Thongchi's writings which is authentically 'Arunachali' rather than 'Assamese'. It is an understanding that emerges from the very texture of the novels without any conscious philosophical intervention by the novelist.

Yeshe Dorje Thongchi represents another significant phase in the lives of the hill communities of Arunachal pradesh, the complex and difficult period of transition from a pre-modern to a modern culture. In his novels and stories one encounters the birth of a new awareness in post-Independence NEFA, about modern concepts like conservation and protection of wild life ('Guard'), a scientific attitude towards diseases including leprosy ('Papor Pukhuri'), and the popularization of modern horticultural techniques ('Apel Burha').[37] He writes about the miraculous transformation that has taken place in the lives of the common folk who had lived in isolation for ages. An illiterate villager who was once terrified by the very sound of an aircraft flying over the hills, has attained the expertise of giving smoke signals to aircrafts in the dropping zone: 'Tachuk's daily life is now timed by new concepts which include "dropping zone", "smoke signal", "wind-choke", "CPO",

---

[36] *Prithibir Hanhi*, p. 71. [Translation mine]
[37] All the stories are from the collection *Papor Pukhuri* (Guwahati, 2000).

"LM", parachute and ski-board.'[38] Such a transformation within the span of a few years, from a stage where a looking glass was the source of greatest wonder for the common folk ('Dapon') to one where villagers can talk easily about the difference between a Dakota, a Caribou, a helicopter or a big AN-32,[39] has been realistically depicted in Thongchi's writings. Thongchi, however is also assailed by doubts about this rapid pace of change in the hills and looks critically at the concepts of 'progress' and 'modernity' in relation to the more healthy values of the past.[40] He has seen the positive effect of modern education and developmental projects like road-building, in a backward region. But, he has also discovered the rapid destruction of those elements of tribal culture which had kept a society together with bonds of kinship, loyalty and trust. The forces of modernization have swept away many of the positive values associated with traditional relationships and Thongchi observes with distress the price one has to pay for 'civilization':

When this road-building project would be completed, many good people would come along this road from the plains to spread the light of knowledge, to offer their services in the health sector and to take up other projects for the good of the hill people. But, along with them would come those hoards of exploiters—the thieves and robbers, the masked gentlemen. Unrest and discontentment would also spread to these hills some day. The tribal culture of the local people would gradually disappear when pitched against the onslaught of an alien culture, language, dress and manners...[41]

The problem of defining the individual's private space in a primitive society where the claims of the self are submerged in those of the community, is again portrayed effectively in Dorje Thongchi's novel *Mouna Ounth Mukhar Hriday*. Rinsin and Yama love each other intensely. But, they can never marry because they belong to different tribes and Yama has already been sold off to another man by her family. So, though there is no dearth of sympathy for the lovers from their young friends and relatives, still there is no protest when Yama is carried away by force by the men from her 'husband's' clan. The situation is almost similar to that in Dai's novels and in Bordoloi's *Miri Jiyori*. Thongchi depicts it realistically without any attempt to romanticize it beyond the limits of plausibility. It shows that the author is aware of the fact

---

[38] Y.D. Thongchi, 'Smoke Signal', in *Papor Pukhuri*.
[39] Ibid.
[40] Y.D. Thongchi, 'Elagi Tasspat', in *Papor Pukhuri*.
[41] Y.D. Thongchi, *Mouna Ounth Mukhar Hriday*, p. 62. [Translation mine]

that the question of the status of women needs to be reviewed urgently if integration of the tribes in the new state is to take place effectively. Mouna Ounth also highlights another interesting dimension of the problem of intra-tribal communication in a multilingual tribal society of Arunachal Pradesh. Most of the diagetic portions of the novel in which the tribal folk from different linguistic groups speak to each other or with people from the plains, are in the pidgin Asamiya. Thongchi makes liberal use of this form of speech in the novel, unlike Dai who rarely uses it. Dai experiments with other interesting devices, including 'translation' of tribal speech into different varieties of Asamiya and even attempting to blend the lexicon of one language with the phonemics of another (as in the speech style of the village idiot Libo in *Prithibir Hanhi*). Thongchi is aware of the fact that the pidgin langue, though it might be a natural mode of communication for the tribals, is not a 'respectable' language, nor is it equipped to convey complex human emotions. He does not refer to this hybrid speech as a distinct creolized language, but merely calls it 'broken Asamiya':

His [Dilip Saikia's] sister and sister-in-law had teased him about this mode of speech when he was getting ready to leave for NEFA. 'Don't pick up that speech as your uncle had done before you', they had warned him. 'If you do, no one would give you a girl in marriage.' Dilip had vowed never to pick up that hybrid and defective mode of speech. But, now he has become so entangled in this new situation that it was impossible to perform his official duties without using the pidgin language.[42]

Mouna Ounth is a novel about building real roads between the hills and the plains, and metaphorically, it is also about cementing relationships between the different communities in the hills. The road-building project leads to the establishment of human relationship between people from different tribes who come together at the work site. The tribes which had been living on the same hills for hundreds of years without ever communicating with each other, except perhaps as enemies, are brought together by work. The ancient silence between communities that had reigned through the centuries is broken by the sounds of dynamite explosion and of the car engine. The primitive fear and suspicion that had kept the tribes apart in their isolated existence, are finally dispelled by the new culture that gradually takes shape at the work site. There is a carnival at the end of the novel to celebrate the opening of the road and the coming of a new era of inter-tribal cooperation and friendship.

[42] *Mouna Ounth*, p. 13.

Thongchi highlights the importance of work in breaking old customary taboos that make the tribes xenophobic. Rinsin, the Sherdukpan youth and Yama, the Bangni woman, are drawn to each other by natural desire. Their relationship does not have the sanction of their tribal societies, but the two enjoy the days of newfound freedom while they are working together at the site. Rinsin even gets the opportunity to establish himself as a romantic hero when he plucks a wild orchid flower for his beloved from a gorge, risking his life. The two lovers are pursued by a series of adverse circumstances, the absence of a common language being one of them. They are incapable of breaking the ancient silence of their lips to articulate their deepest feelings in a language comprehensible to both. So, they communicate in the most primitive of languages, that of touch. This central theme of the novel finds expression in the following poignant passage:

There is a great wall between Yama and Rinsin—the wall of language. How will they reach out to each other through this wall and speak the language of their hearts? They can never do it, never! They are helpless like a pair of dumb doves. Their only language is that of furtive glances, trembling lips.

'I knew I would find you here,' said Yama's heart, 'I don't know where you come from, what is the name of your village, where your home is... But, from the moment I saw you, I have felt that I have always known you... How will you understand my situation, Rinsin? I am an object that has been sold to another. I have no identity of my own, no voice, no opinion. But, if you had been a Bangni man or me a woman born into your society, there would have been no such mighty wall of language and race between us...' (p. 72)

The Bangni woman here has suddenly become aware of the multiple problems of race, gender and culture which affect her identity. The road-building project has at least laid the foundation of a new self-consciousness about individual space and identity amongst the tribal men and women. At the end of the novel, the Sherdukpan man tells his Bangni friend about the inadequacy of a pidgin language to convey the new feelings of a modern man:

Rinsin spoke hesitantly: 'Tadak, I don't know how to speak to you. How easy It would have been to convey my feelings to you had your Bangni tongue been the same as my Bhutiya. I have so much inside here (touching his chest), but I cannot speak in this language of the plains men. God has given our people the same eyes, lips, hands, but different tongues...' (p. 117)

The anguish in Rinsin's words is the anguish also of a writer who is in search of an adequate medium to communicate with his own people.

Yeshe Dorje Thongchi or Lummer Dai's writings are today facing the problem of finding the ideal reader. Will their books be read by their own people whom they love and with whom they would have liked to communicate best, or by the Asamiya speaking people who would be unable to accept the books as a part of their own literature, or by the ideal reader of today who crosses all national and international boundaries? This is the question that has been faced by the popular Turkish writer Orhan Pamuk. In a recent interview, he has stated that since his novels are today read by readers the world over in forty different languages, so he has in mind an ideal reader who belongs to an international community of 'literary readers'. He says,

Writers write for their ideal readers, for their loved ones, for themselves or for no one. All this is true. But, it is also true that today's literary writers also write for those who read them. For this we might infer that today's literary writers are gradually writing less for their own national majorities (who do not read them) than for the small minority of literary readers in the world who do.[43]

The Arunachali writers writing in Asamiya, like many other writers from small nationalities whose readership is also limited, will have to depend more and more on capable translators and publishers who can enable them to reach out to the 'small minority of literary readers' who still read good books.

---

[43] Orhan Pamuk, 2006, 'Name the Reader: Cultural Disquiet and the Inevitable Question', *The Telegraph*, Guwahati, 13 August.

Cherrie L. Chhangte
'Loneliness in the Midst of Curfews'
The Mizo Insurgency Movement and Terror Lore[†]

Terror lore[1] is particularly apt when applied to the northeastern states of India, where such struggles constitute part of each of their very recent histories, and where, as a result, stories and songs and various lores have emerged, reflecting the experiences of entire generations of people who have grown up under the shadow of such terror. This fear, in most cases may be a consequence of the reign of terror inflicted upon a nation or

---

[†] Earlier versions of this paper were presented at the 29th Indian Folklore Congress & National Seminar on Oral Discourse and Ancient Knowledge Systems of North East India at NEHU, Shillong, 20–22 September 2006.

[1] The term 'terror lore' was coined by Dr Desmond Kharmawphlang to denote the type of lore that emerges in a society as a result of the fear and insecurity that people collectively undergo. (In conversation with Dr Desmond Kharmawphlang, Reader and Head, Center for Cultural and Creative Studies, NEHU, Shillong, 20 August 2006.)

society by the dominant political group or a militant group fighting for various causes, with violence being the main force behind their actions in both cases. Terror lore may be a component or variation of what is commonly known as the urban legend, although, of course, the reason for the birth of the terror lore is more specific, and all terror lore may not achieve the status of an urban legend in contemporary culture as it deals with a specific area with the possibility that it may have relevance for only a specific percentage of the population, notably, those who have actually undergone and experienced the trauma.

The Mizo insurgency movement, spearheaded by the Mizo National Front (MNF), took up arms against the Indian government in an effort to preserve its independence. It had the support of the people, and by 1966, many volunteers had joined the MNF, who then went underground. The Central Government responded by sending in its troops who then made every effort to curb the insurgency movement. Their efforts included methodically burning the areas inhabited by the people, including Aizawl, and also many villages; in an effort to make the administration easier to manage, villages were 'grouped' together. Further, the agrarian society suffered considerably and simple village folk were reduced to a state of near starvation. At this point, the army offered rewards to anyone who would act as an informer and report the names of people who were sympathetic to the MNF cause, and compelled by their situation, there were some who could not resist the temptation for the few favours given to them by the army. They therefore, became informers, and, with a cloth covering their faces to hide their identity, they were taken around the villages, and whoever they pointed their fingers at was understood to be a rebel, or someone sympathetic to the movement, and they were rapidly disposed of.

People, therefore lived in perpetual fear of being literally 'pointed at'. Whereas earlier, their fear was directed at the army alone, now it was compounded by a fear of their own people. The MNF, on the other hand, retaliated by ruthlessly killing whoever they believed were traitors and informers. Hence, for the common people, there was another element of the fear they lived in, fear of being accused as an informer. Neither the army nor the MNF wasted time investigating the truth of the allegations and reports; punishment was swift and carried the unmistakable message that others were warned not to repeat such acts of rebellion or betrayal. Under such conditions, people literally lived between the hammer and the anvil.

With the central government and the MNF unable to reach any sort of agreement, the situation reached an impasse and continued in this way for approximately twenty years. During this entire period, although life limped back to normalcy at the surface level, yet the situation was such that there was an intangible fear and insecurity in the psyche of the Mizos, and this unease grew to be part of their everyday life. Curfews continued to be imposed at night all this while, and thus Mizoram gained the dubious distinction of having one of the longest curfews imposed upon any territory in the world. With jet fighters dropping bombs over Aizawl, Mizoram again became the only instance of India bombing its own territory.

Yet, against this tumultuous backdrop, life carried on, and the imagination and creativity of the people could not be stifled. The terror they underwent, in fact, gave rise to a whole new body of creative outpourings largely characterized by pain and pathos. When the movement was at its peak, i.e., in the 60s and early 70s, the act of writing itself posed innumerable risks, and was reason enough to be considered a suspect in the eyes of the army, whose soldiers were often illiterate themselves. Even if they were literate, they did not understand the Mizo language, and therefore, could not differentiate between potentially harmful documents and harmless creative outpourings. Thus, rather than go through the hassle of being accused as rebels and insurgents, people avoided writing as much as possible. Much of whatever little was available by way of written records of this period, such as diaries, journals, and creative writing were burnt either by the army, or by the authors themselves, for fear of punishment. Also, there was a lot of censorship in the media, notably the All India Radio (AIR), which was the media most popular and easily available to the masses. Songs, thus, played an important part in reflecting the state of mind of the people, notably the psychological and emotional impact of terror upon them. In the event, many of the songs that emerged at this time became transmitters of collectively shared feelings and sentiments, with the singers themselves taking on the role of 'vectors'.[2]

---

[2] Jan Harold Brunvand, uses the term 'vector' (after the concept of a biological vector) to describe a person or entity passing along an urban legend or lore in *The Vanishing Hitchhiker: American Urban Legends and Their Meanings* (2003), New York: Norton, p. 2.

Time constraints permit us to take up only a few examples of such songs; these songs gained popularity literally by word-of-mouth, through repetition and imitation, since a majority of them never even found their way into the recording studios to be preserved in the form of audio albums. One such song is called 'Curfew Kara Suihlunglen' ('Loneliness in the Time of Curfews') by K. Rammawia, which poignantly talks about the loneliness of the young men in terror-ridden times. While normal life had come to almost a complete standstill in many aspects, young men were still young men, going through the emotional changes that every young man undergoes at any time, and any place. Romance was especially hard to sustain when circumstances were such that one did not know where one's next meal would be coming from, or whether one would, in fact, survive to partake of the next meal.

Mizo men traditionally woo their women by visiting them at night in their homes. Obviously, with the strict imposition of the curfew, such liberties were a thing of the past. There is an amusing lore that reflects the ingenuity of the young men during this period. Since some of the youth persisted in visiting the women at night, they faced a great risk of running into the patrolling army men during curfew hours. If they happened to run into the soldiers, they would pretend to be village-criers. The practice of using village-criers to inform the community of deaths and other happenings had been continued in the cities as well, and the authorities did not question their existence and role. Thus the young men, on espying the soldiers from a distance, would suddenly shout at the top of their lungs as if announcing something of vital importance. They took care that the community was not unnecessarily alarmed by only shouting some nonsensical words, and the jawans, oblivious to the ridiculous meanings of their words, let them be. In this way, there was a subtle subversion of, and a sly mocking of the authorities. With the heavy constraints imposed upon the liberties of the youth taking its toll on their morale, songs such as these gained popularity:

> Aw, lunglen Curfew karah hian,
> Tuar a har hrilh ka thiam zo love;
> Hmanah Zoram nun leh chim loh Thadangi zun,
> Ngaih hian chin lem a nei thei dawn lo.[3]

---

[3] K. Rammawia, 1995, 'Curfew Kara Suihlunglen', in Ellis Saidenga (ed.), *Mizo Hla Larte*, 3rd edition, Lunglei: Zo-En, p. 11.

(O, loneliness in the midst of curfews,
The anguish of my heart is beyond words;
My longing for Zoram's past and Thadangi's charms
Never will come to an end.)

Another verse laments the curtailing of the individual's freedom and remembers with nostalgia the former life of the Mizos before such intrusions and impositions:

Tlaikhua a lo ngui zantlai bawhar dung thulin,
Riahrun kan bel Curfew hran vang hian;
Leng zawng hian ngai ve maw, hmana kan Zoram nun?
Kei zawng ka ngai, ka dawn sei ngam lo.[4]

(Weary night descends like the lassitude of cocks at dusk,
Curfew instills terror, and we are homebound;
Do you too, yearn for the ways of old Zoram?
As for me, loneliness forbids me to dwell long on it.)

The solitude of the lone singer, while it can be read on one level as the longing for his beloved, goes deeper; the loneliness he talks of is soul-deep. Keeping the context in mind, it can be assumed that he, and many young men and women like him, misses his family (probably scattered, if not dead), his home (probably burnt down), his village (either razed to the ground or desolate because of the grouping of villages), and his friends (most of whom he probably has lost touch with, in the desperate fight for survival where ties like that of friendship cannot afford to bind). In effect, his lament is for an entire way of life, seemingly lost now, forever.

There are songs that tell of the burning of the village of Sialsuk. In one of these songs, after the singer has mourned the destruction of his beloved village, he exhorts his audience to rise up and rebuild the village, and fight back for the freedom they have lost. He envisions the glory which they will reclaim:

Puini tawng kan vangkhua hian lallai a sang tual tual,
Kawrvai i hnawl ang aw, zalen nan kawl a eng mahna;
Rangka dartui ngei an chuan ang aw,
Hlimten i vawr ang thlangsappui biahzai a thang ta e.[5]

---

[4] Ibid.
[5] 'Sialsuk Khaw Kan Hla' © Laltanpuia, 28 December 1966.

(Our village meets with glory, our nobility asserts itself,
Resist the *vai*, freedom's dawn may yet light up the horizon,
Walk we will, on streets paved with gold,
Sing songs of joy, our fame now reaches distant white shores.)

With regard to my queries about the line 'our fame now reaches distant white shores', the common consensus seems to be that Mizos have often seen the white man as their saviour, undoubtedly a result of the influence of white missionaries who came to India in the late 1800s. Missionaries educated the people, built hospitals and schools, and generally helped to uplift the society as part of their mission work, and thus they were held in high esteem. Significantly though, there is very little recollection or reflection concerning the other kind of white person, viz., the government employee. When one looks at nostalgic and appreciative reports of white people, the white people in question are inevitably the missionaries. Anyhow, this view of white people as being superior and capable of saving Mizos from destruction was further reinforced at this time by a widespread rumour that the suffering of Mizos had reached the ears of the UNO, and they would appear to rescue and help form an independent country for Mizos any day now.

People, unable to accept the implications of their new reality, clung on to any hope offered, however distant the possibilities. Another song, also on the burning of Sialsuk village, expresses the bewilderment and anguish collectively felt by the villagers on witnessing the devastation of Sialsuk in the wake of the army's actions:

Hmanah kan pi puten an chawi, vangkhawpui par a chuai,
Kawrvaillian doral an chang ta;
Thinlai kawl eng a var thei lo.
Tlang tinah pheisen lunglian nghosei ang an hrang e.
Vankhawpui leh lallai run mawitu
Chengrang tuilian ang an la e.[6]

(The flower that our forefathers sang of has wilted,
The might of *vais* has become our enemy;
Dawn cannot light up the heart's darkness.
Every hilltop is rife with soldier's anger like wild elephants,
The armor that bedecked every household
Snatched away from us like the ebbing tide.)

---

[6] 'Sialsuk Khaw Kan Hla' © Laltanpuia, August 1966.

One of the best known songs that emerged during this period, 'Khawkhawm Hla' or 'Grouping Song' transmit the agony of villagers who were typically given a day's notice to prepare for such groupings. In the space of twenty-four hours, they had to leave their homes, their fields, their domestic animals, and everything that had given them a sense of security and identity. With just the bare necessities, they were relocated and grouped into one of the bigger villages. Such moves obviously left deep psychological scars in the mentality of the people, and it is a trauma that many have not yet recovered from to this day.

Linguistically, the vocabulary of the common man was irrevocably changed by the reign of terror. For instance, the term *vai* is used by the Mizos to describe a non-tribal or a person from the plain areas, who is easily distinguished by differences in facial features when compared to the mongoloid features of Mizos (much like the Khasis' use of *dkhar* to denote non-tribals). Although this term had been in use right from the time when Mizos first came into contact with non-tribal traders such as traveling salesmen and peddlers who came into Mizoram much earlier, it began to take on negative connotations in common parlance because of the hostility towards the vais. The term itself is said to have originated as a corruption of the Hindi word *bhai*, which these 'outsiders' frequently used. Despite the fact that the term itself has no specific meaning other than this, the non-tribals/vais themselves began to interpret this term as an insult to them, and it was banned from use in the government-run media like the AIR and local newspapers, as well as official correspondence during this time.[7] Interestingly, though, people continue to use the term to this day, although cultural attitudes have changed and it is no longer considered a derogatory word as such. Other linguistic imports include words like 'curfew', 'bandh', 'parole', 'grouping' and 'refugee', among others, which are now part and parcel of common usage in Mizoram.

In any case, what emerges is the significant role that the oral tradition has played and continues to play in the chronicling of events that have happened in the past, especially with reference to the insurgency movement in Mizoram, which spanned 20 years. However, as folklorists have observed, oral records are largely based on memory, and as a scholar has pointed out, human memory is fallible, and information may be lost, misinterpreted or even become untraceable with the passage of

---

[7] Vanneihtluanga, former AIR employee and prominent writer. Personal interview, Aizawl, 21 August 2006.

time.[8] Somewhat similar to what Toni Morrison describes as 'national amnesia',[9] there seems to have been a reluctance to actually put down in writing the horrific experience of that period by those who actually underwent it. Much of what we know has been handed down to us by word-of-mouth. Of late, there has been a revival of interest about the events taking place during 1966–86, but the dearth of written records has given rise to certain discrepancies and inconsistencies by those who have attempted such scholarship. As C. Lalsangliana notes,[10] this could have tragic consequences to the way the history of the Mizos is recorded in the future. Therefore, the need of the hour is to make wholehearted and systematic efforts at documenting such records while the repositories of such lores are still alive.

---

[8] Margaret Ch. Zama, 2006, 'Various Aspects of the Oral Tradition of the Mizo', *ICHR National Seminar*, Department of History and Ethnography, Mizoram University. Aizawl, 2–4 May.

[9] Toni Morrison, black, American writer, uses this term in connection to the avoidance of the issue of slavery by contemporary Americans, black and white alike.

[10] C. Lalsangliana, 2006, 'Ka Tih Reng Kha!', *Vanglaini*, Aizawl: Charity Press, 10 August.

Sukalpa Bhattacharjee
Narrative Constructions of Identity and the Sylheti Experience

Narratives are expressions and representations of lived experiences even though they may not actually have been lived. Narratives essentially link real life forms to art. Likewise, narratives of lived experience and folk stories with its myriad cultural experiences are also an admix of real life and art. Irrespective of how a narrative is formed, be it by an individual or a group of individuals, all narratives have an in-built element or universality at least for the domain for which they are intended and therefore circulation of a story is a must for its artistic survival and appreciation. Such narratives, if domain specific and therefore coherent, are likely to constitute a community that identifies itself with the narrative in terms of a remembered tradition, event or shared reasons and values. Such narratives derive their sustenance not because they essentially speak of something that is true or false but because they make their listeners feel a sense of shared meaning. Rather than being a simple case of the story teller and the narrative in question, inventing and imposing metaphors of agreement, what perhaps actually guide and determine character of the narrative to be told is the traces of lived experiences with all its knowable and unknowable elements. The key issue, in this context, therefore perhaps is to look in details as to how such narratives create the sense it conveys and who are its target audience.

Ingrained within the narratives, the issue, one presumes, calls for a dialogue between a thinking self and a fixed notion of authentic community. Such dialogues are expected to bring into fore all the implicit and explicit elements that accounts for the space between the narrative, its teller and the target audience. Such exercises basically centre on/in tracing the moments of presence and absence of the self, the world and others in an interlocution between the text and the context. It may eventually lead one to possibly end up finding a number of breaks and interruptions within what has so far looked like a coherent story. Consequently, the stable transmission of a fixed essence gives way to a live criss-crossing of signifiers over a dynamic and wide variety of narratives.

Narratives, by virtue of an excess over the comprehension of the tradition, often contain an element of ex-centricity, which implies that they are simultaneously culturally rooted and yet produces a counter cultural domain. While it allows one to speak and not just say what one means, it promotes listening to the unheard, interprets the truth of the world and self in a way that is often unique. In a constant shift between *being* and *becoming* without a realized essence, a realm of the counter factual therefore automatically goes into it signifying a series of contingent, invented and non-narratable ensemble of experiences. Narratives thus, provides for the necessary double bind of belonging to a unified story of life and yet not belonging to what the story merely says. It opens up a different space of living that looks for different cultures, communities other than ones own and engages one with stories/narratives of others.

Tales of ethnographic representations, inhabit the epistemic construction of the migrant or ethnic identity. Tales centred around the oriental as subjects of colonial canons of white anthropology has apparently given rise to a (inter) nationalist discovery of 'noble savages' in the theory and practice of politics of recognition and difference. As such, what seems to be present here is a residue of autonomy, carefully vested on such colonial and late modern national subjects, indignant in their own counter hegemonic aspirations and yet struggling to discover a place of speaking by/for themselves. Caught in the exchanges between the local and the global, the centre and the periphery, the citizenship and the cultural membership, the private and the public, the subjects here are experiencing manifold challenges to locate their self-definition and the narratives of self-identity. Characterized by this existential dilemma, the narratives of mixed-blood, displaced and expatriate identity here is a siege from within, in a transition seeking to link late modern cultural and social capital with tradition. A look at the *self* and the *other*, therefore, constantly poses a crisis in terms of having a stable definition and hence a stable narrative.

In situating a dominant narrative of the Barak Valley of NE-India Sylhet emerges as a distant locale geographically and in the memory, which has been partitioned off from the being of Bengali identity and which has been a historical disruption in the continuity of a self identity for a Sylheti subject. As an interrupted and yet cobbled together idea of identity, the notion of Sylheti in the present Barak Valley acts as a link in the memory that establishes a contact with the partitioned other and at the sane time gives rise to a dynamic of interiority in terms of Hindu–Muslim identities that operated at the core of contemporary Barak valley's Sylheti identity.[1] One such immediate point of reference is the strange inclusion of Cachar district of erstwhile Surma valley into Assam by the British for administrative purposes in the year 1832. In effect a part of what was known to be integrated Sylhet became a part of Assam's administration and the whole process of bringing it under a uniform Special Assam Code in 1837. Looked from another angle, inclusion of a part of Sylhet known as Surma valley into Assam and keeping the rest of Sylhet within the revenue board of Bengal but included within Assam was not just a shrewd administrative manoeuvre on the part of the British, but it presented an enactment of a future policy of territorial division based on the policy of denial of distinctness of Surma valley and turn it into a linguistic and cultural periphery of both Bengal and Assam.

This future plan of territorial division was not just a ploy of the British, but it found its support in the emerging histories of Assam and Sylhet. An event such as imposition of Bengali as the official language of newly constituted Assam (1836–72) by the British had initiated an unbridgeable gulf between the local Bengali-speaking people and the Assamese as a community. This was later mitigated by an act of restitution of Assamese as the medium of instruction, but by then, a comparatively advantageous middle class Bengali-speaking community

[1] Achuyt Charan Tattvanidhi, *c.* 1317, *Srihatter Itibritta* (in Bengali), Sylhet.

had emerged as the dominant class of officials in Assam. This early act of division by the shrewd colonial rulers went a long way in producing a sense of enmity between the educated middle classes of Assamese- and Bengali-speaking communities. This ground level difference had been compounded by the emergence of a sense of dominance of Bengali literature, language and culture that followed directly and indirectly from Kolkata, the center of the so-called Bengal renaissance. One high point of such a sense of dominance of Bengali over Assamese in terms of literature, language and culture has been Tagore's idea of establishment of Bengali as the language of entire Bengal presidency that included Orissa and Assam; which, he, of course, later retracted from by admitting the distinctness of Assamese as a language that had enjoyed a longer ancestry than Bengali.[2] But that didn't have an impact either in propagation of Bengali in Assam by the conspiracy of Bengali administrators nor it had inspired the Sylhetis, the subject of this paper to dream of a Bengali hegemony over Assam.[3] In fact rather Sylhetis had likened the closeness of their dialect with Assamese, despite Sylheti being a dialect of Bengali.[4]

Folk narratives that were born from such a historical rupture presented a subjectivity that was caught in a in-between of real and imagined identity. This became more pronounced in the second and third generation Sylhetis who were born in independent India, who had never visited the land of their ancestors but who were constantly haunted by the presence of an imagined distant locale called Sylhet. This haunting was a result of the reference made to such subjects as refugees or outsiders in a politics of otherization on the one hand and due to the existence of a narrative of immediacy and intimacy with Sylhet on the other, that the older generation lived with and transmitted to the younger generation. Besides, the life-world of Sylhet which is so alien to someone who has not lived but which is always referred to by the older generations

---

[2] Rabindranath Tagore, 1974, 'Bhasabicched', in *Rabindra Rachanabali*, Vol. 6 (in Bengali), Kolkata: Visva-Bharati Prakashan, pp. 740–1; and Dimbeshwar Neog (ed.), 1954, *Dangoria Benudhar Rajkhowa*, Jorhat.

[3] Sivanath Barman and Prasenjit Choudhury, 1986, *Bastab ne Bhibram: Axomot Bangla Bhasa Probortonor Aitihasik Utsa Sandhan* (in Assamese), Dibrugarh. The response of Surma Valley to such an imposition was non-hegemonic, as leaders of the valley didn't articulate any nationalism by that time.

[4] Padmanath Bhattacharya, 1998, 'To the East of Samatata' (mimeo), in Narendra Nath (ed.), *The Indian Historical Quarterly*, reprint Delhi: Caxton, Vol. IV. Miscellany, 17.

is a distant imagery for the new generation. The stories of overnight evacuation and abandonment of land and properties by the victims of partition and riots is a reality that haunts the memory of a Sylheti of the present generation from family narratives of such experiences. These histories of trauma and conflicts in the memory attend forms of exploitation and oppression of contemporary life that operate in the form of ethnic cleansing and competing and contesting the identity of the other, constituting an otherized identity for oneself. This identity is rooted in a sense of dispossession and violence that haunts the memory. Such a history is activated in the repetition of violence that disables genuine dialogue between communities engaged in competition and contestation. So, memory and historicity are central categories linking identity. This opens up a discourse about the principles involved in the 'exchange of memories' and in 'translation' between the Sylheti community and other such communities steeped in memories of loss and no-thingness. In everyday life the sense of a Sylheti self and of a self identity is tied to mundane practices in which the subjects locate themselves by reference to a routine of action or performances enacted by the elder generations. For example, in festivities and marriages Sylheti *dhamail* and *geet* is an integral part, representing Sylheti identity. These forms of performances have come down through word of mouth or occasional demonstrations made by the ladies of the older generations. Present generations living outside Barak Valley or without contact with older generations that are slowly passing away, make attempts to make a dhamail performance making it look like bhangra or the like but attempting to assert her Sylheti identity in one form or the other.

It may be mentioned here that Butler and Derrida[5] point to what is significant about subjectivity in relation to acts, the re-iteration of a particular subjectivity in instances of action that position a self by reference to a previous pattern of behaviour recognized by significant others in this case the older generation of Sylhetis. Pre-established vocabularies of the subjects who have lived in the Sylheti life-world are used as narrative patterns that exist in a discursive form, interiorized in the form of imaginaries, that are enacted and embodied in face to face situations. For example a very popular Sylheti geet narrativizes

---

[5] Judith Butler, 1993, *Bodies that Matter*, London and New York: Routledge; Also see Jacques Derrida, 1998, *Monolingualism of the Other or The Prosthesis of Origin*, translated by Patrick Mensah, Stanford: Stanford University Press.

the first landing of an aeroplane at the Mascot club.[6] This imagery of landing of an aeroplane which is not a unfamiliar sight today for the younger generation is still a very favourite narrative imagery describing Sylhetti experience. The stability of cultural narratives and of social relations between the older generations of Sylhetis and the younger is premised on such patterns of repetition and mutual recognition so that a self exists as a knot in a network of intersubjective action and understanding; they enact the fact that every particular 'who' or self is coupled to a world, both material and social. Thus the trajectory between memory to identity is based on a idea that identity is constituted in relation to narratives of belonging and of the collective—nation, ethnic, religious community, tribe—that inscribe the deep structural aspects of the socio-material life world. Thus, identity or a sense of self is constructed by and through narrative—the stories we tell ourselves and each other about our lives. In the context of the present study Sylheti narratives exist at the interstice and the complex relationships between memory, nostalgia, writing and identity. Sylheti texts of memory shows that remembering the self depends not on restoring an original Sylheti identity but on re-membering, on putting past and present selves together, moment by moment in a process of creative reconstruction of trauma, history and memory.

It may be mentioned in this context that Sylheti women have been very creative narrators of the history of trauma and loss. Women were always kept out of the emerging public spaces in the transitory period between the nineteenth and twentieth century which witnessed riots, partition and the emergence of an Indian Nationalism. They invented alternative mediums of expression through *baromashi* geet, dhamail and *bounach* which described their subjectivities and also incorporated the realities of the times. It is interesting to note how creatively they intervened into spaces of public life by re-creating moments of public and national events like the hanging of Khudiram Bose, in their geet which they also sang along with other songs in marriages.[7] Interestingly, when literate women wrote letters, they wrote *Bande Mataram* on the top replacing Sri Hari or any such conventional words. They also embroidered Bande Mataram on handkerchiefs and presented it to others. In this manner women in their limited way participated in the nationalist reawakening.

---

[6] The song in Sylheti is *Aeroplane uria ailo mascotero club ete*.
[7] S. Deb Laskar, 2002, *Jyotindra Mohan Abong Gram Cacharer Samaj, Rajniti O Sanskriti* (1901–1991), Silchar, p. 89.

In the rural areas women had the unique culture of katha stitching, which became the source of inscribing nationalist imagination through both stitches and discussions pertaining to the situation of the nation they had migrated into. Under the influence of new ideas and idioms of protest, women of rural Surma–Barak valley started embroidering dreams of emancipation and narratives of an emerging new society. They also embroidered the physical structure of important personalities of the Indian freedom movement colouring the entire tapestry with thread taken out of the border of old sarees. Among the women of the rural Muslim in Surma–Barak valley around the same time, *jynamas* and *mehndi* known as *mondi* was a popular medium of expressing individual ideas. Jynamas was another version of *katha*, while mehndi was inscription or design made with the colour extracted from leaves.

Contemporary popular cultural representations of Sylheti identity creatively draw upon the memory of past that is represented in folk belief and religious practices. Drawing from sources of cultural forms and narratives that pre-exist contemporary times, the popular acts as a meta-representation of a mindset that stands to speak for itself. It is in this pastiche of the past that the contemporary draws upon memory and public rites that attract participation of the community. One instance of cultural appropriation of the present generation and a reclaiming of Sylheti identity through popular culture, is the emergence of a group called *Dohar* which draws upon the rich folk tradition of Sylheti origin. This group in the contemporary times of rock and band music has taken upon itself to re-enact a Sylheti past through Sylheti folk songs and performances, which they have collected from various sources. They consciously refrain from using any modern musical instruments and use only the traditional dholok for the Sylheti beat. This re-enactment has re-created the disappearing sense of continuity with what is deemed to be the uncontaminated core of Sylheti identity. In their collection of songs, one finds a re-visiting of the idyllic locale of the rural Sylhet and human relationships that existed.[8] Their songs also represent the sense of Sylheti wit and humour as depicted in the characterization of the stereotypical Shiva as the intoxicated, happy go lucky husband of Durga. The song is an eyewitness view of lord Shiva by a Muslim lad who expresses his astonishment at the merry making journeys and processions that people undertake while worshipping Shiva.

---

[8] The song goes, *Bandhu darao re...* (in Bengali).

In continuation to such a search for latent cultural meanings, one could construct a paradigm of roots as disclosed in songs of mystic and rural poet of eastern Bengal called Hachon Raja. In one of his paradigm statements, the singer and composer Raja sang,

*Khacahr moiydhye achin pakhi komne ase jay
Dhorte parle monobery ditem tari paye...*[9]

(How the unknown birds come and go in their cages, had I caught them, I would have fettered them in their legs, with the yearnings of mind...)

The archetypal yearning to fly like an unknown bird over the infinite space of universe marks a sensibility that cannot possibly be captured by the mind alone. Mind functions here both as a limit as well as an organ of freewill that fails to fetter itself within the limits of the metaphorical 'cage', signifying body, life or being. This also signifies a sense of memory that reclaims itself in images like the bird, which is not merely literary or artistic, but it assumes a concrete narrative act that contextualizes itself historically in a post-partition milieu of re-linking with one's own past. This search for roots culminates into construction of a self-identity in the context of Barak valley of southern Assam.

This experience of being displaced and rooted at the same time has assumed a literary and linguistic dimension in conceptualizing a self-identity that is in exile from the mainland of Bengal. Going by the development and history of this exilic consciousness as it prevails in large part of Bengali-speaking world outside the main centre of Bengali language and culture, Sylheti self-identity is simultaneously affected by the larger world of Bengali language as well as distanced and decentred from any such world. Sylheti as a proper name exists in the world outside, while it presents itself from a position of exile. This exile consciousness is transformative,[10] as it overcomes the distance between Sylheti and Bengali in order to write and speak in Bengali. Authors from Barak valley are caught in a double moment of exile and becoming part of the centre

---

[9] Quoted by Rabindranath Tagore in 'The First Presidential Address' delivered by Tagore in Indian Philosophical Congress in 1925. The full English text is translated with the permission of the poet and published in the monthly magazine *Prabasi*, Magh, *c.* 1332 (Bengali), No. 25, Vol. 2, Issue 4, pp. 542–51 and cited in Amiya Shankar Choudhury, 1999, *Hachon Rajar Sangeetmala* (in Bengali), Kolkata, pp. 245–58.

[10] See A.R. JanMohamed, 'Worldliness-without-World, Homelessness-as-Home', in Michael Sprinker (ed.), 1992, *Edward Said: A Critical Reader*, Oxford: Oxford University Press, pp. 96–120.

of Bengali language and culture. Often they characterize their position as the third world of Bengali literature and culture. The connection between the third world and the first world is that of belonging, struggle and reverence, a mixed bag of sentiments and emotions that guide an internal graduation to the world of Bengali by often terming itself as *ishan* or north east of Bengal.

Such a location is imagined from both the directions. As an outside of Bengal, the valley is deemed to be located in the Northeast. Such an artifact of imagination is articulated in literature as a distant frontier or a periphery only for the purpose of a bottom-up movement towards becoming a part of the world of Bengal. This subjectivity of being the North East has found its paradigmatic expression in Tagore, when he lamented in one of his poems that the scenic land of Sylhet is exiled from the political boundary of Bengal and yet it is connected with the heart of Bengal and therefore, Bengal shall offer its blessings on Sylhet for all the time to come. The unflinching bond of being the blessed child of Bengal in Tagore's imagination connects Sylhet without a territorial fixity with the diasporic world of Bengali literature and culture.[11]

When the Sylhetis of Barak Valley imagine themselves as exiled and yet a part of the diasporic Bengali identity, it produces a self-effacement that is conflated with the current situation of not being-at-home with itself, by being located in the contested trajectory of Assam's history. But from this essential sense of loss and non-coincidences between Sylheti imagination and Assamese linguistic nationalism, what happens is a feeling of being orphaned within the rigid political and linguistic boundaries drawn around. Such external boundaries, of course, constrain the inner mental life, as it produces a picture of unfreedom and coercion.[12] This further results into ghettoization of the identity with its constitutive elements anchoring and rooting itself in a collectivity of pre-displacement of the Sylheti language. Added to that the politics of displacing the mother tongue constituted a politically displaced subjectivity of Sylheti operating at the intersection between culture, identity and belonging to the state of Assam. The conjunction between political and economic *inclusion* within Assam and cultural and

---

[11] An extract from Tagore's poem is reprinted in Ranendra Nath Deb, 1983, *Srihatta Parichay*, Nadiya: Published by author, see back of dedication page.

[12] Partha Pratim Moitra's poem entitled, 'Each Day For A New Ray of Hope', in Bhaskarjyoti Deb, 1999, *Born Again Memoirs: Collection of Verses Translated from Bengali to English*, Silchar: Graphics, p. 15.

linguistic *exclusion* from the dominant develops an identity of the self that is constituted by not just subjectivity, but a network of unstable relationship between the project of state building and cultural belonging. Such a network, on the one hand domesticates the pre-displacement linguistic identity and on the other produces a continuous subjectivity that constrains Sylhetis as an ethnic minority in Assam.

The exilic consciousness of being a Bengali mixed with an anxiety of seeking recognition of ones mother tongue and self-identity from the network of power relations or the abstract other, assumes the form of resistance and collaboration. With this internal sense of exile and resistance and external sense of being displaced and excluded, the articulation of Sylheti identity places itself between languages, boundaries, histories and other interstices of migrancy. Such interstitial spaces are fruitfully utilized in various forms of discursive and non-discursive reasons given for the state and the identity. Looking at Muslims as infiltrators,[13] or finding oneself not in an unequal encounter with the language of power, produces ambivalence in meaning. Sakitapada Brahmacahari, the icon of Bengali poetry from the valley pronounces this ambivalence in his paradigm statement, 'Bengali is my *Maa*'s tongue, while Assamese is my *Ai's*'.[14] The word Ai in Assamese means mother, but he draws a distinction between Maa in Bengali and Ai in Assamese by pointing to their essential non-difference, now philosophically called *identity-in-difference*. The sense of belonging to one's mother tongue is universal, only the mother is different in her name and it is a *difference without alterity*.[15] Such intellectual writing protrudes in time and space, but its occasions are controlled by real power.[16] The sense of being exiled, therefore, is something like being subjected by an 'other' and determined by ethno-cultural oppositions.

[13] Some of the Barak Valley leaders of BJP harp on this theme for electoral reasons

[14] Read a limerick stating this in Barak–Brahmaptura *setubandhan* organized by Axom Sahitya Sabha in August 1986 at Silchar District Library Auditorium.

[15] Gayatri Chakraborty Spivak, 1999, *Critique of Postcolonial Reason: Towards a History of Vanishing Present* Harvard University Press, Harvard, p. 290 explains this idea of alterity as radical when particularism of cultural difference is employed in connecting the different entities with a common conjunction. Saktipada Brahmachari does that in order to evolve a critical determination of difference between the self and the other.

[16] Edward Said, 1984, 'Reflections on Exile', *Granta* 13, p. 172.

Re-membering the Self

It is very interesting to note how the Sylheti literary imagination has re-membered a narrative self in the form of representative characters. The travesty of time has placed such characters at crossroads of lived history. Republication of the novel *Asrumalini* in 1986 has brought to the fore the memory of women of late nineteenth and early twentieth century women, represented by a typical character called Bhubaneswari Devi. She is the central character of the second novel *Asrumalini* (which was also called *Narishakti*) written by Surendra Kumar Chakrabarty in 1924.[17] It may be mentioned here that although women's lives and interventions in historical and political processes mentioned above have not been documented adequately, women did occupy a central position in the male literary imagination. The novel is divided into twenty-three chapters, each of which plays a temporally connected sequence of evolution of Bhubaneswari's authoritative character that grants her the commanding voice in family affairs. The main plot of the story is Bhubaneswari's nonchalant attitude to her husband Prandhon Gupta, who is full of philanthropic and altruistic values. She is very critical of her husband, who is depicted to be an epitome of goodness, but helpness before the wickedness of his wife. Prandhon's parents had died of epidemic in the village leaving him at the age of three in the hands of a midwife. Bhubaneswari decries Prandhon's soft corner for his midwife, whom he treated as equal to his own mother. Bhubaneswari appropriates by treating the midwife just like a maidservant. The novel builds up an implicit irony about the traditional notion of motherhood prevailing in Sylheti society of the period. An apparently intransigent character of Bhubaneswari challenges the culture of treating the midwife as mother, but the deeper sociological reality is that in the era of breakdown of joint Sylheti families, the place of mother or the midwife was not very secure, especially when one has a powerful wife like Bhubaneswari Devi. Mothers assuming the role of head of the family by displacing the male head is also ironized when Bhubaneswari takes total control over her son Paresh and turns him into a puppet in her hands. When Prandhon selects an intelligent and beautiful girl Jogarani to be his daughter-in-law his son Paresh marries her without taking any dowry in order to please

---

[17] For details see, Usha Ranjan Bhattacharjee, 1996, 'Baraker Upanyas o Ashrumalini' (in Bengali), in *Gabeshana Parishad Patrika*, Silchar, First Issue, February, pp. 103–17.

his father. But his mother Bhubaneswari who had always dreamt of a huge dowry from her son's marriage was utterly disappointed. Therefore, from the very first day she takes care to see that her son never gets too close to his wife. For example she is not allowed to meet her husband during daytime. The whole plot represents the presence of a powerful mother-in-law who undermines her nubile and good hearted daughter-in-law and subjugates both her husband and son, making them cower to submission to her power. The novel ends with several personal disasters in the lives of Jogarani, but demonstrates how Bhubaneswari's revengeful nature breaks the family in all the fronts. Of course the novel also re-presents how Jogarani, as the new generation woman appropriates both patriarchy and authority by first avoiding direct confrontation with her husband or mother-in-law despite having the knowledge of the source of her misery. Her patience, tolerance and dutifulness offers her the agency to have the last say in the novel at a time when her husband's family is at a loss both from moral and from economic standpoint. But unlike her revengeful mother-in-law she uses her agency not to destroy the family but to re-unite it forgiving all those who have contributed to her suffering and loss.

This narrative of late nineteenth and early twentieth century brings back the memory of joint family system among the Sylhetis in the pre-partition days on the one hand and consequently presents a re-membering of the female self which celebrates a subjectivity beyond the parameters laid down by patriarchy. Reprint of the novel in 1986 and its renewed reading by the new generation of Sylhetis strike a chord with the rise of women's power within the joint family, where one woman always occupied the central position by sidelining all other women and men as well. This marked a struggle in the family to occupy the central position and construct the place of an elder who would lead the family. But this structure of family fell apart due to partition in 1947, where joint families broke and gave rise to patriarchal power within the displaced families, which had to migrate from the undivided Sylhet to Surma–Barak valley.

However, it is interesting to note how women, as the most affected subjects of social and political histories reconstructed their self in the new geo-political locale of the Surma–Barak Valley As a recuperation of the sense of loss of collective self that grew from the breakdown of joint families owing to displacement consequent upon partition, women of Surma valley engaged themselves in life-world solidarity of inter-community activities. Encompassing the blurred borderlines between

Santhals, Kols, Mundas, Oriyas and Sylhetis, there has been a common celebration of spontaneity in local fairs followed by singing and dancing sessions. At one level, being a part of vagaries and bounties of season, women, through these blurred markers of identity inter-act and re-define new shades of local identity in rituals like Saoni Vrata, worshipping a family of 14 gods and goddesses (locally called Choudda Devata), Mera Meri and many other such micro performances. Such celebrations mark the exteriority of each of the rigidly defined patriarchical notions of identity. At another level, the supposed difference between Hindu and Muslim women are sidestepped in occasions such as Satynarayan and Chandipuja from the Hindu orientation and celebration of remarkable peers such as Panchpeer in commonly recognized altars of godheads. In sharp contrast to profanization of the ritual order, there is an increased mish mash between widely divided pantheons especially in case of some of the dis-gendered gods as mentioned above. Such an affirmation of feminine is a symbolic restitution of the feminine space lost in social domain. The heteronomy of celebrations in common sites bring together un-qualified particularities of godly presence in the fold of the feminine that overcomes male definition of idols and icons. There is also a very interesting subversion of boundaries of caste in female-centric rituals, for example, the Bauri goddess Lakkhinarayan becomes the saviour of upper caste goddess such as Laxmi or Saraswati in local lore. Folklore undercuts the socially defined boundaries to bring together the mutually excluded communities through their feminine myths and stories. Given this subliminal and representational interface, it is possible for women of Surma–Barak valley also to develop overlaps between distinct cultural and linguistic identities.[18] Meitei celebration of their histories of inclusion within India are participated by good number of Bengali women; while Dimasa celebration of their last king Govindrachandra's death is participated by sharing of grief among Bengali women. These real and imagined lives of native faith and histories constitute a vision of self that Hachon raja once sang,[19]

Who is this me and who is this you
Who vows for such one that never differs from the other
You are the master of the universe who made this word 'self'
an untruth

---

[18] For example, between the Dimasas and the Bengalis, the ritual of Manosa Puja and the reading of a folk text called *Padmapuran* are common cultural practices.
[19] *Hachon Udas*, 1st edition, p. 35.

You are the sole law without a counterpart
Vowing me and me only, they do not get the lord (...)

This is a public-reformative denial of male control of identity of women in the master narrative of local discourses that suggest another history and another symbolic constructions. Given this, the symbolic is intimately related to political and social struggles that women embody through resistance and affirmation of difference, thereby exhibiting 'a continuum from pain to healing'[20] through their newly constructed subjectivities.

---

[20] Jason Francisco, 1996, 'In the Heat of Fratricide: The Literature of India's Partition Burning Freshly (A Review Article)' in *The Annual of Urdu Studies*, No. 2, Madison: University of Wisconsin, Centre for South Asia; quoted in Ritu Menon and Kamla Bhasin, 1999, *Borders & Boundaries: Women in India's Partition*, New Delhi: Kali for Women, p. 7.

Charles Chasie
A Naga View of the World[†]

No man, and no people, is without 'roots'. And when we talk of roots, it is not just the family tree that we refer to. We mean much more than that. It is our identity through a set of beliefs, and practices, that sets us apart from all others, and make us unique, that we mean. The solidity of our character depends almost entirely on our culture and value-system. Without them we would all be a colourless homogeneity, completely uprooted and floating around, because without beliefs or identity, there would be no meaning to existence. There would then be no need for any Christ, Allah or the pantheon of gods. Neither would there be Darwin, Marx, capitalism or any talk of systems or ideologies. And, of course, there would be little reason for war or fighting. But it is our roots, and our culture, that give meaning to life and raises mere existence to purpose and living. This, no doubt, also entails all kinds of

---

[†] Charles Chasie, 1999, *The Naga Imbroglio: A Personal Perspective*, Kohima: Standard Printers and Publishers, Chapter 5.

struggles and miseries. But 'meaning' makes it worthwhile and helps us bear the hardships that confront us. Therefore, anyone who belittles his/her culture is only belittling and spiting himself/herself.

Since culture is so essential, it is important to look at it closely. In our context, however, because there is no 'Naga Culture' as such since there are so many Naga tribes with seemingly completely different, often contrasting, cultures and languages, what follows is the Angami culture, in the specific context of Khonoma village from where I come. This is so because even within the tribe there are, frequently, differing practices!

A popular definition of culture is, 'Acquired behaviour of a people over a period of time.' This gives a certain vibrancy because it suggests life and movement. But, 'acquired behaviour' can cover up too many things and carry too many baggages. For instance, could I call myself Western because I happen to have acquired some Western mannerisms or because I wear Western clothes, and could this be my 'acquired' culture? Would Western and 'Indian' ways of greeting others, eating their food, speaking their language and adopting their modes of working, etc. actually make me lose my cultural identity? There could, no doubt, be a lot of grey areas. There are also good and bad in every culture. And, I am convinced that while we may need to shed the bad, we all ought to keep the best in our cultures and traditions because these are the only unique things we could share with the world. Probably, too, sharing our uniqueness is the reason for our having 'collective separateness' and a great part of the reason for our coming into this world.

Since each culture is different and unique, every culture gives its own view of the world. No culture can claim superiority over another. The yardsticks we can use for such measurements and comparison can only be in degrees, at best, as per the prevailing value system in a given community/society at a given time. Naturally, there can be no question of 'better'. It can only be whether a particular culture is complete and total by itself at a given period. Time is important because it is absolutely possible that a particular culture may have been complete but certain aspects may have either been forgotten, mis-interpreted, or got perverted, over time. Or the importance, even relevance, of certain traditional practices may have changed.

What is a 'complete' culture? It means that a particular culture must be able to provide answers to all the basic questions of life, at a given time, to the people whose culture it is. What are these questions?

i. Who am I?
ii. Where have I come from?

iii. Where am I going?
iv. What is the purpose of my life?
v. How do I live?
vi. Is there life after death (the question of God)?, etc.

These are basic questions every human being must have answers to. Or else life would be incomplete. And, against these yardsticks, can one 'civilization' be even considered for comparison with another? The regular archaeological finds of ancient civilizations no longer matter against these. At most, such discoveries can only provide partial answers and a notion of what the particular 'civilization' may have been like! I still remember having an argument, over 10 years ago, with a young European who felt so 'superior' to everyone else because he happened to be from the 'developed' West. Quite annoyed, I remember telling him, 'Do you consider us primitive because we use knives and spears instead of machine-guns and (nuclear) bombs, that you use, to kill? We kill only the guilty while you kill indiscriminately, guilty and innocent laike. And while you pack off your parents to "Old-age Homes" we are duty-bound to take care of our aged parents in gratitude, and respect, for what they have done for us aged parents in gratitude, and respect for what they have done for us while they were able. So, who is more civilized?' My outburst, no doubt, was subjective and only meant to prove a point in an argument.

Alas! We have lost much in the last few decades. Much of the strength in our culture lay in the traditional authority system, our beliefs, and the fact that our economy did not allow too much disparity between rich and poor. Even the British did not disturb these (they initially tried, failed, and decided to let us be) and we were able to maintain our way of life under them. But with the departure of the British things took a completely different turn as a result of the events that followed. And our systems were turned upside-down, often deliberately. It took sometime for the Government of India to realize that the main prop of the Naga movement was the tribal council and that the only effective way of reducing their authority would be to reduce their influence—and that, for this, a break-up of the economic pattern of the Naga people, specifically of land-relationships, would be necessary. Even a rather cursory study of the role of the Indian Army in Nagaland would reveal that, under cover of fighting the insurgents, the entire economic pattern of the Naga people has been attempted to be disrupted. In this connection one may refer to the village re-groupings that were carried out. This disruption of the economic pattern is bound to have far-reaching consequences and will, in the long run, shake the very basis of Naga society—the village 'republics'.[1]

Then, there is the election system which, much more effectively, destroyed the village authority system and completed what the village re-groupings and 'concentration camps' (after villages were burnt) had left still standing. Traditioanlly, we did not elect our leaders. Nagas, at least, never enterd elections. The notion itself would have been a scandal. When you 'go to the people' you are telling them that you are the best person they could possibly have as their leader!—This, in a society, where even a majority or consensus nomination, to be part of a delegation, is often refused several times by the persons concerned, pleading that they are unworthy. In traditional society, such arrogance and absence of fear of God could result in immediate beatings and social ostracism. Leadership qualities were so demanding. Experience, wisdom, depth, quick-wittedness and clarity of expression (because everything was conducted verbally), diplomacy, prowess in battle, persuasiveness, wealth, etc. were expected of a leader. In fact, only an informal recognition as leader, through general acceptance, often grudgingly given, was possible at the time. And this comes about when villagers start directing people, especially strangers, to specific persons for advice, hosting, talking-to (as in foreign relations), etc. Even a widely 'accepted' leader would talk about his unworthiness everytime people press him to take on a certain responsibility or make a certain decision. And, certainly, no leader was accepted on a permanent basis. The moment the person starts boasting, his downfall would begin. And soon, people would lose faith in him, discarding him, finally—while every person is considered valuable, no individual is also considered indispensable.

Having said that, there is possibly no alternative to having elections, today, in a larger democratic set-up, even if this was a Western concept. Neither could we remain completely isolated, without embracing change, in our ways, for all time. The traditional authority system as described above, could function only at the village level where everybody really knew everybody and nothing could be hidden from anyone. Because of such transparency, we were able to practice 'pure democracy' at the village level. But, however ideal a society this was, it is difficult to imagine how it could work beyond the village-republic. Elections empower, however remotely, the common man with a say in the affairs of state. It is also the only workable solution in today's world when

---

[1] Udayon Misra, 1978, *The Naga National Question*.

everyone, armed with a certain amount of knowledge, has his/her own ideas on every subject imaginable. Nagas, on the whole, are actually very adaptive because their entire training and focus in early life is towards survival first, although specialization was not neglected and there is pride in reaping the biggest harvest, in making the most exquisite basket, in facing the biggest danger, etc. In battles, the first to confront the enemy and the last individual rear-guard can wear certain items as part of their traditional regalia. Just to earn accolades, especially in days when there was no war, men also competed (sometimes with bets involved) with each other, going in the dead of night, to pre-arranged 'haunted' places to retrieve certain items placed during the day. These were sometimes several miles away, in the forest, without the benefit of matches and torchlights. So, to such a people, changes would not have been insurmountable. What they were not allowed was adequate time to adjust to work things out in the best way they perceived. This is part of the reason why many failed to fully appreciate the power of the vote. And many still talk about 'Indian elections'.

Without knowing a single word of Hindustani or the English language, our villagers used to undertake long journeys, even individually sometimes, and carry on trade and commerce with people in far-off places like Gujarat and Rajasthan, on the very shores of the Arabian Sea, or down south to Madras, Ceylon (Sri Lanka), etc. Their business was mainly in sea shells and coloured beads. And sign language was usually their means of communication. Bargaining was often done with the help of pebbles! When a young man is setting out on such a journey, or even beyond the confines of the village, a parent or elder usually blesses him: 'May the Spirits look after you and protect you; May good fortune attend to you; May you be always in good health so that you do not lose perspective and can always remain directed towards your goal; And may your achievements surpass that of your rivals. May the smoke of your fire be seen as long as anyone else is making fire; May you be fleet-footed so that you may not stumble and fall either by stone or stump; And having achieved what you set out to do, may you return as quickly as the hand of Providence guides you'. Such blessing can be either long or short. The above is to give an idea of the kind of mental and psychological preparedness with which a person sets out.

The Naga Underground's refusal to carry on military operations during India's wars with her external enemies (Pakistan and China) has usually been misunderstood by most people. On the other hand, his determination, and resilience, in the face of a much more powerful adversary has baffled many. Sekrenyi is the most important Angami festival. But, more than a festival, this is really a religious and spiritual ceremony of the male warrior when he purifies himself and prepares for war. From this ceremony, the Naga warrior will emerge spiritually and psychologically stronger—a bit like the devout Catholic who comes 'floating' out of the Church on 'spiritual wings' after going to confession and receiving holy communion! One of the activities during this time is the unofficial competition to be the first to bathe at the village wells/waterfalls early in the morning while the water is still 'asleep' (before anyone has 'disturbed' it by using the water). While bathing, each man blesses himself with the words, 'May this water cleanse me from all sickness and disease and may I become healthy and strong so that I may overcome all my adversaries, performing feats that others cannot and surpassing everyone in my achievements'. Implicit in this blessing is the prayer to do what others consider impossible—the greater the challenge, the m ore the glory and the desire to achieve. 'What use/benefit is there in doing what everyone else does or can do?' is an attitude that governs a Naga in his daily life. Naturally, 'shameful deeds' or what are considered below the dignity of a man are shunned. And unscrupulous persons who stoop so low as to forget their own dignity will not be respected even today when 'money' has managed to make so many people servile. This is one reason the 'carrot' from Delhi has made addicts of many Naga leaders and led them, but has, so far, failed to make them heed the 'stick'!

Our people had a highly developed sense of diplomacy and how to conduct their relations with others. Each *khel*, even clan, had 'embassies' with complete immunity. No member of the ambassador's household would be harmed by anyone. And the host clan/khel would provide protection. The embassy's responsibility, naturally, was to maintain good relations with the host clan/khel, although intelligence gathering also was part of it's duties. This is a paradox, both curious and natural, in a village society where a drunken fight between two individuals, followed by serious insults, could lead to warfare between the clans/khels and where the ambassador and his household would have had no time to flee! Clans and khels had friendship 'treaties' (frequently just based on a word of honour, without even exchange of articles) which were scrupulously honoured.

The village sense of justice was highly honed and seems far superior to the modern practice. Much of he 'judicial' decisions would depend on the circumstances of the individual case. And care is taken so that even the guilty man/woman is allowed to get away without being totally humiliated before everyone. A lot of the 'punishment' is allowed to hang on social stigma, castigation and ostracism. Certain criminals would suddenly find that no one was willing to accompany them anywhere, apart from family and special friends established earlier (who would do it 'for old times' sake which everyone would 'understand'), and marriage partners would become hard to find. The severity of the social stigma and ostracism would, of course, depend on the crime involved.

Most of the time, the guilty person's family/clan and their honour would be taken into account so that they do not all lose face just for the rash action of one individual. This was necessary because individual identity could only exist alongside that of the family, clan, khel and village—in other words, each of these units were complete in themselves and totally integrated. (It is because of this that two persons' friendship or enmity could lead to either peace and friendship or war among clans, khels and villages!) In minor cases, a simple apology is enough. Frequently, the family would also punish the offender themselves before anyone could complain because this is the honourable thing to do. At the same time, vengeance was, often considered a filial duty, even a virtue, when an insult had been rendered or a life, from one's family or clan, had been taken. The responsibility would be passed on from generation to generation until the right 'opportunity' came along and the wrong was avenged. This was why people like J.H. Hutton wrote that 'the blood-feud of the Naga is what the Corsican vendetta was'. Of course, in cases like murder, prostitution, etc. immediate and permanent exile were prescribed. Often, where murder was concerned, the act of revenge was swifter! In accidental cases of killing, while out hunting, for instance, seven years exile from the village is prescribed for the immediate family. After this period, which was considered adequate punishment, the family would be allowed to return to the village and no further action would follow. In theft cases, seven times the value was usually repaid, except for the *Thevo* or priestly clan for whom the prescribed restitution is less.

In such a volatile situation, third parties and their mediation were very important. This was why every village, right down to families and individuals, would build and maintain their relationships with others. People would be on the look-out to be nice and to befriend each other whenever the opportunity arose. Attempts at other times were futile because they were either suspect or of less value. Naturally, people did not ask for assistance so long as they could help it. This was the delicate balance that had to be maintained because pride and face were important to everyone. Quite often, even to render charity one had to find the proper excuses so that the receiver did not lose face. Naturally, in a case of confrontation, third party mediation was a must. The party usually manages to work out a compromise solution which is generally accepted because failure to accept such solutions could end in the third party losing face! But if the 'solution' was patently unfair, other parties would move in to see that justice is done. The process goes on. This was the kind of check-and-balance that used to be in place and, most times, proved effective in rendering justice, as opposed to proving the power of Law.

With such practices, and in the background of head-hunting, one would be warmly welcomed as an honoured guest with the right kind of introduction or credentials. But, without proper credentials or references, one would be suspect. Worse still one may be considered a spy and an enemy, the penalty for which is not hard to seek although, generally, no hasty steps are taken. Even with the right credentials, special care had to be taken not to cause loss of face. Understandably, most speeches were indirect and one had to make a lot of inferences and search behind what is actually being said in order to discern what is wanting to be said! People also always talked about oneself, and one's family and relations, in self-deprecating terms. One usually made adequate protestations about one's unworthiness whenever a compliment is paid, or before expressions of faith such as a nomination to represent the clan/khel or village, until the insistence becomes strong enough and it becomes apparent that the proposition/nomination was sincere. Although long-winded, the process of selection and decision-making, in such cases, helps create a kind of consensus while the best persons get selected. Also in the event the particular delegation fails in its mission, no one loses face because the clan/village had literally forced the delegates to shoulder the responsibility! And those who had proposed the names of the members are usually the first ones to come forward to defend them and to explain that each member had done his best.

There was a time when I thought our people were very crude in the manner of greeting one another. Although not talking to each other was considered bad manners when you met anyone (not knowing someone was no excuse) on the road, 'Where are you going?', 'What did you eat this morning?', etc. were the standard phrases used. I guess a 'Good morning' or a 'Good afternoon' on a bad day would have made little sense—Most Nagas would just reply 'Yes' or 'No' if, that is, you escape being laughed at for such greetings! Later, I discovered that not too long ago, the speech was so indirect and polite that it had become difficult to communicate! For instance, when you wanted someone's presence you literally said, 'Did I see you come here?' In 'modern' times such manner of speech had become difficult because, invariably, you would get the reply, 'No you didn't?!'

In the life of any people certain words become the driving forces and are too important to ignore. In the lexicon of my own people I find such words and to which we, probably, owe our very souls. The following are some of them:

1. *Kenyu*: The nearest equivalent of this word is 'taboo'. It is just not done when something is kenyu. For instance, it is kenyu to gloat over other people's misfortunes or to take advantage of them (lest similar misfortunes visit you). Explanations are neither sought nor, frequently, available. If it was god enough for your forebears, it better be good enough for you!
2. *Mhosho*: This is an umbrella word that covers pride, integrity, honour, dignity, determination and stickability etc.
3. *Menga*: It suggests a very sophisticated notion of the word 'shame'. For instance, to stoop below what is dignified would be Menga. Perhaps, a combination of mhosho and menga was the reason the Undergrounds ceased operations during India's wars with Pakistan and China although kenyu would also be involved.
4. *Terhomia*: Literally, it means supernatural beings. It can be both singular or plural although plurality is signified. The word can also mean 'ghosts' or 'spirits'. *Ukepenuopfu* (used in the female gender, and usually in the singular) is now, with the coming of Christianity, used more and more. But terhomia is the correct term. And legends prove the fact of history—here legends are also history. But inspite of the suggestion of plurality, our people believed in ONE omniscient God and a number of evil spirits responsible for all the ills of humanity. We believe too in life after death. And we have our own equivalent of St. Peter, in the form of Mecumo, guarding the gate into the next world. People respected and feared God and made all efforts to avoid displeasing Him or committing *phouma* (sin) which is kenyu. This is where, in spite of all the head-hunting practices, which creates a certain image of the Naga, our people believed that the horizontal relationship

with one's fellowmen, had a distinct relationship with the vertical one. God was a personal God and never far from people's minds. One might also add the essential elements of the Christian religion were already in place—concept of good and evil (sin), belief in one God yet with the notion of plurality (the God-head is often the most difficult to explain about Christianity), life after death etc. This, probably, is why Christianity spread so fast among our people although Angamis themselves are, as a rule, slow to accept changes.

5. *Peyu*: This is another word which is, sometimes, not given its due importance. This signifies a man wisdom, depth, possessing clarity of expression, statesmanship, etc. Usually, well-off too. A man would not be accepted as leader, however rich and powerful he happens to be, with many followers, unless he also happened to be peyu. This word, alongwith others, counter-balances the sheer pursuit of material wealth. One often hears people say, 'He is rich, so what? He is not peyu.' But peyu, on its own, is handicapped without mhiasi which brings with it the weight of depth, wisdom and learning, magnanimity, etc. A man who is mhiasi need not, however possess oratorical skills or even clarity of expression. But, without them, and without being well-to-do, he might not become a peyu. Nevertheless, he would command respect. Peyu, without mhiasi, could end up in a lot of modern-day Machiavellis who would be discarded once people discover their tricky machinations. This is where statesmanship is, silently and naturally, woven into the fabric of society. This too is where our people get their ideological outlook because they begin to appreciate things of value that would last and differentiate them from things are ephemeral, however sparkling they may appear for the moment.

An institution, or two institutions combined into one, is the *thehu* (meeting place) and *kichuki* ('kichu' literally means 'sleeping together' and 'ki' is the building housing the dormitory). The verandah or outermost part of the kichuki usually forms the Thehu. Each clan has one of its own. This is a combination of meeting place and dormitory for the men, especially for the young men—the womenfolk have their own dormitory but have no thehu (homosexuality, however, was unknown). It is here that the Angamis prepared their young men for life. All the clan history, the folklores and legends, the songs, traditional practices, etc. are taught here. Any question can be raised here and answered, including intimate man–woman relationships, in the privacy of this fraternal environment. All the disciplining too is done here. From the Thehu would emerge the 'pride' of the clan, fully prepared for life and to play their roles in society. They would already know politics, diplomacy and the various ways of conducting oneself with others including indirect speeches and ready to compete with anyone in any field. Each would know his place within the family, the clan, the khel, the village, and how he ought to behave/act within them. He would give due regard to everyone, choose not to be the first to give offence lest it ends in bringing shame and loss of face to his family and clan. But he would also not brook any insult when offered. He known he is a valuable member of his community and could virtually do what he likes, even go against the decisions of his clan, khel and village so long as he is willing to face the consequences. To this extent he enjoys veto power. But he knows too that he has little or no life beyond his family, clan and village.

There is another very important institution that provided the cementing factor in weaving together the social fabric in the village-republic—this is the age-group. All children, regardless of sex, with age difference of say upto five years (sometimes even more) are organized into a group. This is one age-group. Each khel in the village had one such age-group although the various khel age-groups, formed in the same year would again be treated, informally, as belonging to one. Everyone belongs to one such group. And once a person becomes part of one group, he or she belongs to it for life. The age-group would have a principal host-father whose name would, henceforth, be used to identify the particular age-group. His house also becomes, more or less their club. It is a place of enjoyment, competition, exhibition, even of courting which may lead to deciding and choosing life-partners although most marriages were arranged—the family of the husband-to-be 'hunts' for the wife, instead of the other way round. Discipline, respect for one's peers, honourable social conduct and putting into practice whatever has been learnt in the clan thehu, are an integral part of this place. It is a place of loyalty, of pride and prestige, and gives purpose to social existence which sometimes prove crucial in maintaining the very fabric of village society. It was one such age-group from the three khels that helped bring my own village (Khonoma) back together after it became divided and even warred with each other.

In good and bad times, in life as in death, the members of the same age-group would not desert one another. Everyone competes with the others. But there is never any rancor. The competition is to do more and to do better, not to pull down others which is frowned upon and discouraged through social stigma and even ostracism in serious cases. In an accident, while out hunting or otherwise, they would rush to your help, or even to just inquire how serious the accident was, leaving aside whatever they had been doing and however important that particular activity, at the time, might have been to themselves. You would do likewise. In your success, they would share in your happiness. In failure, they would support and stand by you, not just pity you. Your peers in the age-group would suffer no insult to you, from anyone, within their hearing—often, even relatives would not be allowed to do so to someone from one's age-group, especially when the intended insult was undeserving. Good natured jokes at your expense would be replied to in kind. The same goes for you. This bond, then, is a life-long one. And anyone 'disloyal' to his/her age-group would not get any respect anywhere. So, if family and clan provided the root of our people's identity, and the thehu/kichuki nutured them the age-group helped them to bloom and flower, and to realize their highest potentials.

Our village-society was egalitarian to the extent possible and the basic social premise seemed very sound. The rich did not look down on the poor but looked after them; the poor envied the rich, not hated them. For instance, one of the common social practices was for a rich man to share his wealth by feeding the clan, khel, or village through the 'feasts of merit', differing in scales and degrees, depending on how many times he has been giving these feasts—there is no question of jumping queues! His reward is social acclaim and the right to use certain items in his traditional regalia during special occasions. Wealth for its own sake had little or no meaning in the specific cultural context and it was used to serve a social purpose. Wealth was seen as God's blessing. 'Beware in the days of prosperity', is a warning known to everyone. There is firm belief too that prosperity is only a passing phase. And todays's poor could become rich tomorrow. True, the difference in wealth was not all that much and it was more in degrees than anything else. But wealth was seen in its true perspective—transient and temporary and meant to be a tool in the hands of man to serve a purpose. There was implicit belief that a man's horizontal relationship with his fellowmen has a distinct connection with his vertical relationship with God. I remember pointing out some of these social practices to a Bengali gentleman, a communist, who had come to Kohima a few years back. 'Is this not the ideal of communicism, unfettered by feudal trappings and without suffering the barriers of class?' I asked him. Ours was a vibrant and living culture. Unfortunately, it, probably, could only effectively operate within certain limited scales and confined to the level of village-societies where transparency was ensured. Nevertheless, it made a huge impact on anyone who came into contact with our village societies. And some, like Captain Butler, were to comment, 'it is difficult to conceive as existing for a single day and yet that it does exist here is an undeniable fact.'[2]

A Parsi lady, in Bombay, involved with 'ground-level' artisans and craftsmen, told me she was convinced, the Harappa and Mohenjo-da-ro civilizations had something to do with the Naga people. Her conviction came from the beads and pottery she had seen Nagas wearing and using and from her study of these ancient civilizations. I could say nothing to her because I only had a vague notion of 'Where I came from?' and, necessarily, in the cultural context, I knew little about who I was! I also did not know enough about the civilizations she was talking about. I felt this huge gap, an abyss, in fact. I still do although I am a little clearer now than before. But these are the areas that the Naga people must concentrate on. At the moment, everyone talks 'Naga' but thinks and acts according to their individual tribes. Who is a 'Naga'? What makes a person a Naga? Unhappily, in three-and half-decades of statehood, the government, regardless of who has been 'ruling', has done precious little to carry out any study in this crucial area although the cost would have been a comparative 'pittance'. And most Nagas seem to prefer talking Naga Politics rather than finding out who the Naga is!—'It is an established fact!' is the response of most people. Perhaps, it is part of the larger malady Naga society has been infected with. But unless there is clarity on this front Naga society will, I fear, continue to suffer as from a bone, stuck in the throat, neither able to come up nor go down, and causing much pain and misery in the process.

---

[2] Nagas in the Nineteenth Century, OUP.

Easterine Iralu
Should Writers Stay in Prison?[†]

Of invisible prisons

'We are part human, part stories.'
'Stories can be either bacteria or light: they can infect a system, or illuminate a world.'
'When we started telling stories we gave our lives a new dimension: the dimension of meaning—apprehension—comprehension.'
— Ben Okri, Nigerian storyteller

Every man is a story. Every nation is a bristling galaxy of stories. To be able to share one's story—shouldn't that be a basic human right? Where there is denial of the freedom to tell our stories, invisible prisons are created. Invisible prisons are more poisonous, more effective than visible prisons. The denial of the right to tell our stories violates our humanity. I believe that every story has its space in history. The telling

[†] Speech delivered at the International Congress of PEN in Norway, 2004.

of some stories has been completed while some stories are waiting in the wings to be told at the right time. But when that opportunity is denied, a terrible wrong is committed. Every nation must be given the right to tell its stories, in its own patterns and by the proper storytellers, i.e., its own storytellers. The telling of a story is not only an artistic action, it is a spiritual exercise that is an integral part of the healing of a people's psychological wounds. The imprisoning of stories can prevent the healing of a nation's soul. No one has the right to do this.

What is my story? What is the story of my people?

I live on the edge of the earth. Perhaps, you, too, live on your own edges of the earth. My edge of the earth is called Nagaland. In the minds of its people, Nagaland is a nation. What is its story? The poetry of the hills and dark, dense woods, the spirit stories that nestle in every village, the high romance of star-crossed lovers as well as of the people who turn into stars, and now, in recent years, the long holocaust of genocide, rape and torture of a gentle people.

Naga society was and continues to be a highly oral society. Both men and women take pride in oratory skill, which is an expression of the agility of the mind. We have an overwhelming majority of orators but only a handful of writers. We feel the immense pressure to document our oral literature and native wisdom and simultaneously direct the path Naga writing would like to take. But Naga writing is facing the same fate that Aboriginal writing of Australia had faced some years ago. As Ernie Dingo, Aboriginal actor and poet wrote:

> Aboriginal achievement
> Is like the dark side of the moon
> For it is there
> But so little is known.

Naga writers face the same experience of apathy and more. We have always lived on the periphery. This is my experience, I have been marginalised simply because I am a Naga, twice-marginalised because I am a woman and thrice-marginalised because I am a tribal, a member of an indigenous community. This is the invisible prison that I am referring to.

The absence of major publishing houses in Nagaland makes us totally dependent on the big publishing houses in India to try and publish our writing for a wider audience. But this is where the walls of the prison become visible. There is a dismissive neo-colonial attitude toward Naga writing. This is seen in the mindset that is present in established publishers. Their expectations from this geographical area are very low indeed. It is a stereotyped expectation that Naga writers are capable only of producing politically charged writing or exotic folk literature in mediocre language. Some publishers will publish Naga writing only if it is brought under the umbrella of contemporary Indian writing. This is an exercise that underwrites the peculiar genius of Naga literature. The truth is, there is so much more to Naga writing than the political conflict and the exoticism of the folk. Indeed, we have been profoundly affected by both. We cannot deny the influence of the folk upon our psychological perception of the world. Nor can we extricate the angst of the conflict from our poetry and our writing. But that is all that the outside world, if they are aware of the existence of Nagaland, knows about it. However, I want to assert that Naga writers are capable of writing beyond these strictures imposed upon them. The strictures are themselves part of the invisible prison.

I must dwell a while on the experiences of some Naga writers. A Naga writer of the Naga political conflict had his manuscripts returned to him with the comment that it was 'too explosive'. That particular manuscript contained the Naga side of the conflict. Ironically, an Indian bureaucrat who wrote on the same theme was immediately published. This was because he had presented the Indian version of the conflict. It justified the actions of the Indian armed forces and minimised the genocide, rape and torture of the Nagas. It portrayed the Naga struggle as an insurgency movement and as secession from the Indian Union. This book with only one side of the story was published because it was the politically correct version.

And now, these are some of the things taking place. Some non-Naga researchers have paid money to naïve village women herbalists to make them part with the identity of their closely guarded medicinal herbs. Indian scholars collect data on visits to Nagaland and thus claim to be experts on the Naga context. Indian women academics likewise are representing the Naga story in international forums claiming to be experts on the condition of conflict-ridden Naga women. At an international story festival in Delhi, January 2004, the time given to me to speak about Naga literature was one and a half minutes! Throughout, the moderator kept reminding me to be brief.

Our truths are being distorted. Our stories are being stolen. Our voices are being silenced. These prisons are man-made and invisible. But they are as real as visible prisons.

Unlike Ralph Ellison's protagonist, we do not celebrate invisibility. We fear and reject invisibility.

When does invisibility happen?

When there is rejection because rejection is a way of taking away worth and value. Stories that are devalued cannot be born nor shared. They cannot be.

When does invisibility happen?

When there is theft.

Theft itself is abuse. What theft leaves behind is invisibility.

When does invisibility happen?

When there is disbelief. When you do not believe my stories, you condemn them to invisibility. But when you trust me as a storyteller and begin to accept my stories by believing them, your faith wills them into visibility. Your faith then authenticates them, actualises them and this is the only key that will unlock my invisible prison. I have faith in the stories of my people because listeners from other nations have believed, accepted and appreciated them. A small publishing house in Australia has accepted a manuscript on the cultural life of my village. They agreed to let the voices of the village people who tell the stories be heard in highly cultural translation with the minimum of editing.

Writers in Nagaland do not go to prison. But if their truths are damaging, their freedom of expression is effectively throttled.

How can the outside world help? By creating opportunities for Naga writers and writers in similar situations to be published and read extensively. By listening to our stories. By unmuzzling our truths. By doing this, our invisible prisons will be deconstructed and a new story can be written. If truth and justice are important to the world of writers, then that world has a collective responsibility to work for the Naga voice and all subaltern voices to be heard, read and comprehended.

Could the Romsa Congress be empowered to give this beautiful gift of freedom to imprisoned writers?—The freedom to tell their stories. This alone can liberate us from our visible and invisible prisons.

Chandrakanta Murasingh
Kokborok
Her People and Her Past[†]

Tripura is a small state in the north-eastern region. The mother tongue of the Tripuris, the majority tribe among the indigenous people of the state, is Kokborok. Eight communities of the original inhabitants of Tripura speak this language (Kokborok) which belongs to the Bodo branch of the Tibeto-Burmese family of languages. The communities which speak Kokborok are Tipra, Reang, Noatia, Jamatia, Rupini, Kaloi, Murasingh and Uchai. Besides these communities, some other indigenous people of the state and adjacent areas also use Kokborok as their language for communication. The Tripuris living in Hill-Chittagong of Bangladesh and the Reangs living in Mizoram also speak Kokborok. The total number of Kokborok speakers is approximately nine lakhs. The people of the eight Kokborok speaking communities who are found scattered

---

[†] Introduction to Chandrakanta Murasingh (ed.), 2008, *Tales and Tunes from Tripura Hills*, New Delhi: Sahitya Akademi.

over parts of India and Bangladesh speak in different dialects of the language. In the absence of official recognition over a deplorably long period of time, no script of the language which could be acceptable to all has yet been developed. But despite local dissimilarities between dialects, the Kokborok speakers of different places are able to hold spoken communication among themselves in their mother tongue.

Earlier, the Kokborok language was known by a different name. Sukumar Sen, the great linguist and other researchers did not use the word 'Kokborok' to designate this language. The researchers severally called the language, Tip-ra, Tipra, Tipura, Tiperah, etc. But this language of the indigenous people of Tripura is known in the hills and plains of Tripura as Kokborok only. The meaning of the word 'Kokborok' is 'language of the Borok race'. The word 'Kokborok' was first used in writing by the poet Daulat Ahmed and Muhammad Umat. These two writers wrote a book on Kokborok grammar titled, *Kokboroma* in 1897. In this book, *Kokboro* has been written in place of Kokborok. In 1900 was published another book on Kokborok grammar under the title, *Kokborokma*, written by Thakur Radha Mohan Debbarman.

During the princely rule the Kokborok language suffered worst neglect. Though the language was the mother tongue of the royal family, it did not yet receive its due status and importance. Nevertheless, it deserves to be mentioned that *Rajmala*, the book on the so-called history of the royal family was first written in Kokborok language. In the Bengali version of the book, it is mentioned in the sixth page of the section on Dharma Manikya in the second canto (*Lahar*) of the epic-like history that earlier Rajmala was composed in the verse form in Tripur language so that every one could understand the poem. It is unfortunate that the princely rulers never felt the necessity to preserve this original version of Rajmala written in Tripur (Kokborok) language.

Before he became the king, prince Radha Kishore had taken upon himself the task of compilling a Tipra–Bengali dictionary. The dictionary never saw the light of the day, perhaps because of sheer neglectful and disinterested attitude of the royal family towards their own mother tongue. Even the manuscript of the dictionary was not considered worth preserving by them. That such a dictionary had been written in known from the records on educational matters contained in the Administrative Report of C.W. Bolton, the then officiating Political Agent of the British government for Hill Tipperah. The record ran as follows: 'The Jubaraj is still engaged in the compilation of a Tipperah–Bengali dictionary.'

Since the near-naked hill-people of the princely state, who practiced *jumming* (shifting cultivation), and the poor subjects of the state spoke in Kokborok language, the Maharajas of the state, sitting on the octangular throne held up by a lion, felt ashamed of speaking in the same language. Despite the despise of the royal family and their hangers-on, the Kokborok language continued to be used as the language of the ordinary people living in the hills and forests not only for communication between them on their daily affairs but also for expression of their finer feelings and flights of imagination and for spinning their simple yarns of romances. On one end continued the wishful claim of the royal family to have hailed from the prehistoric lineage of 'Chandra Bamsa' (lunar race or dynasty) voiced through Rajmala, which was later contradicted by Kailash Chandra Sinha, and on the other end flowed on the stream of Kokborok language with its eight tributaries of dialects satiating the thirst for self-expression of the ordinary people who spoke in those dialects. And thus emerged the folk songs and folk tales of Tripura.

Life and living as pictured in Kokborok fold songs

Near the bathing ghat stand the Muibali tree
Janijong, the songbird, sings from there
The new year is back again.

Thus has been described the advent of the new year in a folk song in Kokborok. The songs of janijong birds are heard during the waning days of the spring season from near the forest-enveloped hill-stream. These songs seem to be the welcome harbinger of the new year. The janijong birds, as if, wish to lose themselves in the moist smell of summer clouds and rains.

For the new Baisakh (the first month of the new year), the minds of Tripuris also remain highly eager, for it is then that the worship of their chief deity, Garia, starts. The body and mind of every Tripuri sway and swell with the picture of merriment and festivities that are revived in their minds—the merry songs, the smell and taste of cakes prepared with Maimi rice, of country-liquor, of roasted pork and of stewed meat—all galore. The quick beats of Garia Kham (a sort of drum) call to mind the dances in ecstacy! The walk of the groups of 'magans' going from door to door, carrying Garia deity with them! The courtyards of the houses, ringing with songs that grow louder and louder at every wave of gleeful laughter. Thus begins the new year and along with it starts the season for toil on the hill-slopes coloured with the wild hues of the blooming flowers and the foliage of the trees and creepers, bushes and thickets. New hopes start weaving new dreams.

With sun rising in the east, groups of women and men walk down the slopes to their jum fields with *damra* (a kind of flat headed billhook) held by each in the hand, and a *langa* hanging at their backs in which they carry their mid-day meal, a pack of cooked rice wrapped up carefully in a banana leaf. At noon they wash themselves in the cool and crystal-clear water of a spring, engaging themselves in a sort of merry group bath, thus freshening up their tired bodies. They catch the crabs and the shrimps which hide themselves in the rock-holes and with these catch they prepare *godak*, their favourite dish, in a hollow cone of a strip of bamboo, with bamboo-shoots mixed with the crabs and the shrimps that they have caught. The *gong* (a bamboo-hut raised on bamboo pillars), their resting place, gets filled with the sweet aroma of *jum*-rice, whetting their appetite up. Then comes a spell of welcome shower and both the parched land and the minds of the young men and women get soothingly wetted. The roaring of the clouds get blended with their gleeful cries of 'e-hu-hu'. The forest breeze fans their hopping and dancing bodies. The fragrance of flowers coming out of the braided hair of the loved one fills the air. The youth in his ecstasy sings out:

> From a high branch I picked a flower
> My finger prints are still there
> You and I trod over the path
> The foot-prints linger there still

Life and the consciousness of it have, thus, grown in the Tripuri society in an easy and simple way as shoot up the tender bamboo-shoots with branches and twigs yet to grow. The fingerprints that left their mark while picking the flower or the footprints on the path trodden together have not been effaced even after so many ages. The naivete remains untainted still! The prints perhaps were marked indelibly in the body of love itself, in the deepest core of life-consciousness. The folk songs in Kokborok have thus been enriched by dreams and reality, hopes and joy, deprivations and disturbed peace, feelings and yearnings scattered over both sides of life's path for centuries.

From birth to death, every event is celebrated or mourned over in the folk songs of Tripura. Numerous songs are there on subjects ranging from *Abur-Sumani* of a baby (the baby's first look at the sun), lullaby, the love in youth, marriage, death to the last rites after death. The jum cultivation, description of seasons, hunting, different religious rituals and festivals all come into the songs. Folk songs as a whole are known in the Tripuri society as *Tipra-Bharat*. From when and in what context this name for the folk songs came into vogue is a subject worth researching on. The name may have been coined and may have gained currency in recent past, perhaps, owing to imitation of the Mahabharata, to suggest a wide canvas of life under the influence of Indian culture. The extensive as well as intensive presentation of life and society of the Tripuris in these folk songs in Kokborok may be the reason for the use of this nomenclature for the folk songs of Tripura. The economic base of the Tripuris was jumming or shifting cultivation and on the jum fields and *gayrings* (bamboo-hut) their whole life used to get spent. Hence the abundance of folk songs centred on jum.

For production of jum crops, the jungles on hill-slopes and hill-tops are cleared by setting them on fire. Hence after having carried on jumming at a particular place, jumming cannot be carried on at the same place for several years. After the harvesting is done, the field is left behind in search of fresh hill-slopes and tops. On the deserted jum fields bloom wild flowers as if to give them company and deck them with colours.

A nomadic way of life had developed among the Tripuris who had to move from place to place every year in search of suitable hill-slopes and hill-tops, going deeper and deeper into the dense forests. In course of time some small permanent villages came up in forests and the jumias got used to plough-cultivation on plain and marshy lands. From these remote hamlets they went to their jum fields as well. While going from their habitats to the jum fields and during work on the fields the intimate relationship that grew between the young men and the young women culminated into love between them and such love stories are celebrated in many a folk song. In one such folk song we hear a young lover, sitting on the verandah of a gayring, the bamboo-hut erected on a raised platform for jumias to take rest and keep watch on their jum fields, singing to his beloved, working on the field all by herself, in the following words:

Both of us are of the same age
The desires of our heart are also the same.
By the side of the jum field the Topthai-bird sings
Perhaps his mind is enamoured by you.
Your gayring is rather unstable
My gayring is quite high

> The wind here plays on the body
> Come to my gayring O' my love.

The young maiden listens to his song and cannot decide what she should do. She is abashed in her natural maidenly modesty and shyness. But she feels she must give a reply. In a shy voice she sings softly:

> Your gayring is quite high
> To it come I may
> But I die in fear
> Lest the crows should eat up my crop of maize.

Jumming does not yield a very rich harvest and hence poverty haunts the jumias throughout the year. Perpetually harassed by natural calamities, attack from wild animals, diseases and bereavements, they try to find some consolation by blaming fate for all the adversities of their life. This fatalism has also been reflection in their numerous folk songs, one of which runs as follows:

> I came to the city of men
> But, alas, where am I to find happiness?
> The tool for work is not there at home
> The pot of rice is not there on the loft of the hut
> There isn't any respite even on rainy days
> In the scorching heat of the mid-day sun
> There is only work and sweat
> On the whole of my forehead is written only sorrow
> I am turned an owner of grief alone.

Before we conclude this short introduction to the of folk songs in Kokborok, we may urge upon the discerning reader to take up an in-depth study of the rich store of folk songs of the tribes of Tripura, the songs that speak of the joys and sorrows of the people who live 'far from the madding crowds' ignoble strife' and in the 'cool sequestered vale' of their life and yet are as imaginative and sensitive, as eloquent in their expression of feelings and thoughts as are the affluent, fortunate and sophisticated people of the world.

A Glimpse into the Realm of Kokborok Folk Literature

The traditional jum cultivation demands back-breaking labour from sunrise to sunset. After such a day of toil, evening brings in a welcome respite for recreations. Notes of the *chongpreng* and the *sumui* (indigenous string instrument and flute) float in the evening air. The tune spreads the yearnings of the young hearts. Music from chongpreng, *sumui, dangdu* and *sarinda* seeks new meaning in the familiar moonlight. Audience gathers around. When the group is formed, the elders narrate folk and fairy tales. The stories are interspersed with short rhymes and songs. The teenagers constitute the majority of the audience. The narrators carry them to the world between reality and dreams. Within the kaleidoscopic colours of the tales are reflected the themes of weal and woe, love and separation, hatred and conflict, privation and desire, of natural justice and wish-fulfilment. These tales reflect the social psyche.

The jum being the principal economic activity of the Tripuris, it frequently appears as the background of the stories. Through the stories of the heroes and fools, of love and enterprise, through the tales of social and religious practice and through narratives of socio-political customs like the 'maid-hunt' by king's men, the folk tales reveal the faith, beliefs and values of the Tripuris. In this remote part of the land, away from the so-called 'modernism', these stories bring to light the simple yet vigorous lifestyle, strong sense of values, an innate artistic temperament. Inspite of being one of the most ancient races, no comprehensive history of the Tripuris is available yet. The process of development of their society has remained mostly unknown. The *Rajmala* (history of Tripura kings) composed under royal patronage speaks little of the life of common man. As the material for social history, the folk literature is of great value. To know and understand the customs of the society, its totem and taboos, the folk literature remains the richest source. In this reference the folk tale, 'Kherengbar Bubar' may be cited. The newly wedded wife asks the husband to get her some Kherengbar flowers to wear on her hair. The husband remonstrates but fails. He brings her the flower on condition that she must not smell it. The wife pays no heed and smells the flower. As punishment, the husband turns a hoolock, and the wife a lizard. It is a tale of taboo. In fact, Kherengbar flower has no smell; but on touch it causes itching and eruptions on the skin. The story serves as warning against use of the flower.

Tripuri folk tales are rich in variety and in artistic presentation. Among the stories one finds themes of moral, of social guidance and restrictions, of ancient legends, fertility, taboos, creation and of fate and destiny. There are stories in the form of beast-fable or of abstract character as well. Almost similar stories are found among the different tribes in Tripura. Sometimes through different tales motif of a particular tale is inlaid in a sub-plot. Some of the folk tales of the Tripuris have their close parallels in folk tales of other countries as well.

In some of these folk tales, suggestions of social evolution can be traced. Folk literature evolves with the society, and marks of this evolution are held through symbolic suggestions in the body of the tales. Two such tales are 'Juwangkha' and 'Golden Frog, the Son of Moon.'

In the jum-centric life of the people, the monkey appears in the role of the hero. As the tribal society moved from its abode in the hills towards the plains, the monkey relegates its place to the frog. Cattle, horses and market places appear in the stories. In the story of the golden frog, when the frog discards its skin and becomes the ruling prince, his father, the moon-god comes down and blesses him telling that 'you will be known as a king descending from the lunar dynasty'. It almost echoes the claim made by the Rajmala, that Tripura kings are descendants from the lunar dynasty.

The folk literature of Kokborok is very old. In them, starting from the stellar bodies even the smallest animal speaks the language of man; behaves in human manner. This can be well interpreted as one form of pantheistic creed. These tales have been handed over from generation to generation without much change. Expansions, additions and alterations have not changed their original character much. These folk tales may guide us to the remote unknown past of these people. These are also documents of the rich imaginations and intrinsic artistic skill of these ancient people even in that far-off age.

In English we find categorization of folk lores into folk tales, fairy tales, myths and legends, etc. In Kokborok we do not have such divisions. In Kokborok there is a single term for folk lores, that is *kerang kothoma*. Kerang means the land tortoise, and kothoma means a tale. Folk-tales are, therefore, tales of the wild land tortoise, whether there be a tortoise in it or not. The reason of this nomenclature is not known, but it is in currency from the remotest past. Tortoise belongs to the turtle group, but it is an exception. Instead of water, it lives on land. Even in its shape it has a strange look. This strangeness might have made it a subject of folk tales. There are other stories too, featuring the tortoise, like 'Mui Maising'. There are stories like 'Tentui and the Monkey'. It is believed that even a tiger cannot make an easy prey of a tortoise. At any attack the tortoise draws itself up into its fortress of the shell. The shell is so strong that no wild animal can do any harm to it. The defence system of the tortoise might have attracted the attention of the ancient people who were constantly in need for defence in their fight against nature, the powerful adversary. Before starting of a folk tale many narrators recite the proverb, 'Kerang Kerang biya yabrwi bokhong Khungrang grang' (The tortoise has four legs and a strong shell), calling to mind the priority or defence practiced by the ancient people. When a tortoise moves through the undergrowth a rustling is heard. The watchdog of the jum cultivator starts barking and chasing the tortoise. The owner of the dog follows it and easily catches the slow moving kerang. At times tortoises are caught without the help of dog, and virtually without any effort because of its sluggishness. Jum cultivators believe the tortoise found at jum area as harbinger of good luck and plenty of crop. This faith is expressed in a folk song:

> Under the Muifrai Toksa tree tall,
> I find a Kerang Kormo small.
> Under its shell, in its fold,
> I did find a heap of gold.
> In that heap my lot I find,
> The same as yours, of the same kind.

At the same time, the Kerang is also taken as synonymous with an indolent one. In another folk song there is the allusion:

> Got the tortoise in the slope,
> Without the chasing, barking dog.
> Got the precious 'Mother's boy',
> Without the formal negotiation.

However, in Kokborok folk tales, proverbs, songs and idioms, the tortoise or the kerang holds a prominent place. The term kerang kothoma for folk tales can be an interesting study for scholars.

Patricia Mukhim
Land Ownership Among the Khasis of Meghalaya
A Gender Perspective[†]

Meghalaya has the unique distinction of having retained its customary laws and practices and its traditional institutions. Customary laws have not been codified and leave ample scope for their arbitrary application. No two cases are dealt with in the same manner or with the same yardstick. Very often there is a conflict of interests between traditional bodies, the government and the District Councils which were created as per the spirit of the Sixth Schedule. The prime objective of the District Councils was to control and administer over tribal lands and forests, and to be a custodian of customary laws and practices. District Councils

---

[†] Much of what is recorded in this report is based on the writer's personal visits, discussions with heads of traditional institutions and women's groups, individual women in the villages of West and East Khasi Hills Districts, Ri Bhoi District and Jaintia Hills District.

issue trading licenses to all non-tribals wishing to pursue any business in Meghalaya. Because of the pre-existence of the District Councils, the 73rd and 74th Amendment Acts of the Constitution were not implemented in Meghalaya. The feeling was that grass-roots institutions are already in place. The ambivalence however is whether the Dorbar Shnong (local *dorbar*) which is the grass-roots administrative unit in a village/locality, or the District Council is to assume the status of the Panchayati Raj. The tussle is going on.

In Meghalaya, land belongs to clans, communities and individuals. They are classed as (i) *Ri Raid* (community land) (ii) *Ki Ri Kynti* (land belonging to individuals) and (iii) *Ki Ri Kur* (clan land). No cadastral survey has ever been carried out. Mapping of area belonging to different owners is unheard of. Villagers still adopt the practice of making a river, tree or a hillock as a landmark for their boundaries. This creates enormous problems in the present because the people of Meghalaya are no longer all agrarian nor pastoral nomads engaged in *jhum* or shifting cultivation. A good number are engaged in settled agriculture or are service employees with government or non-government institutions. Many are in businesses of the small, medium and large scale. The problem arises when institutions that are non tribal entities, such as cantonment lands, state and central government establishments which have their boundaries well-marked out happen to lie adjacent to land owned by tribals. There are several instances of boundary disputes between local land owners and the military, and all because the former does not recognize its boundaries while the latter possesses maps and survey records. In 1976 the Meghalaya Land Transfer Act was passed which prohibit sale or transfer of land to non-tribals, except when the land is used for public interests. This would include construction of educational and other institutions and the setting aside of land for industrial purposes.

Meghalaya is noted for its matrilineal culture. Scholars and researchers tend to nurture rosy images of a society where women literally lord it over men. Curious scribes and scholastics descend on Meghalaya with the idea of seeing, literally, a place where women actually live in paradise. Most visitors to Meghalaya are ecstatic and awe-struck by the concept of matriliny itself. It is in fact quite common to hear comments such as, 'how wonderful to know that women enjoy such an enviable status in family and society'. Or, 'how lucky you ladies are to own property in your name', etc. Unfortunately this myth needs to be put in its proper perspective to reflect the ground realities and research into the land holding patterns as practiced by the Khasis in the past and the changing norms need to be documented.

All the three major tribes the Khasis, Jaintia and Garo practice the matrilineal culture. This means that lineage is traced from the mother's clan line. Compared to women in the rest of the region and in the country, women in Meghalaya certainly appear to be better placed because (i) they perpetuate the clan, (ii) there is no dowry system prevailing, (iii) unmarried women are not under any pressure to tie the nuptial knot, (iv) marriage is purely by choice and mutual consent and not arranged, and (v) cohabitation or what modern couples call 'living together' is part, and parcel of Khasi customary practice and not a taboo. In fact Khasi society never considered polygamy to be immoral as long as the husband was in a position to cater to the emotional, financial and material needs of his wives and offsprings.

In one sense, Christianity gave marriage a sanctity that Khasi society and its indigenous faith could not. Cohabitation makes it very easy for the man to abandon his wife and vice versa. This has made marriages very brittle and left a trail of psychological trauma for the abandoned partner but more so for the children who invariably live with their mother. If the mother has no means to support herself, things become even more problematical. Often children have to drop out of school because their mother is unable to support their education. They have to take up some kind of work to supplement the family income. Khasis have tended to depend on the strength of the clan. In the past, the clan did look after its destitute members and therefore it was a sort of buffer against adversities. But with modernization and the attendant economic challenges as well as the tendency to accumulate, as against the old practice of equal distribution of resources, clan ties are weakening. Individual households tend to fend for themselves. If at all the clan helps, it is only by way of a one-off donation for meeting emergencies such as sickness or death in a family.

In Khasi society, the youngest daughter (*ka khatduh*) is the custodian of ancestral and parental property, and not an inheritor as some would like to believe. Scholars interested in deeper understanding of Khasi society will discover that very few clans like the Mawri, Nongkhlaw, Kharkongor, Khyriem, Marbaniang, Blah, Syiem, Lyngdoh, etc. in East Khasi Hills, the Laloo, Rymbai, etc. of Jaintia Hills, the Marwein, Lyngdoh, etc., clans of West Khasi Hills are among those who own fairly large acreage. Not all Khasis own property enough to distribute to all the daughters, with the desirable practice of giving the biggest share to the youngest daughter. Wealthy families owning landed property are becoming fewer as more people in rural areas are dispossessed of their lands on account of poverty. The few affluent families in any case do not discriminate between sons and daughters. In fact, the trend has always been to allocate some portion of the self-acquired property to sons also. The urban middle class educated elite actually has no problem about altering the matrilineal practice and of adopting traits of patriarchy in respect of taking the father's surname instead of the mother's etc.

In a sense therefore there is an intellectual and cultural divide between the rural and urban Khasis, the latter being the real custodians of Khasi culture, folklores, etc. However, it must be admitted, that the urban elite also recognize the harm that gender biases in matriliny has created. Landlessness or the absence of land titles in the name of male members of Khasi society reduces their status as bankable individuals who can access loans for entrepreneurship, etc. This has been very acutely felt by men. Organisations such as the Syngkhong Rympei Thymmai and Mait Shaphrang Movement have been demanding equal rights for both men and women which actually boils down to equitable distribution of parental property. It is unfortunate that these movements are urban centric and have not made much impact beyond Shillong. It is unfortunate too that such movements instead of looking at gender justice then to be male-centric and to focus on the rights of male members of society only.

But there is nothing in Khasi society which debars men from inheriting landed property. Clans like the Khyriem, Kharkongor, Mawri, Nongkhlaw who are virtual owners of land in and around Shillong have been known to divide the money earned from sale of land equally among clan members be they men or women, sons or daughters. It is a myth therefore to say that men have no property rights. But as a rule perhaps men do not inherit property in the manner in which men in patriarchal societies do. All earthly possessions of parents are vested with the khatduh because she fulfils certain responsibilities and obligations which her brothers might be disinclined to take up, more so, because after marriage, a Khasi man leaves his parental home. A man who marries the khatduh has to live in her natal home. If he marries any other sister then the couple starts a nuclear family. When a man marries, he is said to have left for somebody else's home (*leit iing briew*). This does create a sense of psychological alienation for the male as it does for the daughter in a patriarchal society.

The administration of self-acquired property is entirely in the hands of the owners. That land can be sold, or distributed to all children by parents according to their wish. It is the ancestral property that they cannot usually sell without the consent of the maternal uncles and brothers. On the flip side, there are many instances when the youngest daughter is bereft of any property because her parents never owned any property. Some families are too poor to even keep body and soul together. Such instances do not form part of the normal discourse even though their numbers are growing. The reason is because it is easier to perpetuate myths and to be seen as a 'unique society', almost like museum pieces.

The misconception that sons do not and cannot inherit property is not correct. In Khasi matrilineal society, if a khatduh has no daughters, her sons cannot inherit ancestral property but they can be gifted with the self-acquired property of parents. The ancestral property will however pass over to the next elder sister's youngest daughter. One reason why a man usually prefers to buy land in his wife's name is to ensure that on his death, his clan (*kur*) members do not appropriate the property and leave his wife and children in penury, a phenomenon common among the Jaintias. It must be mentioned that the khatduh is a custodian of ancestral property with conditions, albeit unwritten and unspoken. The khatduh must look after her parents as long as they are alive. Her unmarried brothers also live under the same roof. If any of her nieces or nephews are orphaned it is the khatduh who must care for them. If her brothers divorce their wives or vice versa they come back to the 'iing khatduh' or parental home. Looked at from a purely objective prism, therefore, along with the property the khatduh also carries overwhelming responsibilities including loss of social mobility.

As stated earlier, though ancestral property passes through the khatduh she is really not the owner. She is only the stewardess or custodian of ancestral property. Her maternal uncle acts as the chief executor or the administrator over the property. Attempts to sell off ancestral property have often led to court cases because the property is not exactly unencumbered. Every family member has a say which is often not based on the best and most equitable formula. This is actually the weakest link in the matrilineal chain. It is an area that perhaps requires deeper study because of its propensity to create conflict within individuals in society. There are several instances of the khatduh marrying outside her community and her brothers demanding that she should cease to be the inheritor/custodian of ancestral property. One such illustration is that of a Khasi lady marrying a foreigner and the lady herself joining the airlines as an air hostess and therefore having to be out of station most of the time. When the mother became ill, one of the sons shifted to his mother's house and staked a claim to the property on the plea that his sister was hardly available and that he was actually looking after his mother. When the sister heard this she returned home immediately and took her brother to Court citing customary law. The State of Meghalaya takes cognizance of customary law and applies it in cases relating to property disputes. Such disputes are pending with the District Councils and some are settled by the local traditional institution or the Dorbar Shnong. However, since the Dorbar Shnong is not in a position to settle cases that are adversarial in nature but only those with scope for reconciliation, parties most often move to the formal institutions of justice to redress their grievances.

Is Khasi society a gender equitable society? What is the status of men vis-à-vis women? There is no doubt at all that parents unwittingly place greater value on daughters because she is the perpetuator of the lineage. But sons are neither discriminated against or unwanted. In terms of educational opportunities, both sons and daughters get equal opportunities. But like all other societies, Khasis also confuse the biological aspect of being men and women with the cultural construct of male and female. Sexual division of labour is very marked. As a rule, men/boys do not cook, wash the dishes or clothes. Among agrarian families, the woman does more than her share of work beginning at 4 or 5 a.m. and ending only after everyone has had their evening meals. Women are expected to care for the sick and elderly. They fetch water and bring fuel wood home. They are also engaged in kitchen garden during off-farm seasons and get involved in farming during the planting, weeding and harvesting season. Khasi women have the additional burden of marketing because that is a woman's domain. Even among the most educated families where men are expected to be more gender sensitive, the woman spends much of her time in the kitchen and the husband will make an excuse saying, 'Well she enjoys her cooking and the kitchen is her empire.' No one asks the poor wife whether she actually enjoys the drudgery of kitchen chores.

At a seminar organized by the Indigenous Women's Resource Centre (IWRC) where late Mr T.H. Rangad, who was then the home minister, was chief guest, he observed very amusingly that it is not the Khasi woman who says she is privileged. Khasi men have actually been echoing this rhetoric again and again and so often that women have begun to believe it themselves. Mr Rangad came to this conclusion after several engagements with this writer. Gender equality is not just about property and who inherits it. It is about who does what and who has access and control over what resources. A piece of property owned by the khatduh is more often than not administered by her husband or sons. A woman has no right to decide how to use a certain property unless she gets a green signal from her husband and children. If a Khasi woman is still following a clear-cut routine based on gender division of labour and is unable to break free of that social liability, how can a society be called gender equitable. If we look at agrarian communities and these form the major part of the Khasi population, only the male members have contact with government departments. Only male members have access to agricultural trainings, seeds, fertilizers, etc. Decisions about what crops to grow are taken by men. Again, men have more access to the markets because of their social mobility whereas women are restricted by their family responsibilities, such as looking after small children and the elderly and other domestic chores.

Studies conducted in West Khasi Hills by the IWRC on a number of indicators such as decision-making about purchase of jewellery, sale of livestock and other agricultural products, etc., which usually determine the level of gender equity and rights enjoyed by women, found that whereas women have a say in smaller livestock such as chicken, it was men who took decisions on whether to rear cows or pigs and when to sell them and at what price. Decision-making for women was restricted to what is perceived as less important matters. Gender awareness is a very new concept and has not even caught up among the urban population. In fact, women themselves negate their own strengths when they say, 'let men take care of activities outside the home, let them attend the dorbar, why should we women interfere?' This sort of remark from educated, well-placed women such as college teachers and professors reveal that Khasi women are a long way away from understanding gender equality.

Studies on Khasi matriliny have invariably put the spotlight on the khatduh as the progenitor of the Khasi race and the fountainhead of culture. Some scholars believe that there is a discrimination in Khasi society which is based on birth order. To the outside world the khatduh is the powerful heiress who because of her wealth has all the bargaining space she requires. But as explained above, the khatduh is as much a prisoner of gender biases obtaining in other societies. As far as ancestral property is concerned she is only a titular head. The status of other daughters in Khasi society is not so privileged as outsiders would like to observe. Unless parents are very wealthy, daughters do not inherit property. What is their role vis-à-vis the khatduh? The elder sisters and brothers accept the khatduh as the natural custodian of their parent's property and are grateful to her for maintaining the parental home and looking after the parents. Other sisters and brothers do not carry that liability. Hence in cases where parents have only one home, the other daughters have to set up their own units after marriage. They have to live in rented houses until they manage to buy land and construct their own homes. It is therefore a myth to say that all women (read daughters) inherit property. In Shillong and other district headquarters where at least one member in every family is a government employee, the government's house-building advance scheme has enabled families to buy land and construct houses. But the problem still persists in the case of those who live on the fringes of development. Not even 0.01 per cent of those living below poverty line have benefited from government schemes aimed at giving homes to the homeless.

The khatduh enjoys a fair amount of financial independence by virtue of her inherited wealth. However, she is called upon to use this income judiciously and only as a means of benefiting the immediate and extended family, namely her brothers and sister's children, aunts, uncles and sundry relatives. After the demise of her sister, the khatduh takes on the responsibility of caring and nurturing her children as well. She would not be able to take on such responsibilities unless she has this wherewithal. In fact, on proper analysis, the khatduh is a true custodian who is empowered to utilize resources so that she can take on the manifold responsibilities that fall upon her. Should the khatduh's family be a female-headed one there would be greater need to fall back on the resources left behind by her parents so that she is not in penury. It must be understood that the iing khatduh virtually belongs to everyone. Even her brothers are at liberty to live there if they are divorced. The khatduh's unmarried brothers and sisters continue to inhabit their natal home which is the iing khatduh.

Matriliny does not and has not been able to address the problem of rising poverty among a large section of rural population, half of which includes women. Land has traditionally been a community resource. People of a particular clan who reside in a particular village for some length of time are considered part and parcel of that village and are allocated land for farming and housing. This land is called the Ri Raid. For the Khasis the concept of land ownership by individuals is a concept that was pushed in by the market forces. Commodification of land and fixing a monetary value on it has changed the whole contour of Khasi society as an egalitarian society. Privatisation of land started after the British entered these hills and began to create infrastructure. The British entered into hundred year leases with some prominent clans and paid them annual revenue. In some cases, wherever viable, they made outright purchases. This introduced the concept of land valuation. Once the Khasis appreciated the value of land there was a scramble to buy and sell land. Ri Raid land was converted by subterfuge into Ri Kynti or individually owned land. Among the early Khasis, free land not owned by anyone can be claimed by any clan through the process of *skut*, which actually means claiming as much land as a person could lay his eyes on, taking the hills and rivers as natural boundaries. Hence, clans who became the early residents of Shillong actually appropriated almost the entire 10 sq km spanning the city.

Reasons for Landlessness among Khasis

Societies are mobile entities. People from rural areas migrate to the cities in search of better prospects. Individuals move when they marry someone from another village. Those who move to settle down in another village do not have first right to claim the community land or Ri Raid. This type of land is allotted to original inhabitants of a village. So these new settlers become tenants and have to make do with lease-held land for their farming. These leases are very temporary in nature and land can be appropriated by the owners whenever they choose to. It has led to a situation where farmers are unable to undertake plantation farming but have to depend on annual crops like rice, vegetables, etc.

Another reason for landlessness is because of the risks involved in agriculture. When crops fail, families are compelled to mortgage their land to the affluent in order to purchase seeds, fertilisers, etc. If there is crop failure these families lose their land and become landless.

This researcher visited East and West Khasi Hills and Ri Bhoi district and had random interviews with villagers and the village heads. Poverty is on the rise and so is landlessness. In East Khasi Hills in a village of about 120 families at least 20 families lived in homes that were only 10×10 ft in size. Since the average family size is 5–6, that many people lived in these puny houses. The land on which the house stands was reportedly bought for various sums ranging from Rs 20,000 for about 6,000 sq ft of land. The land was, as per custom registered in the woman's (wife's) name. Hence, ownership is with the woman but not control. Men have as much right to decide how to use that land, whether to mortgage it if need be or even to sell it should the family dip into acute poverty. With the erosion of clan and kinship ties families have to fend for themselves. This is another emerging feature in Khasi society.

The practice in early Khasi society was that community land is allocated to every member of the village. So also is jhum land for cultivation. As long as a family resides and cultivates in that allotted land they continue to be the rightful occupiers. If they abandon the allotted land for some reason and it lies uncultivated and unused for three consecutive years then that land reverts back to the *raid* (community). However, the customary laws also have their loopholes. If a holder of community land makes improvements upon it and makes a permanent structure than that person becomes a permanent holder. This is as good as ownership.

Another very interesting observation of this researcher is that community lands are administered by the Dorbar Shnong/Dorbar Raid (Village Council) or Dorbar Hima (Chieftainship). Heads of the Dorbars or the Rangbah Shnong/Sordar are male members only. So also are the chieftains who are called *syiem*. In what can be called a surreptitious stratagem, the syiems, sordar and rangbah shnong have in collaboration with other members of their council converted large areas in their jurisdiction into privately owned land in their own names. In such cases the title holders are male members. This happens especially in the case of forest land. Naturally the community owned land has today shrunken considerably or is non-existent. This phenomenon might become the bases for a complete overhaul of Khasi society. Men as heads of the Dorbars and Chieftainships are increasingly becoming not just owners of land but have appropriated the right to exercise complete control over it. What women will ultimately be left with is the lineage bit. These reversals are happening at a very rapid pace. Ironically, there is very little consciousness in the community about this swift reversal of women's status from owners of land to mere inheritors of ancestral property with all its social encumbrances.

The above instances of re-appropriation of roles are possible because Khasi customary laws have not been codified. The argument that custom is flexible and therefore laws emanating from that custom cannot be set in stone is a valid one. But when that custom tends to upset the equilibrium that has guided the community for generations then there is urgent need to undertake an analytical study to see how far it will also adversely affect the status of women who have hitherto enjoyed a fairly equitable deal.

One factor that has tended to disempower women is their exclusion from traditional institutions involved in local governance. At one time these institutions discussed issues of public welfare, and governance and were to an extent involved in civic administration. The traditional institutions also adjudicated on matters relating to land disputes and other non-compoundable offences. Today these bodies have evolved into power centres which are vested with the authority over land and its distribution. While in the past, the traditional institutions could be trusted to carry out their responsibilities with honour and dignity, always keeping the interests of the community at heart, today those cherished tribal values are diluted. Greed and the desire for accumulation threatens to destroy the fabric of Khasi society.

At this juncture, it is imperative to (i) undertake a cadastral survey of all land in Khasi and Jaintia Hills in order to identify their rightful owners, (ii) legislative action is required to push in for a land ceiling act before the balance is completely tilted towards the affluent and the Khasi society is sharply divided along class lines, (iii) undertake a detailed study of the rapid erosion of women's status from that of land owners to that of powerless, landless ancestresses and (iv) legislation to include women as integral part of traditional institutions is imperative. This will empower them to understand the nuances of governance and help them to check the erosion of tribal values. Women have traditionally been recognized as custodians of culture and tradition but the administration of customary laws and practices was a purely male activity. There needs to be gender equity in this aspect.

Gender sensitive language needs to be introduced into the Khasi milieu. For instance, the nomenclature of the head of the Dorbar—the Rangbah Shnong, literally translated means village headman. The nomenclatures automatically debars women from taking up this responsible position. Women would have to fight for a more gender-equitable language of inclusion.

Any talk of gender equity in Khasi society tends to become acrimonious. This is because men and women are both thinking of their rights and/or the deprivation of those rights. Women believe they have been deprived of the right to decision making in the traditional institution. Men aver that women are already empowered because of their right to lineage and ownership of property. Some traditionalists tend to go as far as saying that a woman's place is in the hearth and home. She should not meddle with politics and matters outside her home. Khasi society in fact has a very pejorative saying for a woman who dabbles in politics. She is termed as a 'crowing hen'. The Khasi adage 'when a hen begins to crow then doomsday is at hand', is meant to keep women tied to their domestic chores. But at the heart of the conflict is also the inability to sit across the table and discuss these ticklish issues. There is need for a non-threatening space where views can be openly shared without fear of criticism or loss of face.

A gender war is the last thing that Meghalaya needs. What is necessary is a climate of dialogue between the sexes. Perhaps the root of conflict today is based on mutual distrust and suspicion. When women speak about equal representation in the Dorbar they are not talking about immediately usurping the man's rights to be head of the Dorbar. They are negotiating for a public space for themselves and to subsequently pave a way for them to shoulder legislative responsibilities. As a progressive society Khasis should not cite tradition as a pretext for avoiding change when it is necessary and to selectively change those facets that tend to disempower women.

References

Ka Meiramew Bad u Hynniewtrep (Mother Earth and the Hynniewtrep People), Hynniewtrep Endeavour Society, 1994.

Report on Land Reforms Commission for Khasi Hills, 1993.

Report on Land Ownership and Natural Resource Management by Khat-ar Shnong Socio-Organisation (KSO), 2004.

Soumen Sen, *Social and State Formation in Khasi-Jaintia Hills, Matriliny*, pp. 89–90.

Statistical Handbook, Government of Meghalaya, Directorate of Economics and Statistics, 2005.

Robin S. Ngangom
Contemporary Manipuri Poetry
An Overview[†]

My intention here is to present a slice of contemporary Manipuri poetry and a brief historical background would be relevant. Manipur was a part of the 'forgotten theatre' of the Second World War, and the seeds of modern Manipuri poetry were perhaps sown amidst the ravages of the Great War. Hijam Irabat, the socialist poet, is considered a trailblazer because of his revolutionary language and subject matter ('Vulture aeroplanes are on the wing/Wolf siren is hooting/It's quite a scene') which constituted a break with the high romantic poetry written by Chaoba and Kamal. A one-time princely kingdom with visions of grandeur, which fell into the clutches of the British colonial regime and ultimately freed, only to become a part of the Indian Union under dubious circumstances, Manipur became just another corrupt and disillusioned state under the new dispensation. After the trauma of World

---

[†] Published in *Muse India*, Issue 16, November–December 2007.

War II, there were distinct transformations in the political and social life of this erstwhile feudal state. Shared areas of experience for many would include loss of traditional values in human affairs, the tyranny of those who wield economic and political power, rootlessness, dispossession, fragmentation of home and family, urbanization, and, interestingly, the disturbing consequence of the struggles of those who cherish freedom in a perceived neo-colonial regime, and the misgivings of those who felt that they were losing their identity and culture.

Poets began responding to the altered circumstances by breaking with their romantic predecessors and choosing a diction which will suit the times. They became more inward-looking and, consequently, tried to adapt the world to themselves by adopting ironic and 'alienated' stances. In short, these modernist Manipuri poets fashioned a skeptical post-Independence poetics in which irony, satire, and detachment or confrontation became the prime means of self-discovery. The new poetry is distinguished by a continuous probing into the social condition and the fractured psyche of modern Manipur. It was the period when Nehruvian optimism, induced by a promised 'tryst with destiny', was giving way to a darker, more sombre, and questioning mood that gradually turned into deep disillusionment with the values on which a modern state had been founded.

The other notable architect of Modern Manipuri poetry is undoubtedly E. Nilakanta, the scholar–poet, who began writing in the 1940s. In spite of his idealistic slant, Nilakanta employed realistic language ('Manipur, I can't help being worried about you') and was an intense witness of shifting realities. L. Samarendra is another outstanding poet with his matter-of-fact colloquial language, tongue-in-cheek humour, and biting satire. His vision is also largely humanist.

But it was during the early seventies that a group of young poets tried to accomplish something radical with a poetic agenda in mind. They were bohemian in their outlook, indecorous, and deliberately tried to shock their readers and mocked everything sacrosanct or sedate. Shri Biren is considered the leader of this new school. R.K. Madhubir is another prominent poet of this group. Then in 1974, Ranjit W., Thangjam Ibopishak and Y. Ibomcha, who called themselves 'angry young poets', published an anthology titled *Challenge* in two volumes. Of this anthology a leading critic wrote: 'Their poems are like sudden bellows by vulgar young men in the dead of night. If you believe that whatever you say should be uttered without inhibitions and regurgitated like vomit, it stinks. That cannot be new art...' He accused them of being shallow, prejudiced and limited in their vision but grudgingly acknowledged their boldness. It was also during the 1970s that Manipuri poets like Brajeshwar and Kheiruddin from Assam published their own collections and joined the modernist bandwagon.

Things went quiet for a while until the publication of an anthology titled *Storm That Came Blowing in '70* in 1979. The poets of this generation are Bhubonsana, M. Barkanya, Chetan Thongam, Hemchandra and others who avoided the excesses of the angry young poet and used subtle imagery and appropriate symbols with a serious intent. Around this time Shahid Chaudhury, Ilabanta, Biswanath, Kalenjao and other young poets made themselves heard from Cachar, Assam. Thus the post-angry young poet years saw a broadening of perspective and deepening of vision.

The 80s and 90s heard new voices who tried to grapple with the paradoxical worlds that surrounded them. Women's issues were taken up in earnest although there are no avowed feminists. There are many practicing poets of this generation which would include Memchoubi, Lanchenba Meitei, Birendrajit Naorem, Saratchand Thiyam, Raghu Leishangthem, Thoudam Netrajit, Doneshwar Konsam, Gambhini (Tripura), Naorem Bidyasagar (Cachar) and others; one too many to be named here.

Manipuri poetry seems to be at the crossroads now. New volumes are being published each year and the churning of the seas continues with the hope that 'the great poem' will come. Many poets seem to be preoccupied with insistent realities such as ethnic violence, corruption, extortion, terrorism, oppression and drug addiction. As a result, experimentation seems to have slowed down a little. While it may not make him or her a better writer, living with the menace of the gun does not permit the Manipuri poet to indulge in verbal wizardry or woolly aesthetics, but is a constant reminder that the poet must perforce master 'the art of witness'. This is an extremely difficult task reminiscent of Camus's mission reserved for the writer: 'Whatever our personal weaknesses may be, the nobility of our craft will always be rooted in two commitments, difficult to maintain: the refusal to lie about what one knows and the resistance to oppression.' In contemporary Manipuri poetry, there is a predominance of images of 'bullets', 'blood', 'mother', the colour 'red' and, paradoxically, 'flowers' too. A poet from Imphal told me of how they've been honing 'the poetry of survival' with guns pressed to both temples: the gun of revolution and the gun of the state. Hardly anyone writes romantic verse or speaks about disturbing aspects of sexuality or anything 'carnal'. There also seems to be a dearth of the confessional or the autobiographical, and an impersonal, detached mannerism seems to be the norm. Is it because contemporary Manipuri poets are absorbed in writing 'the poetry of survival'? All this has resulted in criticism that contemporary Manipuri poetry is hemmed in by extreme realism. There is, of course, a danger of the images listed above becoming hackneyed. And maybe poets should try to strike that fine balance between realism and reflection.

But poets also have to write about the here and now. And writing about it lends a sense of immediacy and vividness to their poetry. This is perhaps what constitutes 'the poetry of witness'. Thankfully, a few fine poets have moved beyond merely recording events and seem to have internalized the complex conflict between themselves and the milieu. In Manipur, when the reality becomes oppressive, these poets frequently seek refuge in absurdist irony often directed towards oneself, in parody, and in satire. It is a rejection by these poets of the extreme realism I've mentioned; they in turn, also reveal an inclination towards the surreal. In Manipuri poet Y. Ibomcha's 'Story of a Dream', murderous bullets turn into luscious fruits, and in Thangjam Ibopishak's 'I Want to be killed by an Indian Bullet', terrorists visit his home in the guise of the five elements. Ibopishak (like Milosz who didn't want to 'kiss' the wounds of his people in order to avoid making them 'holy') also wrote:

> Manipur,
> People call you 'mother'
> Let me also call you 'mother', please.
> But I cannot die for you!
> ....
> ....
> If anyone has to die, let those die
> Who suck your resources dry
> Deceiving stealing intimidating
> Amassing riches for seven generations
> Let them die for you.
> Why should I die?

I wouldn't claim that contemporary Manipuri poetry is as 'sophisticated' as Bengali or even Assamese poetry is, or as 'rooted' as Kokborok poetry of Tripura is with its sense of genuine community. As regards the achievement of contemporary Manipuri poetry, let readers judge for themselves from the poems included in this section.

Anungla Aier
Folklore, Folk Ideas and Gender among the Nagas

Despite the tremendous social and cultural change seen among the Nagas, the fundamental premise of gender relations in the Naga society have remained traditionally inspired till now.

The discipline of oral tradition, folk narrative, on one hand, and gender relationship, on the other, operate on two conceptual polarities. Folklore and oral tradition and narratives border the knowledge sphere of a culture encompassing the literary and creative, symbolic and ritual aspects of culture. But, gender focuses primarily on the structures of social roles, activities, power equation between the sexes. Apparently, the development of the two concepts follows two distinctive paths and fulfills distinctively different purposes. Having said this, it is pertinent that a brief note be made on the two key concepts upon which the analysis of this discussion rests.

† *Eastern Quarterly*, Volume 5, Issues I and II, July–December 2008.

Gender relations are the socially determined relation that differentiates male and female situation in the society and refer to that dimension of social relation that structures the lives of individual men and women. In gender context, women and men are socialized differently and often function in different spheres of the community. An emphasis on gender also highlights the power relation and privileges which is normally legitimized through various cultural denominators. As a result, in every society men and women occupy a different social space that defines their identity and social roles within the household or in the community. Consequently, they have different life experiences, knowledge, perspective and priorities. Cross-cultural studies of these differences the world over have shown that, rather than being pre-determined or natural, almost all such perceived characteristics have been shaped and constructed by the society.

Studies in folklore and oral traditions reflect on a wide variety of knowledge, mode of thought, forms of art, and beliefs of a culture. It encompasses myth, legends, oral traditions, folk belief, and folktales. The very nature of folklore and oral tradition eludes an encompassing definition. However, Jan Brundvand (1978) defines folklore as the 'traditional, non-institutional part of a culture. It encompasses all knowledge, understandings, values, attitudes, assumptions, feelings and beliefs transmitted by word of mouth or by customary exemples'.[1] Despite the seemingly different premises of the two concepts, the argument that is being proposed in this paper is that the construction of gender identity and the nature of gender relationship that follow such constructions are continually strengthened and reinforced through the elements of 'folk ideas' which are sustained in the various forms or genres of folklores.

The term 'folk idea' has been used by Dundes[2] in the sense of 'traditional notions that a group of people have about the nature of man, of the world, and of man's life in the world. Folk ideas would not constitute a genre of folklore but rather would be expressed in a great variety of different genres. Proverbs would almost certainly represent the expression of one or more folk ideas, but the same folk ideas might also appear in folktales, folksongs, and in fact almost every conventional genre of folklore, not to mention non-folkloristic materials. There may well be

---

[1] Jan Brundvand, 1978, *The Study of American Folklore: An Introduction*, 2nd edition, New York: W.W. Norton.

[2] See 'Folk Ideas as Units of Worldview', in Alan Dundes, 1971 'Towards New Perspectives in Folklore', *The Journal of American Folklore*, Vol. 84, No. 331, January–March, pp. 93–103.

other terms that might be considered more appropriate than "folk ideas," for instance, "basic premises", "cultural axioms", or "existential postulates". The particular term is really not the point. What is important is the task of identifying the various underlying assumptions held by members of a given culture. All cultures have underlying assumptions and it is these assumptions or folk ideas which are the building blocks of worldview.'

The notions of masculinity or femininity normally label and justify the accepted norms of behavior and the social roles for men and women. Such assumptions or folk ideas as Dundes pointed go on to build the people's worldview that upholds the basic structure and organization of the society and the gendered relationship of its members. Following this understanding, an effort is made here to look at some aspects of Naga oral tradition, the nature of the folk ideas that spring forth from such tradition and in the ways it contributes towards the construction of gender identity and roles in the Naga society.

The Naga society is a patriarchal, patrilineal society where the structure of the relationship between the genders normally gets the legal sanction through institutions such as the customary laws. The traditional institutions and customary law and practices upheld by various Naga communities are inspired by the belief in male dominance that becomes clearly visible when we consider various oral traditions particularly with reference to origin myth, migration stories, settling of villages that constitute the most important field of oral tradition among the Nagas. Naga origin myths are essentially mythological and describe a supernatural origin and points to a time when human beings and animals were believed to have co-existed. One such origin myth is the story that tells of men, tiger, and spirit[3] who descended from the Ancestral Mother and lived together as brothers. The story is situated at a time when day and night was not separated; humans and animals lived as one communicating with one another. Though different versions are found in different tribes, one common theme that emerges in this myth is that the Nagas clearly demarcate the universe into three parts: one part is controlled by men, the other by the wild animals, usually symbolized by the strength of the tiger, and the third part by the spirits. The story depicts the woman as the mother who gave life to them all, but she is always depicted as a weak, sickly woman who was constantly under the

---

[3] Personal collection of stories by the author. See also *Folktales from Nagaland* (1971), Department of Art and Culture, Government of Nagaland.

threat of the Tiger unless under the care and protection of the man. Eventually she dies and is buried under the hearth to protect the body from being devoured by the tiger.

The folklores and oral narratives of the Nagas indicate a symbolic and ritual representation of the social construction of the role of men and women. The creation stories of the various tribes contains various elements that embrace the idea of women as the caregiver or nurturer equating them with the mother earth while men are equated with the qualities of bravery and strength usually represented by various characters from the animal kingdom, especially the Tiger. She is therefore expected to perform all the tedious, repetitive, and manual works at home, nurturing the proper growth and development of all her family members. The association of beliefs, expected gender roles, and the relationship therein gets ritual expression in the two most important ceremonies of the agricultural cycle—the sowing ceremony and the harvest ceremony. In performing rituals connected with agricultural cycles, the concept of men as seeds are symbolically enacted by the first sower, whereas women as the food manager of the family is ritually declared when she performs the harvest ritual which involves the ritual harvest of the first head of ripened crops, cleaning, pounding, cooking. The ceremony completes only when the new food is given for tasting.[4]

Though Nagas are basically agriculturists, hunting and rearing of livestock has always been an integral part of their household economy with a clear gender divide with respect to the activities involved. The story of the girl who married a water spirit told with slight variations among the different tribes clearly explains why: one day a young girl went to fetch water from the village pond when the water spirit caught hold of her and demanded that she give him her daughter in exchange for her life. Fearing for her life, she agreed. After many years had passed, the girl grew up into a woman, got married and had a beautiful daughter. By this time she had forgotten all about her promise to the water spirit. One day the same spirit appeared to her and demanded the hand of her daughter in marriage. The woman and her husband had no alternative but to give their daughter to the spirit. After some years, the daughter came to visit them and when the mother expressed her wish to visit her daughter in her new home, she said, 'I will leave a trail of rice bran for you to follow me,' And so she went to their daughter's house following

---

[4] See Anungla Aier, 'Agricultural Cycle, Associated Rituals and the Role of Women', in Kunz and Joshi (eds), 2008, *Naga: A Forgotten Mountain Region Rediscovered*, Basel: Museum der Kulturen, pp. 123–9.

the trail she had left behind. When it was time for the mother to return home, the daughter and her husband gave her a closed basket with instruction to open only after reaching home and closing all the doors. But along the way the basket became so heavy that she could no longer carry it. So she opened the basket and to her utter surprise, many animals ran out and escaped into the forest. These animals became wild animals to be hunted by men. She quickly closed her basket and brought home the remaining ones. These animals became the domestic animals to be looked after by women',[5]

According to Malinowski, 'myth expresses, enhances and codifies belief; it safeguards and enforces morality;... and contains practical rules for the guidance of the mass.'[6] Such functional role of folklore in traditional societies has been a subject of interest to both anthropologists and folklorists. In the case of the Nagas, whether the topic is identity, polity, marriage, access and control of land; folklore and oral traditions occupy centerstage. Folklore also comes into play in the area of control and access to land. In the Naga tradition, it is the duty of men to explore new land, demarcate their territory and fight to protect it. Such village founding narratives belong to particular villages which are jealously guarded and preserved.

In yet another oral tradition prevalent among the Ao, Phom, Sangtam, and the Chang tribes, humans are believed to have emerged from stones. This tradition popularly known as the story of the six stones (*Long Terok*), six men (in some versions three men) first originated who became the ancestors of the major clans of the particular tribe. The importance of the story to the community is found in the fact that the detail genealogies of clan descent are always traced back to the first ancestors mentioned in the story.[7] The myth of the magical stone of Khezakenoma, according to Hutton,[8] tells about three brothers who one day quarreled over their rights to use the stone for basking paddy. They eventually separated and became the ancestors of Lotha, Angami,

---

[5] Personal collection of stories by the author. The version that is reproduced in this paper is collected from Zakhama, an Angami Naga village. Similar stories are found in other villages of the same tribe as well as among the Ao and the Chakesang.

[6] B. Malinowski, 1926, *Myth in Primitive Psychology*, New York, p. 19.

[7] A. Aier and Tiatoshi Jamir, 2009, 'Re-interpreting the Myth of Longterok', *Indian Folklife*, July; see also T. Ao, 1990, *The Oral Tradition of the Ao Nagas*, Baroda: Bhasha Publication and P. Longchar, 2002, *History and Development of the Ao Nagas*, Dimapur.

[8] J.H. Hutton, 1921, *The Angami Nagas*, London: Oxford University Press, p. 19.

Sema and the Chakesang tribes. The Angami origin myths trace the descent of their clans to two brothers who came out of the Earth. The descendants of the elder are called Pepoma and the descendants of the younger are called Pepfuma.[9] The Lotha clans consist of three segments—*Tonphyaktsu-rui, Ezomontsu-rui,* and the *Miphongshan-rui.* All those clans under these three segments trace their origin to two ancestors—Limachan and Limathung who are believed to have come out of the earth.[10]

The reason why I have highlighted the origin stories prevalent in various Naga groups is to stress upon the fact that the construction of gender identity within the strictly patriarchal system of the Naga society draws its inspiration from such tradition and narratives that immortalize and revere male ancestors as progenitors whereas the female ancestors, more often than not, are pushed to the background and/or are simply forgotten. This perhaps legitimizes the patriarchal form of the society and the internal arrangement of power structure between men and women. The Naga society being a kin based segmented society, the clan is the central theme around which the entire gamut of their social life revolves. A person is born not only to a set of parents but also into the clan unit and the construction of his/her social identity is primarily drawn from their membership in the clan unit. In this scheme of identity construction based on clan membership, the woman occupies a less significant position as she finds her identity and responsibility shifted to that of the husband's clan after marriage. In the case of men however, they are born to a particular clan and remain attached to it throughout their lives. Reasons such as these are cited to justify as to why women representing the clan in any official or formal capacity are not accepted or recognized. But it is also arguable that perhaps such restrictions on women are imposed more because the patriarchal clan recognizes only their male ancestors and therefore only men are permitted to have the honor of representing them in any social capacity.

We may draw an instance from the traditional decision making institution of the Ao tribe which is called the *Putu Menden* The constitution of this *Putu Menden* follows strict customary practices of clan representation. Once nominated by the clan and inducted into the *Putu Menden*, the person holds the position as a *Tatar* (member of the

---

[9] Ibid., p. 110. Also as narrated to the author by MrKesovito (80 years old) of Jotsoma village in June 2008.

[10] Informant: Myanbemo Kikon, Reader in Anthropology, Kohima Science College.

Putu Menden) for a period of thirty years.[11] Traditionally and even at present, the Ao customary law does not permit women to represent the clan in the *Putu Menden*. So far there is not a single Naga village where women have been given the privilege to become a member of the village councils or are appointed as members of the customary courts such as the *Dobashi courts*.[12] The fact that women are excluded from clan meetings and that they are not allowed to act as representatives of the clan, support the assumption that they are considered as marginal members of the clan though they may carry the name of the clan as their second name or surname. The bar on accepting women as representatives of the clan disfranchises them from exercising their civil rights as citizens on equal terms with men. The consequences of such customary practices effectively disempowers women in participating in all decision making processes.

During the last few decades, the processes of development and education have brought about tremendous changes in the Naga society. Within this changing context, the nature of traditional construction of gender relation and roles have been under pressure specially in view of the fact that many of the traditional institutions of power are replaced by modern institutions with non-traditional guidelines. Further, the introduction of formal education system provided a passport to Naga women to gain access to various modern resources. All these side by side with the general freedom and authority a woman exercises have contributed towards the formation of the assumption that women in Naga society is ascribed a high status. However, as clarified in the preceding discussions, though women have been ascribed a status of respect in the society, they were never recognized as equal to men. The social spheres where women were not accepted or recognized traditionally still continue at present. The arguments put forward in favor of debarring women from those social spheres even in the modern context continue to be inspired and influenced by the oral tradition of the community. An instance of such a case is drawn from the Mokokchung Town Municipal election in 2008, where the *Ao Senden*, the apex tribal organization of the Ao tribe, protested against the Nagaland Municipal Act for reserving 33 per cent of the Municipal Council seats for women. Women candidates were

---

[11] The period/years may vary from village to village but generally in most villages it is thirty years.

[12] The institution of the Dobashi court introduced by the British is a district level court under the Deputy Commissioner with judicial powers to arbitrate based on the customary law of the particular tribe of the district.

not allowed to file their nomination papers and the election was cancelled. The justification given for such strong protest against the entry of women to occupy seats of power in the society are based on the oral tradition and narrative of the community in which traditionally women were never accredited with such positions because access to such positions was reserved for men as only men were involved with headhunting and warfare that protected the villages from enemies. Mention also is made here that in Nagaland, so far not a single woman has ever been elected to the state assembly, nor are there any prominent women in the political stage of the state.

In conclusion, what I have attempted to highlight through this brief discussion is to explore the linkages of cultural ethos embodied in the folklore and oral tradition and the construction of gender identity and in what ways it is expressed through the prescribed gender roles in the society. What has been made tacitly clear in this paper is that despite the tremendous strides of social and cultural change seen among the Nagas, the fundamental premise of gender relations has remained traditionally inspired. Naga women still continue to struggle against the male biased structure of the society and culture whereby they can neither inherit land nor are allowed to occupy seats of political importance and decision making.

This tentative exploration of the realm of the folklore and oral tradition in an effort to understand the intractable patriarchal attitude toward issues of women empowerment and gender justice reveal that it takes more than a few institutional changes with new rules to bring about a change in the mindset of a people. Rather it is found that under the modern situation, patriarchy is expressed even more stringently where the folk ideas or beliefs about gender roles are 're-invented/re-interpreted' to exclude women so that the objective of maintaining the patriarchal 'power structure' is achieved. And in this process, the narratives and traditions and other stories that prescribe the traditionally accepted norms of gender relations are remembered and related as a way of validation.

Contributors

ANUBHAV TULASI (b. 1960; Tulasimukh village, Nagaon, Assam) is a teacher by profession. A graduate from Gauhati University, Tulasi holds postgraduate and MPhil degrees in English from the same university. His first collection of poetry, *Nazma* (1985) was followed by *Doron Phul* and eight other collections of poems in Assamese. He has also translated the poems of Anna Akhmatova, Heinrich Heine, Rainer Maria Rilke, Vasco Popa, Octavio Paz, Marina Tsvetaeva, John Asbury, Mirza Ghalib, and a bunch of Caribbean poetry into Assamese. He has edited several collections of poetry and edits *Discourse*, a journal in English. He has been writing articles on poetry, films, and socio-cultural themes. His poems have been included in various collections, such as *Poetry from the North-East* published by the North-Eastern Hill University (NEHU), Shillong and *North Eastern Poetry* published by Penguin India.

ANUNGLA AIER holds a Masters and a PhD degree in Anthropology. She was the Director of Women's Studies Center, Nagaland University till August 2010. Currently an Associate Professor at the Department of

Anthropology, Kohima Science College, she is engaged in the study of Naga folklore, gender and indigenous knowledge.

ANUPAMA BASUMATARY (b. 1960; Daranggiri village, Goalpara District, Assam) has so far published six poetry collections in Assamese. Amongst these are *Rupali Ratir Ghat* (1994) for which she was awarded the Ishan Puraskar by the Bharatiya Bhasha Parishad, *Anubhutir Bisanna Prantar* (1999), *Dukh Aru Premor Mohanat* (2001), *Jakaranda Sora Ek Rati* (2003), and *Phagunar Dhusar Godhuli* (2007). She has attended several national and international symposiums and poetry festivals and her poems have been translated into Hindi, English, Oriya, Punjabi, Gujarati, Tamil, and Nepali. She holds a Masters in Assamese literature from Gauhati University and works with the Life Insurance Corporation of India in Guwahati.

ARAMBAM ONGBI MEMCHOUBI is the pen-name of Thounaojam Chanu Ibemhal (b. 1957). She holds Masters and PhD degrees in Manipuri Literature and Mythology. A poet, critic, and a social activist, Memchoubi is the recipient of several awards for her contribution to Manipuri literature. She was awarded the Khaidem Pramodini Gold Medal for Literature by Naharol Sahitya Premi Samiti, Imphal for her collection of poems entitled *Androgi Mei* in 1995; the Seram Mukta Mana for Literature by the Manipuri Literary Society for her travelogue *Europagi Mapao* in 2003; the Manipur State Kala Akademi Award for Literature by the Manipur State Kala Akademi for her travelogue *Europagi Mapao* in 2004; and the Ningombam Ongbi Pramodini Ningshing Sahitya Award by Nlanipur Sahitya Samiti, Thoubal in 2007 and the Sahitya Akademi Award in 2008 for *Edu Ningthou*. Her published works include a collection of short biographical sketches of nine prominent women of Manipur entitled *Phou Charong* (1995); a collection of critical essays, *Wakma Maibi* (1999); a research work on the mythology of Manipur entitled *Haoreima Sambudi* (2000); and *Manipuri Sahityada Nupigi Khongjel* (2003). She has also edited an anthology of twentieth-century women's writing in Manipuri literature (Sahitya Akademi, Kolkata, 1998). Memchoubi has published five collections of poetry, one collection of short stories, a travelogue, a narrative poem *Sandrembi Chaishara* on a popular folk tale, and a study on the Shamanism of Manipur based on ancient literature of Manipur entitled *Amaibi: Manipurda Shamanism* (2006).

ARUNI KASHYAP graduated from St Stephen's College, Delhi in 2007. He is the Assistant Editor of the academic research journal *Yaatrâ: The*

Journal of Assamese Literature and Culture. His poems have appeared in *Indian Literature* (Sahitya Akademi), *Postcolonial Text*, *The Daily Star* (Bangladesh), and *Muse India*. He has also written essays, articles, and short stories for *Tehelka*, *The Assam Tribune*, *Sadin*, *Satsori*, and *Dainik Janasadharan*.

BAMAPADA MUKHERJEE (b. 1937) did his Masters in English from Lucknow University and holds a PhD from Calcutta University. He taught English literature at the M.V.B College, Agartala and served as the President of the Tripura Board of Secondary Education. His translations from Kokborok to English have been published in *New Frontiers*, a journal of the North-East Writers' Forum and in Sahitya Akademi publications.

BIBHASH CHOUDHURY teaches English in Gauhati University, Guwahati, Assam. He is the author of *English Social and Cultural History: An Introductory Guide and Glossary* (2005) and has edited *Amitav Ghosh: Critical Essays* (2009), *Charles Dickens: Great Expectations* (2009), and *The Nagaland University Anthology of Poetry* (Macmillan, 2005). He has also written the introduction to the Special Students' Edition of R.K. Narayan's *The Vendor of Sweets* (Mysore, 2004). He has published widely in national and international journals on subjects ranging from modern Assamese literature to contemporary critical theory. His translations of stories and poems from Assamese have been published in different journals and anthologies.

BIJOY KUMAR DEBBARMA (b. 1962; Maharani village, Kamalpur, Dhalai district, Tripura) is an MBBS, MD in Ophthalmology and at present serving as the Head of the Department of Ophthalmology at the IGM Hospital, Agartala. He writes poems, songs, short stories, and novels in his mother tongue, Kokborok. He has published two collections of poems, *Longraini Jambuban* and *Longtraini Ekolobya*; a short story, '*Phola kaitham ni kothoma*' (A story of three souls); and a novel *Dhalai twima naro* (On the bank of the Dhalai River). At present he is the Assistant Secretary of Kokborok Tei Mission (a Kokborok literary society) and also the Treasurer of Movement for Kokborok (a literary and cultural organization).

BIRENDRANATH DATTA (b. 1935) is an eminent educationist and folklorist of Assam. He has held various academic and administrative positions in several institutions. He received his PhD in folklore studies from Gauhati University in 1974 and retired as the Head of the Department of Folklore Research of Gauhati University in 1995. Subsequently, he served Tezpur University as Professor and Advisor in the Department of Traditional Culture and Art Forms until 1999. He has edited various research journals, including the *Assam Academy Review*, *Gauhati University Journal of Arts*, and the research journal of the Anundaram Borooah Institute of Language, Art and Culture. He has edited the Assamese encyclopedia volumes and has also contributed to other national and international encyclopedias. His publications include *A Bibliography of Folklore Material of Assam and Adjoining Areas* (1978), *Folk Toys of Assam* (1986), *Assam: The Emerald Treasure Land* (1990), *A Handbook of Folklore Material of North-East India* (1994), *Folk Paintings in Assam* (1998), *Folkloric Foraging in India's North-East* (1999), and *Folklore and Historiography* (2002). He has also edited several books, including *Traditional Performing Arts of North-East India* (1990), *Folksongs of the Misings* (1992), and has co-edited *Rama-Katha in Tribal and Folk Tradition of India* (1993). He has also several Assamese titles to his credit. He was the President of the Assam Sahitya Sabha from 2003 to 2005 and has been a well-known figure in the world of Assamese music for the last five decades.

CHANDRAKANTA MURASINGH has published five collections of poetry in Kokborok and has edited Tales and Tunes from Tripura Hills (Sahitya Akademi, 2008). He was awarded Sahitya Akademi's Bhasha Samman Award in 1996 for his contribution to the development of the Kokborok language and literature. He is a resident of Agartala and works in a bank.

CHERRIE L. CHHANGTE (b. 1977; Aizawl, Mizoram) was educated at Shillong. She obtained a PhD from the North-Eastern hill University (NEHU), Shillong. Presently a Lecturer in English in Mizoram University, she has published articles in *Indian Literature* (Sahitya Akademi) and *Indian Folklore Congress Journal*. Recently, Romanian translations of five of her poems into were published in *Verso* and a literary and cultural review was published by Babes-Bolyai University, Cluj Napoca, Romania. She has taken part in many poetry festivals and seminars organized by the Sahitya Akademi.

CHARLES CHASIE had his early education in Kohima and graduated from the North-Eastern Hill University (NEHU), Shillong. He later went on to do a course in leadership from Melbourne, Australia and also studied law from Poona. A journalist by profession, Chasie was the President of the Nagaland Journalists Association. He is the author of *The Naga Imbroglio: A Personal Perspective* (1999), *The Search for Peace in North East* (2005), and the co-author of *Subregional Relations in the Eastern South Asia with special focus on India's North-eastern Region* (2005).

DESMOND KHARMAWPHLANG (b. 1964) is a poet and a folklorist. He teaches folkloristics at the Centre for Cultural and Creative Studies of the North-Eastern Hill University (NEHU), Shillong. Kharmawphlang writes in English as well as Khasi and has to his credit three published volumes of poetry. He is currently the Head of the Centre for Cultural and Creative Studies at North-Eastern Hill University (NEHU), Shillong and also the Director, North East Centre for Oral Literature, Sahitya Akademi, Shillong.

D.N. BEZBORUAH (b. 1933; Jorhat, Assam) was the Resident Director of the Assamese daily Natun Asamiya and Editor of the English daily *The Sentinel* (1983–2005). A graduate from the Banaras Hindu University, he obtained a Masters in English from the same university and a postgraduate diploma in Applied Linguistics from Reading University, England. Bezboruah was a Lecturer in English, Lady Keane College, Shillong, J.B. College, Jorhat and Cotton College, Guwahati. He was a Reader and Head of the Department of English, Regional College of Education, Mysore. He was the President, Editors Guild of India; President of North East Writers' Forum; and Member, National Integration Council. He has translated Birendranath Bhattacharyya's novel *Mrityunjay* into English and has published translations of several Assamese short stories and poems. Amongst the many awards received by him are the Katha Award for translation and the B.D. Goenka Award for excellence in journalism.

EASTERINE IRALU is a Reader in the Department of English of Nagaland University. She has published several articles on Naga literature, history, and culture, two volumes of poetry, a number of short stories, and a novel, *A Terrible Matriarchy* (Zubaan, 2007). She has been a guest of Norwegian PEN from 2005 to 2007 and two of her books have been translated and published in Norway.

ESTHER SYIEM (b. 1958) is Professor and Head of the Department of English, North-Eastern Hill University (NEHU), Shillong. She teaches American Literature and Poetry and her special area of interest is oral and folk literature of the Khasis. Her poems have been published in journals like *Chandrabhaga*, *Indian Literature* (Sahitya Akademi), and

Kavya Bharti. Her publications include *The Idiom of the Allegorical Mode: A Study of Six Novels* (NEHU, 2006), a volume of poetry, *Oral Scriptings* (Writers Workshop 2006), and a play in Khasi, *Ka Nam* (2007).

GAMBHINI DEVI (Sorok Khaibam Gambhini) was born in Tripura in 1971 and is a resident of Singibil in the Dhalai District of Tripura. She holds a Masters degree in Sanskrit and a Kavid in Hindi. She writes poetry and short stories in both Manipuri and Bengali. Her published works include a collection of poems in Manipuri with their Bengali versions entitled *Hanglakkanu wahang Aado* (2001), a collection of short stories in Bengali entitled *Subramer Chhota Galpa* (2005), and *Biday! Kangleipak Biday!* (2007), a collection of poems in Manipuri with their Bengali versions. She was awarded the Leihau Tembi Award and the Hemabati Literary Award in 2008.

HAREKRISHNA DEKA (b. 1943) holds a Masters degree in English Literature from Gauhati University. Deka joined the Indian Police Service in 1968 and retired as the Director General of Police, Assam. After retirement he joined the leading English daily of Assam, *The Sentinel* as its Editor. Subsequently, he also edited the Assamese literary journal *Garioshi*. Deka is a prominent poet, short-story writer, and a literary critic. He was awarded the Sahitya Akademi award for his collection of poems, *Aan Ejon* in 1987, and the Katha Award for his story '*Bandiyar*' in 1996. He has written fifteen books and has edited a collection of poetry of the post-independence Assamese poets.

HIREN BHATTACHARJYA (b. 1932; Jorhat, Assam) published his first collection of poems, *Mor Desh Mor Premor Kavita* in 1972. Since then he has published more than twelve collections of poetry, among which are *Bivinna Dinar Kavita* (1974), *Sugandhi Pakhila* (1981), *Saichar Pathar Manuh* (1991), and *Mor Priya Varnamala* (1996). He won the Assam Sahitya Sabha's Raghunath Choudhuri Award in 1976, the Sahitya Akademi Award and the Bharatiya Bhasha Parishad Award for *Saichar Pathar Manuh* in 1992 and 1993 respectively, and the Assam Valley Literary Award in 2000.

HIREN GOHAIN (b. 1939; Golaghat, Assam) did his Bachelors in English from Calcutta University and Masters in the same subject from Delhi University. He also holds a PhD from Cambridge. Gohain taught at Gauhati University from 1969 to 2001 and retired from there as Dean, Faculty of Arts. He writes in Assamese as well as English and has forty books to his credit. He has also published several articles on modern Assamese social history and socio-political affairs of Assam in *Economic and Political Weekly, Frontier, Journal of Modern Thought*, and other national and regional journals. He edited the Assamese journals *Natun Prithivi, Padatic, Kalakhar, Natun Padatic*, and the English daily *North-East Times*. Among his well-known books are *Sahityar Satya* (1970), *Shristi Aru Jukti* (1972), *Sahitya Aru Chetana* (1976), *Asamiya Jatiya Jibanat Mahapurushia Parampara* (1987), *Upanyasar Adhunik Samalochana, Part I & II* (1988–9), and *Uraniya Hanhar Mat* (1998).

JOGAMAYA CHAKMA (b.1960; Gejacherra, North Tripura) is a Deputy Director in the Directorate of Education of the Government of Tripura and a member of the North Eastern Zonal Cultural Centre. She writes poetry in Bengali as well as in her mother tongue Chakma and has published three books of poems, namely, *Aaguner Kache, Halud Chitti*, and *Hillobi Jumma Kadha* (Hill Talks of Jummabi). She has also edited three journals of poetry on behalf of Uttar Purba Kabita Parishad, Agartala, Tripura. She was awarded the Virangana Savitri Bai Phule Fellowship Award by the Bharatiya Dalit Sahitya Academy, Delhi in 2002.

JIBAN NARAH (b. 1970 in Morangial village, Golaghat, Assam) began writing poetry at an early age. He has eight publications to his credit, including poetry, a novel, a collection of personal essays, and a compilation of Mishing folk poetry translated into Assamese from the original Mishing. His poems have been translated into English and several Indian languages and have appeared in anthologies and journals, including *The Telegraph, Indian Literature* (Sahitya Akademi), *Yaatrâ*, and *Samakalin Bharatiya Sahitya*.

KALLOL CHOUDHURY is a poet and short-story writer who writes in Bengali and English; he also translates from Bengali to English and vice versa. His poems, translations, and other writings have been published in leading national and international journals including *Indian Literature, Chandrabhaga, IIC Quarterly*, and *South Asian Review*. He has published four titles, including one of poetry. He has translated Jayanta Mahapatra's Sahitya Akademi Award winning book of poetry *Relationship* into Bengali.

KRISHNA DULAL BARUA is a teacher of English language by profession and is also an honorary music teacher. He has been consistently translating prose and poetry from Assamese to English. His published works include a book on music entitled *Sangeetar Byawaharik Sutra aru Guitar* and a collection of translated poems, *Selected Poems of Nilamani Phookan* published by the Sahitya Akademi. He received the Katha Award for translation in 2005.

KYNPHAM SING NONGKYNRIH (b. 1964; Cherrapunjee, Meghalaya) is a poet, short-story writer, and translator. He writes in both Khasi and English and his writings have been published in some of the leading journals of the country. He has to his credit twelve publications in Khasi and seven in English besides edited volumes and translation works of poetry and short stories in both Khasi and English. He is currently a Reader in English, North-Eastern Hill University (NEHU). The first recipient of the Veer Shankar Shah-Raghunath Shah National Award for literature conferred by the Government of Madhya Pradesh in 2008, he was also awarded the first North-East Poetry Award in 2004 from the North-East India Poetry Council, Tripura, besides a 'Fellowship for Outstanding Artists 2000' from the Government of India.

LALRINMAWII KHIANGTE (b. 1961) is a senior lecturer in the Government College, Aizawl.

LALTLUANGLIANA KHIANGTE (b. 1961), recipient of the Padmasree, is a Professor in the Department of Mizo, Mizoram University.

MAMANG DAI (b. 1957; Pasighat, East Siang District, Arunachal Pradesh) was formerly a civil servant. She is at present a journalist and writer. Her published works include *Arunachal Pradesh: The Hidden Land*, *River Poems*, *Mountain Harvest: The Food of Arunachal Pradesh*, and *The Legends of Pensam*.

MARGARET ZAMA is a BA from St Mary's College, Shillong and MA from the North-Eastern Hill University (NEHU). She is also a PhD from the same university. Her publications include *The Dark Beastie: A Study of Golding's Protagonists* (Calcutta: Writers Workshop, 1996), a scholarly Introduction to the collection of short stories *Heart of the Matter* (New Delhi: Katha, 2004), translation of a Mizo novella *The Beloved Bullet* by James Dokhuma, published in Fresh Fictions (New Delhi: Katha, 2005), transcreation of 'Origin Myths of the Mizo', in Geeti Sen (ed.), *Where the Sun Rises When Shadows Fall: The North-East* (New Delhi: OUP, 2006), and 'Globalization and the Mizo Story' in *Indian Folklife* (Chennai: National Folklore Support Centre).

MRINAL MIRI (b. 1940), a philosopher and educationalist, graduated from the University of Cambridge in 1966 and gained his doctorate in 1970. He has taught philosophy in St Stephen's College, Delhi University and North-Eastern Hill University (NEHU), Shillong. He has also been a Visiting Professor in several universities in the country and abroad and served as the Vice-Chancellor of NEHU. He was the Director of the Indian Institute of Advanced Study (IIAS), Shimla, from 1993 to 1999; the Chairman of the Indian Council of Philosophical Research; and is a member of the National Advisory Council. He is the author of several books and articles published in professional journals. Amongst his publications are *Identity and the Moral Life* (New Delhi: OUP, 2002), *Philosophy of Psychoanalysis* (Shimla: IIAS, 1997), *Five Essays on Kant* (Shillong: NEHU, 1987) and an edited volume entitled *Continuity and Change in Tribal Society* (Shimla: IIAS, 1993).

MOUSHUMI KANDALI spent her early years in Diphu, the district headquarters of the Karbi Anglong autonomous district of Assam. She obtained a Masters in Philosophy from Gauhati University in 1998 and in art criticism from the Department of Art History & Aesthetics of MS University, Baroda in 2001. Though she writes her articles on art, culture, and other subjects mostly in English, her short fictions are in her mother tongue Assamese. She has published two collections of short stories, *Lambada Nachor Seshot* and *Tritiyottor Golpo*. She was awarded the National Award for the Young Authors by Rastriya Bhasha Parishad Kolkata in 2005. Earlier, she had received the Munin Borkotoki Memorial Award for young writers of Assam in 2000. Kandali was also invited to present her stories at the curtain raiser event of the Frankfurt World Book Fair, 2006. She has curated several exhibitions of the North-East artists, both within and outside the state. She has translated the oral poetry of the Mishing tribes of Assam from Assamese to English and the Diary of a Genius by Salvador Dali from English to Assamese.

NARENDRA DEBBARMA (b. 1964; North Maharanipur village of the Khowai sub-division of Tripura West) writes poems, short stories, and plays in Kokborok. He has also written several radio-plays and plays for children. His published works include a book of poems, *Kuklia Nwng Twmani Aswk Pung* and a collection of short stories, *Imangni Yakhilik* (Stairs of Dreams). He is a Government teacher by profession.

NAVAKANTA BARUA (1926–2002) was born in Guwahati, Assam. He graduated with an Honours degree in English from Visva-Bharati,

Santiniketan and obtained a postgraduate degree in English from Aligarh Muslim University. He served as a Lecturer in English in Cotton College from 1954 and retired as the Vice-Principal of the institution. His first publication was a slender volume of verse, *He Aranya He Mahanagar* (1951), after which he published ten volumes of verse that ushered in a new era in Assamese poetry. These include *Samrat* (1962), *Ravana* (1963), *Mor Aru Prithivir* (1973), *Ratnakar* (1983), *Ekhon Swachha Mukhare* (1990), and *Dalangat Tamighora* (1999). Barua has also published five novels: *Kapili Pariya Sadhu* (1953), *Kakadeutar Haar* (1973), *Goroma Kunwari* (1980), *Manuh Ataibor Dweep* (1980), and *A- padartha* (1981) apart from seven collections of prose writings and eight books of children's literature. He also has to his credit eleven literary translations, among which are his translations of the poems of Rabindranath Tagore and Kazi Nazrul Islam. He has also edited two children's magazines and one journal of art and culture besides compiling and editing several volumes of poetry. He was also the co-editor of *Adhunik Asomiya Abhidhan*. Navakanta Barua was awarded the Publication Board Award for his book of poems *Mor Aru Prithivir* and the Sahitya Akademi Award for his novel *Kakadeutar Haar*.

NILIM KUMAR (b. 1961) has authored seventeen collections of Assamese poetry. English translations of his poems have been published in two collections. He has also published two Assamese novels. He participated in the India Festival in Bangladesh in 1996 and in 2001 and visited France as an Indian poet for cultural exchange between India and France sponsored by the Sahitya Akademi. He was awarded the Uday Bharati National Award for poetry in 1994.

NILMANI PHOOKAN (b. 1933; Dergaon, Assam) was educated at Dergaon High School and Cotton College, Guwahati. With a Masters in History from Gauhati University, he served as a Lecturer in History at Aryavidyapeeth College, Guwahati from where he retired in 1992. He has published eight collections of poetry, including *Surjya Heno Nami Ahe Ei Nadiyedi* (1963), *Kavita* (1980), *Nrityarata Prithibi* (1985), and *Alap Agate Ami Ki Katha Pati Asilo* (2003). His poems have also featured in several anthologies, including *Golapi Jamur Lagna* (1977), *Sagartalir Sankha* (1994), *Nilmani Phookan: Sampurna Kavita* (2006), and in Krishna Dulal Barua (ed.), *Selected Poems of Nilmani Phookan* (Sahitya Akademi, 2007). He has also authored several books on art criticism and art history, including *Rup Barna Bak*, *Silpakala Darshan*, and *Lok Kalpa Drishti*. Phookan has edited an anthology of modern Assamese poetry and has edited *Sanjaya*, an Assamese literary and cultural quarterly. He has also translated the poems of Garcia Lorca and of Chinese and Japanese poets into Assamese and has published an anthology of Indian tribal love poems, *Aranyar Kavita*. He has received several awards, including the Raghunath Choudhary Award of Assam Sahitya Sabha in 1972, Sahitya Akademi Award for poetry in 1981, the Kamalkumari National Award in 1994, the Assam Valley Award in 1998, and the Bharatiya Bhasha Parishad Award in 2000.

NINI LUNGALANG was educated at Loreto Convent and St Edmund's College, Shillong and later did her Masters from Delhi University. Currently, she is teaching Literature and Classical Music at the Baptist College, Kohima. Her poems have been published in various journals and anthologies. Her book of poems entitled *The Morning Years* was published in 1994.

NIRENDRA NATH THAKURIA (b. 1960; Bhojkuchi, Nalbari district, Assam) did his Masters in English from Gauhati University. He is currently a Senior Lecturer in English at Pragjyotish College, Guwahati. He is also an Associate Editor of the journal *Yaatrâ* published from Guwahati. Thakuria has been translating the works of various Assamese writers into English. He has recently published two collections: *Seven Days* (a collection of Sameer Tanti's prose and poetry) and *Rupiyabathanar Kabi Prantikar Kabita* (translations of selected poems of Bijayshankar Barman).

PATRICIA MUKHIM (b. 1954; Shillong,) is an educationist, activist, and journalist. She is currently the editor of *The Shillong Times* and a columnist for *The Telegraph* and *The Statesman*. She is also the Director, Indigenous Women's Resource Centre, North East India and has worked relentlessly in the field of consumer rights, gender rights, and rural development. Mukhim was awarded the Padmashree in 2000. Earlier, in 1996, she received the Chameli Devi Jain Award for outstanding woman media person from the Media Foundation, New Delhi. She is also the recipient of an award for excellence in journalism given by FLO, the women's wing of the Federation of Indian Chamber's of Commerce and Industry (FICCI) at Mumbai in 2008 and the UN Brahma, Soldier of Humanity Award in May 2008.

PIJUSH RAUT (b. 1940) is a Bengali poet who has published fourteen collections of poetry, including *Bishanna Udyane Baishakh* and *Janma*

Jowari. He also has to his credit a collection of short stories. He lives in Dharmanagar, Tripura.

PRADIP ACHARYA (b. 1948) taught English literature at Cotton College, Guwahati. He has translated extensively from Assamese into English, including the works of a large number of Assamese poets.

RAJKUMAR BHUBONSANA (b. 1951; Manipur) is an MA from Gauhati University. Bhubonsana started writing poems from his schooldays and his poems have been published in various journals since 1969. He has to his credit seven publications, including five volumes of poetry—*Jarasandha* (1991), *Mamising-Pambomsing* (1996), *Mei Mamgera Budhi Mamgera* (1999), *Ashangba Unaagee Mami* (2002), and *Mei Eshing Nungshit Leibak Atiya* (2006); a volume of children's stories—*Sanakokchao* (1999); and the Manipuri translation of 'Laughing Together'—*Eikhoi Punna Nokminnasi* (2000). He was awarded the 'Telem Abir Cash Award' by the Manipuri Sahitya Parishad for *Mamising-Pambomsing*, the Sahitya Akademi Award for *Mei Mamgera Budhi Mamgera*, the Telem Ningol Atoibemma Award (Children Literature) by the Naharol Sahitya Premee Samiti, Imphal for *Sanakokchao*, and the Minaketan Memorial Award of the Manipuri Sahitya Parishad for *Mei Eshing Nungshit Leibak Atiya*.

ROBIN S. NGANGOM was born in Imphal, Manipur and studied literature at St Edmund's College and at the North-Eastern Hill University (NEHU), Shillong, where he teaches literature at present. His poems have been published in various literary journals and anthologies, such as *The New Statesman* (London), *Verse* (Georgia), *Planet: The Welsh International* (Ceredigion), *Kavya Bharati* (Madurai), *Chandrabhaga* (Cuttack), *Confronting Love: Poems* (Penguin Books India), and *Khasia in Gwalia* (Alun Books, Wales). Among his published books of poems are *Time's Crossroads* and *The Desire of Roots*.

RUPANJALI BARUAH writes poetry, short stories, and translates both poetry and fiction from Assamese to English. Her translations have been published in several leading journals and newspapers. *All Things Passing* (Kolkata: Writers Workshop, 2005) is her first published volume of poetry and *Amrita* (2005) is a collection of short fiction by her. Currently, she runs a publishing house called Wordsmith which publishes *Sabd*, a journal of creative writing in both English and Assamese.

SAMEER TANTI (b. 1955; Mikirchang Tea Estate, Golaghat, Assam) has fourteen published books to his credit, including eleven collections of poetry and three books of lyrical and critical essays. These include *Yuddhabhumir Kavita* (1985), *Kaffri Kavita* (1987), *Shokakul Upatyaka* (1990), *Samay Sabda Sapon* (1996), *Tez Andharar Nao* (2004), *Ekak Chinta* (2007), and *Seven Days* (2008). His works have been translated into English and eight Indian languages. He has participated in the World Poetry Festival (2008), the SAARC Writers' Conference (2007), and several other writers' meets. He has worked with several Assamese journals and newspapers and is at present with the Directorate of Tourism, Government of Assam.

SANJOY HAZARIKA (b. 1954; Shillong, Meghalaya), a writer, journalist, and political consultant, was formerly a correspondent of *The New York Times* and held fellowships from the universities of Harvard, Tufts, and Kentucky. He was formerly a member of the first National Security Advisory Board of India, the Review Committee on the Armed Forces Special Powers Act, and the ICSSR. Currently, he is the Managing Trustee of the Centre for North-East Studies and Policy Research. His published works include *Bhopal, the Lesson of a Tragedy*; *Strangers of the Mist: Tales of War* and *Peace from India's North-East*; *Rites of Passage: Border Crossings*; and *Imagined Homelands-India's East and Bangladesh*.

SARATCHAND THIYAM (b. 1961; Imphal, Manipur) is an engineer by profession but is better known as a poet, sports writer, and columnist. Thiyam started writing poetry at an early age and his first book *Tengali Karaba Podon* (1980), an anthology of poems, was published when he was only nineteen. His other published works include *Chho Chaboon* (poetry, 1989), *Africa* (poetry, 1993), *Hajillakpa Eshing-gi Manakta* (travelogue, 1994), *The Waves* (poetry, 1995) *Yumlingdabasing-gi yum* (poetry, 2001), *Nungshibi Greece* (travelogue, 2002), and *Tsunami* (poetry, 2006). He participated as the Indian delegate in the World Peace Conference at Athens, Greece organized by the World Peace Council in 2000. His poems have been translated into various Indian and foreign languages. Thiyam is the recipient of the Dingko Sportswriter Award, the Jamini Sunder Guha Gold Medal of the Manipuri Sahitya Parishad, and the Sahitya Akademi Award in 2006.

SAROJ CHAUDHURY retired as teacher of English literature at the MBBS College, Agartala and translates from Bengali and Kokborok into English.

SUKALPA BHATTACHARJEE teaches English at the North-Eastern Hill University (NEHU), Shillong. She has authored *Post-Colonial Literature: Essays on Gender, Theory and Genres* and is one of the Editor-Contributors for *Human Rights and Insurgency: The North-East India* (2002) and *Ethno-Narratives: Identity and Experience in North-East India* (2005). She has contributed to anthologies on Multi-Ethnic Literatures of the United States (MELUS), Literary Theory, Cultural Studies, and journals on Postcolonial Studies and Gender Studies.

TAYENJAM BIJOYKUMAR SINGH (b. 1957) has a Bachelors degree in Electrical Engineering and a Postgraduate Diploma in Business Management. He writes short stories and poems in English and Manipuri and has translated many Manipuri short stories and poems into English. He has authored Turoi Ngamloiba Wagi Lanban, an anthology of Manipuri short stories and Manipur Trilogy, an English translation of Ratan Thiyam's Manipuri plays. His English writings and translations have appeared in several journals and anthologies including *Indian Literature, Chandrabhaga, IIC Quarterly Journal, The Sentinel, Imphal Free Press, New Frontiers, Sabd, Ishani,* and Katha publications. His Manipuri writings and translations have appeared in *Sahitya, Wakhal, Poknapham*. He was awarded the Katha Translation Award in 2005.

TEMSULA AO (b. 1945) is a Professor in the Department of English and Dean of the School of Humanities and Education in the North-Eastern Hill University (NEHU), Shillong. She was also the Director of the North East Zone Cultural Centre, Dimapur. She has published five volumes of poetry: *Songs that Tell* (Writers Workshop, 1988), *Songs that Try to Say* (Writers Workshop, 1992), *Songs of Many Moods* (1995), *Songs from Here and There* (EHU, 2003), *Songs from the Other Life* (2007), and a volume of short stories *These Hills Called Home: Stories from A War Zone* (2006). Amongst her other publications are a book on the folk tradition of the Ao Nagas (The Ao-Naga Oral Tradition) and several articles on the myths and folk songs of the Ao Nagas.

MONALISA CHANGKIJA (b. 1960; Jorhat, Assam) did her schooling in Jorhat and Kohima. An alumni of the Patkai Christian College, Chumukedima, she graduated from Hindu College, Delhi University, and also has a Masters degree from the same university. She began her career in journalism as a columnist with the two Dimapur-based weeklies, *Nagaland Times* and *Ura Mail*. She has also been a correspondent for several newspapers and magazines outside the state of Nagaland. Currently, she is the Proprietor, Publisher, and Editor of a daily English newspaper, *Nagaland Page*. Her poems and short stories have been published in several national and regional newspapers and magazines and was invited by the International Indigenous Peoples' Forum to present her poems in 1997 at Oslo, Norway, where she presented her collection *Monsoon Mourning*. Her first volume of poetry was *Weapons of Words of Pages of Pain* (1993). A Fellow of the National Foundation of India (NFI), she is a member of the Planning Commission's National Steering Committee/Working Group on Women's Empowerment for the Eleventh Five-Year Plan and a member of the Governing Body of the North East Zonal Cultural Centre, Dimapur.

THANGJAM IBOPISHAK SINGH (b. 1948; Imphal) is a Manipuri poet who has published several volumes of poetry, including *Apaiba Thawai* (The Hovering Soul, 1969), *Shingnaba* (Challenge, in two volumes, 1974), *Norok Patal Prithivi* (This Earth is Hell, 1985), *Boot Amsung Maikhum* (The Ghost and Mask, 1994), *Mayadesh* (1999), *Meegee Manam* (The Human Scent, 2003), and *Shrimati Tomcha Babu* (2007). Thangjam Ibopishak has received several awards, including the Sahitya Akademi Award for *Bhoot Amasung Maikhum* in 1997, the Manipur State Kala Akademi Award in 1986, the Jamini Sunder Guha Gold Medal in 1989, the Jananeta Irabot Award in 1997, the Ashangbam Minaketan Memorial Award in 2005, and the Tayenjam Jayanta Poetry Award in 2008.

THINGNAM KISHAN SINGH (1972–2009) was born in Imphal and graduated with an Honours degree in English from Jamia Millia Islamia, New Delhi in 1992. He also obtained a postgraduate degree in English from the same university in 1994 and a PhD from Manipur University in 2004. He started his career as a lecturer in English at Shyam Lal College, New Delhi and then moved to Manipur to serve as a lecturer at the D.M College, Imphal. He worked briefly as a lecturer in English in the Manipur University and then joined the Manipur Civil Service in 2007. While on government duty as a conscientious officer he was kidnapped by members of a militant group and brutally assassinated in February 2009. During his short span of life, Kishan Singh wrote books and articles on various aspects of Manipuri literature, society, and contemporary political and economic problems of north-east India. He was the founder-editor of the quarterly journal *Alternative Perspectives* published from Manipur. Besides various articles published in journals, he authored *Rethinking Colonialism* (2006) and *India's Look East Policy and India's Northeast* (2009).

MONA ZOTE is in government service in Aizwal, Mizoram. She writes poetry in English. Some of her poems have been included in *IIC Quarterly Journal, Indian Literature Journal,* and *Anthology of North East Poetry* published by NEHU.

TILOTTOMA MISRA (b. 1947; Shillong) had her early education in Shillong. She graduated from Calcutta University, and holds a Masters Degree in English from Delhi University and a PhD from Gauhati University. She taught English literature at Indraprastha College, Delhi and subsequently joined the Department of English, Dibrugarh University, Assam from where she retired as a Professor in 2007. Her published books include *Literature and Society in Assam: A Study of the Assamese Renaissance* 1826–1926 (Guwahati, 1987), two novels *Swarnalata* (1991) and *Louhitya Sindhu* (1997), and *Ramnabami-Natak: The Story of Ram and Nabami,* a translation of Gunabhiram Barua's *Ramnabami-Natak* (New Delhi: OUP, 2007). She was awarded the Ishan Puraskar by Bharatiya Bhasha Parishad in 1995 for her novel *Swarnalata*.

UDAYON MISRA (b. 1945; Shillong), former Professor and Head of the Department of English of Dibrugarh University, had his school and college education at St Edmund's College, Shillong. He did his post-graduation in English Literature and his LLB and PhD from Gauhati University. Apart from his research in post-colonial literature, Misra has been writing extensively on the society and politics of North-East India. His publications include *The Raj in Fiction, The Periphery Strikes Back: Challenges to the Nation-State in Assam and Nagaland* (IIAS, Shimla), *North-East India: Quest for Identity,* and *The Transformation of Assamese Identity*. He has been a Fellow of the Indian Institute of Advanced Study (IIAS), Shimla and is currently an ICSSR National Fellow.

YUMLEMBAM IBOMCHA (b. 1949; Imphal, Manipur) is a poet, a short-story writer, and columnist. He has two anthologies of poems, *Sandrembi Thoraklo Nahum Ponjen Sabige* (Manipuri, 1973) and *Rajkumari Amasung Uchek Machasing* (Manipuri, 1994) and one of short stories, *Numitti Asum Thengjillaklee* (Manipuri, 1990) besides a number of articles, satires, and parodies published in various journals and newspapers under various pseudonyms. He was awarded the Manipur State Kala Akademi Award in 1974 for his book of poetry *Sandrembi Thoraklo Nahum Ponjen Sabige* and the Sahitya Akademi Award in 1991 for his book of short stories, *Numitti Asum Thengjillaklee*.

Copyright Statement

Poetry

ARUNACHAL PRADESH
- Mamang Dai, 'The Voice of the Mountain'. Reprinted here with permission from the poet.
- Mamang Dai, 'The Sorrow of Women'. Reprinted here with permission from the poet.
- Mamang Dai, 'An Obscure Place'. Reprinted here with permission from the poet.

ASSAM
- Navakanta Barua, 'Judas', translated from Assamese by D.N. Bezboruah. Reprinted here with permission from the poet's heir and the translator.
- Navakanta Barua, 'Bats', translated from Assamese by D.N. Bezboruah. Reprinted here with permission from the poet's heir and the translator.

- Navakanta Barua, 'Silt', translated from Assamese by Pradip Acharya. Reprinted here with permission from the poet's heir and the translator.
- Nilmani Phookan, 'Poem', translated from Assamese by Hiren Gohain. Reprinted here with permission from the poet and the translator.
- Nilmani Phookan, 'After a Couple of Days', translated from Assamese by Nirendra Nath Thakuria. Reprinted here with permission from the poet and the translator.
- Nilmani Phookan, 'Mating Music', translated from Assamese by Nirendra Nath Thakuria. Reprinted here with permission from the poet and the translator.
- Hiren Bhattacharya, 'The Lone Prayer for Poetry', translated from Assamese by Pradip Acharya. Reprinted here with permission from the poet and the translator.
- Hiren Bhattacharya, 'The Earth My Poem', translated from Assamese by Pradip Acharya. Reprinted here with permission from the poet and the translator.
- Hiren Bhattacharya, 'Sylvan Song', translated from Assamese by Rupanjali Baruah. Reprinted here with permission from the poet and the translator.
- Hiren Bhattacharya, 'Let there be crop', translated from Assamese by Rupanjali Baruah. Reprinted here with permission from the poet and the translator.
- Harekrishna Deka, 'Another One', translated from Assamese by Bibhash Choudhury. Reprinted here with permission from the poet and the translator.
- Harekrishna Deka, 'A Word for Love', translated from Assamese by Bibhash Choudhury. Reprinted here with permission from the poet and the translator.
- Harekrishna Deka, 'Towards Freedom', translated from Assamese by Bibhash Choudhury. Reprinted here with permission from the poet and the translator.
- Nilim Kumar, 'I had Nothing to Offer', translated from Assamese by Rupanjali Baruah. Reprinted here with permission from the poet and the translator.
- Nilim Kumar, 'To My Son', translated from Assamese by Rupanjali Baruah. Reprinted here with permission from the poet and the translator.
- Sameer Tanti, 'The Night of Kadams in Bloom', translated by Nirendra Nath Thakuria. Reprinted here with permission from the poet and the translator.

- Sameer Tanti, 'As the Night Thickens the Stars Nod Off', translated by Nirendra Nath Thakuria. Reprinted here with permission from the poet and the translator.
- Anubhav Tulasi, 'The Prodigal', translated from Assamese by Hiren Gohain.
- Anubhav Tulasi, 'Infernal Playground', translated from Assamese by Hiren Gohain. Reprinted here with permission from the poet and the translator.
- Jiban Narah, 'Rhythm', translated from Assamese by Krishna Dulal Barua. Reprinted here with permission from the poet and the translator.
- Jiban Narah, 'Colours', translated into English by Pradip Acharya. Reprinted here with permission from the poet and the translator.
- Jiban Narah, 'Mother', translated into English by Pradip Acharya. Reprinted here with permission from the poet and the translator.
- Jiban Narah, 'The Subaltern', translated into English by Krishna Dulal Barua. Reprinted here with permission from the poet and the translator.
- Saktipada Brahmachari, 'One Birth of Love, Another of Household Duties', translated from Bengali by Kallol Choudhury. Reprinted here with permission from the translator.
- Saktipada Brahmachari, 'Assassin, Turn Horse', translated from by Kallol Choudhury. Reprinted here with permission from the translator.
- Anupama Basumatary, 'Seasons', translated from Assamese by Pradip Acharya. Reprinted here with permission from the translator.
- Anupama Basumatary, 'Earthy', translated from Assamese by Pradip Acharya. Reprinted here with permission from the translator.
- Aruni Kashyap, 'Journeys'. Reprinted here with permission from the poet.
- Aruni Kashyap, 'Me'. Reprinted here with permission from the poet.

Manipur
- Rajkumar Bhubonsana, 'Should Light be Put Out or Mind Kept in Dark', translated from Manipuri by Tayenjam Bijoykumar Singh. Reprinted here with permission from the translator.
- Rajkumar Bhubonsana, 'The Smell of Pomegranate', translated from Manipuri by Tayenjam Bijoykumar Singh. Reprinted here with permission from the translator.

- Rajkumar Bhubonsana, 'E-nga', translated from Manipuri by Tayenjam Bijoykumar Singh. Reprinted here with permission from the translator.
- Robin S. Ngangom, 'Poetry'. Reprinted here with permission from the poet.
- Robin S. Ngangom, 'Gangok, February 1998'. Reprinted here with permission from the poet.
- Robin S. Ngangom, 'The First Rain'. Reprinted here with permission from the poet.
- Robin S. Ngangom, 'Everywhere I Go ...' Reprinted here with permission from the poet.
- Yumlembam Ibomcha, 'For the Next Birth', translated from Manipuri by Robin S. Ngangom. Reprinted here with permission from the translator.
- Saratchand Thiyam, 'Shillong', translated from Manipuri by Robin S. Ngangom. Reprinted here with permission from the translator.
- Saratchand Thiyam, 'Hillworld', translated from Manipuri by Robin S. Ngangom. Reprinted here with permission from the translator.
- Saratchand Thiyam, 'Hill', translated from Manipuri by Robin S. Ngangom. Reprinted here with permission from the translator.
- Saratchand Thiyam, 'Pokhran Kargil Gaisal', translated from Manipuri by Robin S. Ngangom. Reprinted here with permission from the translator.
- Gambhini Devi, 'Hansapadika', translated from Manipuri by Robin S. Ngangom. Reprinted here with permission from the poet and the translator.
- Gambhini Devi, 'A Village Girl', translated from Manipuri by Robin S. Ngangom. Reprinted here with permission from the poet and the translator.
- Memchoubi, 'Red Chingthrao', translated from Manipuri by Tayenjam Bijoykumar Singh. Reprinted here with permission from the poet and the translator.
- Memchoubi, 'Goddess of Lightning', translated from Manipuri by Tayenjam Bijoykumar Singh. Reprinted here with permission from the poet and the translator.
- Thangjam Ibopishak, 'I Want to be Killed by an Indian Bullet', translated from Manipuri by Robin S. Ngangom. Reprinted here with permission from the translator.

Meghalaya
- Desmond L. Kharmawphlang, 'The Conquest', translated from Khasi by the author. Reprinted here with permission from the poet.
- Desmond L. Kharmawphlang, 'Letter from Pahambir'. Reprinted here with permission from the poet.
- Desmond L. Kharmawphlang, 'Poems During November'. Reprinted here with permission from the poet.
- Desmond L. Kharmawphlang, 'They'. Reprinted here with permission from the poet.
- Esther Syiem, 'Retelling Nam's Tale'. Reprinted here with permission from the poet.
- Kynpham Sing Nongkynrih, 'The Colours of Truth'. Reprinted here with permission from the poet.
- Kynpham Sing Nongkynrih, 'The Ancient Rocks of Cherra'. Reprinted here with permission from the poet.
- Kynpham Sing Nongkynrih, 'A Day in Sohra'. Reprinted here with permission from the poet.
- Kynpham Sing Nongkynrih, 'A Farewell Letter of Cherries'. Reprinted here with permission from the poet.

Mizoram
- Mona Zote, 'What Poetry Means to Ernestina in Peril'. Reprinted here with permission from the poet.
- Mona Zote, 'Girl, with Black Guitar and Blue Hibiscus'. Reprinted here with permission from the poet.
- Cherrie L. Chhangte, 'Rain'. Reprinted here with permission from the poet.
- Cherrie L. Chhangte, 'Night'. Reprinted here with permission from the poet.
- Cherrie L. Chhangte, 'Plea'. Reprinted here with permission from the poet.
- Cherrie L. Chhangte, 'What Does an Indian Look Like?' Reprinted here with permission from the poet.
- Lalrinmawii Khiangte, 'Betrayal'.
- Lalrinmawii Khiangte, 'For A Better Tomorrow'.
- L. Biakliana, 'Cry of Mizo Women', translated from Mizo by Laltluangliana Khiangte
- L. Biakliana, 'True Love', translated from Mizo by Laltluangliana Khiangte.

Nagaland

- Temsula Ao, 'Blood of Other Days'. Reprinted here with permission from the poet.
- Temsula Ao, 'The Old Story-Teller'. Reprinted here with permission from the poet.
- Temsula Ao, 'The Spear'. Reprinted here with permission from the poet.
- Easterine Iralu, 'Genesis'. Reprinted here with permission from the poet.
- Monalisa Changkija, 'Mist over Brahmaputra'. Reprinted here with permission from the poet.
- Monalisa Changkija, 'One of these decades'. Reprinted here with permission from the poet.
- Monalisa Changkija, 'Shoot'. Reprinted here with permission from the poet.
- Nini Lungalang, 'Mirror'. Reprinted here with permission from the poet.
- Nini Lungalang, 'I will be'. Reprinted here with permission from the poet.
- Nini Lungalang, 'Rock'. Reprinted here with permission from the poet.

Tripura

- Chandrakanta Murasing, 'O, Poor Hachukrai', translated from Kokborok by Bamapada Mukherjee. Reprinted here with permission from the poet and the translator.
- Chandrakanta Murasing, 'Of A Minister', translated from Kokborok by Saroj Chowdhury. Reprinted here with permission from the poet and the translator.
- Chandrakanta Murasing, 'The Python's Call from the Deserted Tong', translated from Kokborok by Bamapada Mukherjee. Reprinted here with permission from the poet and the translator.
- Chandrakanta Murasing, 'Your Dreams', translated from Kokborok by Udayan Ghosh. Reprinted here with permission from the poet.
- Pijush Raut, 'Feelings', translated from Bengali by Kallol Choudhury. Reprinted here with permission from the translator.
- Pijush Raut, 'Picnic', translated from Bengali by Kallol Choudhury. Reprinted here with permission from the translator.

- Bijoy Kumar Debbarma, 'Ekalavya of the Longtarai', translated from Kokborok by Bhaskar Roy Burman. Reprinted here with permission from the translator.
- Jogmaya Chakma, 'The Martyr's Altar', translated from Chakma by Mihir Deb. Reprinted here with permission from the translator.
- Narendra Debbarma, 'The Border', translated from Kokborok by Bamapada Mukharjee. Reprinted here with permission from the translator.

Essays

- Mrinal Miri, 'The Moral and the Spiritual'. Reprinted here with permission from the author.
- Birendranath Datta, 'North-East India and its Socio-Cultural Milieu', in Birendranath Datta, N.C. Sarma, P.C. Das (eds), 1994, *A Handbook of Folklore Material of North-East India*, Guwahati: Anundaram Barua Institute of Language, Art and Culture. Reprinted here with permission from the author.
- Esther Syiem, 'Social Identity and the Liminal Character of the Folk: A Study in the Khasi Context'. Reprinted here with permission from the author.
- Thingnam Kishan Singh, 'Encounters and Literary Engagements: A Critique of History and Literature in Manipur'.
- Sanjoy Hazarika, 'There are No Shangri-Las Left', from 'Note from the Author', in Sanjoy Hazarika, 1994, *Strangers of the Mist: Tales of War and Peace from India's Northeast*, Penguin-Viking. Reprinted here with permission from the author and publisher.
- Udayon Misra, 'Peasant Consciousness as Reflected in the Oral Literature of Assam: A Study of Two Assamese Ballads'. Reprinted here with permission from the author.
- Moushumi Kandali, 'The Colonial Impression on Vaisnavaite Art Form of Assam: A Study of Sculptural Reliefs of the Srihati Satra'.
- Tayenjam Bijoykumar Singh, '"Kurukshetragi Peerang"—Ratan Thiyam's Gift to Mothers'. Reprinted here with permission from the author.
- Margaret Ch. Zama, 'Mizo Literature: An Overview'. Reprinted here with permission from the author.

- Tilottoma Misra, 2007, 'Crossing Linguistic Boundaries: Two Arunachali Writers in Search of Readers', Economic and Political Weekly, Vol. XLII, No. 36, 8 September. Reprinted here with permission from the author.
- Cherrie Lalnunziri Chhangte, '"Lonliness in the Midst of Curfews": The Mizo Insurgency Movement and Terror Lore'. Reprinted here with permission from the author.
- Sukalpa Bhattacharjee, 'Narrative Constructions of Identity and the Sylheti Experience', in Sukalpa Bhattacharjee and Rajesh Dev (eds), 2006, *Ethno-Narratives: Identity and Experience in North East India*, Delhi. Reprinted here with permission from the author.
- Charles Chasie, 1999, 'A Naga View of the World', *The Naga Imbroglio: A Personal Perspective*, Kohima: Standard Printers and Publishers. Reprinted here with permission from the author.
- Easterine Iralu, 2004, 'Should Writers Stay in Prison?', Speech delivered at the International Congress of PEN, Norway. Reprinted here with permission from the author.
- Chandrakanta Murasingh, 2008, 'Kokborok: Her People and Her Past', *Tales and Tunes from Tripura Hills*, New Delhi: Sahitya Akademi. Reprinted here with permission from the author.
- Patricia Mukhim, 'Land Ownership Among the Khasis of Meghalaya: A Gender Perspective'. Reprinted here with permission from the author.
- Robin S. Ngangom, 2007, 'Contemporary Manipuri Poetry: An Overview', *Muse India*, Issue 16, November–December. Reprinted here with permission from the author.
- Anungla Aier, 2008, 'Folklore, Folk Ideas and Gender among the Nagas', *Eastern Quarterly*, Volume 5, Issues II and II, July–December. Reprinted here with permission from the author.